# The Beatles Recording Reference Manual

Volume 1

*My Bonnie* through *Beatles For Sale*

(1961-1964)

Jerry Hammack

Edited by
Gillian G. Gaar

First edition published 2017
Second edition published 2018
Third edition published 2019
Fourth edition published 2020



Library of Congress Control Number: 2017909370

CreateSpace Independent Publishing Platform, North Charleston, SC

Hammack, Jerry, 1961-
The Beatles Recording Reference Manual: Volume 1: My Bonnie through Beatles For Sale (1961-1964)
Includes appendices, indexes, and bibliographical references.

ISBN-10: 1548023930
ISBN-13: 978-1548023935

Gearfab Books, Ltd. Toronto, Ontario, Canada

*For Beatles fans here, there, and everywhere*
*and for my love, Aimee*

# Contents

# ACKNOWLEDGMENTS

This book would not have been possible without the cooperation and previous work of a number of authors. In particular, Mark Lewisohn; Andy Babiuk; Kevin Ryan and Brian Kehew and John C. Winn.

For their assistance in the development and verification of this book's content and accuracy, I would like to thank: Richard Langham, former Beatles engineer; Ken Scott, former Beatles engineer; David Allen at Abbey Road Studios; Dr. Ingbert Blüthner-Haessler and Kristina Richards at Julius Blüthner Pianofortefabrik GmbH; Graham Calkin; Johannes Teigl; Ben Rieveley; Josh McGee, Mike Lewis, and Fred Gretsch from Fender Musical Instruments; Jill Jokisch at Getty Images; Aaron Bremner at Apple Corps LTD; Gary Astridge; Ben Rowling; The Toronto Public Library Research Library and staff, Sebastian Wohlfeil, Rob Langley, and Jorge Nasta.

I would like to thank all my dear friends and family who have supported this effort over the many years it has been in development. A special thanks to Aimee Park, Jeff Hammack, Rod Moody, Tina Anderson, Albert and Janet Hammack, Jim and Susan Hammack, Jim and Debbie Lusebrink, Joon and Young Park, Jim and Lisa Park, Steven Hammack, Zoro, Linda Sharp, Cindi Shirock, Stacey Ivanchuk, Michael Brockow, Rashana Smith, Charles R. Cross, and Art Chantry.

A special thanks to my brilliant editor, Gillian G. Gaar for her invaluable feedback, encouragement, and keen eye. Also thank you to Frank Miranda for his careful scrutiny and helping to make this book as good and internally consistent as possible.

# Introduction

History is a knotted string of fact, myth and memory. Unravelling it to create some accurate linear rendering of time and events is rarely anything but a complex undertaking. The history of The Beatles' recording sessions and the songs that emerged from them is no exception.

Chronicling the recording history of The Beatles started in earnest in 1982 when a young balance engineer at Abbey Road Studios named John Barrett was given the job of listening to and logging the details of every Beatles tape in the studio's collection. From this detailed account Mark Lewisohn's landmark 1988 book *The Beatles Recording Sessions: The Official Abbey Road Studio Session Notes 1962-1970* was born.

Lewisohn's book added factual organizational detail to Barrett's initial work by linking Barrett's research with his own from EMI Recording Studios' files (the name of the facility during The Beatles era), interviews with the engineers and producers who worked on the sessions, and other sources, such as the British Musicians' Union. Through this research he documented studio session dates and times, some of the musicians who participated on sessions, and other relevant narrative details to bring this chronology to life.

Lewisohn's book has long been the standard source of information regarding the Beatles recording sessions and his additional iterations, corrections, and new works continue to shed light on the band's recording history.

Beyond Lewisohn, other information has come to light regarding this golden age of pop music. Andy Babiuk published *Beatles Gear* in 2001 (revised in 2015), an account of a number of the instruments owned and used by the band to create their music. In 2008, Kevin Ryan and Brian Kehew published *Recording The Beatles*, an exhaustive look at the recording gear and techniques used to create their historic sound at EMI Recording Studios and other studios around the world. In another area of research, John C. Winn's books provided an exhaustive narrative to the multiplicity of songs in their released and bootleg versions, as well as bringing Barrett's raw logs to the light of day in an organized manner.

Autobiographies and biographies of participants in The Beatles recording sessions were written; critical examinations of the music The Beatles produced; and many hundreds of bootlegs of song takes and remixes surfaced for study. With each new asset, the picture of what went into creating the top selling recordings of all time came into focus.

Despite these wonderful resources there has always been a gap, or perhaps more accurately, some glue missing in the chronicle of The Beatles recording history. There has never been a single source where the core technical details of their recording sessions have been researched and organized into a narrative detailing the recording of the songs that mean so much to fans around the world.

We are aware of most of the "when" and "where", but the "what was done?" or the "who played that part?" isn't always clear. We rarely know what guitars or amplifiers were used. There is even less knowledge about the format of the recordings or the studio equipment used on a specific song. It takes a lot of detective work to figure some of these facts out; and a number of popular sources for the information are in conflict, out of date, or just plain wrong. A picture of the work that compromised the creation of each song must be assembled like a jigsaw puzzle.

Thus began my quest to research, gather and organize both the narrative and core technical details of each of the classic Beatles recording sessions on a song-by-song as well as session-by-session basis.

This book contains song-by-song reconstructions of the session work behind and technical specifications for each of The Beatles' singles, EPs and albums from the start of their recording career through the release of the *Beatles For Sale* album, spanning 1961 through 1964.

I created these reconstructions from the most reliable and authoritative resources and research available, including EMI Recording Studios documentation, the engineers who worked on the sessions themselves, studio photographs of the band at work, film and video assets, and analysis of available session recordings and remixes.

The song narratives include information on backing tracks, edit pieces, superimpositions (overdubs), remixes, and other details that comprise the creation of each song. Each narrative is followed by a diagram providing a graphical representation of the song's recording process at each major milestone of production.

The narrative detail of the work performed on each song is as complete as the record allows, and is derived from recognized, reliable sources; or where evidenced from my own exhaustive examination and analysis of session recordings (takes), numbered remixes, a photographic, film or video record of the events, and interviews with participants.

Notes associated with the session-by-session listings make mention of situations where the historical record is in conflict regarding what occurred during a session for a song, or the technical details presented. I made every attempt to document and reconcile these discrepancies and provide well-considered justification whenever my own interpretation of the facts is included.

Each song's narrative follows a common format. As the narratives are meant to encompass the work on a specific song, there are a number of elements that you will find repetitive. The reason behind this is that I want you to be able to learn about any one song and get a complete picture of its recording without having to rely on information covered in relation to a previous one.

For instance: The historic February 11th, 1963 session where The Beatles recorded the majority of the *Please Please Me* album consisted of 11 individual songs that all share nearly the same core narrative in that Lennon played one electric guitar and one acoustic that night (as did Harrison), McCartney played his Hofner bass throughout, Starr played the 1960 Premier 58 Mahogany Duroplastic drum set, and so on.

On a song-by-song basis, the narratives for the *Please Please Me* era tunes are very similar. While I understand that for some readers this repetition might be monotonous, I made the conscious choice that the song-by-song integrity of the text and the ability to read about any one song in its entirety outweighed the issue of repetition of some narrative content.

Some "songs" are left out of the narratives. These omissions relate primarily to the off-the-cuff creations for various Beatles *Christmas flexi-discs* sent to fan club members. Information on the sessions for these recordings is included in the Appendix of recording sessions.

At the start of each song narrative you will find a reference to the song's session dates. Appendix 2 at the end of the book includes exhaustive technical details of every Beatles recording session for the songs included in this book.

The session details include:

- The session date and time
- The session location
- What work was performed on the song during the session
- Who played on the session
- What instruments were played

- What amplifiers were in use
- What recording gear was in use
- What effects were in use
- What microphones were in use

In addition to my own original research, I have scoured the published record of books, magazines, photography, audio, film and video relating to The Beatles recording sessions to assist me in generating the most accurate picture of the sessions that follow. This includes dozens of books and magazine articles, hours of archival video, hundreds of photographs and thousands of both official releases and unauthorized audio tracks.

Through this research, I determined that aside from works that contain information gained from period-specific documentary sources (such as archives, audio, photo or film) or personal interviews, vetted for accuracy, there are few reliable sources for the information presented here prior to 1988.

Beyond the previously stated, none of the works prior to that year had the benefit of Lewisohn's documentation from actual EMI archives, or Barrett's log books. This makes the conclusions reached by those authors highly subjective and suspect. So, while many fan-favourite books regarding this subject matter were parsed, only a select few were found reliable or relevant in the development of this book.

I made no attempt in this book to recreate or regurgitate the brilliant narrative work of my predecessors. If you want to read the story of the New Year's Day drive to the Decca audition, read Lewisohn, or any one of the fine Beatles biographies. If you want to understand the frequency ranges and boost or cut increments of an EMI RS127 Presence Box, and how it was applied to a track or remix, or the deep technical details of tape delay effects, look to Ryan and Kehew for the answer. If you want to learn the provenance of ownership behind Lennon's original Gibson J-160E acoustic guitar, read about it in Babiuk.

Reconstructing a technical profile of The Beatles' revolutionary recording sessions has been a strenuous exercise in research, with the constant requirement of maintaining the historic context of many individual factors including equipment acquisition and usage, personnel and recording practise.

The sound of The Beatles classic recordings is, like all art, both the product of its times and the restrictions associated with them.

Any student of the history of The Beatles can be overwhelmed by the abundance of material at their disposal. This book is both an assimilation of this generous data, a recollection of the events as recorded by those who participated, and my own original research; the conclusions, omissions and errors within this book, if any, are mine and mine alone.

I hope this book will become a useful addition to your Beatles library. I can only hope that it answers questions for you similar to the ones that caused it to be born in the first place, provokes your curiosity, and acts as a gateway for your deeper enjoyment and appreciation of the music of The Beatles.

*Jerry Hammack*
Toronto, Ontario
Canada

**Notes on the Third Edition**

There were a few minor differences between the first edition of Volume 1 and the second. They included a correction to one song narrative (*You Can't Do That*), release date corrections for 1963 and 1964, one mis-dated diagram (*A Taste Of Honey*), an incomplete diagram (*It Won't Be Long*), and two post-era mixing sessions from 1966 that were previously omitted. Starr's Ludwig Set 3 was also corrected for the accuracy of cymbal selections. A handful of formatting and embarrassing typographic errors were also corrected.

With this third edition, only a couple of changes have been made, though they are important ones. Consultations with Beatles drum experts have refined model information on Best's kit (previously noted as a Premier Marine Pearl "53"/"55", now correctly identified as a model "54"). Starr's drum information has also been clarified. His Ludwig Sets 2 and 4, which I previously believed to be in play for certain sessions were actually used exclusively for live and film performances. The only recordings they appeared on were the post-career, 1977 release, *The Beatles At The Hollywood Bowl*. There were also minor errors associated with Lennon's original Rickenbacker 325 guitar (it originally had a Kaufmann vibrato) and the assignment of Harrison's Futurama guitar to the Sheridan session.

Diagrams for the Tony Sheridan sessions have also been clarified to better reflect the initial twin-track stereo recordings. The diagram for *From Me To You* has also been modified to include a previously omitted tape syncing step.

# 1961

---

# 1963

## ”Not to mince words, Mr. Epstein, we don’t like your boys’ sound.”

- Dick Rowe, Decca A&R

# 1961-1963 Releases

## January 5, 1962

**Location**
London, England

**Release Title (composer) (version)**
*My Bonnie* (Traditional, arranged by Tony Sheridan) *b/w The Saints** (Traditional, arranged by Tony Sheridan) (mono)

* credited to Tony Sheridan and The Beat Brothers

**Release label**
Polydor

**Catalogue number**
NH 66 833

**Studio Personnel**

- Producer: Bert Kaempfert

**Sources** – "The Beatles Club - My Bonnie." Digital image. *The Beatles Club*. 31 May 2017. <http://the-beatles.club/wp-content/uploads/1964/04/the-beatles-germany-single-polydor-nh-24-673-the-first-commercial-pressing-of-a-beatles-record-tony-sheridan-the-beat-brothers.jpg>.

## October 5, 1962

**Location**
London, England

**Release Title (version)(composer)**
*Love Me Do b/w P.S. I Love You* (mono) (John Lennon and Paul McCartney)

**Publisher**
Ardmore & Beechwood, Ltd. 1962

**Release label**
Parlophone

**Catalogue number**
45-R 4949

**Sources -** Lewisohn, Mark (1). p. 22.

## January 11, 1963

**Location**
London, England

**Release Title (version)(composer)**
*Please Please Me b/w Ask Me Why* (mono) (John Lennon and Paul McCartney)

**Publisher**
Dick James Music, 1963

**Release label**
Parlophone

**Catalogue number**
45-R 4983

**Studio Personnel**

- Producer: George Martin

**Sources -** Lewisohn, Mark (1). p. 24.

# March 22, 1963

**Location**
London, England

**Release Title (version)(composer)**

*Please Please Me (with Love Me Do and 12 other songs)"* (mono)

Side A

*I Saw Her Standing There* (John Lennon and Paul McCartney)
*Misery* (John Lennon and Paul McCartney)
*Anna (Go To Him)* (Arthur Alexander)
*Chains* (Gerry Goffin and Carole King)
*Boys* (Luther Dixon and Wes Farrell)
*Ask Me Why* (John Lennon and Paul McCartney)
*Please Please Me* (John Lennon and Paul McCartney)

Side B

*Love Me Do* (John Lennon and Paul McCartney)
*P.S. I Love You* (John Lennon and Paul McCartney)
*Baby It's You* (Burt Bacharach, Mack David and Barney Williams)
*Do You Want To Know A Secret* (John Lennon and Paul McCartney)
*A Taste Of Honey* (Ric Marlow and Bobby Scott)
*There's A Place* (John Lennon and Paul McCartney)
*Twist And Shout* (Phil Medley and Bert Berns)

**Publishers (songs)**

- Aldon Music, Charles Bens (*Chains*)
- Ambassador Music, Ltd. (*A Taste Of Honey*)
- Ardmore & Beechwood, Ltd. (*Boys, Love Me Do, P.S. I Love You*)
- Dick James Music (*I Saw Her Standing There, Misery, Ask Me Why, Please Please Me, Do You Want To Know A Secret, There's A Place*)
- Ludix Music (*Baby It's You*)
- Sapiro, Bernstein & Co., Inc.(*Anna*)
- Sherwin Music (*Twist And Shout*)

**Release label**
Parlophone

**Catalogue number**
PMC 1201 (UK)

**Studio Personnel**

- Producer: George Martin

**Sources -** Lewisohn, Mark (1). p. 32. / "Please Please Me album – original label.." Digital image. *Beatle Net.* 31 May 2017. www.beatle.net/wp-content/uploads/UK0139.jpg.

# April 11, 1963

**Location**
London, England

**Release Title (version)(composer)**
*From Me To You b/w Thank You Girl* (mono) (John Lennon and Paul McCartney)

**Publisher**
Dick James Music, 1963

**Release label**
Parlophone

**Catalogue number**
R 5015

**Studio Personnel**

- Producer: George Martin

**Sources -** Lewisohn, Mark (1). p. 32.

## April 26, 1963

**Location**
London, England

**Release Title (version)(composer)**
*Please Please Me (with Love Me Do and 12 other songs)* (stereo)

Side A

*I Saw Her Standing There* (John Lennon and Paul McCartney)
*Misery* (John Lennon and Paul McCartney)
*Anna (Go To Him)* (Arthur Alexander)
*Chains* (Gerry Goffin and Carole King)
*Boys* (Luther Dixon and Wes Farrell)
*Ask Me Why* (John Lennon and Paul McCartney)
*Please Please Me* (John Lennon and Paul McCartney)

Side B

*Love Me Do* (John Lennon and Paul McCartney)
*P.S. I Love You* (John Lennon and Paul McCartney)
*Baby It's You* (Burt Bacharach, Mack David and Barney Williams)
*Do You Want To Know A Secret* (John Lennon and Paul McCartney)
*A Taste Of Honey* (Ric Marlow and Bobby Scott)
*There's A Place* (John Lennon and Paul McCartney)
*Twist And Shout* (Phil Medley and Bert Russell)

**Publishers (songs)**

- Aldon Music, Charles Bens (*Chains*)
- Ambassador Music, Ltd. (*A Taste Of Honey*)
- Ardmore & Beechwood, Ltd. (*Boys, Love Me Do, P.S. I Love You*)
- Dick James Music (*I Saw Her Standing There, Misery, Ask Me Why, Please Please Me, Do You Want To Know A Secret, There's A Place*)
- Ludix Music (*Baby It's You*)
- Saphiro, Bernstein & Co., Inc.(*Anna*)
- Sherwin Music (*Twist And Shout*)

**Release label**
Parlophone

**Catalogue number**
PCS 3042 (UK)

**Studio Personnel**

- Producer: George Martin

**Sources -** Lewisohn, Mark (1). p. 32.

# July 12, 1963

**Location**
London, England

**Release Title (version)(composer)**
*Twist And Shout* (mono)

Side A

*Twist And Shout* (Phil Medley and Bert Russell)
*A Taste Of Honey* (Ric Marlow and Bobby Scott)

Side B

*Do You Want To Know A Secret* (John Lennon and Paul McCartney)
*There's A Place* (John Lennon and Paul McCartney)

**Publishers (songs)**

- Ambassador Music, Ltd. (*A Taste Of Honey*)
- Dick James Music (*Do You Want To Know A Secret, There's A Place*)
- Sherwin Music (*Twist And Shout*)

**Release label**
Parlophone

**Catalogue number**
GEP 8882 (UK)

**Studio Personnel**

- Producer: George Martin

**Sources** - Lewisohn, Mark (1). p. 200.

# August 23, 1963

**Location**
London, England

**Release Title (version)(composer)**
*She Loves You b/w I'll Get You* (mono) (Lennon and McCartney)

**Publisher**
Northern Songs, Ltd., 1963

**Release label**
Parlophone

**Catalogue number**
R 5055 (UK)

**Studio Personnel**

- Producer: George Martin

**Sources** - Lewisohn, Mark (1). p. 35.

# September 6, 1963

**Location**
London, England

**Release Title (version)(composer)**
*The Beatles Hits* (mono)

Side A

*From Me To You* (John Lennon and Paul McCartney)
*Thank You Girl* (John Lennon and Paul McCartney)

Side B

*Please Please Me* (John Lennon and Paul McCartney)
*Love Me Do* (John Lennon and Paul McCartney)

**Publisher**
Northern Songs, Ltd.

**Release label**
Parlophone

**Catalogue number**
GEP 8880 (UK)

**Studio Personnel**

- Producer: George Martin

**Sources -** Lewisohn, Mark (1). p. 200.

# November 1, 1963

**Location**
London, England

**Release Title (version)(composer)**
*The Beatles (No. 1)* (mono)

Side A

*I Saw Her Standing There* (John Lennon and Paul McCartney)
*Misery* (John Lennon and Paul McCartney)

Side B

*Anna (Go To Him)* (Arthur Alexander)
*Chains* (Gerry Goffin and Carole King)

**Publishers (songs)**

- Aldon Music, Charles Bens (*Chains*)
- Northern Songs, Ltd. (*I Saw Her Standing There, Misery*)
- Sapiro, Bernstein & Co., Ltd.(*Anna*)

**Release label**
Parlophone

**Catalogue number**
EP 8883 (UK)

**Studio Personnel**

- Producer: George Martin

**Sources -** Lewisohn, Mark (1). p. 200.

# November 22, 1963

**Location**
London, England

**Release Title (version)(composer)**
*With The Beatles* (mono) (stereo)

Side A

*It Won't Be Long* (John Lennon and Paul McCartney)
*All I've Got To Do* (John Lennon and Paul McCartney)
*All My Loving* (John Lennon and Paul McCartney)
*Don't Bother Me* (George Harrison)
*Little Child* (John Lennon and Paul McCartney)
*Till There Was You* (Meredith Willson)

*Please Mister Postman* (Georgia Dobbins, William Garrett, Freddie Gorman, Brian Holland, and Robert Bateman)

Side B

*Roll Over Beethoven* (Chuck Berry)
*Hold Me Tight* (John Lennon and Paul McCartney)
*You Really Got A Hold On Me* (Smokey Robinson)
*I Wanna Be Your Man* (John Lennon and Paul McCartney)
*Devil In Her Heart* (Richard Drapkin)
*Not A Second Time* (John Lennon and Paul McCartney)
*Money (That's What I Want)* (Janie Bradford and Berry Gordy)

**Publishers (songs)**

- Dominion Music (*Please Mister Postman, You Really Got A Hold On Me, Money*)
- Frank Music (*Till There Was You*)
- JAEP Music (*Don't Bother Me*)
- Jewel Music (*Roll Over Beethoven*)
- Leeds Music (*Devil In Her Heart*)
- Northern Songs, Ltd., 1963 (*It Won't Be Long, All I've Got To Do, All My Loving, Little Child, Hold Me Tight, I Wanna Be Your Man, Not A Second Time*)

**Release label**
Parlophone

**Catalogue number**
(mono) PMC 1206 (UK)
(stereo) PCS 3045 (UK)

**Studio Personnel**

- Producer: George Martin

**Sources -** Lewisohn, Mark (1). p. 37.

# November 29, 1963

**Location**
London, England

**Release Title (version)(composer)**

*I Want To Hold Your Hand b/w This Boy* (mono) (John Lennon and Paul McCartney)

**Publisher**
Northern Songs, Ltd., 1963

**Release label**
Parlophone

**Catalogue number**
R 5084 (UK)

**Studio Personnel**

- Producer: George Martin

**Sources**

- Lewisohn, Mark (1). p. 37.

# Early Recordings

For The Beatles, it was always about the wax. It was the wax that inspired them, either in their bedrooms at home or in the listening booths at NEMS Record Shop in Liverpool. Music came to them on a record, and being on a record meant that you had arrived — you were a real musician. As they mastered their art in marathon live sessions in Hamburg's Reeperbahn district and developed relationships with other artists, their first opportunities to create some wax for themselves were born. Later, with the diligent aid and persistence of their new manager Brian Epstein, they found their way to a real recording contract and a chance to make their dreams come true.

# My Bonnie (The first Tony Sheridan session)

**Sessions**

- June 22, 1961 (possible additional session on June 23, 1961)

Audio recording in 1961 was a basic affair from a technical perspective, though for the act being recorded, it could be demanding and exacting. When The Beatles entered Friedrich-Ebert-Halle in Hamburg, a large gymnasium, cum concert hall on June 22nd, 1961 to back Tony Sheridan's recording session for Polydor, their work was cut out for them (history is not clear on the exact date, or dates. While it's definitive a session occurred on June 22nd, it is possible that the work extended to June 23rd as well).

Seven songs were on the schedule for the session, two of which featured The Beatles in a leading role. *Beatle Bop (Cry For Shadow)* and *Ain't She Sweet* may have been seen by The Beatles as an opportunity to impress producer Bert Kaempfert, though his mind was likely on the business at hand — cutting a solid single for the star of the session, Sheridan.

Through rehearsals and a series of unnumbered takes, the band recorded live backing tracks for *My Bonnie* (a traditional Scottish folk song, arranged by Tony Sheridan), James Milton Black and Katharine Purvis' *The Saints*, Bill Crompton and Tony Sheridan's *Why*, John Lennon and George Harrison's *Beatle Bop (Cry For Shadow)*, Cy Coben and Mel Foree's *Nobody's Child*, Jesse Stone's *Take Out Some Insurance On Me Baby*, and Milton Ager and Jack Yellen's *Ain't She Sweet*.

Lewisohn notes these sessions were recorded and remixed live to two-track stereo, though audio examination indicates that while some entire songs were indeed recorded live, backing vocals and handclaps for both *My Bonnie* and *Why* appear to have been recorded as superimpositions.

The backing tracks featured Sheridan on his 1959 Gibson ES-175 electric guitar, Lennon on his 1958 Rickenbacker 325 Capri electric guitar with Kaufmann vibrato, Harrison on his 1958/1959 Resonet Futurama electric guitar, McCartney on his 1961 Hofner 500/1 bass, and Best on his 1960 Premier Marine Pearl 54 drum set.

From the start, one member of the backing band put The Beatles hopes at getting noticed in jeopardy. Pete Best was simply not a great timekeeper. According to Lewisohn, he was only allowed to play part of his drum set because of tempo issues — Kaempfert took the kick drum away from him.

At least the shoddy amplifiers the band had with them in Hamburg were not an issue: Kaempfert provided his own amplifiers for this session.

The stereo backing track for *My Bonnie* featured Sheridan on guitar and lead vocals, Lennon and Harrison on guitars, McCartney on bass, and Best on drums. A simple superimposition followed of Lennon, McCartney, and Harrison adding backing vocals and handclaps.

*The Saints*, with all performances recorded live to stereo, again featured Sheridan on guitar and lead vocals, Lennon and Harrison on guitars, McCartney on bass, and Best on drums.

*Why* was recorded live to stereo, featuring Sheridan on lead vocals, Lennon and Harrison on guitars, McCartney on bass and Best on drums. A simple superimposition followed of Lennon, McCartney, and Harrison adding backing vocals and handclaps.

*Nobody's Child* was the simplest of the recordings created during the session. Recorded live to stereo, it featured Sheridan on guitar and lead vocals, McCartney on bass and Best on drums.

*Take Out Some Insurance On Me Baby*, recorded live to stereo, featured Sheridan on lead vocals, Lennon and Harrison on guitars, McCartney on bass and Best on drums.

At some point The Beatles took a star turn with John Lennon and George Harrison's instrumental, *Beatle Bop (Cry for A Shadow)*. The live stereo recording featured Lennon and Harrison on guitars, McCartney on bass and Best on drums.

With Sheridan's work completed (the order of the songs performed in the recording session is not known), The Beatles raced through a second effort for Kaempfert, *Ain't She Sweet*, recorded live to stereo and featuring Lennon on guitar and lead vocals, McCartney on bass, Harrison on guitar and Best on drums.

When push came to shove, the Sheridan recordings were a powerful document of the type of rave ups the Hamburg rockers created on a nightly basis. This was not second-class rock-n-roll, even if it came from a minor British act on a German label.

The Beatles, while not top of the bill, were now recording artists.

June 22, 1961

# My Bonnie session

*All songs recorded to twin-track stereo

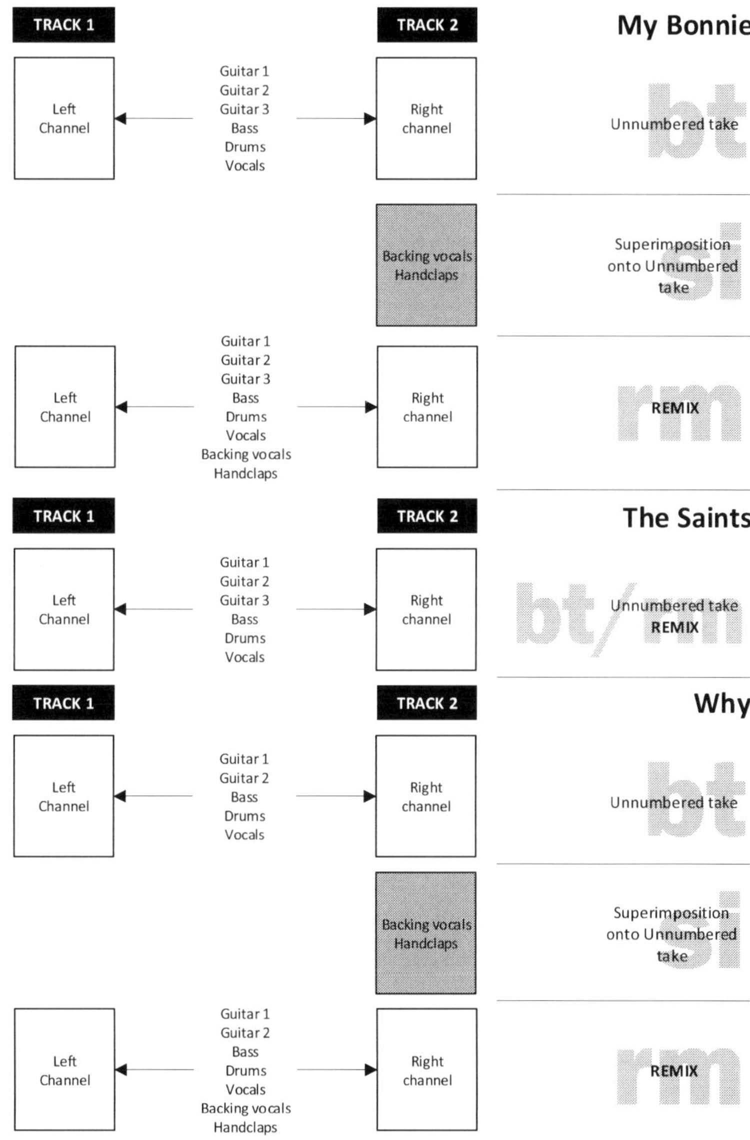

June 22, 1961

# My Bonnie session

*All songs recorded to twin-track stereo

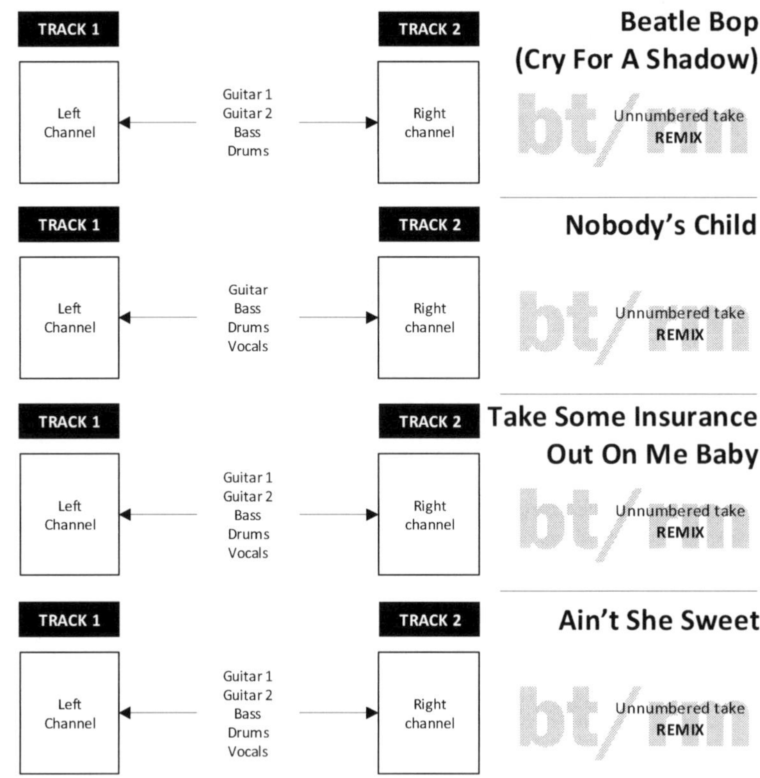

# The Decca Records Audition

**Sessions**

- January 1, 1962

Happy New Year 1962 for The Beatles. Brian Epstein secured the band a January 1st audition with Decca Records at their Broadhurst Gardens studios in North London and once again the band was put through some heavy paces for the session. For a group of young rockers, the 11AM start of the session was less than ideal, but The Beatles played more than their share of lunchtime sessions at Liverpool's Cavern Club, where Decca's A&R man originally saw them in action.

The 15 tracks recorded during the session were cut live to the twin-track EMI TR90 primary tracking machine, with some reverb added through an EMT 140 plate reverb.

The tracks featured Lennon on his 1958 Rickenbacker 325 Capri electric guitar with Bigsby vibrato, McCartney on his 1961 Hofner 500/1 bass, Harrison on his 1957 Gretsch G6128 Duo Jet electric guitar, and Best on his 1960 Premier Marine Pearl 54 drum set. Lennon, McCartney, and Harrison took turns at lead vocals which sounded tired and strained.

As with the 1961 Sheridan sessions, The Beatles didn't use their own amplifiers for the recordings. Decca provided in-house amplification. This fact may account for the clinical sound of the guitars on the session. There's none of the grit and drive evident in live Beatles recordings from this same period.

The session started with John Lennon and Paul McCartney's *Like Dreamers Do*, with McCartney's lead vocal. Perhaps a portent of things to come in the session, the number found McCartney reaching for notes, running short of breath, giving it the old show-biz go.

Berry Gordy and Janic Bradford's *Money (That's What I Want)* was next up, with Lennon's lead vocals and McCartney and Harrison's backing vocals. Lennon's vocals were thin and warbled in the version, as if his voice was worn at the end of a show, but Best's jungle beat was impressive.

Meredith Willson's *Till There Was You* with McCartney's lead vocals followed. His phrasing and enunciation, distracting at times, gave the impression he wasn't certain of how he wanted to approach the song. To add to the trouble, Harrison's solo work missed more notes than it hit.

Ted Snyder, Harry B. Smith, and Francis Wheeler's *The Sheik of Araby*, with Harrison's lead vocal, was the fourth song of the session. The novelty tune may have been intended to show the versatility of The Beatles repertoire, but Lennon's vocal asides caused the song to stray into territory more akin to Spike Jones than rock-and-roll. In fairness, Harrison did make a good go of the lead.

Phil Spector's girl group hit and live standard of the band from their Hamburg days, *To Know Her Is to Love Her* featured Lennon's lead vocals and McCartney and Harrison's backing vocals. The song was a template for what went wrong for The Beatles in the Decca session. Just where the song climaxes at the middle eight, where it should soar with the "Why can't she see? How blind can she be?" vocal, Lennon chose to back off vocally and emotionally, his voice a whimper where it could have been a roar.

Gerry Goffin and Carole King's *Take Good Care of My Baby*, with Harrison's lead vocals and McCartney's harmony vocals was another nervous, lightweight effort, with McCartney's odd choice of vocal tone and Best limited to playing a hi-hat cymbal.

Chuck Berry's *Memphis, Tennessee*, with Lennon's lead vocals, fared much better than most of the session's songs. The Beatles channeled a taste of what club goers in Hamburg and Liverpool experienced — the relentless beat and solid vocals. Unfortunately, Harrison once again ham fisted the song's solo.

Carl Perkins, Bill Cantrell, and Quinton Claunch's *Sure to Fall (In Love with You)* featured Lennon and McCartney on lead vocals. The song was a solid effort, but McCartney's crooning vibrato and artificial twang didn't ring true.

John Lennon and Paul McCartney's Everly Brothers-esque *Hello Little Girl* featured Lennon on lead vocals and McCartney and Harrison on backing vocals. The song was an early taste of what The Beatles sound would become, and easily one later fans of the band would recognize as a Beatles tune — in particular, the familiar close harmonies. At a short 1:37, it's likely if it had ever fallen into George Martin's hands, the song would have found a more mature arrangement. Without any expectations of emulating someone else's hit, it was the most natural performance of the entire Decca session.

Jerry Leiber and Mike Stoller's *Three Cool Cats* featured another Harrison lead vocal, with Lennon and McCartney providing backing vocals. The song was solid and the band finally hit their stride ten songs into the audition. Whether the Decca A&R men were still listening at this point is impossible to know.

Buddy Holly's *Crying, Waiting, Hoping*, featured Harrison's lead vocals, with Lennon and McCartney's on backing vocals. Harrison acquitted himself with some fine lead guitar work as well as a solid vocal on the track.

John Lennon and Paul McCartney's *Love Of The Loved* featured McCartney's lead vocals and Lennon and Harrison's backing vocals. Again free of a previous model, the vocals were more natural. The song, however, was instantly forgettable.

Harry Warren and Al Dubin 's *September in the Rain* was stuck between a rocker and a ballad with McCartney's strident lead vocals attempting to force energy into Best's lagging backbeat. As the session neared its completion, you can almost hear the band raise the white flag of surrender.

Consuelo Velázquez's *Bésame Mucho* featured McCartney's lead vocals and Lennon and Harrison's backing vocals. A popular live favourite for the band, The Beatles rolled through the number easily and with plenty of energy, though Harrison again flubbed some of the key guitar work.

Finally, Jerry Leiber and Mike Stoller's *Searchin'*, with McCartney's lead vocals and Lennon and Harrison's backing vocals, ended the New Year's Day audition. The song was a final, competent effort.

All in all, the Decca recordings captured the sound of a group of young men trying desperately to please. McCartney's vocals in particular are overreaching, if expressive, and both he and Lennon's addition of falsetto in unnatural places on a few of the numbers was distracting at best.

The biggest surprise of the session is Pete Best. Despite his accurate reputation as a marginal timekeeper and unoriginal drummer, his work in the session didn't stand out as inconsistent with the rest of the band's. His weakest performance was *Till There Was You*, where he was uneven and plodding.

Surprisingly, it is the young Harrison who was the weakest link in this unsuccessful audition.

January 1, 1962

# Decca Records audition

*All songs recorded
to twin-track stereo

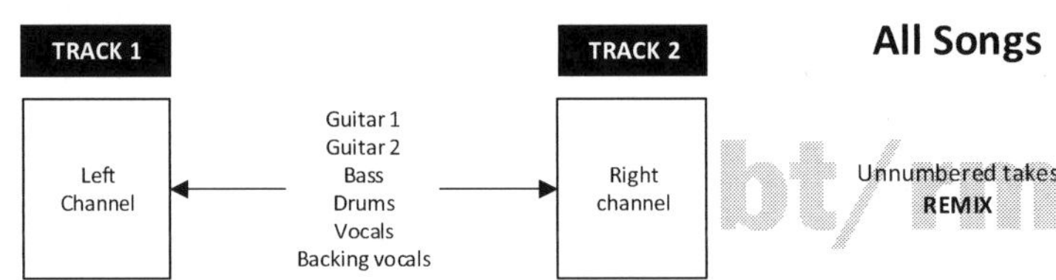


- *Like Dreamers Do*
- *Money (That's What I Want)*
- *Till There Was You*
- *The Sheik of Araby*
- *To Know Her Is to Love Her*
- *Take Good Care of My Baby*
- *Memphis, Tennessee*
- *Sure to Fall (In Love with You)*
- *Hello Little Girl*
- *Three Cool Cats*
- *Crying, Waiting, Hoping*
- *Love of the Loved*
- *September in the Rain*
- *Bésame Mucho*
- *Searchin'*

# Swanee River (The second Tony Sheridan session)

**Sessions**

- May 24, 1962

On May 24th, 1962, The Beatles, with Tony Sheridan and pianist Roy Young met at Studio Rahlstedt in Hamburg's sleepy eastern suburbs to work on Sheridan's follow up single to *My Bonnie.*

This session was most likely recorded live to two-track.

Two songs were recorded during the session; Stephen Foster's *Swanee River* and Ben Bernie, Maceo Pinkard, and Kenneth Casey's *Sweet Georgia Brown.*

As evidenced by *Sweet Georgia Brown*, Sheridan played his 1959 Gibson ES-175 electric guitar and sang lead vocals, Lennon played his 1958 Rickenbacker 325 Capri electric guitar with Bigsby vibrato, McCartney, his1961 Hofner 500/1 bass, and Best played the snare drum and ride cymbal from his 1960 Premier Marine Pearl 54 drum set. Harrison did not play guitar, but provided backing vocals, along with McCartney. The track was filled out by Roy Young on piano.

It is assumed that as with the earlier Hamburg session, Kaempfert provided the amplifiers.

*Swanee River* is another story. The song was released by Sheridan, but it is unlikely that the version recorded with The Beatles is the released version of the song.

An examination of the single release indicates a backing band that included a full drum set (as opposed to the snare and cymbal work of Best on *Sweet Georgia Brown*), as well as a saxophone player. Additionally, the production of the sessions differs dramatically.

Months before the May 24th session, on December 21st, 1961, Sheridan recorded ten songs for Kaempfert in Hamburg. The Beatles were in Liverpool on that day, playing a lunchtime session at The Cavern Club.

According to Gottfridsson's research, Sheridan's session included Roy Young on piano, Colin Melander on bass, Ricki Barnes on saxophone and either Jimmy Doyle or Johnny Watson on drums.

It is likely that this lineup recorded *Swanee River* during this session, and that it's their version, not

The Beatles', that appeared as the release version of the song.

In a coda to this session, on January 3rd, 1964, Sheridan re-recorded his vocals for *Sweet Georgia Brown*, attempting to cash in on Beatlemania by adding the novelty lyrics, "In Liverpool she even dared/To criticize The Beatles hair/With their whole fan club standing there/Ah, meet Sweet Georgia Brown."

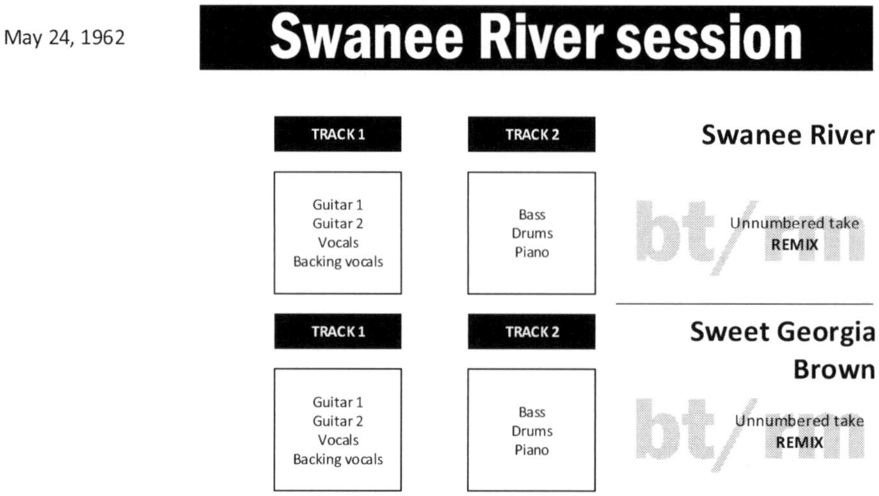

May 24, 1962

## Swanee River session

**Swanee River**

| TRACK 1 | TRACK 2 |
|---|---|
| Guitar 1<br>Guitar 2<br>Vocals<br>Backing vocals | Bass<br>Drums<br>Piano |

bt/rm
Unnumbered take
**REMIX**

**Sweet Georgia Brown**

| TRACK 1 | TRACK 2 |
|---|---|
| Guitar 1<br>Guitar 2<br>Vocals<br>Backing vocals | Bass<br>Drums<br>Piano |

bt/rm
Unnumbered take
**REMIX**

# Please Please Me

---

Spanning 281 days between June 6th, 1962 and March 14th, 1963, the *Please Please Me* era launched The Beatles into star status in the UK. In less than one year, the band leaped from being local Liverpool favourites to a national sensation, sowing the seeds of Beatlemania.

Not having fully earned the trust of their producer, George Martin, their recordings during the era included not only Lennon and McCartney originals, but also the obscure B-side American hits they loved so much and covered in their live shows. In fairness to Martin, who recognized Lennon and McCartney's promise (all the A-sides of their singles featured original material, and their debut album opened with the raucous *I Saw Her Standing There*), there was likely some relief at Parlophone when their song selection for the first album contained a handful of tested hits.

It's also important to remember at this stage that The Beatles were just another rock-n-roll band making recordings. Record companies were businesses, and their products were recordings. The musicians were workers that created the product, and recording studios were merely factories where that product was created.

In addition to the *Please Please Me* album, the era also produced the hit singles *Love Me Do*, *Please Please Me*, and *From Me To You*.

---

# Bésame Mucho

**Sessions**

- June 6, 1962

The Beatles' first recording session for EMI on June 6th, 1962 was held in the room that became as closely identified with the band as EMI Recording Studios itself — Studio 2. The session's goal was to track the band's first single. But first, they needed to break the ice.

Consuelo Velázquez's *Bésame Mucho*, long a part of the band's Liverpool and Hamburg sets, was the first song The Beatles ever recorded for Parlophone.

The technical team for the song's only session included producer Ron Richards, balance engineer Norman Smith, and tape operator Chris Neal.

The song was recorded to both the twin-track EMI BTR3 and mono EMI BTR2 primary tracking machines.

The track featured Lennon on his 1958 Rickenbacker 325 Capri electric guitar with Bigsby vibrato and vocals, McCartney on his 1961 Hofner 500/1 bass and vocals, Harrison on his 1957 Gretsch G6128 Duo Jet electric guitar, and Best on his 1960 Premier Marine Pearl 54 drum set.

Unlike their experience in Germany and in the Decca audition, EMI engineers were willing to work with The Beatles' amplification. Lennon used his 15-watt 1960 Fender Narrow Panel Tweed Deluxe amplifier, while Harrison played through his 16-watt 1960 Gibson GA-40 amplifier.

McCartney's 40-watt Quad II/22 amplifier with "Coffin" cabinet was another story. Initially mic'ed, but immediately considered unsuitable for recording, it was replaced by studio engineer Ken Townsend with a Leak Point One preamplifier and Leak TL-12 Plus amplifier with Tannoy Dual Concentric 15" speaker and cabinet from the studio's echo chamber 1. This combination continued to be used in the studio for McCartney's bass amplification until he improved his rig in March 1963.

Four takes were attempted of the song, with take 4 being deemed best. No other work occurred on the song after this session and no remix was ever created.

# Love Me Do

**Sessions**

- June 6, 1962
- September 4, 1962
- September 11, 1962
- February 25, 1963

The Beatles began work on what would be their first single, the John Lennon and Paul McCartney original, *Love Me Do*, on June 6$^{th}$, 1962, at EMI Recording Studios, Studio 2. It was unusual at the time for an untested band to be permitted to record an original song — there were professional songwriters to do that work. But The Beatles always projected an aura of confidence and as luck would have it, Parlophone head George Martin was open to giving the new writers a shot.

The technical team for the song's first session included producer Ron Richards, balance engineer Norman Smith, and tape operator Chris Neal.

The song was recorded to the twin-track EMI BTR3 and the mono EMI BTR2 primary tracking machines.

The backing track featured Lennon on his 1958 Rickenbacker 325 Capri electric guitar with Bigsby vibrato, and Hohner harmonica (either an Echo Vamper or Super Chromonica), Harrison on his 1957 Gretsch G6128 Duo Jet electric guitar, McCartney on his 1961 Hofner 500/1 bass, and Best on his 1960 Premier Marine Pearl 54 drum set.

For amplification, Lennon used his 15-watt 1960 Fender Narrow Panel Tweed Deluxe amplifier, while Harrison played through his 16-watt 1960 Gibson GA-40 amplifier. McCartney's 40-watt Quad II/22 amplifier with "Coffin" cabinet had been ruled out for use in the session by technical engineer Ken Townsend due to the noise it generated in favour of a Leak Point One preamplifier and Leak TL-12 Plus amplifier with Tannoy Dual Concentric 15" speaker and cabinet from the studio's echo chamber 1.

The band proceeded through a five takes of the "McCartney and Lennon" original (the order of the songwriting credit for the time being), the backing track including live vocals by Lennon and McCartney. Take 5 was considered best at this point.

George Martin joined the session part way through, beginning his career-long relationship with the band. It's his post-session chemistry with The Beatles that is credited with piquing Martin's interest that first evening in what must have seemed like just another band, just another session.

While the overall impression was positive, there was one thing amiss: Over the course of the four songs attempted that first evening, Pete Best's lazy beat and lacklustre performance were getting in the way of making a finished recording. Best may have been fine for the clubs, but he simply wasn't a studio-grade drummer. Martin communicated this impression to manager Brian Epstein over the days between the first and second sessions for *Love Me Do.*

When Martin met The Beatles again on September 4th in Studio 2, he was acting as producer and a new drummer sat on the throne. As events transpired that evening, Ringo Starr's welcome to EMI also turned out to be a little rocky.

Unlike the initial session for the song, this evening the technical team chose to work in monaural.

At least 15 attempts were made at *Love Me Do* during Starr's first session and the overall impression was that he didn't represent a great improvement over Best. However, the backing track of Lennon on guitar and harmonica, Harrison on his 1962 Gibson J-160E acoustic guitar, McCartney on bass, and Starr on his 1960 Premier 58 Mahogany Duroplastic drum set was good enough.

By the end of the session, Lennon and McCartney's lead vocals had been superimposed along with handclaps and an unnumbered remix mono (RM) was created from an unnumbered take.

But Martin remained unsatisfied with *Love Me Do.* Could it still be the drumming? To find out, Ron Richards (back in the producer's chair) hired studio veteran Andy White for the next session on September 11th in Studio 2, leaving Starr to play tambourine on the track.

Eighteen more takes were made of the song with White playing his 1956 Ludwig Black Diamond Pearl Buddy Rich Super Classic drum set (and once again recorded to mono). The takes included new vocal and handclap superimpositions.

By the end of the evening, it appeared the song was in the can, with an unnumbered mono remix being created from take 18.

The song was revisited on February 25th, 1963, in a Studio 2 control room session where an unnumbered remix stereo (RS) was created from take 18.

In the end, both Starr's September 4th and White's September 11th versions of the song ended up as official releases.

Starr's version was the UK single (released in mono), while White's performance appeared on both the mono and stereo *Please Please Me* albums. How can you tell the two apart? Starr's version doesn't include the tambourine.

September 4, 1962 thru
February 25, 1963

# Love Me Do

## Version 1 (Starr)

**TRACK 1**

| Track 1 |  |
|---|---|
| Guitar<br>Acoustic guitar<br>Bass<br>Drums<br>Harmonica | bt — Takes 1-15+ |
| Vocal 1<br>Vocal 2<br>Handclaps | si — Superimposition onto unknown take |
| Guitar<br>Acoustic guitar<br>Bass<br>Drums<br>Harmonica<br>Vocal 1<br>Vocal 2<br>Handclaps | rm — REMIX |

## Version 2 (White)

**TRACK 1**

| Track 1 |  |
|---|---|
| Guitar 1<br>Acoustic guitar<br>Bass<br>Drums<br>Harmonica<br>Tambourine | bt — Takes 1-18 |
| Vocal 1<br>Vocal 2<br>Handclaps | si — Superimposition onto unknown take |
| Guitar<br>Acoustic guitar<br>Bass<br>Drums<br>Harmonica<br>Tambourine<br>Vocal 1<br>Vocal 2<br>Handclaps | rm — REMIX |

# P.S. I Love You

**Sessions**

- June 6, 1962
- September 11, 1962
- February 25, 1963

*P.S. I Love You*, another John Lennon and Paul McCartney original, would become the B-side of the *Love Me Do* single (as well as eventually find a home on the *Please Please Me* album) and was first recorded at the band's initial June 6th, 1962 session at EMI Recording Studios, Studio 2.

The songwriters were developing their early voices and recognized the power of speaking directly to their fans. Likened by Lennon to songs like Luther Dixon and Florence Greenberg's *Soldier Boy*, the song also featured the kind of clever narrative device that McCartney always appreciated (the closest analogy being Brian Hyland's 1962 hit version of Gary Geld and Peter Udell's, *Sealed With A Kiss*). This direct approach in singing to their fans in an "I, me, you" voice would be a signature of their early hits.

The technical team for the song's first session on June 6th, 1962 included producer Ron Richards, balance engineer Norman Smith, and tape operator Chris Neal.

The song was recorded to the twin-track EMI BTR3 primary tracking machine and simultaneously to a mono EMI BTR2 primary tracking machine.

The backing track featured McCartney on his 1961 Hofner 500/1 bass and lead vocals, Lennon on his 1958 Rickenbacker 325 Capri electric guitar with Bigsby vibrato and Hohner harmonica (either an Echo Vamper or Super Chromonica model), as well as singing backing vocals, Harrison on his 1957 Gretsch G6128 Duo Jet electric guitar and backing vocals, and Best on his 1960 Premier Marine Pearl 54 drum set.

For amplification, Lennon used his 15-watt 1960 Fender Narrow Panel Tweed Deluxe amplifier, while Harrison played through his 16-watt 1960 Gibson GA-40 amplifier. McCartney used a Leak Point One preamplifier and Leak TL-12 Plus amplifier with Tannoy Dual Concentric 15" speaker and cabinet provided by the studio.

Three takes were attempted, with take 2 being considered best for the moment.

The song sat idle until September 11th, when a remake was attempted in Studio 2, this time with session drummer Andy White on his 1956 Ludwig Black Diamond Pearl Buddy Rich Super Classic drum set, and new Beatles drummer Ringo Starr on maracas. Unlike the initial session for the track, the technical team chose to work purely in monaural for this day's work.

With a new backing track that also included Lennon and Harrison on guitars and McCartney on bass, 10 takes, including superimpositions of McCartney on lead vocals and Lennon and Harrison on backing vocals, completed the recording of the song.

Before the session ended, an unnumbered remix mono (RM) of the song was created from take 10 which served as the mono release version of the song for the single. *P.S. I Love You* was the only Beatles single produced by Ron Richards ever released.

The song was revisited on February 25th, 1963 in a Studio 2 control room session where an unnumbered remix stereo (RS) was created from take 10. Making a stereo remix from mono master tapes was achieved by recording the mono version to two tracks, then applying slight variations in the equalization between the tracks. This remix served as the stereo release version of the song.

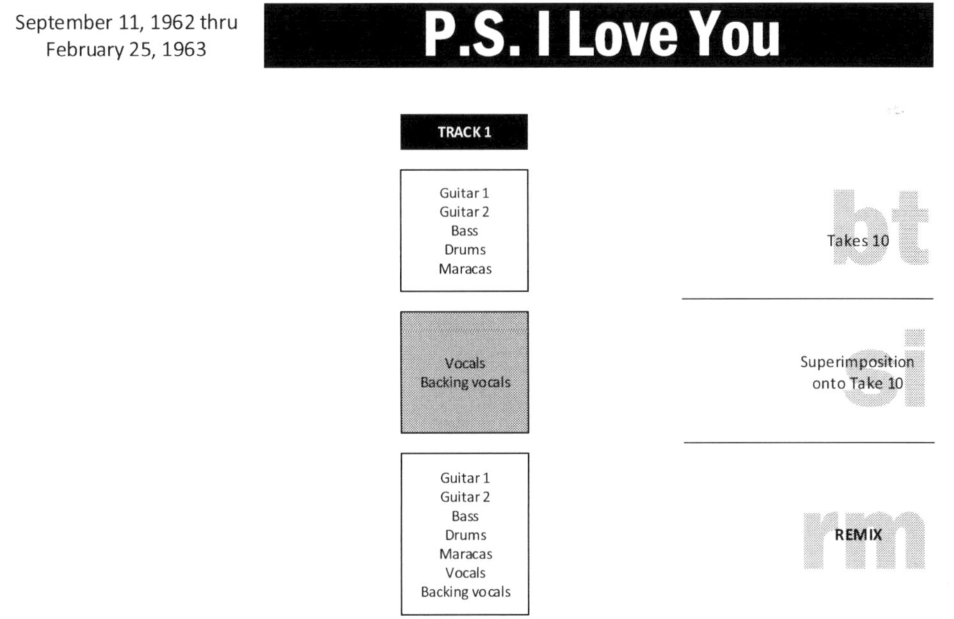

# Ask Me Why

**Sessions**

- June 6, 1962
- November 26, 1962
- November 30, 1962
- February 25, 1963

The June 6th, 1962 session at EMI Recording Studios, Studio 2, wrapped up with the first attempt at John Lennon and Paul McCartney's *Ask Me Why*, another song dating back to The Beatles' Hamburg and Liverpool live sets. Their songwriting approach at the time featured direct appeals to the objects of their affections. It was just the kind of quality that inspired Beatlemania, as every girl could believe she was the focus of their attentions.

The technical team for the session included producer Ron Richards, balance engineer Norman Smith, and tape operator Chris Neal.

The song was recorded to the twin-track EMI BTR3 primary tracking machine and simultaneously to an additional mono EMI BTR2 primary tracking machine.

The backing track featured Lennon on his 1958 Rickenbacker 325 Capri electric guitar with Bigsby vibrato, Harrison on his 1957 Gretsch G6128 Duo Jet electric guitar, McCartney on his 1961 Hofner 500/1 bass, and Best on his 1960 Premier Marine Pearl 54 drum set.

For amplification, Lennon used his 15-watt 1960 Fender Narrow Panel Tweed Deluxe amplifier, while Harrison played through his 16-watt 1960 Gibson GA-40 amplifier. McCartney used a Leak Point One preamplifier and Leak TL-12 Plus amplifier with Tannoy Dual Concentric 15" speaker and cabinet provided by the studio.

Only one take was attempted, with the backing track featuring live vocals by Lennon, McCartney, and Harrison. Work on this version went no further.

Work on the song recommenced on November 26th with George Martin now in charge of the sessions as producer and a new drummer in place. Again in Studio 2, the new backing track featured Lennon trading his Rickenbacker 325 for his 1962 Gibson J-160E acoustic guitar and singing lead vocals, McCartney on bass and backing vocals, Harrison on guitar and backing vocals, and Starr on his 1960 Premier 58 Mahogany Duroplastic drum set.

By this date, Lennon and Harrison had retired their well-worn club amplifiers in favour of a pair of 30-watt 1962 JMI Vox AC30/6 Twin amplifiers. Lennon's Gibson was also mic'ed acoustically with a Neumann U48 microphone. Engineer Smith blended the acoustic signal with the amplified one to create a unique acoustic guitar tone.

Six new takes were made of the song, with take 6 being the best.

Four days later on November 30th in a Studio 2 control room session, the technical team created an unnumbered remix mono (RM) from take 6, which served as the B-side of the *Please Please Me* (mono) single released on January 11th, 1963.

On February 25th, 1963 another Studio 2 control room session for the *Please Please Me* album, the song was remixed again for both mono and stereo from take 6, the remix stereo (RS) being a direct copy of the twin-track with added echo according to Winn. These unnumbered remixes served as the respective mono and stereo release versions for the *Please Please Me* album.

November 26, 1962 thru
February 25, 1963

**Ask Me Why**

| TRACK 1 | TRACK 2 |
| --- | --- |
| Guitar<br>Bass<br>Drums | Acoustic guitar<br>Vocal<br>Backing vocals |

bt/rm Take 6 **REMIX**

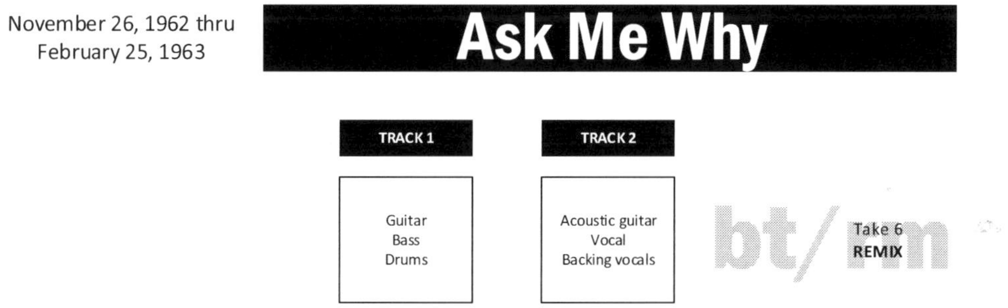

# How Do You Do It

**Sessions**

- September 4, 1962

George Martin was looking for a hit for the Beatles, and his first session with them didn't convince him that either *Love Me Do* or *P.S. I Love You* had any hit-making potential. So, for their second session at EMI Recording Studios, Studio 2, on September 4th, 1962, he put them to work on a song he believed did have the magic — Mitch Murray's *How Do You Do It*. The song had been making the rounds in London, being shopped to two other artists before Martin decided to give The Beatles a go at it.

The technical team for the song's only session included producer George Martin and balance engineer Norman Smith.

The song was recorded to the mono EMI BTR2 primary tracking machine.

The backing track featured Lennon on an unknown acoustic guitar, Harrison on his 1957 Gretsch G6128 Duo Jet electric guitar, McCartney on his 1961 Hofner 500/1 bass and Ringo Starr, in his first Beatles recording session, on his 1960 Premier 58 Mahogany Duroplastic four-piece drum set.

For amplification, Harrison used the 30-watt 1962 JMI Vox AC30/6 Twin amplifier. For bass amplification, McCartney used technical engineer Ken Townsend's makeshift bass setup comprised of the studio's Leak Point One preamplifier and Leak TL-12 Plus amplifier with Tannoy Dual Concentric 15" speaker and cabinet.

At least two takes of the song were recorded, take 2 being the best (the total number of takes is unknown). After the instrumental backing track was complete, superimpositions to take 2 included Lennon and McCartney on vocals and handclaps.

By the end of the session, an unnumbered remix mono (RM) was created from take 2. The remix represented the release-ready version of the song, though it was replaced by *Love Me Do* for the band's first single, which Martin conceded in the end to be a better tune.

*How Do You Do It* remained unreleased until it finally appeared in a remixed stereo version on *Anthology 1* in 1995. The song was a hit for Gerry and The Pacemakers in 1964; another George Martin-produced act.

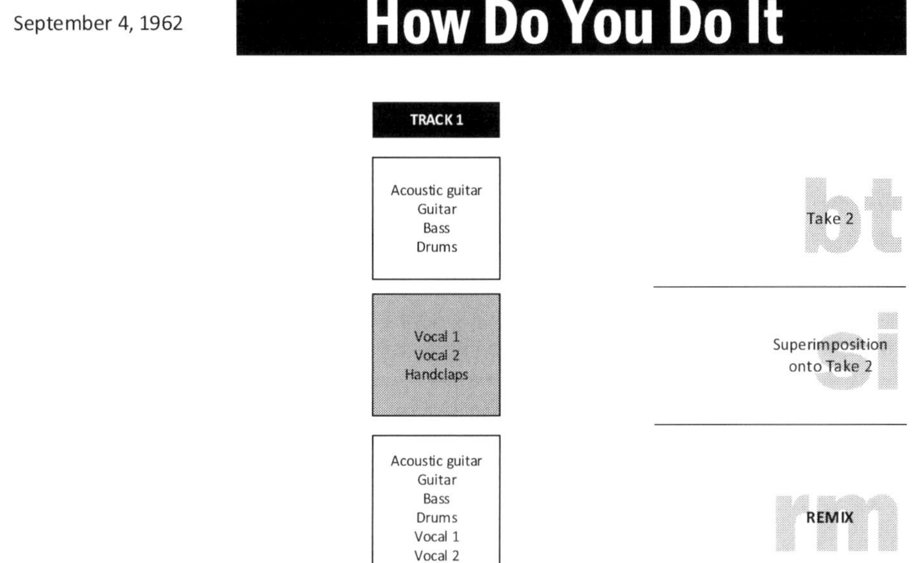

# Please Please Me

**Sessions**

- September 11, 1962
- November 26, 1962
- November 30, 1962
- February 25, 1963

The Beatles first UK No. 1 record didn't have the most auspicious of starts. John Lennon and Paul McCartney viewed their song, *Please Please Me* as a slowly building, smouldering Roy Orbison-style ballad. Martin hated the arrangement, even with the rock-solid Andy White providing the backbeat for the song's first takes. In the end, the solution to Martin's problem was simple. The song needed to rock — and The Beatles had no problem with that.

The technical team for the song's first session on September 11th, 1962 at EMI Recording Studios, Studio 2, included producer Ron Richards and balance engineer Norman Smith.

The song was recorded to the twin-track EMI BTR3 primary tracking machine.

The backing track featured Lennon on his 1958 Rickenbacker 325 Capri electric guitar with Bigsby vibrato, Harrison on his 1957 Gretsch G6128 Duo Jet electric guitar (his 1962 Rickenbacker 425 was also available, though not likely used), McCartney on his 1961 Hofner 500/1 bass and the aforementioned White sitting in for Starr on his on his 1956 Ludwig Black Diamond Pearl Buddy Rich Super Classic drum set.

For amplification, Lennon and Harrison used the 30-watt 1962 JMI Vox AC30/6 Twin amplifiers. For bass amplification, McCartney used technical engineer Ken Townsend's makeshift bass rig, comprised of a Leak Point One preamplifier and Leak TL-12 Plus amplifier with Tannoy Dual Concentric 15" speaker and cabinet from the studio's echo chamber 1.

While the original tapes no longer exist, it is likely that given the nature of their other work during this period that Lennon, McCartney, and Harrison's vocals for the song were attempted as a superimposition to the instrumental backing track during the session.

However the song was tracked, the results weren't satisfying. The saving grace was that Martin liked the song itself. On November 26th, the band returned to Studio 2, this time with Starr firmly in place as drummer, to record a remake.

Lennon's 1958 Rickenbacker 325 Capri electric guitar with Bigsby vibrato had been repainted black by this date, but no other changes to the instrumental or amplification setup were made for the session. Starr played his 1960 Premier 58 Mahogany Duroplastic drum set.

The remake was recorded to the twin-track EMI BTR3 primary tracking machine and simultaneously to a mono EMI BTR2 primary tracking machine.

Eighteen takes, including the instrumental backing track with unnumbered superimpositions, were attempted during the session. The superimpositions included Lennon, McCartney, and Harrison's vocals and Lennon's Hohner harmonica (either an Echo Vamper or Super Chromonica model) in places.

Unnumbered edit pieces were also recorded during the session. The edit piece featured the ending of the song performed by the entire band.

On November 30th, the technical team returned to Studio 2 to create an unnumbered remix mono (RM) from an unnumbered November 26th take (likely either takes 16, 17 or 18, which would be the basis of later remixes). This remix served as the mono release version of the song used for the single. Unlike the later mono and stereo remixes of the song, this mono version did not use any echo effect.

On February 25th in a Studio 2 control room session, *Please Please Me* was remixed for mono and stereo from an edit of takes 16, 17 and 18, this time with echo added to both versions. The stereo version of the song, according to Winn, was a direct copy of the twin-track edit. These unnumbered remixes served as the mono and stereo release versions of the song used for the *Please Please Me* album.

September 11, 1962 thru February 25, 1963

# Please Please Me

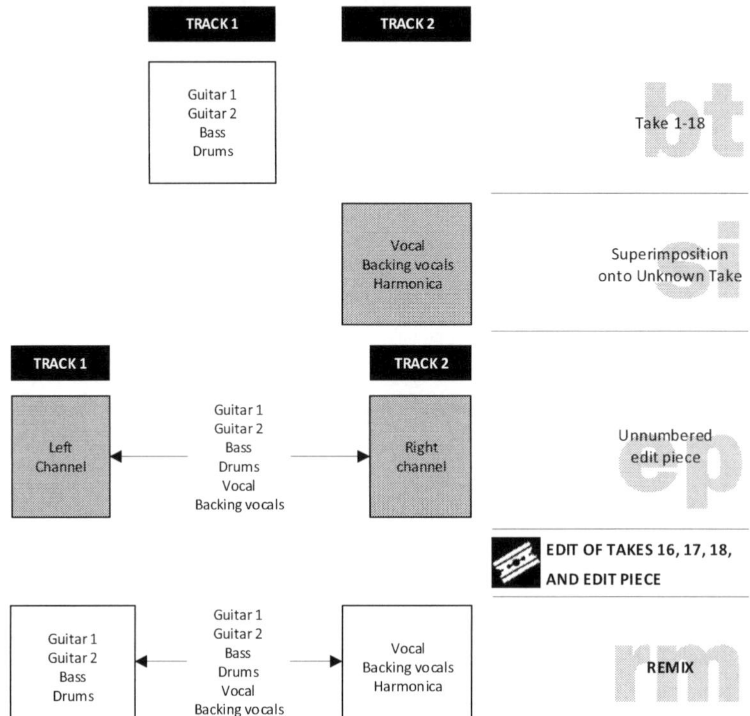

# There's A Place

### Sessions

- February 11, 1963
- February 25, 1963

*Please Please Me* was a hit; The Beatles first No. 1 charting UK single. On February 11th, 1963, one month after its release, the band was back at EMI Recording Studios, Studio 2, to record a follow-up — this time, an album. In the rapid-fire world of pop music, the rule is, "strike while the iron is hot". Popularity, after all, is fleeting; or so everyone believed.

Returning to Studio 2, the plan was to spend the day recording essentially the band's current live set, comprised of both cover tunes and originals. Brian Epstein, aware of the fact that the real money in the music business was in publishing, was keen on placing as many Lennon and McCartney originals as possible on the upcoming album. In the end, Epstein got his wish. Five of the tracks recorded at the session (and eight songs on the final album) were John Lennon and Paul McCartney originals, including *There's A Place.*

The technical team for the session included producer George Martin, balance engineer Norman Smith, and tape operator Richard Langham.

The song was recorded to the twin-track EMI BTR3 primary tracking machine.

The backing track featured Lennon on his 1958 Rickenbacker 325 Capri electric guitar with Bigsby vibrato and lead vocals, McCartney on his 1961 Hofner 500/1 bass and lead vocals, Harrison on his 1957 Gretsch G6128 Duo Jet electric guitar and backing vocals, and Starr on his 1960 Premier 58 Mahogany Duroplastic drum set.

For amplification, Lennon and Harrison used the 30-watt 1962 JMI Vox AC30/6 Twin amplifiers. For bass amplification, McCartney used technical engineer Ken Townsend's makeshift bass setup comprised of the studio's Leak Point One preamplifier and Leak TL-12 Plus amplifier with Tannoy Dual Concentric 15" speaker and cabinet.

Ten takes of the backing track were attempted, though only seven takes (1, 2, 4, 6, 8, 9, and 10) were complete.

Take 10, being the best, was superimposed in three additional takes with Lennon's harmonica part later in the same session (takes 11 through 13). With take 13, recording of the song was completed.

On February 25th, in a Studio 2 control room session, unnumbered mono and stereo remixes (RM and RS) were created from take 13. These remixes served as the mono and stereo release versions of the song.

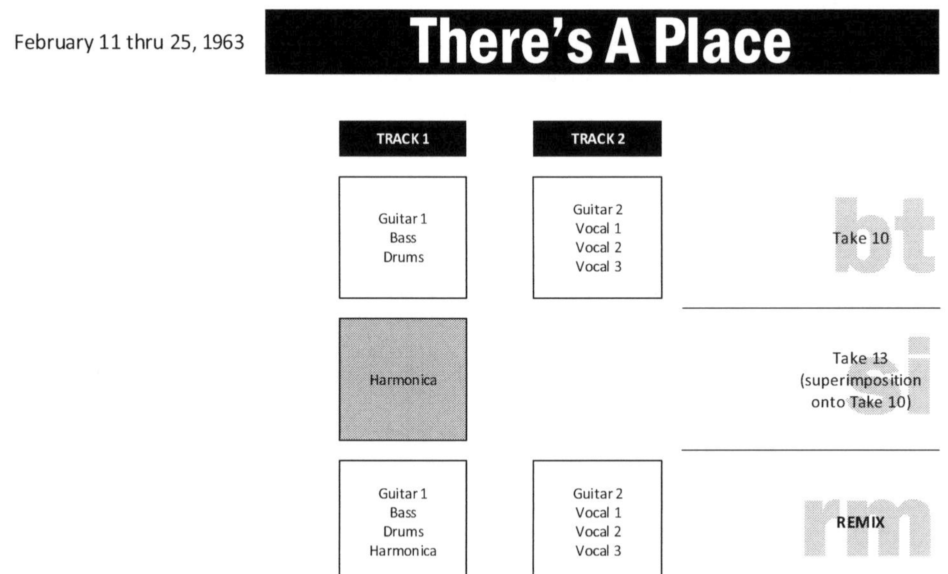

# I Saw Her Standing There

**Sessions**

- February 11, 1963
- February 25, 1963

What became the leadoff tune for the *Please Please Me* album, John Lennon and Paul McCartney's *I Saw Her Standing There* was the second song recorded during their historic February 11th, 1963 session at EMI Recording Studios, Studio 2. Going by the title *Seventeen* at the time of recording, the song was one of the duo's first compositions and a favourite of their Liverpool and Hamburg live shows.

The technical team for the session included producer George Martin, balance engineer Norman Smith, and tape operator Richard Langham.

The song was initially recorded to the twin-track EMI BTR3 primary tracking machine, with later superimpositions simultaneously recorded to a mono EMI BTR2 primary tracking machine.

The backing track featured McCartney on his 1961 Hofner 500/1 bass and lead vocals, Lennon on his 1958 Rickenbacker 325 Capri electric guitar with Bigsby vibrato and backing vocals, Harrison on his 1957 Gretsch G6128 Duo Jet electric guitar, and Starr on his 1960 Premier 58 Mahogany Duroplastic drum set.

For amplification, Lennon and Harrison used the 30-watt 1962 JMI Vox AC30/6 Twin amplifiers. For bass amplification, McCartney used technical engineer Ken Townsend's makeshift bass setup comprised of the studio's Leak Point One preamplifier and Leak TL-12 Plus amplifier with Tannoy Dual Concentric 15” speaker and cabinet.

The band first tracked two complete takes of the song, with take 1 being the favoured performance.

Takes 3, 4 and 5 were edit pieces in which Martin tried unsuccessfully to coax a better guitar solo out of Harrison; in retrospect, it's hard to imagine what he didn't like about the original.

Take 6 was another full take attempt, though it fell apart after a minute. Takes 7 and 8 didn't make it out of the gate with tempo problems and Starr, completely out of character, dropping a beat.

Take 9 was another complete pass, and while no match for take 1, McCartney's spirited count-in was edited to the front of take 1 in the final version of the song.

Later in the day (the day's work was broken into three sessions; *I Saw Her Standing There*'s backing track was recorded in the first session, with superimpositions in the second), takes 10 through 12 comprised the superimpositions to takes 2 and 1.

Take 10 was used to reinforce vocals onto take 2 of the song, the superimposition marking the end of work on that version as all the attention shifted to take 1.

Onto take 1, takes 11 and 12 involved the addition of handclaps for the duration of the song, take 12 being the best. With this superimposition, recording on the song was completed.

On February 25$^{th}$ in a Studio 2 control room session, the edit of McCartney's count-in ("One, two, three, FAWR!") from take 9 was added in an edit to take 12. Next, an unnumbered remix mono (RM) and stereo (RS) were created from the edit of takes 9 and 12. These remixes served as the respective mono and stereo release versions of the song.

February 11 thru 25, 1963

# I Saw Her Standing There

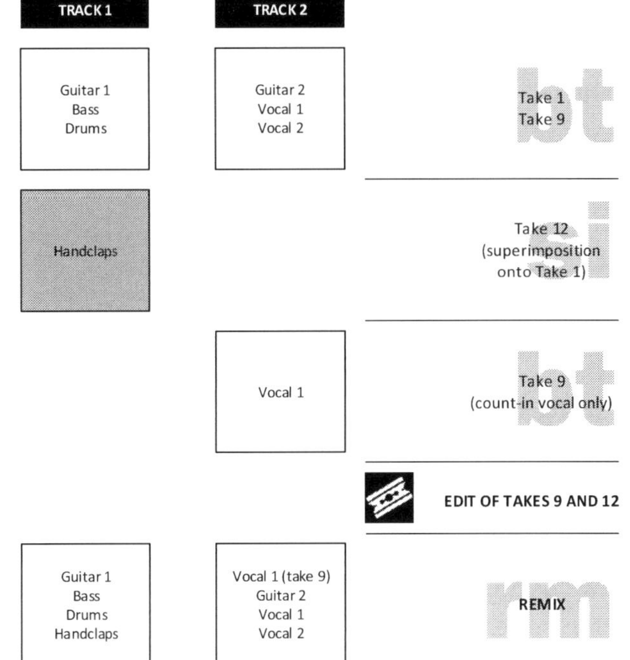

# A Taste Of Honey

**Sessions**

- February 11, 1963
- February 25, 1963

Ric Marlow and Bobby Scott's *A Taste Of Honey* was the third song recorded for the *Please Please Me* album at EMI Recording Studios, Studio 2, on February 11th, 1963. Owing significantly in its arrangement to the Lenny Welch version released by Cadence Records in 1962, the song had long been part of The Beatles' live set in Liverpool and Hamburg.

The technical team for the session included producer George Martin, balance engineer Norman Smith, and tape operator Richard Langham.

The song was recorded to the twin-track EMI BTR3 primary tracking machine and, starting with take 6, simultaneously to an additional mono EMI BTR2 primary tracking machine.

The backing track featured McCartney on his 1961 Hofner 500/1 bass and lead vocals, Lennon on his 1962 Gibson J-160E acoustic guitar and backing vocals, Harrison on his 1957 Gretsch G6128 Duo Jet electric guitar and backing vocals, and Starr on his 1960 Premier 58 Mahogany Duroplastic drum set.

For amplification, Lennon and Harrison used the 30-watt 1962 JMI Vox AC30/6 Twin amplifiers. Lennon's Gibson was also mic'ed acoustically with a Neumann U48 microphone. Engineer Smith blended the acoustic signal with the amplified one to create a unique acoustic guitar tone. For bass amplification, McCartney used technical engineer Ken Townsend's makeshift bass setup comprised of the studio's Leak Point One preamplifier and Leak TL-12 Plus amplifier with Tannoy Dual Concentric 15" speaker and cabinet.

Five takes were attempted of the backing track (only takes 1, 3 and 5 were complete), take 5 being judged the best.

Later in the session, takes 6 and 7 comprised the superimposition of McCartney's double-tracked lead vocals during the "I will return..." sections of the song. With take 7 being the best of these minor additions, recording on the song was completed.

On February 25th in a Studio 2 control room session, unnumbered mono and stereo remixes (RM and RS) were created from take 7. These remixes served as the respective mono and stereo release versions of the song.

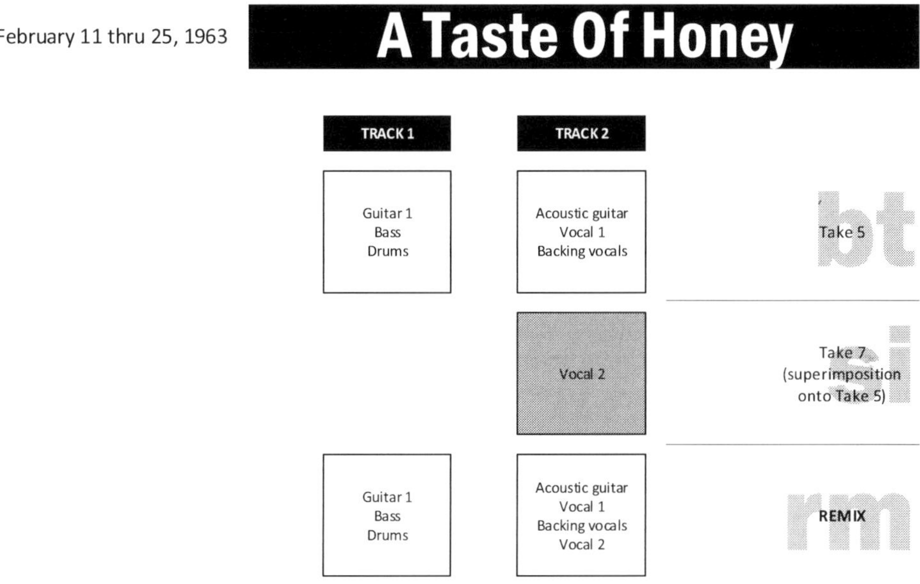

# Do You Want To Know A Secret

**Sessions**

- February 11, 1963
- February 25, 1963

John Lennon and Paul McCartney's *Do You Want To Know A Secret* was the fourth song recorded for the *Please Please Me* album at EMI Recording Studios, Studio 2, on February 11th, 1963, and second song recorded during the afternoon session, following *A Taste of Honey*. It was one of two vocal contributions to the album by Harrison.

The song is a throwback to the type of tune not heard in a generation, with an introductory section that never repeats; the kind of prologue shared by songs like Harold Arlen and E.Y. Harburg's *Somewhere Over The Rainbow* that had largely fallen out of fashion. Throughout The Beatles' career, they would call upon influences from the '30s, '40s and '50s without a thought as to whether they were hip or not. Simply by being themselves, they made these compositional approaches new again.

The technical team for the session included producer George Martin, balance engineer Norman Smith, and tape operator Richard Langham.

The song was recorded to the twin-track EMI BTR3 primary tracking machine, and starting with take 7, simultaneously to an additional mono EMI BTR2 primary tracking machine.

The backing track featured Harrison on his 1962 Gibson J-160E acoustic guitar and lead vocals, Lennon on his 1962 Gibson J-160E acoustic guitar, McCartney on his 1961 Hofner 500/1 bass, and Starr on his 1960 Premier 58 Mahogany Duroplastic drum set.

For amplification, Lennon and Harrison played through the 30-watt 1962 JMI Vox AC30/6 Twin amplifiers. The Gibson guitars were also mic'ed acoustically with Neumann U48 microphones. Engineer Smith blended the acoustic signal with the amplified one to create a unique acoustic guitar tone. For bass amplification, McCartney used technical engineer Ken Townsend's makeshift bass setup comprised of the studio's Leak Point One preamplifier and Leak TL-12 Plus amplifier with Tannoy Dual Concentric 15" speaker and cabinet.

Six takes of the backing track were attempted, two of them false starts (takes 1 and 5) and four of them complete (takes 2, 3, 4 and 6). Take 6 was considered the best of these takes.

Superimposition takes 7 and 8 followed, including Lennon, McCartney, and Harrison's harmony vocals, and Starr on drumsticks that he used as a percussion instrument by clicking them together. With these additions, recording on the song was completed.

On February 25th in a Studio 2 control room session, unnumbered mono and stereo remixes (RM and RS) were created from take 8. These remixes served as the respective mono and stereo release versions of the song.

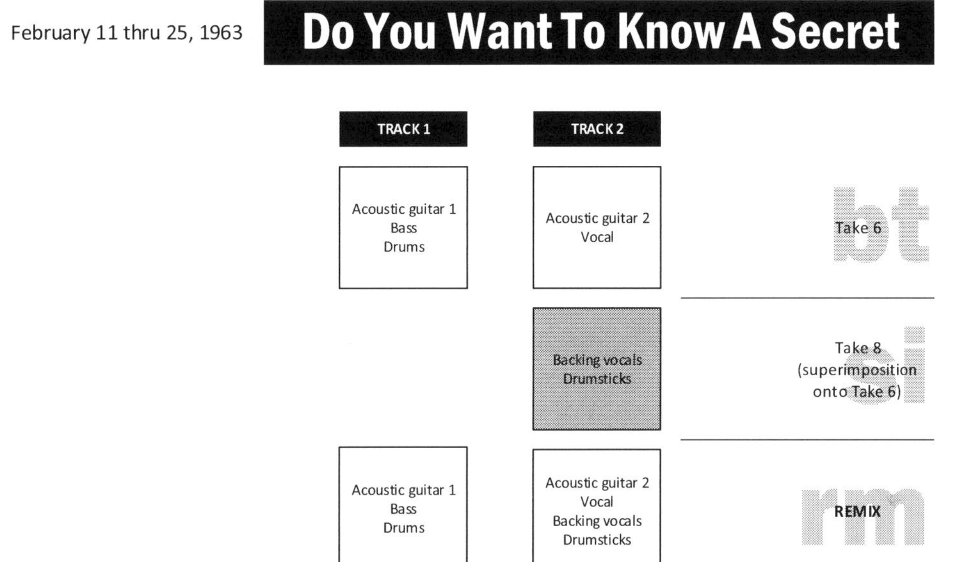

# Misery

**Sessions**

- February 11, 1963
- February 20, 1963
- February 25, 1963

John Lennon and Paul McCartney's *Misery* was the fifth song recorded for the *Please Please Me* album at EMI Recording Studios, Studio 2, on February 11th, 1963 (and the last song recorded during the afternoon session). The song was originally intended for Helen Shapiro, a 16-year-old UK teen idol The Beatles toured with early in 1963. When her management passed on the song, it was a natural choice for the new album.

The technical team for the song's first session included producer George Martin, balance engineer Norman Smith, and tape operator Richard Langham.

The song was recorded to the twin-track EMI BTR3 primary tracking machine and simultaneously to a mono EMI BTR2 primary tracking machine.

The backing track featured Lennon on his 1962 Gibson J-160E acoustic guitar and lead vocals, McCartney on his 1961 Hofner 500/1 bass and lead vocals, Harrison on his 1957 Gretsch G6128 Duo Jet electric guitar, and Starr on his 1960 Premier 58 Mahogany Duroplastic drum set.

For amplification, Lennon and Harrison played through the 30-watt 1962 JMI Vox AC30/6 Twin amplifiers. Lennon's Gibson was also mic'ed acoustically with a Neumann U48 microphone. Engineer Smith blended the acoustic signal with the amplified one to create a unique acoustic guitar tone. For bass amplification, McCartney used technical engineer Ken Townsend's makeshift bass setup comprised of the studio's Leak Point One preamplifier and Leak TL-12 Plus amplifier with Tannoy Dual Concentric 15” speaker and cabinet.

Eleven takes of a backing track were recorded, though in the end Martin was left with only a handful of performances from which to choose.

Take 1 was complete, while take 2 broke down after a minute (Harrison's amplifier volume was a little loud for the engineers, who first asked him if he had changed guitars — they couldn't see him from their control room vantage point high above Studio 2). Takes 3, 4 and 5 also broke down, this time due to Lennon forgetting the words to his own song, which was not an unusual occurrence.

Take 6 was a complete performance, though McCartney flubbed an early chord change on the bass and Starr rushed the beat. These takes were followed by a pedestrian effort on take 7, false starts on takes 8, 9 and 10, and finally an inspired take 11 that was just what Martin was after. But recording on the song wasn't complete yet.

On February 20th, while The Beatles were busy with live performance commitments, George Martin, balance engineer Stuart Eltham, and tape operator Geoff Emerick returned to Studio 3 to add a piano part to the middle eight of the song. Martin played the studio's Steinway "Music Room" Model B Grand Piano, which was recorded at half-speed to the twin-track EMI BTR3.

With this technique, the primary tape machine ran at half its normal 15 inch-per-second speed while Martin executed his part. This accomplished two things. First, it made it easier for Martin to play the runs. Secondly, on playback at the normal tape speed, the part was transposed an octave above the pitch it was recorded at, giving the instrument a shimmering quality as the piano's overtones rang at twice their normal rate.

Takes 12 through 16 were created with Martin perfecting the superimposition on take 16. With this addition, recording on the song was completed.

On February 25th in a Studio 2 control room session, unnumbered mono and stereo remixes (RM and RS) were created from take 16. These remixes served as the respective mono and stereo release versions of the song.

February 11 thru 25, 1963

# Misery

| TRACK 1 | TRACK 2 | |
|---|---|---|
| Guitar<br>Bass<br>Drums | Acoustic guitar<br>Vocal 1<br>Vocal 2 | bt Take 11 |
| | Piano | si Take 16 (superimposition onto Take 11) |
| Guitar<br>Bass<br>Drums | Acoustic guitar<br>Vocal 1<br>Vocal 2<br>Piano | rm REMIX |

# Hold Me Tight (unreleased)

**Sessions**

- February 11, 1963

John Lennon and Paul McCartney's *Hold Me Tight* never made it to the *Please Please Me* album. The sixth song recorded at EMI Recording Studios, Studio 2, on February 11th, 1963 (and the first of the evening session), was what McCartney described as a "work" song (a song that got the job done, but wasn't special in any way), and apparently the version created that night was not a memorable one.

The technical team for the session included producer George Martin, balance engineer Norman Smith, and tape operator Richard Langham.

The song was recorded to the twin-track EMI BTR3 primary tracking machine and simultaneously to an additional mono EMI BTR2 primary tracking machine.

The backing track featured Lennon on his 1958 Rickenbacker 325 Capri electric guitar with Bigsby vibrato and lead vocals, McCartney on his 1961 Hofner 500/1 bass and lead vocals, Harrison on his 1957 Gretsch G6128 Duo Jet electric guitar, and Starr on his 1960 Premier 58 Mahogany Duroplastic drum set.

For amplification, Lennon and Harrison played through the 30-watt 1962 JMI Vox AC30/6 Twin amplifiers. For bass amplification, McCartney used technical engineer Ken Townsend's makeshift bass setup comprised of the studio's Leak Point One preamplifier and Leak TL-12 Plus amplifier with Tannoy Dual Concentric 15" speaker and cabinet.

The band struggled with the song. False starts and breakdowns plagued the first five takes; and nine takes of the song resulted in only two complete performances (takes 6 and 9, with take 9 being considered the best).

An attempt by Martin to make the best of a bad situation followed with an edit piece (takes 10 through 13). The section of the song which the piece was intended for is unknown. With take 13 of the edit piece being considered the best, Martin created an edit joining take 9 with 13. The work completed, this version of the song was put aside.

No remixes were ever created of this version of *Hold Me Tight*, and the tape containing it was later destroyed before anyone at EMI thought to archive anything and everything The Beatles recorded.

A remake of the song finally saw the light of day as a part of the *With The Beatles* sessions seven months later.

# Anna (Go To Him)

**Sessions**

- February 11, 1963
- February 25, 1963

The seventh song recorded for the *Please Please Me* album at EMI Recording Studios, Studio 2, on February 11th, 1963 was Arthur Alexander's *Anna (Go To Him)*. Originally released in 1962 on the Dot label, the song was another example of how The Beatles mined the pop and R&B charts for quality cover songs most regarded as lesser hits. The original version of the track didn't even break the top 50 in the US pop charts and only reached #10 on the US R&B charts.

The technical team for the session included producer George Martin, balance engineer Norman Smith and, tape operator Richard Langham.

The song was recorded to the twin-track EMI BTR3 primary tracking machine and simultaneously to an additional mono EMI BTR2 primary tracking machine.

The backing track featured Lennon on his 1962 Gibson J-160E acoustic guitar and lead vocals, McCartney on his 1961 Hofner 500/1 bass and backing vocals, Harrison on his 1957 Gretsch G6128 Duo Jet electric guitar and backing vocals, and Starr on his 1960 Premier 58 Mahogany Duroplastic drum set.

For amplification, Lennon and Harrison used the 30-watt 1962 JMI Vox AC30/6 Twin amplifiers. Lennon's Gibson was also mic'ed acoustically with a Neumann U48 microphone. Engineer Smith blended the acoustic signal with the amplified one to create a unique acoustic guitar tone. For bass amplification, McCartney used technical engineer Ken Townsend's makeshift bass setup comprised of the studio's Leak Point One preamplifier and Leak TL-12 Plus amplifier with Tannoy Dual Concentric 15" speaker and cabinet.

With *Anna (Go To Him)*, The Beatles hit their stride in the marathon recording session. After two false starts, take 3 was not only a complete performance, but also the definitive one, with the band firing on all cylinders. Lennon's lead and McCartney and Harrison's backing vocals were spot-on.

Martin as producer was experienced enough to understand that he had what he needed on tape and no further work was required.

The track was in such good shape that come the first dedicated mixing session for the album on February 25th in Studio 2, an unnumbered remix mono (RM) from take 3 was the first work completed. Later in the same session, an unnumbered remix stereo (RS) was created from the same take. These remixes served as the respective mono and stereo release versions of the song.

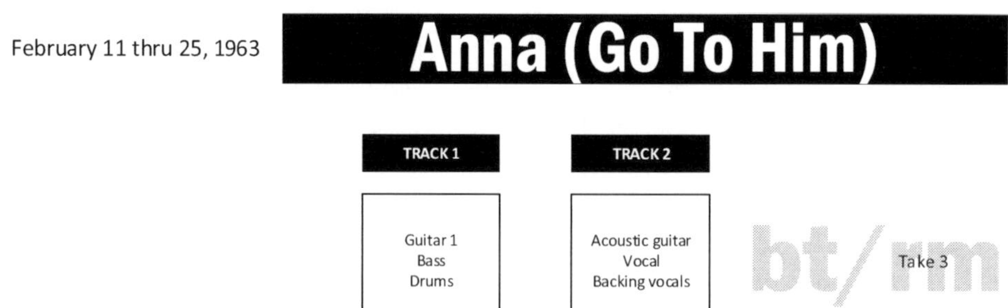

# Boys

**Sessions**

- February 11, 1963
- February 25, 1963

Luther Dixon and Wes Farrell's *Boys* was the eighth song recorded for the *Please Please Me* album at EMI Recording Studios, Studio 2, on February 11th, 1963.

Yet another hidden gem, this time the song was mined from the B-side of The Shirelles single, *Will You Love Me Tomorrow*, appearing on the Scepter label in 1960. The Beatles, huge fans of the "girl group" sound from the States, didn't even think to change the gender of the song for the recording as they had with their Decca audition track, *To Know Her Is To Love Her* (originally, *To Know Him Is To Love Him*).

How closely did the band identify with the girl group sound? *Please Please Me* would feature another Shirelles song, *Baby It's You*, as well as The Cookies' *Chains* — three of the album's 14 tracks.

The technical team for the session included producer George Martin, balance engineer Norman Smith, and tape operator Richard Langham.

The song was recorded to the twin-track EMI BTR3 primary tracking machine and simultaneously to an additional mono EMI BTR2 primary tracking machine.

The backing track featured Starr on his 1960 Premier 58 Mahogany Duroplastic drum set and lead vocals, Lennon on his 1958 Rickenbacker 325 Capri electric guitar with Bigsby vibrato, McCartney on his 1961 Hofner 500/1 bass and backing vocals, and Harrison on his 1957 Gretsch G6128 Duo Jet electric guitar and backing vocals.

For amplification, Lennon and Harrison played through the 30-watt 1962 JMI Vox AC30/6 Twin amplifiers. For bass amplification, McCartney used technical engineer Ken Townsend's makeshift bass setup comprised of the studio's Leak Point One preamplifier and Leak TL-12 Plus amplifier with Tannoy Dual Concentric 15" speaker and cabinet.

One take was good enough for producer Martin and the band, with Starr nailing a rousing vocal performance.

On February 25th in a Studio 2 control room session, unnumbered remixes of the song in mono and stereo (RM and RS) were created from take 1. These remixes served as the respective mono and stereo release versions of the song.

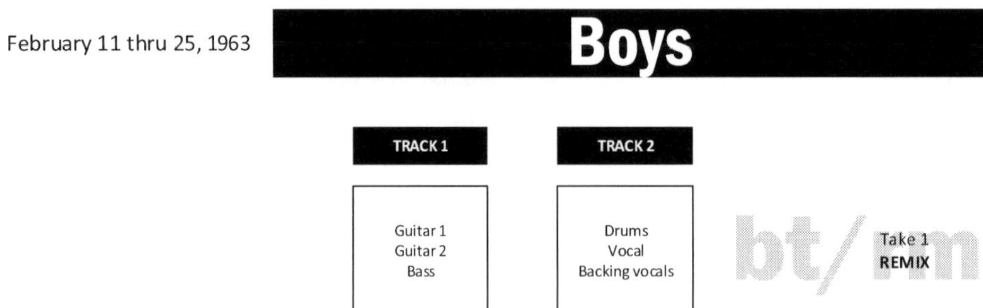

# Chains

**Sessions**

- February 11, 1963
- February 25, 1963

Gerry Goffin and Carole King's *Chains* was the ninth song recorded for the *Please Please Me* album at EMI Recording Studios, Studio 2, on February 11th, 1963. The song had been a top 20 hit in the US for The Cookies in 1962 on Dimension Records and released in the UK on the London label, where the band likely originally heard it. The song featured Harrison's second lead vocal on the album.

The technical team for the session included producer George Martin, balance engineer Norman Smith, and tape operator Richard Langham.

The song was recorded to the twin-track EMI BTR3 primary tracking machine and simultaneously to an additional mono EMI BTR2 primary tracking machine.

The backing track featured Harrison on his 1957 Gretsch G6128 Duo Jet electric guitar and lead vocals, Lennon on his 1958 Rickenbacker 325 Capri electric guitar with Bigsby vibrato, Hohner harmonica (either an Echo Vamper or Super Chromonica model), and backing vocals, McCartney on his 1961 Hofner 500/1 bass and backing vocals, and Starr on his 1960 Premier 58 Mahogany Duroplastic drum set.

For amplification, Lennon and Harrison used the 30-watt 1962 JMI Vox AC30/6 Twin amplifiers. For bass amplification, McCartney used technical engineer Ken Townsend's makeshift bass setup comprised of the studio's Leak Point One preamplifier and Leak TL-12 Plus amplifier with Tannoy Dual Concentric 15" speaker and cabinet.

Four takes of the song were attempted, with takes 1 and 4 being complete, while takes 2 and 3 were false starts. Take 1 ended up being the best of the two complete takes and with it, recording on the song was done as no superimpositions were required.

The pace at which the *Please Please Me* album sessions were recorded can be readily illustrated with this track. Distortion and crackling are present in Lennon's guitar part, likely caused by a loose guitar connection to his amplifier (starting at around the 1:02 mark). This flaw isn't evident in the mono remix of the song, but stands out in the left channel of the stereo version. While the engineers must have known the flaw was there, it wasn't enough to hold up the work at hand.

On February 25th in a Studio 2 control room session, unnumbered mono and stereo remixes of the song (RM and RS) were created from take 1. The remixes served as the respective mono and stereo release versions of the song.

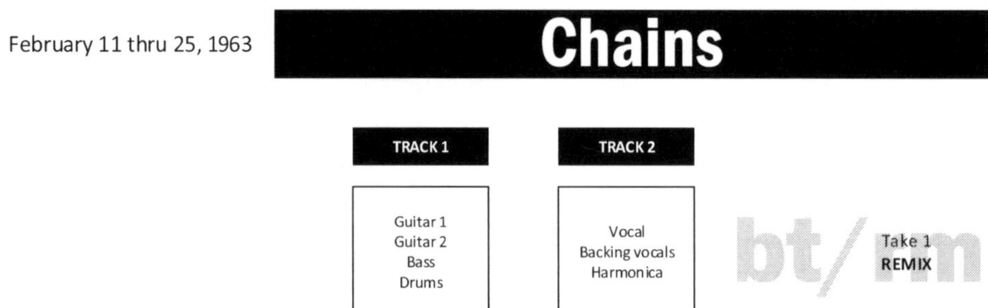

# Baby It's You

**Sessions**

- February 11, 1963
- February 20, 1963
- February 25, 1963

Burt Bacharach, Mack David, and Barney Williams' *Baby It's You* was the tenth song recorded for the *Please Please Me* album at EMI Recording Studios, Studio 2, on February 11th, 1963. The song was a Top 10 hit in the US for The Shirelles in 1961 on Scepter Records.

The technical team for the song's first session included producer George Martin, balance engineer Norman Smith, and tape operator Richard Langham.

The song was recorded to the twin-track EMI BTR3 primary tracking machine and simultaneously to an additional mono EMI BTR2 primary tracking machine.

The backing track featured Lennon on his 1958 Rickenbacker 325 Capri electric guitar with Bigsby vibrato and lead vocals, McCartney on his 1961 Hofner 500/1 bass and backing vocals, Harrison on his 1957 Gretsch G6128 Duo Jet electric guitar and backing vocals, and Starr on his 1960 Premier 58 Mahogany Duroplastic drum set.

For amplification, Lennon and Harrison played through the 30-watt 1962 JMI Vox AC30/6 Twin amplifiers. For bass amplification, McCartney used technical engineer Ken Townsend's makeshift bass setup comprised of the studio's Leak Point One preamplifier and Leak TL-12 Plus amplifier with Tannoy Dual Concentric 15" speaker and cabinet.

Three takes of the song were attempted, with takes 1 and 3 being complete, while take 2 was a false start. Take 3 ended up being the best of the two complete takes and the song went no further during the session.

On February 20th with The Beatles busy with live performance commitments, George Martin, balance engineer Stuart Eltham and tape operator Geoff Emerick returned to Studio 2 to add a keyboard part to the song's instrumental break.

First, Martin played the studio's Schiedmayer celeste onto takes 4 and 5 (take 5 being the best), then the studio's Steinway "Music Room" Model B Grand Piano onto take 6. The piano did not appear on the final remix, as the celeste version on take 5 was considered the best addition to the song.

On February 25th in a Studio 2 control room session, an unnumbered remix stereo (RS) of the song was created from take 5. Later in the evening, in Studio 3, an unnumbered remix mono (RM) was created from the same take. These remixes served as the respective mono and stereo release versions of the song.

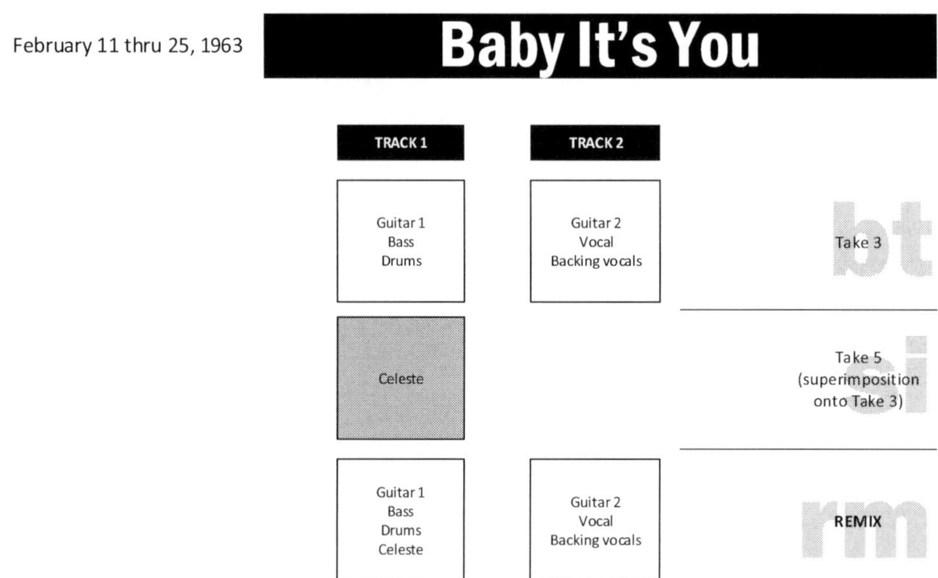

# Twist And Shout

**Sessions**

- February 11, 1963
- February 25, 1963

Phil Medley and Bert Burns' *Twist And Shout* was the final song on the *Please Please Me* album, and the final song recorded at EMI Recording Studios, Studio 2, on February 11th, 1963. Originally a Top 20 hit in the US for The Isley Brothers in 1962 on the Wand label, it would be The Beatles' version that history would remember.

The technical team for the session included producer George Martin, balance engineer Norman Smith, and tape operator Richard Langham.

The song was recorded to the twin-track EMI BTR3 primary tracking machine.

The backing track featured Lennon on his 1958 Rickenbacker 325 Capri electric guitar with Bigsby vibrato and lead vocals, McCartney on his 1961 Hofner 500/1 bass and backing vocals, Harrison on his 1957 Gretsch G6128 Duo Jet electric guitar and backing vocals, and Starr on his 1960 Premier 58 Mahogany Duroplastic drum set.

For amplification, Lennon and Harrison played through the 30-watt 1962 JMI Vox AC30/6 Twin amplifiers. For bass amplification, McCartney used technical engineer Ken Townsend's makeshift bass setup comprised of the studio's Leak Point One preamplifier and Leak TL-12 Plus amplifier with Tannoy Dual Concentric 15" speaker and cabinet.

With Lennon's voice shredded from singing either lead or backing vocals on the majority of the other 75 takes during a full day's work on 11 songs, it's something of a miracle that *Twist And Shout* only required two takes to perfect, with take 1 being the best of the two complete performances.

Nothing more was needed. No superimpositions. No edit pieces. The song was a perfect rock-and-roll moment.

Before the session was completed, and because of the excitement generated by the performance, a rough unnumbered remix mono of the tune (RM) was created from take 1.

On February 25th in a Studio 2 control room session, unnumbered mono and stereo remixes (RM and RS) were created from take 1. These remixes served as the respective mono and stereo release versions of the song.

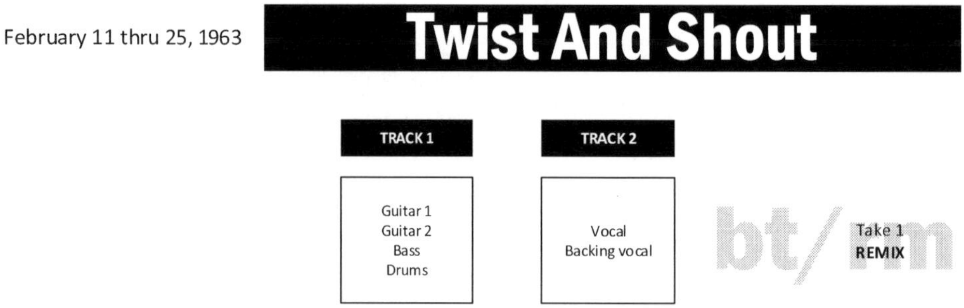

February 11 thru 25, 1963

## Twist And Shout

| TRACK 1 | TRACK 2 | |
|---|---|---|
| Guitar 1<br>Guitar 2<br>Bass<br>Drums | Vocal<br>Backing vocal | bt/rm Take 1 **REMIX** |

# From Me To You

**Sessions**

- March 5, 1963
- March 14, 1963

Due for release in late March, work on the *Please Please Me* album was completed on February 25th, 1963, but just over a week later on March 5th, The Beatles were back at EMI Recording Studios, Studio 2, to record their next single.

*From Me To You* was another John Lennon and Paul McCartney original, and with it the songwriters started hitting an early stride. Through the craftsmanship of the tune and its arrangement you can hear the duo gaining confidence, though the performances this time around were another issue altogether.

The technical team for the session included producer George Martin, balance engineer Norman Smith, and tape operator Richard Langham.

The song was recorded to the twin-track EMI BTR3 primary tracking machine and simultaneously to an additional mono EMI BTR2 primary tracking machine.

The backing track featured Lennon on his 1962 Gibson J-160E acoustic guitar and lead vocals, McCartney on his 1961 Hofner 500/1 bass and lead vocals, Harrison on his 1957 Gretsch G6128 Duo Jet electric guitar (while his 1962 Rickenbacker 425 was available for the session, it's unlikely that it was used), and Starr on his 1960 Premier 58 Mahogany Duroplastic drum set.

For amplification, Lennon and Harrison played through the 30-watt 1962 JMI Vox AC30/6 Twin amplifiers. Lennon's Gibson was also mic'ed acoustically with a Neumann U48 microphone. Engineer Smith blended the acoustic signal with the amplified one to create a unique acoustic guitar tone. For bass amplification, McCartney used technical engineer Ken Townsend's makeshift bass setup comprised of the studio's Leak Point One preamplifier and Leak TL-12 Plus amplifier with Tannoy Dual Concentric 15" speaker and cabinet.

The seven takes of the backing track show the band trying to find their way with the song. Take 1 broke down before the end; take 2 was complete, though it had a rough ending; take 3 was also complete, but uninspired; and take 4 was complete, but also suffered a rough ending.

In take 5, a change in the arrangement took place — for the first time, a break was made for a solo. Take 6 had a false start, but finally in take 7 the band created a full and usable version of the song.

Martin moved the session forward at a brisk pace, setting the band to work on a few edit pieces to tighten up take 7. Edit pieces during this period were referred to by a pair of reference numbers that increased together. So the first take of an edit piece in this instance was referred to as, "edit piece 1, take 8" (the work based on take 7), the next as "edit piece 2, take 9" and so on.

The edit pieces included Lennon on harmonica, Harrison's guitar solo and Lennon and McCartney's vocal harmony introduction.

Martin assembled a complex edit of *From Me To You* from takes 12, 8, 9, and 10 (in that order), the best of the performances and edit pieces.

On March 14th in a Studio 2 control room session, both the mono and stereo remixes (RM and RS) of the song were created. The final unnumbered mono version of the song was an edit of takes 12, 8, 9, and 10, manually synced with take 8. The stereo version of the song was never remixed, but instead derived from the edit of takes 12, 8, 9, and 10 only (the master twin-track edit).

The unnumbered mono remix served as the release version of the song. The stereo version was not released until 1966 on the greatest hits collection, *A Collection Of Beatles Oldies*.

March 5 thru 14, 1963

# From Me To You

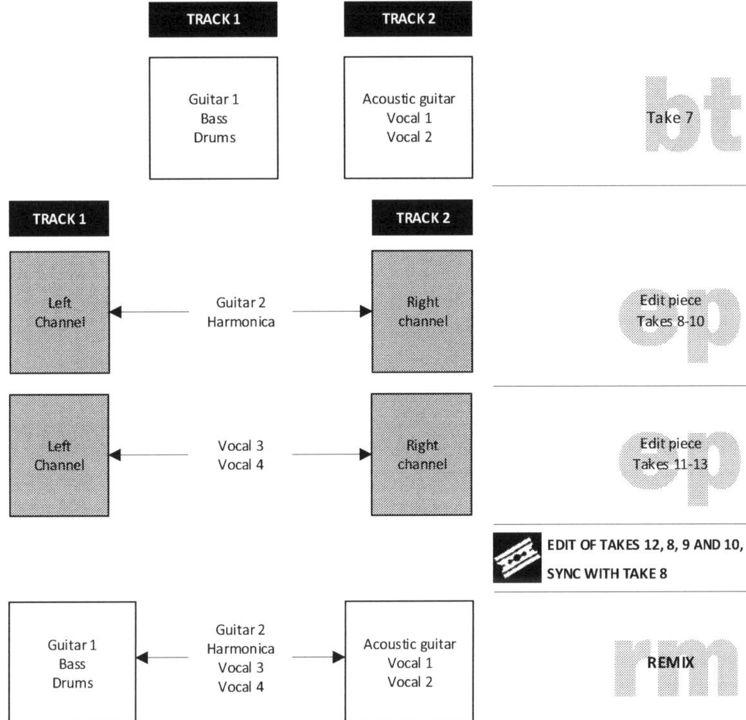

# Thank You Girl

**Sessions**

- March 5, 1963
- March 13, 1963

The same recording session on March 5th, 1963 at EMI Recording Studios, Studio 2, for *From Me To You* also included work on the B-side of the next Beatles single. *Thank You Girl* was another John Lennon and Paul McCartney original, and while the song is a solid pop offering, just as with the single's A-side, it would take some heavy editing of the performances to make the most of its potential.

The technical team for the song's first session included producer George Martin, balance engineer Norman Smith, and tape operator Richard Langham.

The song was recorded to the twin-track EMI BTR3 primary tracking machine and simultaneously to an additional mono EMI BTR2 primary tracking machine.

The backing track featured Lennon on his 1962 Gibson J-160E acoustic guitar and lead vocals, McCartney on his 1961 Hofner 500/1 bass and lead vocals, Harrison on his 1962 Gibson J-160E acoustic guitar, and Starr on his 1960 Premier 58 Mahogany Duroplastic drum set.

For amplification, Lennon and Harrison played through the 30-watt 1962 JMI Vox AC30/6 Twin amplifiers (now re-covered in black material from their original fawn finish). The Gibson guitars were also mic'ed acoustically with Neumann U48 microphones. Engineer Smith blended the acoustic signal with the amplified one to create a unique acoustic guitar tone. In this instance, he balanced Harrison's guitar sound in favour of the amplified signal in order to distinguish it from Lennon's, which was weighted to the more natural, acoustic sound. For bass amplification, McCartney used technical engineer Ken Townsend's makeshift bass setup comprised of the studio's Leak Point One preamplifier and Leak TL-12 Plus amplifier with Tannoy Dual Concentric 15" speaker and cabinet.

*Thank You Little Girl* (the song's original title) began with six takes of the backing track. Take 1 was a successful run through; takes 2 and 3 false starts; and takes 4 and 5 were complete (though the ending of take 5 was flubbed somewhat). Take 6 was a complete performance and considered the best, though the ending still needed work.

Edit pieces 8 through 13 followed — all attempts to tighten up the ending of the song.

On March 13th, the band returned to Studio 2 where Lennon added a harmonica superimposition to the song in 15 additional takes (takes 14 through 28).

Next, Martin and the technical team again set to cutting tape to create the ultimate version of the song. The compiled edit of takes 6, 13, 17, 20, 21 and 23 was called take 30 and the basis of both the unnumbered mono and stereo master remixes (RM and RS) created during the session. These remixes served as the respective mono release and stereo version of the song. The stereo version of the song was unreleased contemporary to The Beatles' recording career.

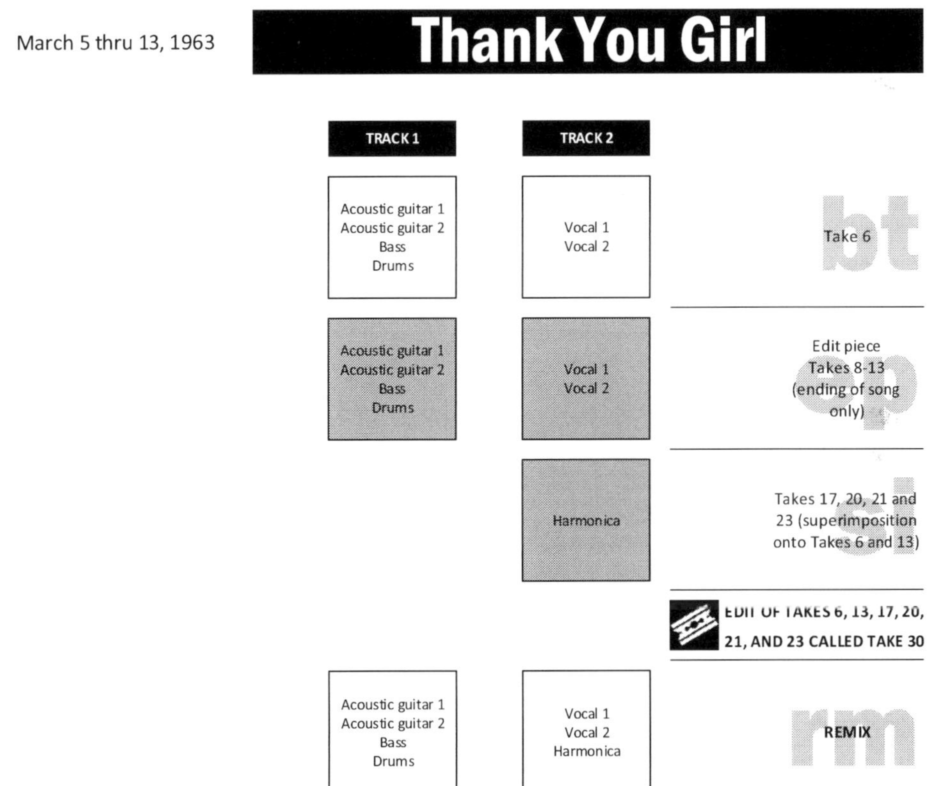

# The One After 909 (unreleased)

**Sessions**

- March 5, 1963

The final song recorded during the March 5th, 1963 session at EMI Recording Studios, Studio 2, was another John Lennon and Paul McCartney original, and one of the earliest tunes the pair had written together, *The One After 909.*

The technical team for the session included producer George Martin, balance engineer Norman Smith, and tape operator Richard Langham.

The song was recorded to the twin-track EMI BTR3 primary tracking machine and simultaneously to an additional mono EMI BTR2 primary tracking machine.

The backing track featured Lennon on his 1962 Gibson J-160E acoustic guitar and lead vocals, McCartney on his 1961 Hofner 500/1 bass and lead vocals, Harrison on his 1957 Gretsch G6128 Duo Jet electric guitar (while his 1962 Rickenbacker 425 was also available for the session, it's unlikely he used it), and Starr on his 1960 Premier 58 Mahogany Duroplastic drum set.

For amplification, Lennon and Harrison played through the 30-watt 1962 JMI Vox AC30/6 Twin amplifiers. Lennon's Gibson was also mic'ed acoustically with a Neumann U48 microphone. Engineer Smith blended the acoustic signal with the amplified one to create a unique acoustic guitar tone. For bass amplification, McCartney used technical engineer Ken Townsend's makeshift bass setup comprised of the studio's Leak Point One preamplifier and Leak TL-12 Plus amplifier with Tannoy Dual Concentric 15" speaker and cabinet.

Take 1 broke down after a little over a minute, while take 2 was complete (though Harrison dropped a few bars in the beginning of the song and McCartney commented at the end, "What kind of solo was that?").

Take 3 broke down again, with an irritated Lennon asking McCartney, "What are you doing?" and McCartney responding that he couldn't keep the relentless ⅛ note bass part going. "It's murder, man, I can't do it; can't keep it up..." Apparently McCartney didn't have a pick and was playing with his fingers.

Take 4 was another breakdown, though McCartney changed his part enough to play through the song. None of the takes was identified as a "best" take.

A final edit piece, take 5, included the entire band from the middle eight guitar solo through the end of the song, filling in the back end of take 4. With this edit piece, recording on the song was completed.

No remixes of this early version of the song were created. A modern stereo remix would be included in the *Anthology 1* release in 1995.

The Beatles would remake a release-worthy version of the song in January of 1969 during the *Get Back/Let It Be* sessions.

March 5, 1963

## The One After 909

| TRACK 1 | TRACK 2 | |
|---|---|---|
| Acoustic guitar 1<br>Acoustic guitar 2<br>Bass<br>Drums | Vocal 1<br>Vocal 2 | bt/ep<br>Take 4<br>and<br>Edit piece Take 5 |

# With The Beatles

Spanning 144 days from July 1st until November 22nd, 1963, the *With The Beatles* era witnessed the band become a global phenomenon, including the birth of Beatlemania. Eventually the adoration of fans drove the band off the live stage and into the studio, but for now they were still climbing and striving to arrive at, in Lennon's words, “the toppermost of the poppermost”.

Lennon and McCartney's growing sophistication as songwriters was on full display during the era with songs like *She Loves You* and *This Boy*, as was the band's role as global influencers, introducing the UK to US Motown and girl group hits, and, in the long run, re-introducing the US to its own musical heritage.

In addition to the *With The Bea*tles album, the era included the release of the global hit singles *She Loves You* and *I Want To Hold Your Hand*, and multiple EPs cashing in on fan hunger for product (even if they were only reconfigurations of earlier releases): *Twist And Shout*, *The Beatles Hits* and *The Beatles (No. 1)*.

---

# She Loves You

**Sessions**

- July 1, 1963
- July 4, 1963
- November 8, 1966

Early in the summer of 1963, The Beatles' schedule included recording their autumn and winter releases for Parlophone. On July 1st, 1963 the band was back at EMI Recording Studios, Studio 2, to record their next single and B-side, the John Lennon and Paul McCartney originals *She Loves You* and *Get You In The End* (later, *I'll Get You*).

With a technical team that included producer George Martin, balance engineer Norman Smith, and recently hired tape operator Geoff Emerick (who went on to an influential career as a Grammy Award-winning engineer for later Beatles recordings), the band set to work on the A-side of the new single; *She Loves You.*

The song was recorded to the twin-track EMI BTR3 primary tracking machine.

The backing track featured Lennon on his 1962 Gibson J-160E acoustic guitar and lead vocals, McCartney on his 1961 Hofner 500/1 bass and lead vocals, Harrison on his 1962 Gretsch 6122 Chet Atkins Country Gentleman electric guitar with Gretsch Bigsby B6G vibrato and backing vocals, while Starr stepped up from his 1960 Premier 58 Mahogany Duroplastic drums, now playing his 1963 Ludwig Oyster Black Pearl Downbeat drum set (the first of five Ludwig sets he played on with the band).

For amplification, Lennon and Harrison continued to play through the 30-watt 1962 JMI Vox AC30/6 Twin amplifiers. Lennon's Gibson was also mic'ed acoustically with a Neumann U48 microphone. Engineer Smith blended the acoustic signal with the amplified one to create a unique acoustic guitar tone. McCartney improved his bass amplification and was now using a 60-watt 1963 Vox T60 head with a Vox T60 speaker cabinet.

A series of unnumbered takes were made of the backing track, and audio evidence reveals at least one superimposition was performed. Harrison's guitar fills at the introduction, between stanzas and at the end of the song all appear to be superimpositions. With Harrison's additional work, recording on the song was completed.

On July 4th in a Studio 2 control room session, Martin, with an unidentified technical team, created an edit of the song from unnumbered/unknown takes, followed by a mono remix from the edited result. This unnumbered remix mono (RM) served as the mono release version of the song, The Beatles' first million-seller.

Over three years later on November 8th, 1966 after work had completed on *Revolver*, Geoff Emerick returned to Room 53 at EMI Studios to create the first stereo remix of the song from the mono master.

But why not use the original session tapes to create the stereo master? The sad fact is that by 1966, the original master tapes for the song had been lost. The "mock stereo" remix was created by duplicating the mono track on a second track and then using audio equalization to create different tonal qualities between the left and right channels while maintaining the integrity of the original track's sound.

Emerick completed two stereo remixes (RS 1 and 2), RS 1 being the best, which ended up as the stereo release version on the 1966 album *A Collection Of Beatles Oldies*.

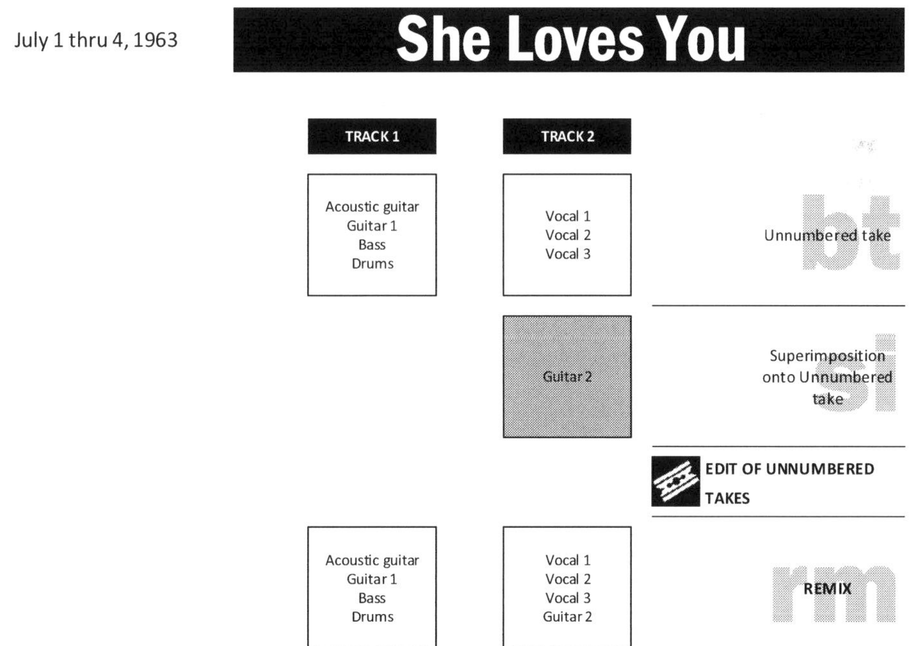

# I'll Get You

**Sessions**

- July 1, 1963
- July 4, 1963

The July 1st, 1963 session at EMI Recording Studios, Studio 2, for *She Loves You* included the recording of that single's B-side, the John Lennon and Paul McCartney original *Get You In The End* (later, *I'll Get You*).

The technical team for the session included producer George Martin, balance engineer Norman Smith, and tape operator Geoff Emerick.

The song was recorded to the twin-track EMI BTR3 primary tracking machine.

The backing track featured Lennon on his 1958 Rickenbacker 325 Capri electric guitar with Bigsby vibrato and lead vocals, McCartney on his 1961 Hofner 500/1 bass and lead vocals, Harrison on his 1962 Gretsch 6122 Chet Atkins Country Gentleman electric guitar with Gretsch Bigsby B6G vibrato and backing vocals, and Starr on his 1963 Ludwig Oyster Black Pearl Downbeat drum set.

For amplification, Lennon and Harrison played through the 30-watt 1962 JMI Vox AC30/6 Twin amplifiers. For bass amplification, McCartney used the 60-watt 1963 Vox T60 head with a Vox T60 speaker cabinet.

A series of unnumbered takes were made of the backing track. Audio examination reveals that at least two performances were created as a superimposition; Lennon's Hohner harmonica touches and McCartney and Harrison on handclaps. With these additions, recording on the song was completed.

On July 4th in a Studio 2 control room session, Martin, with an unidentified technical team, created an unnumbered remix mono (RM) from an unnumbered take. This remix served as the mono release version of the song.

The song was never remixed in stereo for the UK market, although it was, on an unknown date and location, remixed for the US market, where it appeared on *The Beatles' Second Album* in 1964.

July 1 thru 4, 1963

# I'll Get You

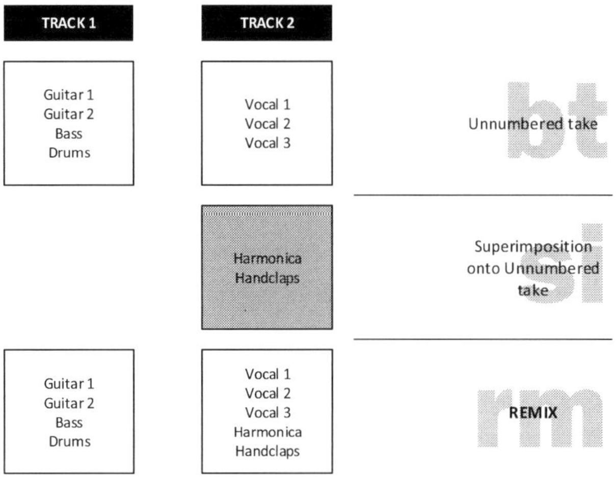

| TRACK 1 | TRACK 2 | |
|---|---|---|
| Guitar 1<br>Guitar 2<br>Bass<br>Drums | Vocal 1<br>Vocal 2<br>Vocal 3 | bt Unnumbered take |
| | Harmonica<br>Handclaps | si Superimposition onto Unnumbered take |
| Guitar 1<br>Guitar 2<br>Bass<br>Drums | Vocal 1<br>Vocal 2<br>Vocal 3<br>Harmonica<br>Handclaps | rm **REMIX** |

# You Really Got A Hold On Me

**Sessions**

- July 18, 1963
- August 21, 1963
- October 17, 1963
- October 29, 1963

The first full session for what became the *With The Beatles* album commenced on July 18th, 1963, with four tracks recorded at EMI Recording Studios, Studio 2. The first song to be tracked was a Motown favourite, Smokey Robinson's *You Really Got A Hold On Me*, which had been a Top 10 hit in the US in 1962 for The Miracles on the Tamla label.

The technical team for the session included producer George Martin, balance engineer Norman Smith, and tape operator Richard Langham.

The song was recorded to the twin-track EMI BTR3 primary tracking machine.

The backing track featured Lennon on his 1962 Gibson J-160E acoustic guitar, McCartney on his 1961 Hofner 500/1 bass, Harrison on his 1962 Gretsch 6122 Chet Atkins Country Gentleman electric guitar with Gretsch Bigsby B6G vibrato, and Starr on his 1963 Ludwig Oyster Black Pearl Downbeat drum set.

For amplification, Lennon and Harrison played through the 30-watt 1963 JMI Vox AC30/6 Twin Treble amplifiers. Lennon's Gibson was also mic'ed acoustically with a Neumann U48 microphone. Engineer Smith blended the acoustic signal with the amplified one to create a unique acoustic guitar tone. For bass amplification, McCartney used the 30-watt 1963 Vox AC30 head with a Vox T60 speaker cabinet.

Takes 1, 4 and 5 were complete, while takes 2 and 3 were false starts. Take 5 was considered the best and the subject of additional work.

Superimpositions to take 5 followed, adding Lennon's lead vocals, McCartney and Harrison's backing vocals and Harrison's few touches of additional lead guitar.

Superimposition takes 6 and 7 featured George Martin on the studio's Steinway "Music Room" Model B Grand Piano.

Next, three edit pieces were created (takes 8 through 10) comprised of McCartney adding a short backing vocal segment at around the 2:22 mark of the song (the "Baby!" heard during the last full verse).

Finally, edit piece take 11 had Martin back on the grand piano, reinforcing Harrison's guitar with a matching phrase for the introduction.

On August 21st, in a Studio 3 control room session, the best backing track with superimposition (take 7) and edit piece takes (takes 10 and 11) were remixed to mono and edited together to created the edit master. From this edit, the master mono remix (RM) was compiled. This compilation remix served as the mono release version of the song.

On October 17th in Studio 2, additional work was done on the song, but exactly what is a mystery. Barrett's tape logs record a twin-track tape with the song, noted as "Take 12", sandwiched between messages destined for The 1963 Christmas flexi-disc, the first of what would become an almost annual thank you to their fan club members. It is possible that this twin-track is the duplication of the master mono edit meant to be used for the stereo remix of the song, though the log does not reveal this.

On October 29th in a Studio 3 control room session, the two-track edit master was used to create the stereo master (RS). This compilation remix, RS 7/10/11 served as the stereo release version of the song.

July 18 thru
October 29, 1963

# You Really Got A Hold On Me

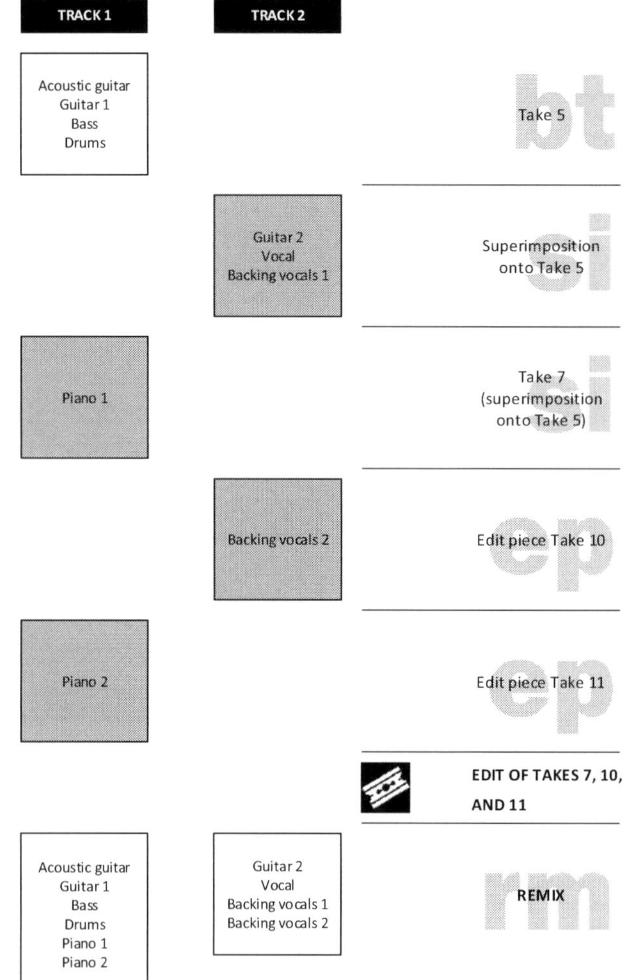

# Money (That's What I Want)

**Sessions**

- July 18, 1963
- July 30, 1963
- August 21, 1963
- September 30, 1963
- October 29, 1963
- October 30, 1963

The second song to be tracked during the first full session for what became the *With The Beatles* album on July 18th, 1963 at EMI Recording Studios, Studio 2, was another Motown favourite, Janie Bradford and Berry Gordy's *Money (That's What I Want)*. Released in 1959 by Barrett Strong on the Tamla and Anna labels, it was Motown's first hit single. The Beatles had previously recorded the song during their Decca tryout and it was a perfect follow-up in spirit to *Please Please Me*'s *Twist And Shout*.

The technical team for the session included producer George Martin, balance engineer Norman Smith, and tape operator Richard Langham.

The song was recorded to the twin-track EMI BTR3 primary tracking machine.

The backing track featured Lennon on his 1958 Rickenbacker 325 Capri electric guitar with Bigsby vibrato guitar and lead vocals, McCartney on his 1961 Hofner 500/1 bass, Harrison on his 1962 Gretsch 6122 Chet Atkins Country Gentleman electric guitar with Gretsch Bigsby B6G vibrato, and Starr on his 1963 Ludwig Oyster Black Pearl Downbeat drum set.

For amplification, Lennon and Harrison played through the 30-watt 1963 JMI Vox AC30/6 Twin Treble amplifiers. For bass amplification, McCartney used the 30-watt 1963 Vox AC30 head with a Vox T60 speaker cabinet.

Tracking on the song only produced two complete performances — takes 1 and 5 (takes 2, 3 and 4 were false starts).

After the completion of take 5, Martin headed to the floor of Studio 2 to record an edit piece of the first two bars of the introduction on the studio's Steinway "Music Room" Model B Grand Piano, while Starr tapped out a brief percussion part by tapping his drumsticks together (take 6).

Take 7 followed with the superimposition of more piano by Martin and additional backing vocals and handclaps by Lennon, McCartney, and Harrison.

Work resumed on the song on July 30th in Studio 2, where Martin attempted seven more takes with the grand piano, noted as a "piano test". None of Martin's work from this session was used.

Returning nearly a month later on August 21st to the control room of Studio 3, takes 6 and 7 of the song were edited together to create remix mono (RM) 6/7 — but was the song complete?

One more session sorted that question out. On September 30th, Martin again took a shot at improving the song's piano part. Three new versions, noted as RM 7 (versions 1 through 3) were created from the edit of takes 6 and 7, along with the simultaneous superimposition of a new piano part during the remix (again using the studio's Steinway "Music Room" Model B Grand Piano).

The experiment was ultimately unsuccessful and RM 6/7 became the mono release version of the song.

On October 29th, remix stereo (RS) 7 was created from the edit of takes 6 and 7. The remix was not quite right, and on the following day another RS 7 was created, this time from take 7 only. RS 7 from October 30th served as the stereo release version of the song.

Because the stereo version uses Martin's complete take 7 piano superimposition, it omits Starr's drumstick percussion on the introduction heard in the mono release version.

July 18 thru
October 30, 1963

# Money (That's What I Want)

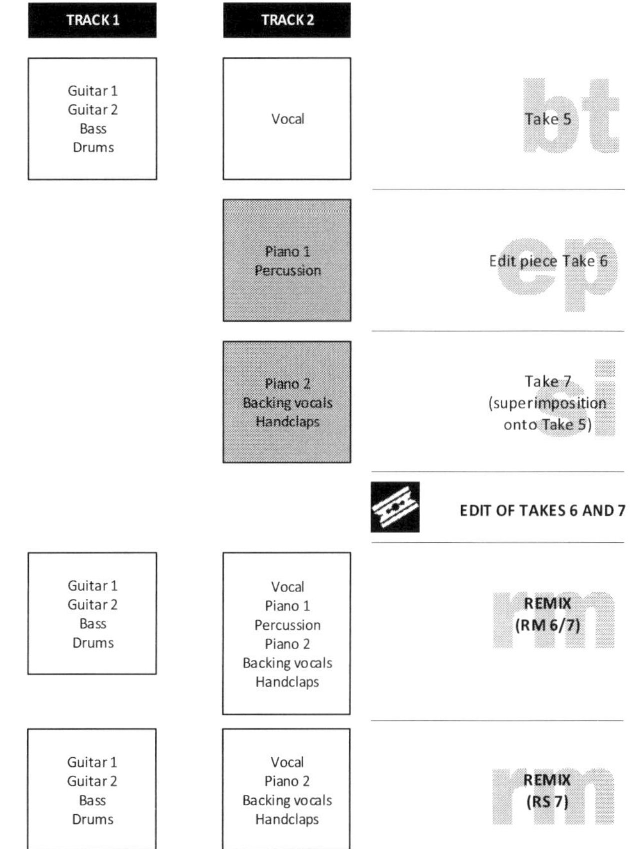

# Devil In Her Heart

**Sessions**

- July 18, 1963
- August 21, 1963
- October 29, 1963

The third song to be tracked during the first full session for what became the *With The Beatles* album on July 18th, 1963 at EMI Recording Studios, Studio 2, was Richard Drapkin's *Devil In Her Heart*. Originally titled, *Devil In His Heart* (the title change by The Beatles reflecting the updated gender orientation), it was a girl group favourite of the band, first recorded by Detroit's The Donays and released in the UK in 1962 on the Oriole label.

The technical team for the session included producer George Martin, balance engineer Norman Smith, and tape operator Richard Langham.

The song was recorded to the twin-track EMI BTR3 primary tracking machine.

The backing track featured Harrison on his 1962 Gretsch 6122 Chet Atkins Country Gentleman electric guitar with Gretsch Bigsby B6G vibrato and lead vocals, Lennon on his 1958 Rickenbacker 325 Capri electric guitar with Bigsby vibrato guitar and backing vocals, McCartney on his 1961 Hofner 500/1 bass and backing vocals, and Starr on his 1963 Ludwig Oyster Black Pearl Downbeat drum set.

For amplification, Lennon and Harrison played through the 30-watt 1963 JMI Vox AC30/6 Twin Treble amplifiers. For bass amplification, McCartney used the 30-watt 1963 Vox AC30 head with a Vox T60 speaker cabinet.

It took just three takes to perfect the backing track (take 2 being a false start), Harrison singing for the majority of the song, save when playing the delicate descending lead guitar part of the song.

Superimposition takes followed with Harrison patching the primary lead vocal and double-tracking the performance in places, while Starr contributed maracas. After two false starts on takes 4 and 5, take 6 was solid and no further work was required.

Returning nearly a month later on August 21st to the control room of Studio 3, remix mono (RM) 6 was created from take 6. RM 6 served as the mono release version of the song.

On October 29th in another Studio 3 control room session, remix stereo (RS) 6 was created from take 6. For this version, some tape echo was added to Harrison's guitar introduction. RS 6 served as the stereo release version of the song.

July 18 thru
October 29, 1963

## Devil In Her Heart

| TRACK 1 | TRACK 2 | |
|---|---|---|
| Guitar 1<br>Guitar 2<br>Bass<br>Drums | Vocal 1<br>Backing vocals | bt Take 3 |
| Maracas | Vocal 1 (fixes)<br>Vocal 2 | si Take 6 (superimposition onto Take 3) |
| Guitar 1<br>Guitar 2<br>Bass<br>Drums<br>Maracas | Vocal 1<br>Backing vocals<br>Vocal 1 (fixes)<br>Vocal 2 | rm REMIX |

# Till There Was You

**Sessions**

- July 18, 1963
- July 30, 1963
- August 21, 1963
- October 29, 1963

The last song to be tracked during the first full session for what became the *With The Beatles* album on July 18th, 1963 at EMI Recording Studios, Studio 2, was Meredith Willson's *Till There Was You*, from the musical *The Music Man* (which opened on Broadway in 1957, and released as a film in 1962). The song was part of The Beatles' set going back to Hamburg, and had been attempted at their Decca audition. This new version displayed a confidence sorely lacking in that first attempt.

The technical team for the song's first session included producer George Martin, balance engineer Norman Smith, and tape operator Richard Langham.

The song was recorded to the twin-track EMI BTR3 primary tracking machine.

The backing track featured McCartney on his 1961 Hofner 500/1 bass and lead vocals, Lennon on his 1962 Gibson J-160E acoustic guitar, Harrison on his nylon string Jose Ramirez Guitarra de Estudio acoustic guitar, and Starr on Premier bongos.

For amplification, Lennon played through the 30-watt 1963 JMI Vox AC30/6 Twin Treble amplifier. Lennon's Gibson was also mic'ed acoustically with a Neumann U48 microphone. Engineer Smith blended the acoustic signal with the amplified one to create a unique acoustic guitar tone. For bass amplification, McCartney used the 30-watt 1963 Vox AC30 head with a Vox T60 speaker cabinet.

After a false start on take 1, two complete takes of the song were completed during the session (takes 2 and 3), though Martin wasn't convinced he had the best the band could offer.

On July 30th, the band returned to Studio 2 for a remake of the song. There was no change in the instrumentation. Takes 4 and 5 were false starts, but then the band laid down three solid takes (takes 6 through 8); of these, take 8 was considered the best.

Unlike any other track recorded for *With The Beatles*, *Till There Was You* was complete as originally tracked — no superimpositions were required.

Nearly a month later, on August 21st in a Studio 3 control room session, remix mono (RM) 8 was created from take 8. RM 8 served as the mono release version of the song.

On October 29th in another Studio 3 control room session, a remix stereo (RS) 8 was created from take 8. RS 8 served as the stereo release version of the song.

July 18 thru
October 29, 1963

**Till There Was You**

| TRACK 1 | TRACK 2 | |
|---|---|---|
| Acoustic guitar 1<br>Acoustic guitar 2<br>Bass<br>Drums | Vocal | bt/rm<br>Take 8<br>**REMIX** |

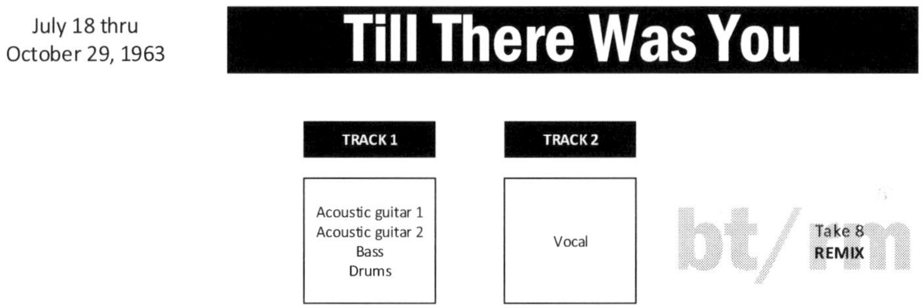

# Please Mister Postman

**Sessions**

- July 30, 1963
- August 21, 1963
- October 29, 1963

Work proceeded in earnest on the *With The Beatles* album during its second major session on July 30th, 1963 at EMI Recording Studios, Studio 2. The first song of the session was Georgia Dobbins, William Garrett, Freddie Gorman, Brian Holland, and Robert Bateman's *Please Mister Postman*. The song was originally recorded by The Marvelettes in 1961 for the Tamla label and became the first "Motown" No. 1 hit on the Billboard Hot 100 charts.

The technical team for the session included producer George Martin, balance engineer Norman Smith, and tape operator Richard Langham.

The song was recorded to the twin-track EMI BTR3 primary tracking machine.

The backing track featured Lennon on his 1958 Rickenbacker 325 Capri electric guitar with Bigsby vibrato and lead vocals, McCartney on his 1961 Hofner 500/1 bass and backing vocals, Harrison on his 1962 Gretsch 6122 Chet Atkins Country Gentleman electric guitar with Gretsch Bigsby B6G vibrato and backing vocals, and Starr on his 1963 Ludwig Oyster Black Pearl Downbeat drum set.

For amplification, Lennon and Harrison played through the 30-watt 1963 JMI Vox AC30/6 Twin Treble amplifiers. For bass amplification, McCartney used the 30-watt 1963 Vox AC30 head with a Vox T60 speaker cabinet.

Takes 1 and 2 were solid enough that Martin proceeded to superimpose a double-tracked lead vocal onto the best of these, take 2. Once complete however, it was thought that the core performance could be improved upon.

Starting over with take 4, the band and Martin got what they were looking for in four additional takes (takes 4 through 7). Take 7 was deemed the best of the new backing tracks and two superimposition takes followed (takes 8 and 9), featuring Lennon's double-tracking of his lead vocals and McCartney and Harrison double-tracking their backing vocals with the addition of handclaps. Take 9 was the best of the two takes.

Returning nearly a month later on August 21st to the control room of Studio 3, remix mono (RM) 9 was created from take 9. RM 9 served as the mono release version of the song.

On October 29th in another Studio 3 control room session, remix stereo (RS) 9 was created from take 9. RS 9 served as the stereo release version of the song.

July 30 thru
October 29, 1963

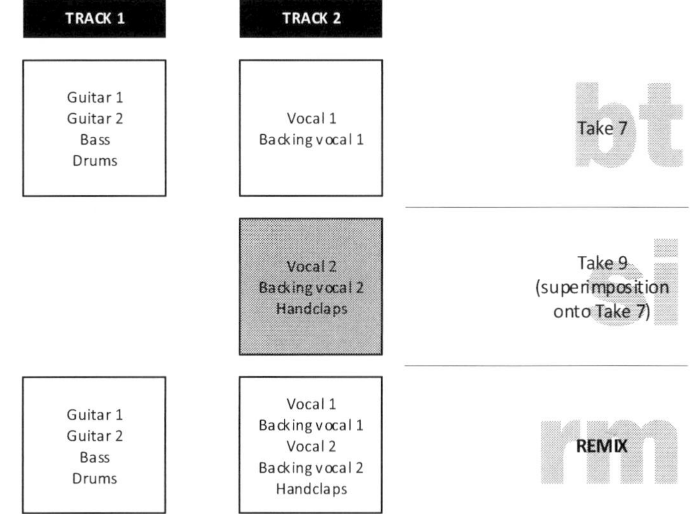

# It Won't Be Long

**Sessions**

- July 30, 1963
- August 21, 1963
- October 29, 1963

The second of six songs recorded during the session for the *With The Beatles* album on July 30th, 1963 at EMI Recording Studios, Studio 2, was John Lennon and Paul McCartney's *It Won't Be Long.* Another song of the period that might be considered a "work song", it's nonetheless heads and tails above the majority of pop fare from the era.

The technical team for the session included producer George Martin, balance engineer Norman Smith, and tape operator Richard Langham.

The song was recorded to the twin-track EMI BTR3 primary tracking machine.

The backing track featured Lennon on his 1958 Rickenbacker 325 Capri electric guitar with Bigsby vibrato and lead vocals, McCartney on his 1961 Hofner 500/1 bass and backing vocals, Harrison on his 1962 Gretsch 6122 Chet Atkins Country Gentleman electric guitar with Gretsch Bigsby B6G vibrato and backing vocals, and Starr on his 1963 Ludwig Oyster Black Pearl Downbeat drum set.

For amplification, Lennon and Harrison played through the 30-watt 1963 JMI Vox AC30/6 Twin Treble amplifiers. For bass amplification, McCartney used the 30-watt 1963 Vox AC30 head with a Vox T60 speaker cabinet.

It took seven takes to nail down the backing track for the song. While take 7 ended up being the best version of the song, Martin had the band continue for three more takes (takes 8 through 10) before deciding he already had what he was looking for.

Lennon's double-tracked lead vocals and Harrison's lead guitar were the focus of superimposition takes 11 through 17, and finally work was completed on the song with edit piece takes 18 through 23, in which the entire band focused on a stronger ending for the song. Take 21 was the best of these edit pieces.

Returning nearly a month later on August 21st to the control room of Studio 3, takes 17 and 21 were edited together to create a master edit, then remix mono (RM) 17/21 was created from the master edit. RM 17/21 served as the mono release version of the song.

On October 29th in another Studio 3 control room session, remix stereo (RS) 17 was created from the edit of takes 17 and 21. RS 17 served as the stereo release version of the song.

July 30 thru
October 29, 1963

# It Won't Be Long

| TRACK 1 | TRACK 2 | |
|---|---|---|
| Guitar 1<br>Guitar 2<br>Bass<br>Drums | Vocal 1<br>Backing vocals | bt Take 7 |
| Guitar 3 | Vocal 2 | si Take 17 (superimposition onto Take 7) |
| Guitar 1<br>Guitar 2<br>Bass<br>Drums | Vocal 3<br>Backing vocals 2 | ep Edit piece Take 21 |
| | | EDIT OF TAKES 17 AND 21 |
| Guitar 1<br>Guitar 2<br>Guitar 3<br>Bass<br>Drums | Vocal 1<br>Backing vocals<br>Vocal 2<br>Vocal 3<br>Backing vocals 2 | rm REMIX |

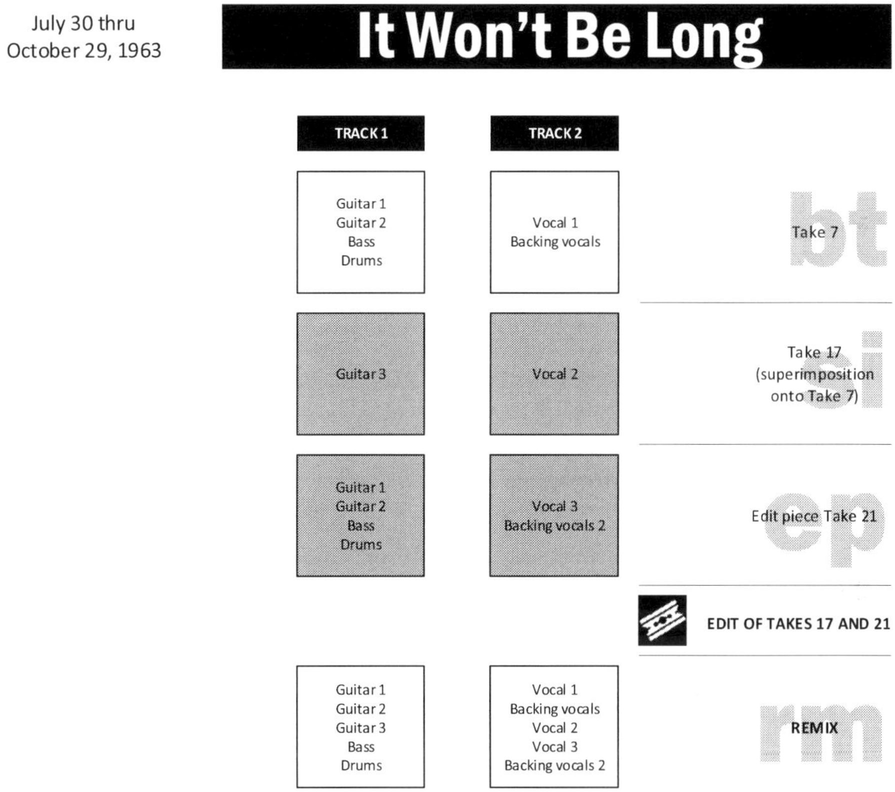

# Roll Over Beethoven

**Sessions**

- July 30, 1963
- August 21, 1963
- October 29, 1963

The third song recorded during the July 30th, 1963 session at EMI Recording Studios, Studio 2, for the *With The Beatles* album was Chuck Berry's classic, *Roll Over Beethoven.* The Beatles had been playing the song live in both their Liverpool and Hamburg club sets for years and it provided a particularly strong showcase for Harrison's guitar and voice.

The technical team for the session included producer George Martin, balance engineer Norman Smith, and tape operator Richard Langham.

The song was recorded to the twin-track EMI BTR3 primary tracking machine.

The backing featured Harrison on his 1962 Gretsch 6122 Chet Atkins Country Gentleman electric guitar with Gretsch Bigsby B6G vibrato and lead vocals, Lennon on his 1958 Rickenbacker 325 Capri electric guitar with Bigsby vibrato, McCartney on his 1961 Hofner 500/1 bass, and Starr on his 1963 Ludwig Oyster Black Pearl Downbeat drum set.

For amplification, Lennon and Harrison played through the 30-watt 1963 JMI Vox AC30/6 Twin Treble amplifiers. For bass amplification, McCartney used the 30-watt 1963 Vox AC30 head with a Vox T60 speaker cabinet.

Three complete takes emerged from the first five takes of the backing track (takes 2, 4 and 5 — takes 1 and 3 were false starts).

Take 5 being the best was then the focus of two superimposition takes (takes 6 and 7) that comprised Harrison's double-tracked lead vocals, lead guitar solo, and handclaps. Take 7 was the best of the two attempts (take 6 was another false start).

Lastly, with edit piece take 8, the band replaced the song's final chord.

Nearly a month later on August 21st in a Studio 3 control room session, takes 7 and 8 were edited together to create a master edit, then remix mono (RM) 7/8 was created from the master edit. RM 7/8 served as the mono release version of the song.

On October 29th in another Studio 3 control room session, remix stereo (RS) 7/8 was created from the two-track edit of takes 7 and 8. RS 7/8 served as the stereo release version of the song.

July 30 thru
October 29, 1963

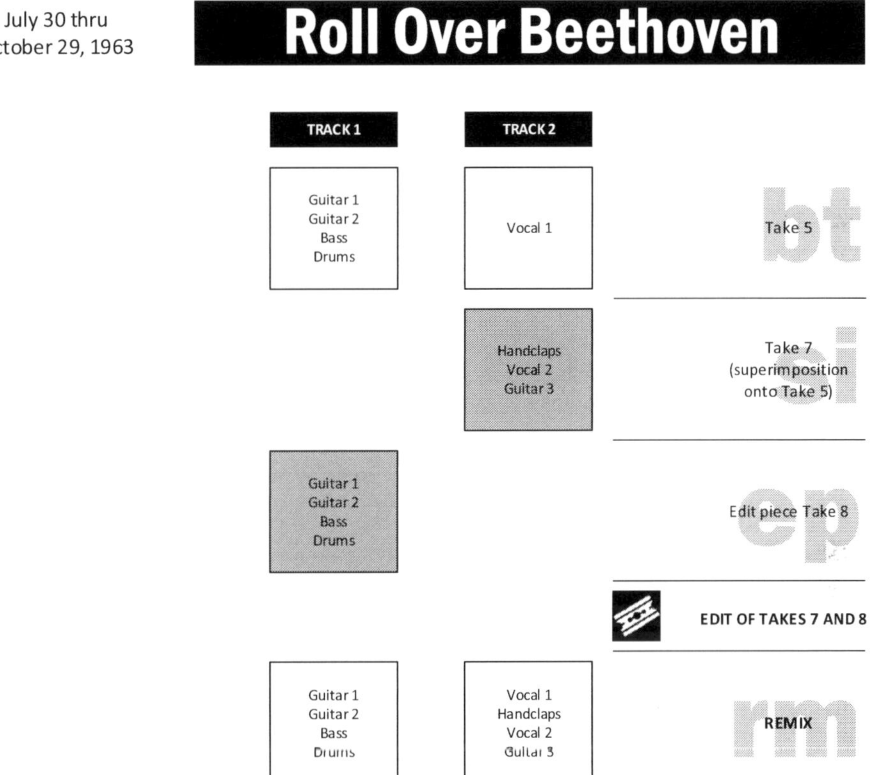

# All My Loving

**Sessions**

- July 30, 1963
- August 21, 1963
- October 29, 1963

*All My Loving* was the final song of the July 30th, 1963 session at EMI Recording Studios, Studio 2, for the *With The Beatles* album. The John Lennon and Paul McCartney original was deceptively straightforward, featuring McCartney's walking bass part and one of Harrison's finest solos to date. In a period filled with memorable tunes from the band, the song was still a standout.

The technical team for the session included producer George Martin, balance engineer Norman Smith, and tape operator Richard Langham.

The song was recorded to the twin-track EMI BTR3 primary tracking machine.

The backing track featured McCartney on his 1961 Hofner 500/1 bass and lead vocals, Lennon on his 1958 Rickenbacker 325 Capri electric guitar with Bigsby vibrato and backing vocals, Harrison on his 1962 Gretsch 6122 Chet Atkins Country Gentleman electric guitar with Gretsch Bigsby B6G vibrato and backing vocals, and Starr on his 1963 Ludwig Oyster Black Pearl Downbeat drum set.

For amplification, Lennon and Harrison played through the 30-watt 1963 JMI Vox AC30/6 Twin Treble amplifiers. For bass amplification, McCartney used the 30-watt 1963 Vox AC30 head with a Vox T60 speaker cabinet.

Take 1 was complete, though like many first takes, it was not a finished backing track. That required 10 more attempts to accomplish. Takes 2 and 3 were false starts, while takes 4, 6 and 7 were complete (there was no take 5). In the end, take 11 captured the performance everyone was looking for.

An addition to take 11 of McCartney's double-tracked lead vocals followed, with superimposition takes 12 through 14 — take 14 being the best. With this addition, recording on the song was completed.

Nearly a month later on August 21st in a Studio 3 control room session, remix mono (RM) 14 was created from take 14. RM 14 served as the mono release version of the song.

On October 29th in another Studio 3 control room session, remix stereo (RS) 14 was created from take 14. RS 14 served as the stereo release version of the song.

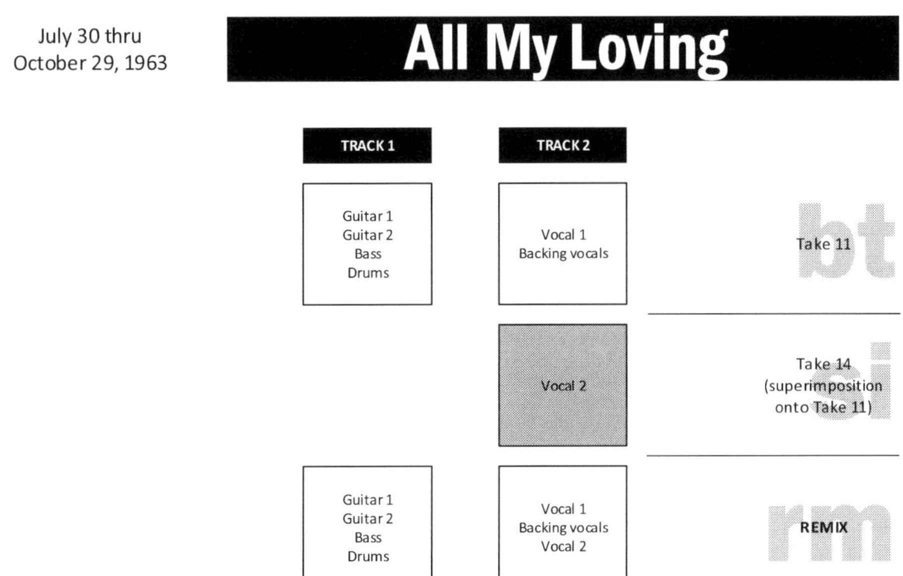

# I Wanna Be Your Man

**Sessions**

- September 11, 1963
- September 12, 1963
- September 30, 1963
- October 3, 1963
- October 23, 1963
- October 29, 1963

After over a month away from the studio, The Beatles began the second round of sessions for the *With The Beatles* album on September 11th, 1963, at EMI Recording Studios, Studio 2. The session included the initial work on five songs, the first of which provided Starr's sole lead vocal contribution to the album, John Lennon and Paul McCartney's *I Wanna Be Your Man*. For such a simple song, it would take quite an effort to complete.

The technical team for the song's initial session included producer George Martin, balance engineer Norman Smith, and tape operator Richard Langham.

The song was recorded to the twin-track EMI BTR3 primary tracking machine.

The backing track featured Starr on his 1963 Ludwig Oyster Black Pearl Downbeat drum set, Lennon on his 1958 Rickenbacker 325 Capri electric guitar with Bigsby vibrato, McCartney on his 1961 Hofner 500/1 bass, and Harrison on his 1962 Gretsch 6122 Chet Atkins Country Gentleman electric guitar with Gretsch Bigsby B6G vibrato.

For amplification, Lennon and Harrison played through the 30-watt 1963 JMI Vox AC30/6 Twin Treble amplifiers. For bass amplification, McCartney used the 30-watt 1963 Vox AC30 head with a Vox T60 speaker cabinet.

Only one take of the song was created during the session, and the band quickly moved on to the second song of the day, *Little Child*.

Returning to the song the following day, this time at the tail end of an afternoon and evening recording session, the band made six more attempts at the backing track for the song (takes 2 through 7). Take 7 was a solid performance and further work on the track proceeded from this take.

On September 30th in Studio 2, a series of unusual mono remixes were created. Martin must have felt the song needed a little something more as he added the studio's Hammond RT3 Organ to the song as a superimposition during the remixes. Remix mono (RM) 8-13 each included this simultaneous superimposition, though in the end, Martin was still not content with the track and the work went unused.

On October 3rd in Studio 2, Starr's double-tracked lead vocals, Lennon and McCartney's backing vocals, and maracas were added to the track. Martin also finalized his organ work on the song. Two superimposition takes were required to cover the work (takes 14 and 15).

Finally, on October 23rd a last superimposition to take 15 (named take 16) featured Starr on tambourine.

Before the session ended, remix mono (RM) 16 was created from take 16. RM 16 served as the mono release version of the song.

On October 29th in another Studio 3 control room session, remix stereo (RS) 16 was created from the two-track master of take 16. RS 16 served as the stereo release version of the song.

September 11 thru October 29, 1963

# I Wanna Be Your Man

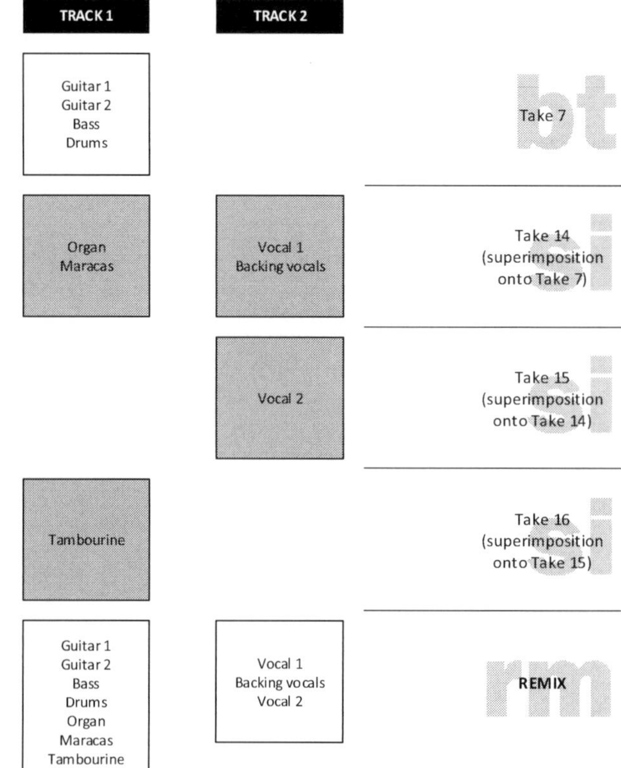

# Little Child

**Sessions**

- September 11, 1963
- September 12, 1963
- September 30, 1963
- October 3, 1963
- October 23, 1963
- October 29, 1963

The September 11th, 1963 session at EMI Recording Studios, Studio 2, for the *With The Beatles* album included the initial work on five songs, the second of which was John Lennon and Paul McCartney's *Little Child.* As with a number of songs on the album, though catchy, it was simple fare, a "work song".

The technical team for the session included producer George Martin, balance engineer Norman Smith, and tape operator Richard Langham.

The song was recorded to the twin-track EMI BTR3 primary tracking machine.

The backing track featured Lennon on his 1958 Rickenbacker 325 Capri electric guitar with Bigsby vibrato, McCartney on his 1961 Hofner 500/1 bass, Harrison on his 1962 Gretsch 6122 Chet Atkins Country Gentleman electric guitar with Gretsch Bigsby B6G vibrato, and Starr on his 1963 Ludwig Oyster Black Pearl Downbeat drum set.

For amplification, Lennon and Harrison played through the 30-watt 1963 JMI Vox AC30/6 Twin Treble amplifiers. For bass amplification, McCartney used the 30-watt 1963 Vox AC30 head with a Vox T60 speaker cabinet.

Two takes of the song's instrumental backing track were created during the session, neither of which were used.

The following day, ten more takes of the backing track were recorded (takes 3 through 12), with take 12 being the best of these.

To this, superimposition take 13 included Lennon and McCartney's lead vocals. Superimposition takes 14 and 15 followed, comprised of Lennon's Hohner harmonica part and McCartney's turn on the studio's Steinway "Music Room" Model B Grand Piano.

Work on the track finished for the day with an edit piece that focused on Lennon's harmonica solo (takes 16-18).

On September $30^{th}$ the technical team created an edit of takes 15 (the best of the backing track, plus superimpositions) and 18 (the best edit piece of Lennon's harmonica solo). The edit is obvious in the contemporary stereo remix of the song, with the harmonica moving jarringly from the left to the right channel of the stereo field at around the 0:54 mark.

Work on the song finished for the day with an unnumbered remix mono (RM) created from the edit of takes 15 and 18.

On October $3^{rd}$ a final superimposition was created for the song. The simple addition included Lennon doubling his "Come on, come on, come on" vocal over three new takes (takes 19 through 21), take 21 being the best.

Returning to the song on October $23^{rd}$, remix mono (RM) 21 was created from take 21. RM 21 served as the mono release version of the song.

On October $29^{th}$ in a Studio 3 control room session, remix stereo (RS) 21 was created from the two-track master of take 21. RS 21 served as the stereo release version of the song.

September 11 thru October 29, 1963

# Little Child

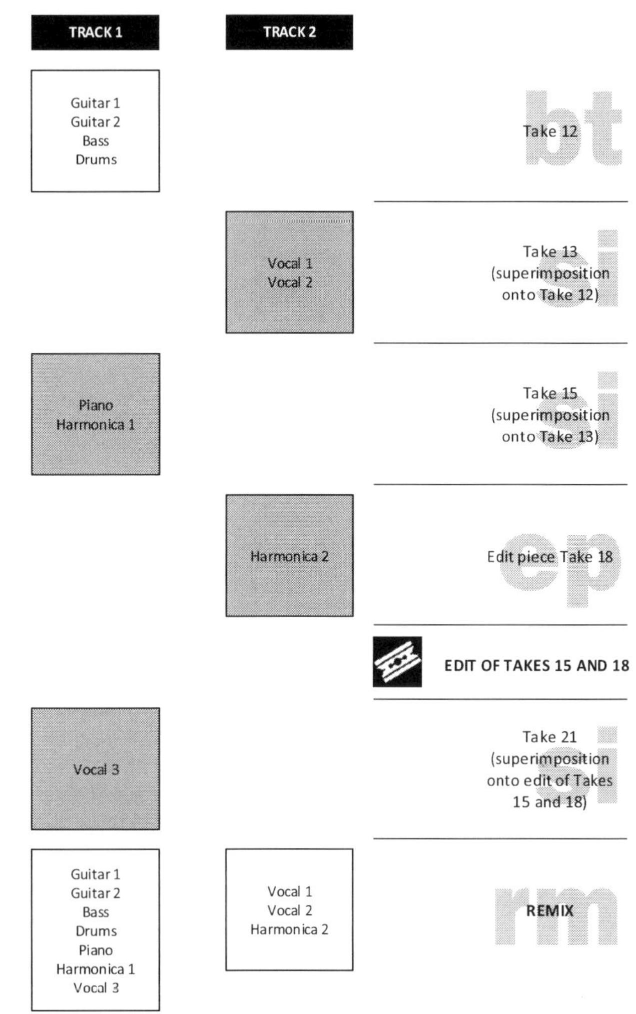

# All I've Got To Do

**Sessions**

- September 11, 1963
- September 30, 1963
- October 29, 1963

John Lennon and Paul McCartney's *All I've Got To Do* was the third song recorded during the September 11th, 1963 session at EMI Recording Studios, Studio 2, for the *With The Beatles* album. The song was a step above the ordinary if only due to the unique arrangement of the vocal harmonies — always one of the band's strong points.

The technical team for the session included producer George Martin, balance engineer Norman Smith, and tape operator Richard Langham.

The song was recorded to the twin-track EMI BTR3 primary tracking machine.

The backing track featured Lennon on his 1958 Rickenbacker 325 Capri electric guitar with Bigsby vibrato and lead vocals, McCartney on his 1961 Hofner 500/1 bass and backing vocals, Harrison on his 1962 Gretsch 6122 Chet Atkins Country Gentleman electric guitar with Gretsch Bigsby B6G vibrato, and Starr on his 1963 Ludwig Oyster Black Pearl Downbeat drum set.

For amplification, Lennon and Harrison played through the 30-watt 1963 JMI Vox AC30/6 Twin Treble amplifiers. For bass amplification, McCartney used the 30-watt 1963 Vox AC30 head with Vox T60 speaker cabinet.

Though the band fumbled through the backing track (eight takes being false starts), by take 14 they had a beauty on their hands. Lennon's lead vocal and the gentle touch of the rest of the band were masterful.

A simple superimposition of McCartney and Harrison on backing vocals at the chorus were all that was needed to finish the song; the work completed in a single take (take 15).

On September 30th in Studio 2, remix mono (RM) 15 was created from take 15. RM 15 served as the mono release version of the song.

On October 29th in a Studio 3 control room session, remix stereo (RS) 15 was created from the two-track master of take 15. RS 15 served as the stereo release version of the song.

September 11 thru
October 29, 1963

## All I've Got To Do

| TRACK 1 | TRACK 2 | |
|---|---|---|
| Guitar 1<br>Guitar 1<br>Bass<br>Drums | Vocal 1<br>Vocal 2 | bt<br>Take 14 |
| | Backing vocals | si<br>Take 15<br>(superimposition onto Take 14) |
| Guitar 1<br>Guitar 1<br>Bass<br>Drums | Vocal 1<br>Vocal 2<br>Backing vocals | rm<br>REMIX |

# Not A Second Time

**Sessions**

- September 11, 1963
- September 30, 1963
- October 29, 1963

John Lennon and Paul McCartney's *Not A Second Time* was the fourth of five songs recorded during the September 11th, 1963 session at EMI Recording Studios, Studio 2, for the *With The Beatles* album. Another "work song" from the duo, it took no special effort to create or perform.

The technical team for the session included producer George Martin, balance engineer Norman Smith, and tape operator Richard Langham.

The song was recorded to the twin-track EMI BTR3 primary tracking machine.

The backing featured Lennon on his 1962 Gibson J-160E acoustic guitar and lead vocals, McCartney on his 1961 Hofner 500/1 bass and backing vocals, Harrison on his 1962 Gibson J-160E acoustic guitar, and Starr on his 1963 Ludwig Oyster Black Pearl Downbeat drum set.

For amplification, Lennon and Harrison played through the 30-watt 1963 JMI Vox AC30/6 Twin Treble amplifiers. The Gibson acoustics were also mic'ed with a Neumann U48 microphone. Engineer Smith blended the acoustic signal with the amplified one to create a unique acoustic guitar tone. For bass amplification, McCartney used the 30-watt 1963 Vox AC30 head with a Vox T60 speaker cabinet.

Five takes of the backing track were all it took to perfect the core of the song, take 5 being the best.

Superimposition takes 6 through 9 focused on Lennon's double-tracked lead vocals and George Martin's addition of the Steinway "Music Room" Model B Grand Piano.

On September 30th remix mono (RM) 9 was created from take 9. RM 9 served as the mono release version of the song.

On October 29th in a Studio 3 control room session, remix stereo (RS) 9 was created from the two-track master of take 9. RS 9 served as the stereo release version of the song.

September 11 thru
October 29, 1963

# Not A Second Time

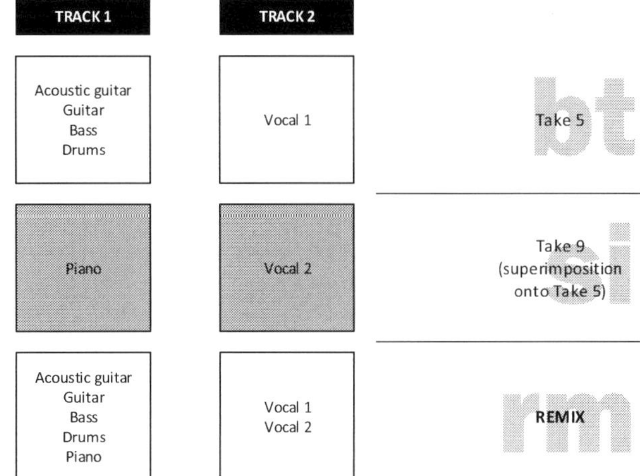

# Don't Bother Me

**Sessions**

- September 11, 1963
- September 12, 1963
- September 30, 1963
- October 29, 1963

George Harrison's first original songwriting contribution to a Beatles album, *Don't Bother Me* was the final song recorded during the September 11th, 1963 session at EMI Recording Studios, Studio 2, for the *With The Beatles* album. While the lessons and influence of Lennon and McCartney are plain to see, Harrison's lyrical voice is a unique one; a little darker, a little more personal. Rejection was always one of the themes of the pop song formula and there's something pointed in Harrison's song that leaves you feeling he's connected to it.

The technical team for the session included producer George Martin, balance engineer Norman Smith, and tape operator Richard Langham.

The song was recorded to the twin-track EMI BTR3 primary tracking machine.

The backing track featured Harrison on his 1962 Gretsch 6122 Chet Atkins Country Gentleman electric guitar with Gretsch Bigsby B6G vibrato and lead vocals, Lennon on his 1958 Rickenbacker 325 Capri electric guitar with Bigsby vibrato, McCartney on his 1961 Hofner 500/1 bass, and Starr on his 1963 Ludwig Oyster Black Pearl Downbeat drum set.

For amplification, Lennon and Harrison played through the 30-watt 1963 JMI Vox AC30/6 Twin Treble amplifiers. For bass amplification, McCartney used the 30-watt 1963 Vox AC30 head with a Vox T60 speaker cabinet.

Four takes were made of the backing track, take 4 being the best of these.

Next, three superimposition takes were made to the song (takes 5 through 7), evidence pointing to a doubling of Harrison's lead vocal, though the actual superimpositions are unknown.

None of the work on the song in this session was good enough for Martin or the band and they returned the next day for a remake.

The September 12th remake was tracked identically to the previous day's work, with the instrumental backing track including Harrison's live lead vocals. Again, it only took four takes to get the song right (for reasons unknown, the day's work on the song began with take 10, not take 8), and by take 13 it was time to move onto the superimpositions.

Superimposition takes 15 through 19 (there was no take 14) included Harrison on double-tracked lead vocals, Lennon on tambourine, McCartney on wood block, and Starr on doumbek (a small Egyptian hand drum). Take 15 was the best of these five superimposition takes and the basis of the final remixes of the song.

On September 30th in Studio 2, remix mono (RM) 15 was created from take 15. RM 15 served as the mono release version of the song.

On October 29th in a Studio 3 control room session, remix stereo (RS) 15 was created from the two-track master of take 15. RS 15 served as the stereo release version of the song.

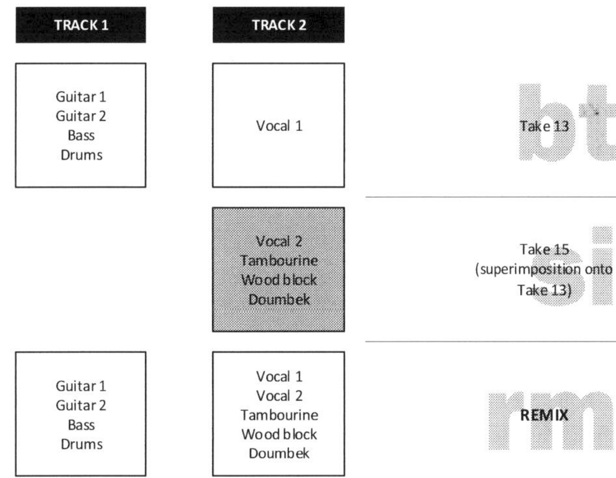

# Hold Me Tight (remake)

**Sessions**

- September 12, 1963
- September 30, 1963
- October 23, 1963
- October 29, 1963

A song originally attempted for the *Please Please Me* album in February, John Lennon and Paul McCartney's *Hold Me Tight* resurfaced for the *With The Beatles* album. Work on the remake commenced on September 12th, 1963 at EMI Recording Studios, Studio 2, with the band running through numerous rehearsal takes of the song before recording. The lessons learned from Martin about the importance of catching the listener's attention were on full display, with the song breaking immediately into full bloom after a single bar of the introduction. The overall sound hearkened back to the stomping beats of the sweaty Hamburg and Liverpool clubs they had left behind not too long before.

The technical team for the session included producer George Martin, balance engineer Norman Smith, and tape operator Richard Langham.

The song was recorded to the twin-track EMI BTR3 primary tracking machine.

The backing track featured McCartney on his 1961 Hofner 500/1 bass and lead vocals, Lennon on his 1958 Rickenbacker 325 Capri electric guitar with Bigsby vibrato and backing vocals, Harrison on his 1962 Gretsch 6122 Chet Atkins Country Gentleman electric guitar with Gretsch Bigsby B6G vibrato and backing vocals, and Starr on his 1963 Ludwig Oyster Black Pearl Downbeat drum set.

For amplification, Lennon and Harrison played through the 30-watt 1963 JMI Vox AC30/6 Twin Treble amplifiers. For bass amplification, McCartney used the 30-watt 1963 Vox AC30 head with a Vox T60 speaker cabinet.

Starting with take 20 (though it was actually take 1 of the remake), the band worked through a breakdown and full take (takes 20 and 21), false start (take 22) and a blown take (take 23) before completing the backing track on take 24 (a peeved Norman Smith slating the take with some level of exasperation, "TWENTY-FOUR!").

Five superimposition takes followed (takes 25 through 29), including McCartney's harmony lead vocals and Lennon and Harrison on backing vocals and handclaps. Between takes 26 and 29, Martin had what he needed and work on the track was complete.

On September 30th in Studio 2, an edit of takes 26 and 29 was completed and became the basis of remix mono (RM) 26 + RM 29. On examination, the remix was close, but not quite right.

On October 23rd, remix mono (RM) 26 was created from take 26. RM 26 served as the mono release version of the song.

On October 29th in a Studio 3 control room session, remix stereo (RS) 29 was created from take 29. RS 29 served as the stereo release version of the song.

September 12 thru
October 29, 1963

**Hold Me Tight**

| TRACK 1 | TRACK 2 | |
|---|---|---|
| Guitar 1<br>Guitar 2<br>Bass<br>Drums | Vocal 1 | bt<br>Take 24 |
| | Vocal 2<br>Backing vocals<br>Handclaps | si<br>Takes 26 and 29<br>(superimposition onto Take 24) |
| Guitar 1<br>Guitar 2<br>Bass<br>Drums | Vocal 1<br>Vocal 2<br>Backing vocals<br>Handclaps | rm<br>**REMIX**<br>**(RM 26 and RS 29)** |

# I Want To Hold Your Hand

**Sessions**

- October 17, 1963
- October 21, 1963
- November 7, 1966

The October 17th, 1963 session at EMI Recording Studios, Studio 2, that included John Lennon and Paul McCartney's *I Want To Hold Your Hand* was the last full recording session for the band in 1963 (there would be a superimposition session for *I Wanna Be Your Man* on the 23rd and a handful of editing and remix sessions for the technical team before the year's end). The Beatles fifth single for Parlophone was also their first to be recorded to four-track.

The move to four-track could be viewed in a couple of lights historically. Pop producers in the US routinely used three and four-track machines to exert more control over their sound, not discounting the fact that stereo releases were much more prominent in the US market. Simply to be competitive in the quality of recordings they produced, EMI would have had to eventually make the move beyond twin-track. In terms of engineering, it was also simply much easier to produce the increasingly layered recordings pop acts were producing using four-track. Decisions about how to arrange the recording process and schedule musicians to facilitate different arrangements, as well as recording songs non-contiguously, was also made easier with the move to four-track.

The technical team for the session included producer George Martin, balance engineer Norman Smith, and tape operator Geoff Emerick.

The song was recorded to the four-track Telefunken M10 primary tracking machine.

Work commenced on a backing track featuring Lennon on his 1958 Rickenbacker 325 Capri electric guitar with Bigsby vibrato and lead vocals, McCartney recording for the first time with his 1962-1963 Hofner 500/1 bass and also singing lead vocals, Harrison likely on his 1962 Gretsch 6122 Chet Atkins Country Gentleman with Gretsch Bigsby B6G vibrato (his 1962 Rickenbacker 425 was also an option during the session), and Starr on his 1963 Ludwig Oyster Black Pearl Downbeat drum set.

For amplification, Lennon and Harrison played through the 30-watt 1963 JMI Vox AC30/6 Twin Treble amplifiers. For bass amplification, McCartney used the 30-watt 1963 Vox AC30 head with a Vox T60 speaker cabinet.

Only 10 out of 17 takes of the backing track were complete to any extent, take 17 being the best (takes 1, 2, 9, and 14 through 16 were false starts, while take 13 was a breakdown).

In this new era of four-track recording, superimpositions were noted as being made "to" a take (in this case, take 17) as opposed to being noted as an additional take in and of themselves, which was the past practise (though this new studio standard for track numbering wasn't fully in effect yet as witnessed by *This Boy*, recorded in the same session).

The superimpositions to take 17 included Harrison on guitar and Lennon and McCartney both on handclaps and doubling the vocals of the second "And when I touch you I feel happy inside..." section. With these additions, recording on the song was complete.

Everett notes that Harrison superimposed a bass part on *I Want To Hold Your Hand* during this session. However, examination of both the 1963 and 1966 remixes do not reveal any additional bass performance. It is likely those such as Everett noting a bass part are actually referring to the baritone figure Harrison plays on a standard electric guitar between stanzas of the verse (e.g. before the words, "I think you'll understand").

On October 21st in Studio 1, both mono and stereo remixes (RM and RS) were created from take 17. RM 1 and RS 17 served as the respective mono and stereo release versions of the song.

One final stereo version of the song was remixed on November 7th, 1966 in Studio 1. RS 1 from take 17 was released in 1966 in place of RS 17 on the greatest hits collection, *A Collection Of Beatles Oldies*.

October 17 thru 21, 1963

# I Want To Hold Your Hand

| TRACK 1 | TRACK 2 | TRACK 3 | TRACK 4 | |
|---|---|---|---|---|
| Guitar 1<br>Guitar 2<br>Bass<br>Drums | Vocal 1<br>Vocal 2 | | | bt<br>Take 17 |
| | | Guitar 3 | Handclaps<br>Backing vocals | si<br>Superimposition onto Take 17 |
| Guitar 1<br>Guitar 2<br>Bass<br>Drums | Vocal 1<br>Vocal 2 | Guitar 3 | Handclaps<br>Backing vocals | rm<br>REMIX |

# This Boy

**Sessions**

- October 17, 1963
- October 21, 1963
- November 10, 1966

The October 17th, 1963 session at EMI Recording Studios, Studio 2, for The Beatles fifth single (*I Want To Hold Your Hand*) also included its B-side, John Lennon and Paul McCartney's magnificent *This Boy*. While other artists might have used the advantage of four-track recording technology to eliminate the challenge of playing a solid backing track while simultaneously singing close three-part harmonies, The Beatles, still performers at this point in their careers, developed songs much in the way they would be played on stage. Playing and singing together were the natural initial approach.

The immaculate harmonies for the song developed along with Martin and based on a combination of simple triads, produced a result that was sublimely sophisticated.

The technical team for the session included producer George Martin, balance engineer Norman Smith, and tape operator Geoff Emerick.

The song was recorded to the four-track Telefunken M10 primary tracking machine; the first session in which The Beatles recorded to this format.

The backing track featured Lennon on his 1962 Gibson J-160E acoustic guitar and vocals, McCartney on his 1962-1963 Hofner 500/1 bass and also singing vocals, Harrison on his 1962 Gretsch 6122 Chet Atkins Country Gentleman electric guitar with Gretsch Bigsby B6G vibrato (his 1962 Rickenbacker 425 was also an option during the session), singing the third part of the three-part harmony vocals, and Starr on his 1963 Ludwig Oyster Black Pearl Downbeat drum set.

For amplification, Harrison played through the 30-watt 1963 JMI Vox AC30/6 Twin Treble amplifier. For bass amplification, McCartney used the 30-watt 1963 Vox AC30 head with a Vox T60 speaker cabinet.

Work began with 14 takes of the song, including numerous false starts and partial takes, before the band hit its stride. Takes 2, 7, 10, 13 and 15 were complete takes; take 15 being the best.

Superimposition takes 16 and 17 completed the song, which included Lennon's double-tracked lead vocals, McCartney and Harrison's double-tracked backing vocals and Harrison on the song's ending lead guitar figures.

On October 21st, remix mono (RM) 1 and 2 from an edit of takes 15 and 17 was created. Then RM 1 and 2 were edited just after the middle eight of the song to create the master remix of the song. This edited version served as the mono release version of the song.

During the same session, remix stereo (RS) 15 from the edit of takes 15 and 17 was also created. The stereo version of the song significantly downplays the backing track instruments, with particular emphasis on Starr's work throughout the remix. RS 15 served as the stereo version of the song. This version of the song was unreleased contemporary to The Beatles' recording career.

On November 10th 1966 in Room 65, two new stereo remixes were created. RS 1 and 2 from takes 15 and 17 were also left on the shelf during The Beatles career.

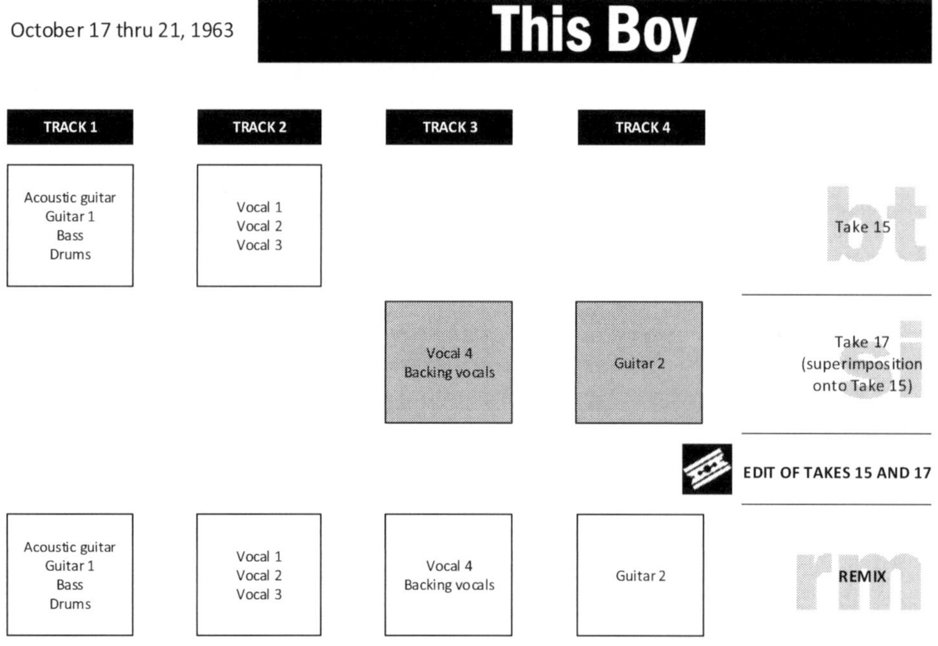

# 1964

## " Musically they are a near disaster, guitars and drums slamming out a merciless beat that does away with secondary rhythms, harmony and melody."

- *Newsweek*, February 24, 1964

# 1964 Releases

## February 7, 1964

**Location**
London, England

**Release Title (version)(composer)**

*All My Loving* (mono)

Side A

*All My Loving* (John Lennon and Paul McCartney)
*Ask Me Why* (John Lennon and Paul McCartney)

Side B

*Money (That's What I Want)* (Janie Bradford and Berry Gordy)
*P.S. I Love You* (John Lennon and Paul McCartney)

**Publishers (songs)**

- Ardmore & Beechwood, Ltd. (*P.S. I Love You*)
- Dick James Music (*Ask Me Why*)
- Dominion Music (*Money*)
- Northern Songs, Ltd., 1963 (*All My Loving*)

**Release label**
Parlophone

**Catalogue number**
GEP 8883 (UK)

**Studio Personnel**

- Producer: George Martin

**Sources** - Lewisohn, Mark (1). p. 200.

## March 20, 1964

**Location**
London, England

**Release Title (version)(composer)**

*Can't Buy Me Love b/w You Can't Do That* (mono) (John Lennon and Paul McCartney)

**Publisher**
Northern Songs, NCB, 1964

**Release label**
Parlophone

**Catalogue number**
PMC 1230 (UK)

**Studio Personnel**

- Producer: George Martin

**Sources** - Lewisohn, Mark (1). p. 44.

# June 19, 1964

**Location**
London, England

**Release Title (version)(composer)**
*Long Tall Sally* (mono)

Side A

*Long Tall Sally* ((Enotris Johnson, Richard Penniman, and Robert Blackwell)
*I Call Your Name* (John Lennon and Paul McCartney)

Side B

*Slow Down* (Larry Williams)
*Matchbox* (Carl Perkins)

**Publishers (songs)**

- Carl Perkins Music (*Matchbox*)
- Hal Leonard Corporation (*Slow Down*)
- Northern Songs, 1964 (*I Call Your Name*)
- Southern Music Publishing (*Long Tall Sally*)

**Release label**
Parlophone

**Catalogue number**
GEP 8913

**Studio Personnel**

- Producer: George Martin

**Sources** - Lewisohn, Mark (1). p. 200.

# July 10, 1964

**Location**
London, England

**Release Title (version)(composer)**
*A Hard Day's Night b/w Things We Said Today* (mono) (John Lennon and Paul McCartney)

*A Hard Day's Night* (mono) (stereo)

Side A

(Songs from the film *A Hard Day's Night*)

*A Hard Day's Night* (John Lennon and Paul McCartney)
*I Should Have Known Better* (John Lennon and Paul McCartney)
*If I Fell* (John Lennon and Paul McCartney)
*I'm Happy Just To Dance With You* (John Lennon and Paul McCartney)
*And I Love Her* (John Lennon and Paul McCartney)
*Tell Me Why* (John Lennon and Paul McCartney)
*Can't Buy Me Love* (John Lennon and Paul McCartney)

Side B

*Any Time At All* (John Lennon and Paul McCartney)
*I'll Cry Instead* (John Lennon and Paul McCartney)
*Things We Said Today* (John Lennon and Paul McCartney)
*When I Get Home* (John Lennon and Paul McCartney)
*You Can't Do That* (John Lennon and Paul McCartney)
*I'll Be Back* (John Lennon and Paul McCartney)

**Publisher**
Northern Songs, 1964

**Release label**
Parlophone

**Catalogue number**

- (single) R 5160
- (album) PMC 1230 (mono)
- (album) PCS 3058 (stereo)

**Studio Personnel**

- Producer: George Martin

**Sources** - Lewisohn, Mark (1). p. 47.

# November 6, 1964

**Location**
London, England

**Release Title (version)(composer)**
*A Hard Day's Night (extracts from the film)* (mono)

Side A

*I Should Have Known Better* (John Lennon and Paul McCartney)
*If I Fell* (John Lennon and Paul McCartney)

Side B

*Tell Me Why* (John Lennon and Paul McCartney)
*And I Love Her* (John Lennon and Paul McCartney)

**Publisher**
Northern Songs, Ltd., 1964

**Release label**
Parlophone

**Catalogue number**
GEP 8920 (UK)

**Studio Personnel**

- Producer: George Martin

**Sources** - Lewisohn, Mark (1) p. 200.

# November 6, 1964

**Location**
London, England

**Release Title (version)(composer)**
*A Hard Day's Night (extracts from the album)* (mono)

Side A

*Any Time At All* (John Lennon and Paul McCartney)
*I'll Cry Instead* (John Lennon and Paul McCartney)

Side B

*Things We Said Today* (John Lennon and Paul McCartney)
*When I Get Home* (John Lennon and Paul McCartney)

**Publisher**
Northern Songs, Ltd.

**Release label**
Parlophone

**Catalogue number**
GEP 8924 (UK)

**Studio Personnel**

- Producer: George Martin

**Sources** - Lewisohn, Mark (1). p. 200.

# November 27, 1964

**Location**
London, England

**Release Title (version)(composer)**
*I Feel Fine b/w She's A Woman* (mono) (John Lennon and Paul McCartney)

**Publisher**
Northern Songs, NCB 1964

**Release label**
Parlophone

**Catalogue number**
R 5200 (UK)

**Studio Personnel**

- Producer: George Martin

**Sources** - Lewisohn, Mark (1). p. 53.

# December 4, 1964

**Location**
London, England

**Release Title (version)(composer)**
*Beatles For Sale* (mono) (stereo)

Side A

*No Reply* (John Lennon and Paul McCartney)
*I'm A Loser* (John Lennon and Paul McCartney)
*Baby's In Black* (John Lennon and Paul McCartney)
*Rock And Roll Music* (Chuck Berry)
*I'll Follow The Sun* (John Lennon and Paul McCartney)
*Mr. Moonlight* (Roy Lee Johnson)
*Kansas City/Hey-Hey-Hey-Hey!* (Jerry Leiber and Mike Stoller/Richard Penniman)

Side B

*Eight Days A Week* (John Lennon and Paul McCartney)
*Words Of Love* (Buddy Holly)
*Honey Don't* (Carl Perkins)
*Every Little Thing* (John Lennon and Paul McCartney)
*I Don't Want To Spoil The Party* (John Lennon and Paul McCartney)
*What You're Doing* (John Lennon and Paul McCartney)
*Everybody's Trying To Be My Baby* (Carl Perkins)

**Publishers**

- Belinda Music (*Honey Don't, Everybody's Trying To Be My Baby*)
- Chappell Music (*Mr. Moonlight*)
- Jewel Music (*Rock And Roll Music*)

- Macmelodies (*Kansas City/Hey-Hey-Hey-Hey!*)
- Northern Songs, NCB, 1964 (*No Reply, I'm a Loser, Baby's In Black, I'll Follow The Sun, Eight Days A Week, Every Little Thing, I Don't Want To Spoil The Party, What You're Doing*)
- Southern Music (*Words Of Love*)

**Release label**
Parlophone

**Catalogue number**

- (mono) PMC 1240 (UK)
- (stereo) PCS 3062 (UK)

**Studio Personnel**

- Producer: George Martin

**Sources** - Lewisohn, Mark (1). p. 53.

# A Hard Day's Night

If there was one project that firmly established The Beatles in the world's imagination (and, for better or for worse, provided the easy stereotypes that would be attached to them for life), it was the motion picture *A Hard Day's Night*. Through that film, Lennon became "the clever one", McCartney "the cute one", Harrison "the quiet one", and Starr "the lovable (if dim-witted) one". While none of these images of the four musicians were either complete or accurate, they did allow the world's press to quickly frame each of the Beatles for their readers and viewers through the lens of mass fan consumption that was Beatlemania.

Musically, the period was one where the band hit their full stride in mastering the pop forms they had created. The level of ease and confidence on display caused an entire industry to pause and take notice. The Beatles were a band rapidly playing at a higher level. For emerging artists, they would become an aspirational model. To be able to write and record your own songs, to communicate with a breezy confidence, and appear as four limbs of the same body — these became the goals of generations of artists to follow. Spanning a period of 163 days between January 29th and July 10th, 1964, the era included the recording and release of the film's soundtrack album and title single, the *Can't Buy Me Love* single, and *All My Loving* and *Long Tall Sally* EPs.

---

# Komm, Gib Mir Deine Hand

**Sessions**

- January 29, 1964
- March 10, 1964
- March 12, 1964

George Martin had been convinced by Parlophone's German subsidiary that in order to really move units in the country, The Beatles had to record German language versions of their songs. So on January 29th, 1964, in the midst of a visit to France for 19 days of shows at Paris' Olympia Theatre, Martin booked the band into EMI Pathe' Marconi Studios, EMI's French recording studio located in the western suburbs of the city, for a day spent rerecording two of their hits specifically for the German market. The first song they worked on was their latest hit, *I Want To Hold Your Hand*, or in this incarnation, *Komm, Gib Mir Deine Hand.*

The technical team for this session included producer George Martin, balance engineer Norman Smith, and tape operator Jacques Esmenjaud.

The song was recorded to the twin-track EMI BTR3 primary tracking machine.

The instrumental backing track for the song was taken from the original recording. Omitting the vocals, it had been transferred to two-track in a remixing session at EMI Recording Studios, Studio 1, in London on January 24th. Work on the song in Paris focused solely on the vocals.

Over 11 takes (including an understandable four false starts), Lennon and McCartney eventually got the words right, though not in one complete take. Martin next assembled an edit of takes 5 and 7 – the two best performances.

Onto this edit, handclaps were superimposed by Lennon and McCartney, and work on the song was completed.

At some point prior to its German release on March 6th, 1964, an unnumbered mono remix was created from the edit of takes 5 and 7. This unnumbered remix served as the mono release version of the song.

On March 10th, back in London's EMI Recording Studios, Studio 2, remix mono (RM) 1 was created from the edit of takes 5 and 7. RM 1 is not known to have been released.

On March 12th during a quick control room session in Studio 3, remix stereo (RS) 1 was created from the two-track master edit of takes 5 and 7. There was no contemporary release of this stereo version of the song; it later found its way onto the *Past Masters* compilation in 1988.

January 29 thru
March 12, 1964

**Komm, Gib Mir Deine Hand**

*From two-track copy of *I Want To Hold Your Hand*

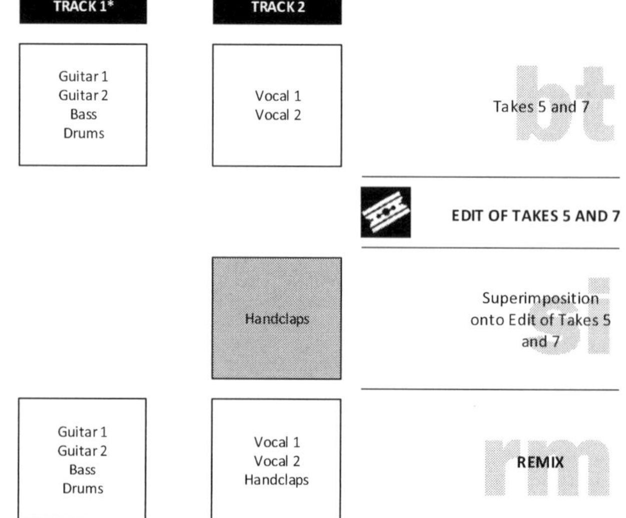

# Sie Liebt Dich

**Sessions**

- January 29, 1964
- March 10, 1964
- March 12, 1964

During the same January 29th, 1964 session at EMI Pathe' Marconi Studios in the Parisian suburbs during which The Beatles recorded *Komm, Gib Mir Deine Hand*, a second German language version of one of their hits was tracked to serve as a B-side to the market-specific single: *She Loves You*, or in this incarnation, *Sie Liebt Dich*.

Unfortunately, as the original session tapes for *She Loves You* had been destroyed prior to the session, there was no way to record the song in the same way the German version of *I Want to Hold Your Hand* been done; superimposing the German language vocals onto a remix of the original backing track. This time, the band had to start from scratch. Of course, they were pretty familiar with the material.

The technical team for this session included producer George Martin, balance engineer Norman Smith, and tape operator Jacques Esmenjaud.

As with *Komm, Gib Mir Deine Hand*, the song was recorded to the twin-track EMI BTR3 primary tracking machine.

The backing track featured Lennon on his 1958 Rickenbacker 325 Capri electric guitar with Bigsby vibrato, McCartney on his 1962-1963 Hofner 500/1 bass, Harrison on either his 1963 Gretsch PX6122 Chet Atkins Country Gentleman with Gretsch Bigsby B6G vibrato or 1963 Gretsch 6119 Chet Atkins Tennessean with Gretsch Bigsby vibrato electric guitar (both were available to him on this date), and Starr on his 1963 Ludwig Oyster Black Pearl Downbeat drum set.

For amplification, while the 30-watt 1963 JMI Vox AC30/6 Twin Treble amplifiers were still available to Lennon and Harrison, it is more likely that they utilized their newer amplifiers for this session; the 50-watt 1963 JMI Vox AC50 Small Box (Mk. I) amplifiers with Vox AC50 cabinets. McCartney's rig also was updated by this date. For bass amplification he used a 100-watt 1963 Vox AC100 head with a Vox AC100 custom cabinet.

While rehearsal tracks reveal an attempt to track the song live with vocals, when it came to recording the song, the backing track was instrumental only. Thirteen takes were required to perfect the backing track, take 13 being the best of these.

Superimposition take 14 included Lennon, McCartney, and Harrison's vocals. With this addition, work on the track was completed.

At some point prior to its German release on March 6th, 1964, an unnumbered mono remix was created from take 14. This unnumbered remix served as the mono release version of the song.

On March 10th, back in London's EMI Recording Studios, Studio 2, remix mono (RM) 1 was created from take 14. RM 1 is not known to have been released.

On March 12th during a quick control room session in Studio 3, remix stereo (RS) 1 was created from the two-track master of take 14. There was no contemporary release of this stereo version of the song; it later found its way onto the *Past Masters* compilation in 1988.

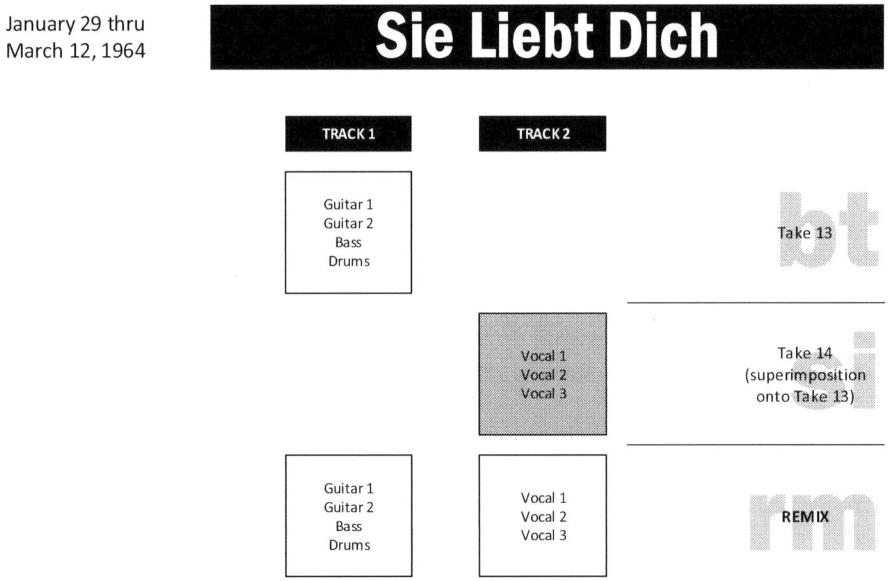

January 29 thru
March 12, 1964

**Sie Liebt Dich**

| TRACK 1 | TRACK 2 | |
|---|---|---|
| Guitar 1<br>Guitar 2<br>Bass<br>Drums | | bt Take 13 |
| | Vocal 1<br>Vocal 2<br>Vocal 3 | si Take 14 (superimposition onto Take 13) |
| Guitar 1<br>Guitar 2<br>Bass<br>Drums | Vocal 1<br>Vocal 2<br>Vocal 3 | rm REMIX |

# Can't Buy Me Love

**Sessions**

- January 29, 1964
- February 25, 1964
- February 26, 1964
- March 10, 1964

John Lennon and Paul McCartney's *Can't Buy Me Love* was a high point of the *A Hard Day's Night* album as well as the soundtrack to one of the film's most memorable scenes. During the same January 29th, 1964 session at EMI Pathe' Marconi Studios in the Parisian suburbs in which the band recorded *Komm, Gib Mir Deine Hand*, and *Sie Liebt Dich* for the German market, work on one of the band's early classic singles was initiated. Martin's decision to start the song with the chorus provided another example of his masterful touch at production.

The technical team for the song's first session included producer George Martin, balance engineer Norman Smith, and tape operator Jacques Esmenjaud.

Unlike the earlier work in the session, *Can't Buy Me Love* was tracked to four-track, using one of the studio's Telefunken primary tracking machines (either the Telefunken T9u or M10).

The backing track featured McCartney on his 1962-1963 Hofner 500/1 bass and lead vocals, Lennon on Harrison's 1962 Gibson J-160E acoustic guitar and backing vocals (his own J-160E had been stolen in November 1963), Harrison on either his 1963 Gretsch PX6122 Chet Atkins Country Gentleman with Gretsch Bigsby B6G vibrato or 1963 Gretsch 6119 Chet Atkins Tennessean with Gretsch Bigsby vibrato electric guitar (both were available to him on this date), also singing backing vocals, and Starr on his 1963 Ludwig Oyster Black Pearl Downbeat drum set.

For amplification, while the 30-watt 1963 JMI Vox AC30/6 Twin Treble amplifiers were still available to Lennon and Harrison, it is more likely that they utilized their newer amplifiers for this session; the 50-watt 1963 JMI Vox AC50 Small Box (Mk. I) amplifiers with Vox AC50 cabinets. Lennon's Gibson was also mic'ed acoustically with a Neumann U48 microphone. Engineer Smith blended the acoustic signal with the amplified one to create a unique acoustic guitar tone. For bass amplification, McCartney used the 100-watt 1963 Vox AC100 head with a Vox AC100 custom cabinet.

Takes 1 and 2, both performed in a higher key than the final track, featured Lennon and Harrison's counterpoint harmonies answering McCartney's lead vocal throughout. Take 3 adopted what became the key of the final version of the song, lower than the original two takes. The take broke down before the second verse ended.

Take 4 was the finished backing track, the final version omitting Lennon and Harrison's backing vocals. Harrison's guitar solo, while serviceable, was the subject of later improvement.

Back at EMI Recording Studios, Studio 2, on February 25th, final superimpositions to take 4 were added to the song. McCartney double-tracked his lead vocal, while Harrison improved his guitar solo. Examination of audio evidence indicates Harrison double-tracked both the solo and additional rhythm guitar (heard in the right channel of the stereo remix during the introduction and choruses). The doubled rhythm guitar is played in octave mode relative to the backing track, giving the impression of a 12-string guitar.

On February 26th in a Studio 2 control room session, five mono remixes (RM) were created from take 4 (RM 1 through 5). The technical team then went about determining which of the remixes was the best. They created an edit of RM 1 and 2, then an edit of RM 4 and 5. In the end neither of these edits made the cut.

Winn noted that tape box notation documents *Can't Buy Me Love* RM 3 as the master remix used for the UK release, and RM 4+5 for the US release. Lewisohn noted RM 4 was used for both the UK and US markets. In actuality, both territories received RM 3 as the mono release version of the song.

An interesting thing happened after these mono remixes were created.

Emerick recalled in his autobiography that in a remixing session on March 10th in Studio 2, balance engineer Smith noticed a technical issue with Starr's drum part (a loss in the high frequencies that manifested itself in dulling the sound of the hi-hat on Starr's drum part). The loss was not significant enough to be noticed in the mono remix, but come the stereo version, it apparently was blatant enough to cause concern.

Smith, according to Emerick, "...headed down into the studio to overdub a hastily set-up hi-hat onto a few bars of the song..." leaving Emerick at the controls for the superimposition — his first time in the balance engineer's chair.

While Smith's contributions were not documented until Emerick's autobiography, audio evidence demonstrates a variation in the drum work between the mono and stereo versions of the song.

This difference supports Emerick's claim about Smith's contribution, as no mono remixing on the song occurred during this March 10th session, and the February 26th mono remix (RM 3) was never replaced as the mono release version.

The likelihood of Starr having contributed the hi-hat work on this day is low, considering the date and time of the session conflicts with the fact that The Beatles spent the day on location in Middlesex for the filming of scenes for their upcoming movie.

By the end of the March 10th session, remix stereo (RS) 1 was created from take 4. RS 1 served as the stereo release version of the song.

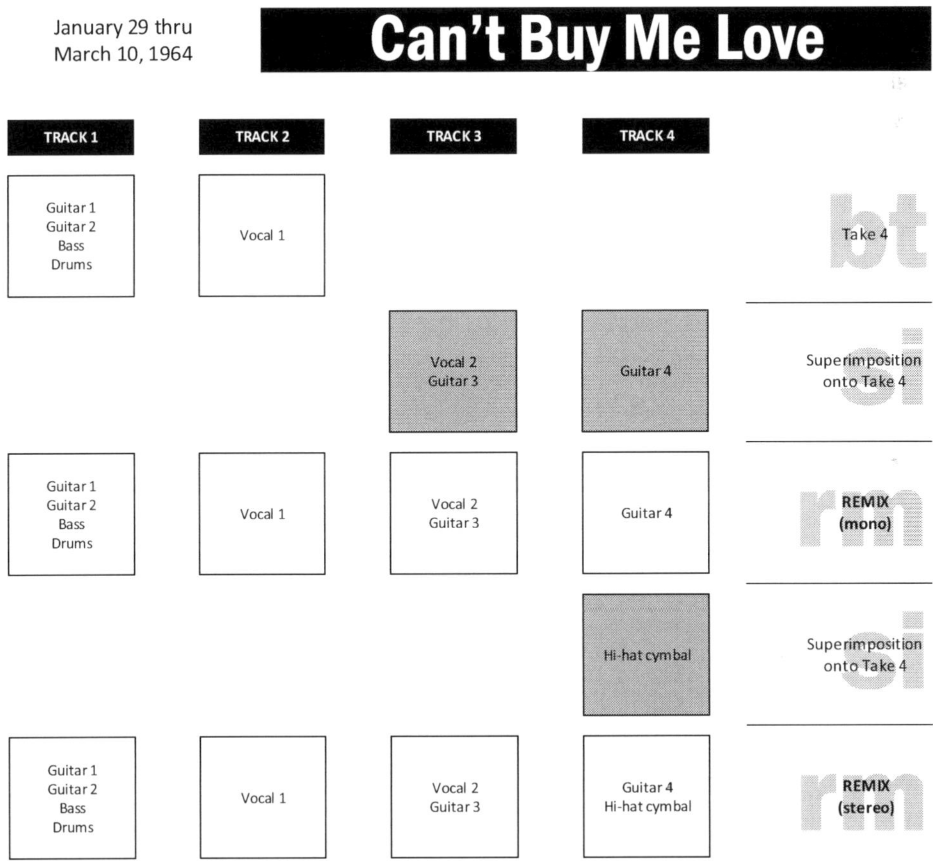

# You Can't Do That

**Sessions**

- February 25, 1964
- February 26, 1962
- March 10, 1964
- May 22, 1964

On February 25th, 1964 at EMI Recording Studios, Studio 2, recording began in earnest for the *A Hard Day's Night* album, as well as work completing the next single. With *Can't Buy Me Love* slated as the A-side, a B-side was needed. John Lennon and Paul McCartney's *You Can't Do That* filled the void.

With today's pop stars putting out albums years apart, on their own schedules and sometimes taking years to even record them, it's hard to appreciate the fact that The Beatles faced huge time constraints. Not only now the biggest band in the world, with demands for live shows, television, print and radio interviews; they were expected to put out two albums and two singles (or four "sides") a year on average.

And they were filming a movie.

The technical team for the session included producer George Martin, balance engineer Norman Smith, and tape operator Richard Langham.

The song was recorded to the four-track Telefunken M10 primary tracking machine.

The backing track featured Lennon on his 1964 Rickenbacker 325 Capri electric guitar and lead vocals, McCartney on his 1962-1963 Hofner 500/1 bass, Harrison recording for the first time with his 1963 Rickenbacker 360-12 twelve-string electric guitar (an instrument key to The Beatles mid-60s sound and influence on guitar players globally, not the least of which being The Byrds' Roger McGuinn), and Starr on his 1963 Ludwig Oyster Black Pearl Downbeat drum set.

For amplification, while the 30-watt 1963 JMI Vox AC30/6 Twin Treble amplifiers were still available to Lennon and Harrison, it is more likely that they utilized their newer amplifiers for this session; the 50-watt 1963 JMI Vox AC50 Small Box (Mk. I) amplifiers with Vox AC50 cabinets. For bass amplification, McCartney used the 100-watt 1963 Vox AC100 head with a Vox AC100 custom cabinet.

The backing track was perfected in eight takes, with take 8 being the best of these. Lennon provided the guitar solo on the song.

It might be argued that the song was the first to put the four-track to use in a more rounded way. The backing track is split between two channels with Lennon's guitar on a separate track than Harrison's, which shares space with the drums and bass. This simple separation widens the sound of the band and is an evident departure from previous engineering approaches to the backing track, most pronounced in the stereo remix of the song.

Superimposition take 9 followed, featuring Lennon's double-tracked lead vocals at the middle eight, McCartney and Harrison on backing vocals (McCartney also playing a Ludwig Clear Tone cowbell), and Starr on a pair of Premier bongos. With these additions, recording on the song was completed.

On February 26th in Studio 2, remix mono (RM) 1 through 3 from take 9 were created. RM 3 was the best of these remixes and served as the mono release version of the song.

Returning to Studio 2 on March 10th, remix stereo (RS) 1 was created from take 9. RS 1 served are the stereo release version of the song.

On May 22nd, two months after the release of the *Can't Buy Me Love* single with *You Can't Do That* as the B-side, George Martin booked a brief one-hour session in Studio 2 to try a piano superimposition on the song using the studio's Steinway "Music Room" Model B Grand Piano (take 10). The work completed in the session did not find its way to any release version of the song.

February 25 thru
May 22, 1964

# You Can't Do That

| TRACK 1 | TRACK 2 | TRACK 3 | TRACK 4 | |
|---|---|---|---|---|
| Guitar 1<br>Bass<br>Drums | Vocal 1 | Guitar 2 | | bt Take 8 |
| | | | Vocal 2<br>Backing vocals<br>Cowbell<br>Bongos | si Take 9<br>(superimposition<br>onto Take 8) |
| Guitar 1<br>Bass<br>Drums | Vocal 1 | Guitar 2 | Vocal 2<br>Backing vocals<br>Cowbell<br>Bongos | rm **REMIX** |

# And I Love Her

**Sessions**

- February 25, 1964
- February 26, 1964
- February 27, 1964
- March 3, 1964
- June 22, 1964

On February 25th, 1964, at EMI Recording Studios, Studio 2, work began in earnest for the *A Hard Day's Night* album on two songs slated for inclusion in the movie. John Lennon and Paul McCartney's *And I Love Her* was the first of these. Two unique approaches would be taken to recording the song, revealing in the process that The Beatles could adapt and change direction in order to find the best key, tempo, or arrangement. The ballad was only the second to feature a Jose Ramirez nylon string guitar as a primary instrument, a choice that made all the difference in the world to the finished track.

The technical team for the song's first session included producer George Martin, balance engineer Norman Smith, and tape operator Richard Langham.

The song was recorded to the four-track Telefunken M10 primary tracking machine.

The initial backing track for the song was unlike the final version of the song in many regards. It featured McCartney on his 1962-1963 Hofner 500/1 bass and lead vocals, Lennon on Harrison's 1962 Gibson J-160E acoustic guitar, Harrison on his 1963 Rickenbacker 360-12 twelve-string electric, and Starr on his 1963 Ludwig Oyster Black Pearl Downbeat drum set.

For amplification, while the 30-watt 1963 JMI Vox AC30/6 Twin Treble amplifiers were still available to Lennon and Harrison, it is more likely that they utilized their newer amplifiers for this session; the 50-watt 1963 JMI Vox AC50 Small Box (Mk. I) amplifiers with Vox AC50 cabinets. Lennon's Gibson was also mic'ed acoustically with a Neumann U48 microphone. Engineer Smith blended the acoustic signal with the amplified one to create a unique acoustic guitar tone. For bass amplification, McCartney used the 100-watt 1963 Vox AC100 head with a Vox AC100 custom cabinet.

Two takes of the backing track were recorded in this initial session, though the feel for the song was somehow wrong. The band and Martin recognized this and moved on to *I Should Have Known Better* after abandoning take 2.

The following day, work proceeded with a new arrangement. Softening the previous day's rock-n-roll approach to the tune, this version saw Harrison move to a Jose Ramirez nylon string acoustic guitar (either the Guitarra de Estudio or A1 Segovia model) and Starr, after starting again on drums, moving to bongos and claves (at some point around take 8). Of the 17 new takes attempted during the session (takes 3 through 19), none were satisfactory.

On the third straight day of tracking for the song, the band finally had a take of the backing track that struck the right chord (take 20). Starr's percussion now was simply the Premier bongos, while all other elements of the song remained the same as the work of the 26th.

Superimposition take 21 followed with McCartney's double-tracked lead vocals and Starr on claves. With these simple additions, recording on the song was completed.

On March 3rd in a Studio 1 control room session, remix mono (RM) 1 was created from take 21. RM 1 served as the mono version of the song that was used in the film.

On June 22nd, in another Studio 1 control room session, both RM 2 and remix stereo (RS) 1 were created, both from take 21. RM 2 and RS 1 served as the mono and stereo release versions of the song.

February 25 thru
June 22, 1964

# And I Love Her

| TRACK 1 | TRACK 2 | TRACK 3 | TRACK 4 | |
|---|---|---|---|---|
| Acoustic guitar 1<br>Bass<br>Drums | Acoustic guitar 2 | Vocal 1 | | bt Take 20 |
| | | | Vocal 2<br>Claves | si Take 21<br>(superimposition onto Take 20) |
| Acoustic guitar 1<br>Bass<br>Drums | Acoustic guitar 2 | Vocal 1 | Vocal 2<br>Claves | rm REMIX |

# I Should Have Known Better

**Sessions**

- February 25, 1964
- February 26, 1964
- March 3, 1964
- June 22, 1964

John Lennon and Paul McCartney's *I Should Have Known Better* was the second song slated for the *A Hard Day's Night* film and album, work beginning at EMI Recording Studios, Studio 2, on February 25th, 1964. Hitting a sweet spot with a swinging beat and Lennon's harmonica contributions, the song was a natural next step from *Love Me Do* and *Please Please Me.* The recording is a great early example of how the band used the four-track format to execute a difficult live arrangement, as well as sweeten an already great song.

The technical team for the song's first session included producer George Martin, balance engineer Norman Smith, and tape operator Richard Langham.

The song was recorded to the four-track Telefunken M10 primary tracking machine.

The backing featured Lennon on Harrison's 1962 Gibson J-160E acoustic guitar, Hohner harmonica and lead vocals, McCartney on his 1962-1963 Hofner 500/1 bass, Harrison on a Jose Ramirez nylon string acoustic guitar (either the Guitarra de Estudio or A1 Segovia model), and Starr on his 1963 Ludwig Oyster Black Pearl Downbeat drum set.

Lennon and Harrison's guitars were mic'ed acoustically with Neumann U48 microphones. For bass amplification, McCartney used the 100-watt 1963 Vox AC100 head with a Vox AC100 custom cabinet.

For amplification, while the 30-watt 1963 JMI Vox AC30/6 Twin Treble amplifiers were still available to Harrison, it is more likely that he utilized their newer amplifier for this session; the 50-watt 1963 JMI Vox AC50 Small Box (Mk. I) amplifier with a Vox AC50 cabinet.

The first three takes of the song went unused as, if the following day's work was any sign, Lennon struggled to play guitar, harmonica, and sing the lead vocal at the same time. It was a lot to keep track of for a man who routinely forgot the words to his own songs.

The following day the band entered Studio 2 once more, this time to complete the song with a remake, though starting again with take 1. By take 8 Lennon realized he wasn't going to make it through the song with the challenge of the harmonica part, and decided soon thereafter that the part would be added later. By take 21, a complete backing track was in place.

Superimposition take 22 included Lennon's double-tracked lead vocals and harmonica, as well as Harrison's 12-string 1963 Rickenbacker 360-12 electric guitar contributions. With these additions, the recording for the song was completed.

On March 3rd in a Studio 1 control room session, remix mono (RM) 1 was created from take 22. RM 1 served as the mono release version of the song used in both the film and album.

On June 22nd in another Studio 1 control room session, remix stereo (RS) 1 was created from take 22. RS 1 served as the stereo release version of the song.

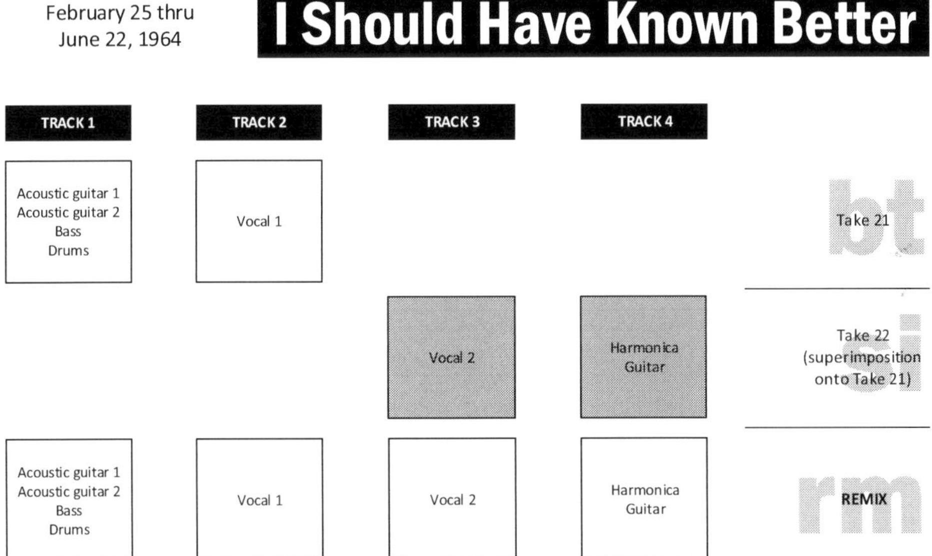

# Tell Me Why

**Sessions**

- February 27, 1964
- March 3, 1964
- June 22, 1964

As recording proceeded on songs for the film *A Hard Day's Night* at EMI Recording Studios, Studio 2, on February 27th, 1964, The Beatles made quick work of the John Lennon and Paul McCartney rocker, *Tell Me Why*. The straightforward song didn't demand much in the way of performance or production, its biggest challenge being the falsetto vocals during the middle eight.

The technical team for the session included producer George Martin, balance engineer Norman Smith, and tape operator Richard Langham.

The song was recorded to the four-track Telefunken M10 primary tracking machine.

The backing track featured Lennon on Harrison's 1962 Gibson J-160E acoustic guitar and lead vocals, McCartney on his 1962-1963 Hofner 500/1 bass and backing vocals, Harrison on his 12-string 1963 Rickenbacker 360-12 electric guitar, also on backing vocals, and Starr on his 1963 Ludwig Oyster Black Pearl Downbeat drum set.

For amplification, while the 30-watt 1963 JMI Vox AC30/6 Twin Treble amplifiers were still available to Lennon and Harrison, it is more likely that they utilized their newer amplifiers for this session; the 50-watt 1963 JMI Vox AC50 Small Box (Mk. I) amplifiers with Vox AC50 cabinets. Lennon's Gibson was also mic'ed acoustically with a Neumann U48 microphone. Engineer Smith blended the acoustic signal with the amplified one to create a unique acoustic guitar tone. For bass amplification, McCartney used the 100-watt 1963 Vox AC100 head with a Vox AC100 custom cabinet.

Seven takes of the backing track were created (with at least one breakdown on take 4), take 7 being the best.

Superimposition take 8 included Lennon on double-tracked lead vocals and an unknown player on the studio's Steinway "Music Room" Model B Grand Piano (likely George Martin). With these additions, recording on the song was completed.

On March 3rd in a Studio 1 control room session, remix mono (RM) 1 was created from take 8. RM 1 served as the mono release version of the song used in both the film and album.

On June 22nd in another Studio 1 control room session, remix stereo (RS) 1 was created from take 8. RS 1 served as the stereo release version of the song.

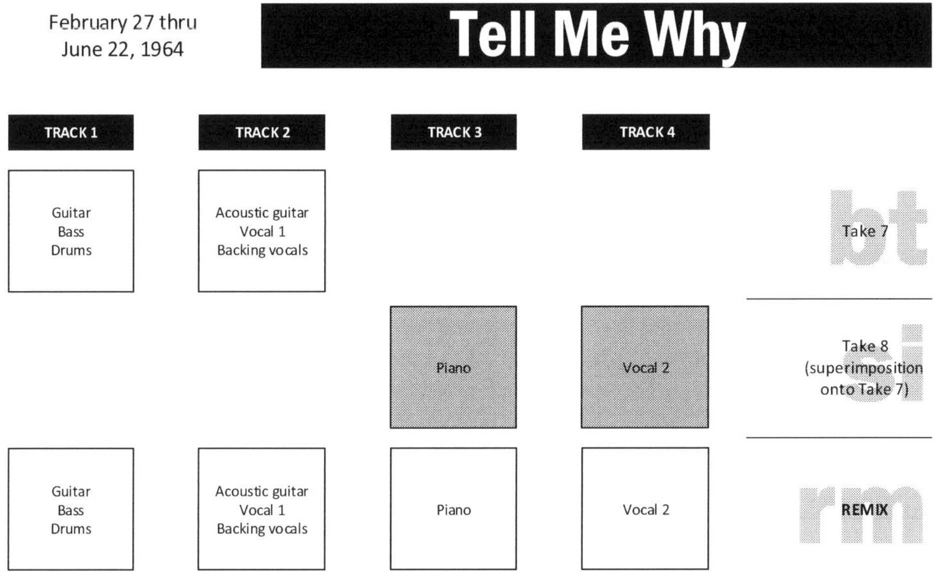

# If I Fell

**Sessions**

- February 27, 1964
- March 3, 1964
- June 22, 1964

The third and final song tracked on February 27th, 1964, at EMI Recording Studios, Studio 2, for the *A Hard Day's Night* film was the John Lennon and Paul McCartney ballad, *If I Fell*. The song was another demonstration of the duo's growth as songwriters, both in the subtle beauty of its composition and its vocal arrangement.

The technical team for the session included producer George Martin, balance engineer Norman Smith, and tape operator Richard Langham.

The song was recorded to the four-track Telefunken M10 primary tracking machine.

The backing track included Lennon on Harrison's 1962 Gibson J-160E acoustic guitar and lead vocals, McCartney on his 1962-1963 Hofner 500/1 bass and backing vocals, Harrison on his 12-string 1963 Rickenbacker 360-12 electric guitar, and Starr on his 1963 Ludwig Oyster Black Pearl Downbeat drum set.

For amplification, while the 30-watt 1963 JMI Vox AC30/6 Twin Treble amplifiers were still available to Harrison, it is more likely that he utilized the newer amplifier for this session; the 50-watt 1963 JMI Vox AC50 Small Box (Mk. I) amplifier with a Vox AC50 cabinet. For bass amplification, McCartney used the 100-watt 1963 Vox AC100 head with a Vox AC100 custom cabinet.

It took fourteen takes to perfect the backing track, with take 14 being the best.

The simple superimposition take 15 followed with Lennon and McCartney double-tracking their vocal work across the entire song, and Harrison adding a handful of 12-string electric guitar flourishes to the backing track. With these additions, recording on the song was completed.

On March 3rd in a Studio 1 control room session, remix mono (RM) 1 was created from take 15. RM 1 served as the mono release version of the song used in both the film and on the album.

On June 22nd in another Studio 1 control room session, remix stereo (RS) 1 was created from take 15. RS 1 served as the stereo release version of the song.

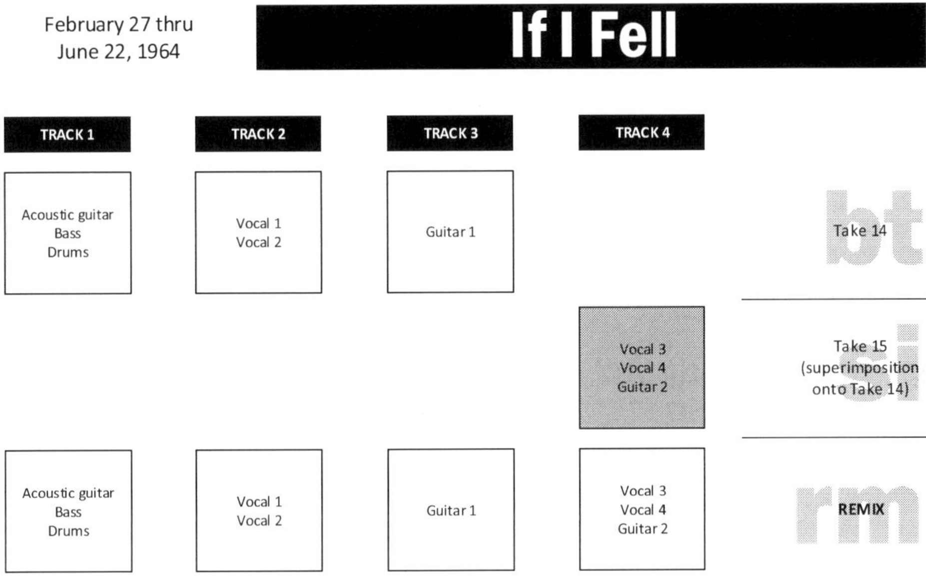

# I'm Happy Just To Dance With You

**Sessions**

- March 1, 1964
- March 3, 1964
- June 22, 1964

Recording continued on the *A Hard Day's Night* project on March 1st, 1964, at EMI Recording Studios, Studio 2, during a session that included work on three new tracks. The first song of the day was another one destined for the film, with Harrison's turn on lead vocals — John Lennon and Paul McCartney's *I'm Happy Just To Dance With You.* Though an unremarkable song, Martin made some interesting choices in having Starr reinforce his drum part with some tom-tom strikes during the superimposition phase of the work.

The technical team for the session included producer George Martin, balance engineer Norman Smith, and tape operator Richard Langham.

The song was recorded to the four-track Telefunken M10 primary tracking machine.

The backing track featured Harrison on either his 1963 Gretsch PX6122 Chet Atkins Country Gentleman with Gretsch Bigsby B6G vibrato or 1963 Gretsch 6119 Chet Atkins Tennessean with Gretsch Bigsby vibrato electric guitar (both were available to him) and lead vocals, Lennon on his 1964 Rickenbacker 325 Capri electric guitar and backing vocals, McCartney on his 1962-1963 Hofner 500/1 bass and backing vocals, and Starr on his 1963 Ludwig Oyster Black Pearl Downbeat drum set.

For amplification, while the 30-watt 1963 JMI Vox AC30/6 Twin Treble amplifiers were still available to Lennon and Harrison, it is more likely that they utilized their newer amplifiers for this session; the 50-watt 1963 JMI Vox AC50 Small Box (Mk. I) amplifiers with Vox AC50 cabinets. For bass amplification, McCartney used the 100-watt 1963 Vox AC100 head with a Vox AC100 custom cabinet.

Quick work was made of the song with the backing track completed by take 3.

Superimposition take 4 included Harrison's double-tracked lead vocals and Starr on tom-tom fills. With these quick additions, recording on the song was completed.

On March 3rd in a Studio 1 control room session, remix mono (RM) 1 was created from take 4. RM 1 served as the mono release version of the song used in both the film and album.

On June 22nd in another Studio 1 control room session, remix stereo (RS) 1 was created from take 4. RS 1 served as the stereo release version of the song.

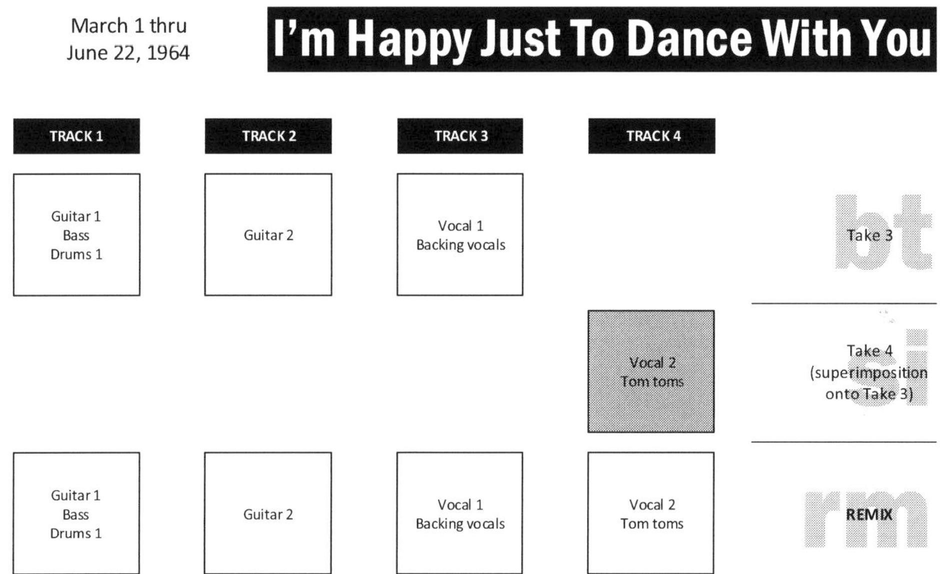

# Long Tall Sally

**Sessions**

- March 1, 1964
- March 10, 1964
- June 4, 1964
- June 22, 1964

Recording continued on the *A Hard Day's Night* project at EMI Recording Studios, Studio 2, on March 1st, 1964 during a session that included work on three new tracks. The second song of the day was Enotris Johnson, Richard Penniman (also known as Little Richard), and Robert Blackwell's *Long Tall Sally*. Originally released in 1956 in the US on the Specialty Records label, the song had long been part of The Beatles' live sets. McCartney had learned Little Richard's vocal styling from the man himself in 1962.

The technical team for the session included producer George Martin, balance engineer Norman Smith, and tape operator Richard Langham.

The song was recorded to the four-track Telefunken M10 primary tracking machine.

The backing track featured McCartney on his 1962-1963 Hofner 500/1 bass and lead vocals, Lennon on his 1964 Rickenbacker 325 Capri electric guitar, Harrison on either his 1963 Gretsch PX6122 Chet Atkins Country Gentleman with Gretsch Bigsby B6G vibrato or 1963 Gretsch 6119 Chet Atkins Tennessean with Gretsch Bigsby vibrato electric guitar (both were available to him), and Starr on his 1963 Ludwig Oyster Black Pearl Downbeat drum set.

The Beatles also had a piano player for this backing track: None other than producer George Martin, taking on Little Richard's role on the Steinway "Music Room" Model B Grand Piano.

For amplification, while the 30-watt 1963 JMI Vox AC30/6 Twin Treble amplifiers were still available to Lennon and Harrison, it is more likely that they utilized their newer amplifiers for this session; the 50-watt 1963 JMI Vox AC50 Small Box (Mk. I) amplifiers with Vox AC50 cabinets. For bass amplification, McCartney used the 100-watt 1963 Vox AC100 head with a Vox AC100 custom cabinet.

One take — no superimpositions, no edits. What you hear is what you get. The immediacy and power of a rock-n-roll band confident in their material and themselves. Martin knew they had put the song to bed. Next, please.

On March 10th, in a Studio 2 control room session, a series of remixes were created for the song. Remix stereo (RS) 1 and remix mono (RM) 1 were created from take 1, both intended for the US market, where they were released on *The Beatles' Second Album.*

On June 4th in Studio 2, another RM 1 (marked RM1 #2) was created from take 1. This RM 1 served as the mono release version of the song.

On June 22nd in a Studio 1 control session, another RS 1 (marked RS 1 #2) was created from take 1. The stereo version of the song was unreleased contemporary to The Beatles' recording career.

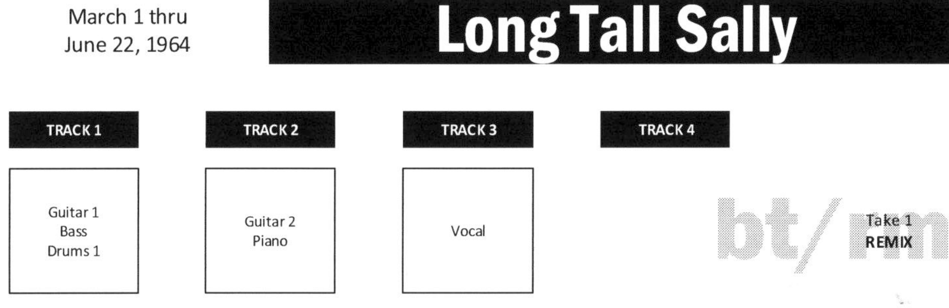

# I Call Your Name

**Sessions**

- March 1, 1964
- March 3, 1964
- March 10, 1964
- June 4, 1964
- June 22, 1964

Recording continued on the *A Hard Day's Night* project on March 1st, 1964, at EMI Recording Studios, Studio 2, during a session that included work on three new tracks. The last song of the day was another John Lennon and Paul McCartney original, *I Call Your Name*. The straightforward rock-n-roller, with some clever and well-placed variations, declared Lennon and McCartney's mastery of the form.

The technical team for the session included producer George Martin, balance engineer Norman Smith, and tape operator Richard Langham.

The song was recorded to the four-track Telefunken M10 primary tracking machine.

The backing track featured Lennon on his 1964 Rickenbacker 325 Capri electric guitar and lead vocals, McCartney on his 1962-1963 Hofner 500/1 bass, Harrison on his 12-string 1963 Rickenbacker 360-12 electric guitar, and Starr on his 1963 Ludwig Oyster Black Pearl Downbeat drum set.

For amplification, while the 30-watt 1963 JMI Vox AC30/6 Twin Treble amplifiers were still available to Lennon and Harrison, it is more likely that they utilized their newer amplifiers for this session; the 50-watt 1963 JMI Vox AC50 Small Box (Mk. I) amplifiers with Vox AC50 cabinets. For bass amplification, McCartney used the 100-watt 1963 Vox AC100 head with a Vox AC100 custom cabinet.

Only six takes of the backing track were necessary to lock the song down, take 5 being the best.

A single superimposition take (take 7) was used to add Lennon's double-tracked lead vocals and Starr on a Ludwig Clear Tone cowbell. With these additions, the song was completed.

Before the session ended, an edit was made of takes 5 and 7. Take 7 made up the bulk of the song, save for a few seconds of the introduction and the entire solo section of the song, which came from take 5. It is unclear whether a tape copy was made to perform this edit, as later on both these takes were remixed independently and then edited together for both mono and stereo versions.

On March 3rd in a Studio 1 control room session, remix mono (RM) 1 was created from the edit of takes 5 and 7 created on the 1st. This remix was destined for the US market, where it ended up on the mono version of *The Beatles' Second Album*.

On March 10th in a Studio 2 control room session, remix stereo (RS) 1 was created from the edit of takes 5 and 7 created on March 1st. This remix was also destined for the US market, where it ended up on the stereo version of *The Beatles' Second Album*.

On June 4th in Studio 2, the song was remixed again for mono. This time, take 5 was remixed in mono, becoming RM 1(#2) (ignoring the version created on March 3rd), and take 7 also remixed, becoming RM 2. Then an edit was created from RM 1 (#2) and 2. This edit served as the mono release version of the song.

On June 22nd in a Studio 1 control room session, the song was remixed a final time for stereo, this time with take 5 remixed, becoming RS 1 (#2) and take 7 also remixed, becoming RS 3. Then an edit was created from RS 1 and 3. This edit served as the stereo release version of the song.

March 1 thru
June 22, 1964

# I Call Your Name

| TRACK 1 | TRACK 2 | TRACK 3 | TRACK 4 | |
|---|---|---|---|---|
| Guitar 1<br>Bass<br>Drums 1 | Guitar 2 | Vocal 1 | | Take 5 |
| | | | Vocal 2<br>Cowbell | Take 7<br>(superimposition onto Take 5) |
| Guitar 1<br>Bass<br>Drums 1 | Guitar 2 | Vocal 1 | | **REMIX FROM TAKE 5** |
| Guitar 1<br>Bass<br>Drums 1 | Guitar 2 | Vocal 1 | Vocal 2<br>Cowbell | **REMIX FROM TAKE 7** |
| | | | | **EDIT OF REMIXES** |
| Guitar 1<br>Bass<br>Drums 1 | Guitar 2 | Vocal 1 | Vocal 2<br>Cowbell | **RELEASE VERSION** |

# A Hard Day's Night

**Sessions**

- April 16, 1964
- April 20, 1964
- April 23, 1964
- June 22, 1964

The recording session of April 16th, 1964 at EMI Recording Studios, Studio 2, had a single focus — recording the title song for the film, *A Hard Day's Night.* The John Lennon and Paul McCartney original was central to the film soundtrack and had only been composed a few days earlier. The title, a "Ringoism", provided a perfect summation of life at the centre of The Beatles' hurricane. The song was one of those Lennon and McCartney pairings in which the contributions of each artist could be clearly delineated — Lennon providing the verse, McCartney, the middle eight.

The technical team for the evening session included producer George Martin, balance engineer Norman Smith, and tape operator Geoff Emerick.

The song was recorded to the four-track Telefunken M10 primary tracking machine.

The backing track featured Lennon on Harrison's 1962 Gibson J-160E acoustic guitar and lead vocals, McCartney on his 1962-1963 Hofner 500/1 bass and backing vocals (or co-lead vocals, as he sings lead on the middle eight of the song), Harrison on his 12-string 1963 Rickenbacker 360-12 electric guitar, and Starr on his 1963 Ludwig Oyster Black Pearl Downbeat drum set.

For amplification, while the 30-watt 1963 JMI Vox AC30/6 Twin Treble amplifiers were still available to Lennon and Harrison, it is more likely that they utilized their newer amplifiers for this session; the 50-watt 1963 JMI Vox AC50 Small Box (Mk. I) amplifiers with Vox AC50 cabinets. Lennon's Gibson was also mic'ed acoustically with a Neumann U48 microphone. Engineer Smith blended the acoustic signal with the amplified one to create a unique acoustic guitar tone. For bass amplification, McCartney used the 100-watt 1963 Vox AC100 head with a Vox AC100 custom cabinet.

Take 1 demonstrates that Martin had plans for a dramatic first chord from the start, with a rapid slapback, repeat echo effect applied live to the chord. Also evident from the fumbling first take was the intent to end the song with the $F^9$ to F-major chord sequence, repeating into a fade.

The false starts on takes 2 and 3 led to another sloppy, but complete take 4. In retrospect, it makes sense that a song Lennon and McCartney had just written was still being locked down. Harrison's solo was as unformed as the rest of the performances. Only Starr seemed to have found the song's pocket. A second "take 4" (actually the fifth take) eliminated the slapback echo and any attempt by Harrison at a solo. Apparently at that point it had been decided that a solo would be recorded in a superimposition, not with the backing track.

Takes 6 and 7 comprised two more rough attempts. Take 6 broke down before the song was complete, while in take 7, McCartney missed cues throughout and Harrison palmed the ending chord. To top it off, Lennon broke a string before the take finished.

Finally, after a false start on take 8, take 9 struck not only the right chord to start the song, but was the strong core performance Martin had been seeking for the film's important title track.

Next, multiple superimpositions were added to take 9. The first of these included Lennon and McCartney double-tracking their lead vocals, Starr adding a Ludwig Clear Tone cowbell, and Norman Smith adding bongos (leaving the balance engineer's chair once again to Emerick).

The solo superimposition for the song was recorded at half-speed with Martin on piano and Harrison on guitar. Audio evidence indicates that while Harrison used the Rickenbacker 360-12 to record the rhythm track, he used one of his Gretsch guitars to play the solo. The 360-12 was used one final time to reinforce the final chord of the song.

Emerick noted in his autobiography that Martin played an "out of tune upright piano" for his part, doubling the solo of the song. The likely suspect was the 1905 Steinway Vertegrand piano, known for being intentionally left slightly out of tune (the so-called "Mrs. Mills" upright piano was named after an unlikely star, Parlophone recording artist Gladys Mills, who in her mid 40's made her mark as "Mrs. Mills" with piano sing-along versions of pop standards). With these additions, recording on the song was completed.

On April 20th, in a brief Studio 2 control room session, remix mono (RM) 1 and remix stereo (RS) 1 were created from take 9. The mixes were made for United Artists, though neither were used.

On April 23rd, an even briefer, 15-minute Studio 2 control room session was all that was needed to create RM 10 from take 9. RM 10 served as the mono release version of the song.

On June 22nd in a Studio 1 control room session, another RS 1 was created from take 9. This RS 1 served as the stereo release version of the song.

April 16 thru
June 22, 1964

# A Hard Day's Night

| | TRACK 1 | TRACK 2 | TRACK 3 | TRACK 4 |
|---|---|---|---|---|
| bt — Take 9 | Guitar 1<br>Bass<br>Drums 1 | Acoustic guitar 1<br>Vocal 1<br>Vocal 2 | | |
| si — Superimposition onto Take 9 | | | Vocal 3<br>Vocal 4<br>Bongos<br>Cowbell | Guitar 2<br>Piano<br>Guitar 3 |
| rm — REMIX | Guitar 1<br>Bass<br>Drums 1 | Acoustic guitar 1<br>Vocal 1<br>Vocal 2 | Vocal 3<br>Vocal 4<br>Bongos<br>Cowbell | Guitar 2<br>Piano<br>Guitar 3 |

# Matchbox

**Sessions**

- June 1, 1964
- June 4, 1964
- June 22, 1964

Songs for the film *A Hard Day's Night* had been completed, and all that was left for The Beatles was to complete the additional songs for the upcoming UK album. The session on June 1st, 1964 at EMI Recording Studios, Studio 2, saw three of those songs started along with Carl Perkins' *Matchbox*, which was Starr's vocal contribution during the era. The song didn't end up on the soundtrack album, but instead found itself allocated to the *Long Tall Sally* EP. And it just so happened that its writer, rockabilly legend Perkins, was present for the session.

The technical team of producer George Martin and balance engineer Norman Smith included one new face who, like Geoff Emerick before him, came to play a key part in The Beatles recording career — tape operator Ken Scott.

The song was recorded to the four-track Telefunken M10 primary tracking machine.

The backing track featured Starr on lead vocals and his newly acquired third Ludwig drum set, this one a 1964 Ludwig Oyster Black Pearl Super Classic. The biggest difference between this and his earlier, road-weary Downbeat set was a 22" bass drum. He continued to use his favourite 1963 Jazz Festival snare with the new drum set.

In addition to Starr, the backing track included Lennon on his 1964 Rickenbacker 325 Capri electric guitar, Harrison on either his 1963 Gretsch PX6122 Chet Atkins Country Gentleman with Gretsch Bigsby B6G vibrato or 1963 Gretsch 6119 Chet Atkins Tennessean with Gretsch Bigsby vibrato electric guitar (both were available to him), McCartney on his 1962-1963 Hofner 500/1 bass, and George Martin on the studio's Steinway "Music Room" Model B Grand Piano.

For amplification, while the 30-watt 1963 JMI Vox AC30/6 Twin Treble amplifiers were still available to Lennon and Harrison, it is more likely that they utilized the newer 50-watt 1963 JMI Vox AC50 Small Box (Mk. I) amplifiers with Vox AC50 cabinets. For bass amplification, McCartney used the 100-watt 1963 Vox AC100 head with a Vox AC100 custom cabinet.

It only took four takes to complete the backing track, with take 4 being the best, before moving onto the superimposition take 5.

Superimpositions to the song included Starr doubling his lead vocals and Harrison double-tracking his guitar solo.

In a June 4th session in Studio 2, remix mono (RM) 1 was created from take 5. RM 1 served as the mono release version of the song.

On June 22nd in a Studio 1 control room session, remix stereo (RS) 1 was created from take 5. This version was unreleased contemporary to The Beatles' recording career in the UK, though it did find release on *Something New* in the US market.

In the mono remix, Harrison's double-tracked guitar solo lasts for the entire solo section, but in the stereo version, the initial guitar solo can be heard at around the 1:00 mark for just a few seconds in the centre pan before it's replaced by the superimposition solo in the right pan.

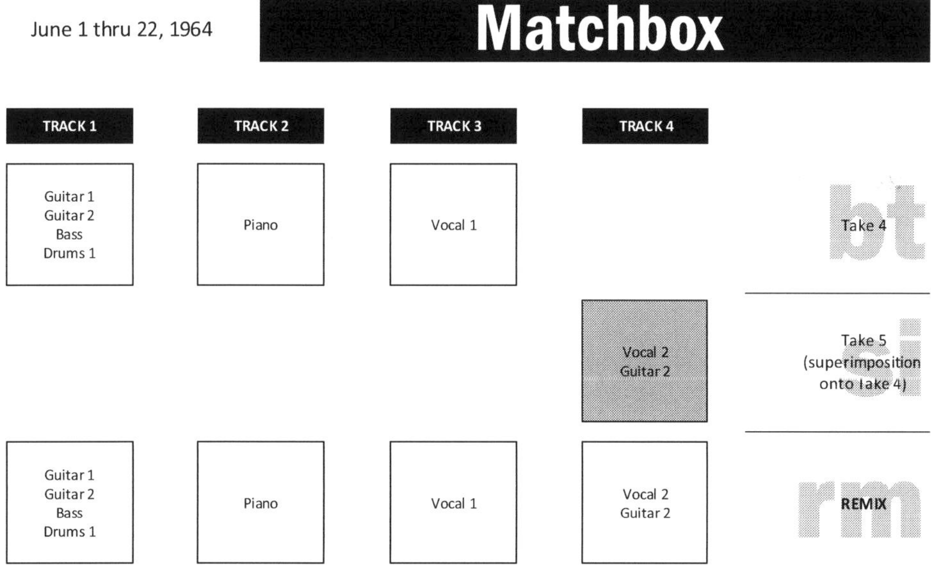

# I'll Cry Instead

**Sessions**

- June 1, 1964
- June 4, 1964
- June 9, 1964
- June 22, 1964

The second song recorded on June 1st, 1964, at EMI Recording Studios, Studio 2, was another John Lennon and Paul McCartney tune initially under consideration for the *A Hard Day's Night* film, though in the end it ended up on the B-side of the album.

*I'll Cry Instead* was recorded in two parts, though history does not reveal why (Winn speculates it may have had to do with movie production requirements for a song that could be edited to a specific time duration, as it was thought to be originally intended to slot into the film during what became the *Can't Buy Me Love* sequence).

It wasn't uncommon for The Beatles to record edit pieces in which the band played entire sections of a song to be cut in where Martin believed the performances needed improvement, but *I'll Cry Instead* was different — specifically created with a "Section A" and a "Section B".

The technical team for the session included producer George Martin, balance engineer Norman Smith, and tape operator Ken Scott.

The song was recorded to the four-track Telefunken M10 primary tracking machine.

The backing track featured Lennon on Harrison's 1962 Gibson J-160E acoustic guitar and lead vocals, McCartney on his 1962-1963 Hofner 500/1 bass, Harrison on either his 1963 Gretsch PX6122 Chet Atkins Country Gentleman with Gretsch Bigsby B6G vibrato or 1963 Gretsch 6119 Chet Atkins Tennessean with Gretsch Bigsby vibrato electric guitar (both were available to him), and Starr on his 1964 Ludwig Oyster Black Pearl Super Classic drum set.

For amplification, while the 30-watt 1963 JMI Vox AC30/6 Twin Treble amplifiers were still available to Lennon and Harrison, it is more likely that they utilized their newer amplifiers for this session; the 50-watt 1963 JMI Vox AC50 Small Box (Mk. I) amplifiers with Vox AC50 cabinets. Lennon's Gibson was also mic'ed acoustically with a Neumann U48 microphone. Engineer Smith blended the acoustic signal with the amplified one to create a unique acoustic guitar tone. For bass amplification, McCartney used the 100-watt 1963 Vox AC100 head with a Vox AC100 custom cabinet.

Five takes of Section A were created, take 5 being the best. Take 5 was then edited, becoming take 6. Next, one take of Section B was created, named take 7. As with Section A, it was then edited, becoming take 8.

Before work on the song ended for the day, Lennon added a double-tracked lead vocal and Starr added tambourine to both Sections A and B (these superimpositions were not numbered). With these additions, recording on the track was complete.

On June 4th, the technical team returned to Studio 2 for editing and remixing work on the track. First, unnumbered mono remixes of take 6 (Section A) and take 8 (section B) were created, then these remixes were edited together. At least two versions of take 8 were compiled into release versions of the song. While Section B appears to make up only the last 0:40 of the song in the UK version, adding a second pass of the middle eight section (the total running time being 1:49), a U.S. mono single release version of the song extends an additional 0:20 with a third verse (the total running time being 2:09).

The edited result of the UK version was referred to as remix mono (RM) 1. RM 1 served as the mono release version of the song. There is no note of a remix number assigned to the U.S. version of the song.

On June 9th, a copy of RM 1 was made for consideration as a part of the *A Hard Day's Night* film soundtrack, but ultimately it wasn't included.

On June 22nd in a Studio 1 control room remix session, stereo editing and remixing work occurred on the track. First, unnumbered remixes of take 6 (Section A) and take 8 (section B) were created, then the remixes were edited together. The resulting edit served as the stereo release version of the song though it was never given a remix number.

June 1 thru 22, 1964

# I'll Cry Instead

| TRACK 1 | TRACK 2 | TRACK 3 | TRACK 4 | |
|---|---|---|---|---|
| Guitar 1<br>Bass<br>Drums 1 | Acoustic guitar | Vocal 1 | | bt<br>Takes 5 and 7 |
| | | | | **EDIT OF TAKE 5, NAMED TAKE 6 AND EDIT OF TAKE 7, NAMED TAKE 8** |
| | | | Vocal 2<br>Tambourine | si<br>Superimposition onto Take 6 and Take 8 |
| Guitar 1<br>Bass<br>Drums 1 | Acoustic guitar | Vocal 1 | Vocal 2<br>Tambourine | rm<br>**REMIX OF TAKE 6 AND TAKE 8** |
| | | | | **EDIT OF REMIXES** |
| Guitar 1<br>Bass<br>Drums 1 | Acoustic guitar | Vocal 1 | Vocal 2<br>Tambourine | rv<br>**RELEASE VERSION** |

# Slow Down

**Sessions**

- June 1, 1964
- June 4, 1964
- June 22, 1964

The third song recorded for the B-side of the *A Hard Day's Night* album at EMI Recording Studios, Studio 2, on June 1st, 1964, was the Larry Williams rocker, *Slow Down* (the track ended up on the *Long Tall Sally* EP instead). As with earlier straightforward rock-n-roll songs, the band made short work of the recording.

The technical team for the session included producer George Martin, balance engineer Norman Smith, and tape operator Ken Scott.

The song was recorded to the four-track Telefunken M10 primary tracking machine.

The backing track featured Lennon on his 1964 Rickenbacker 325 Capri electric guitar and lead vocals, McCartney on his 1962-1963 Hofner 500/1 bass, Harrison on either his 1963 Gretsch PX6122 Chet Atkins Country Gentleman with Gretsch Bigsby B6G vibrato or 1963 Gretsch 6119 Chet Atkins Tennessean with Gretsch Bigsby vibrato electric guitar (both were available to him), and Starr on his 1964 Ludwig Oyster Black Pearl Super Classic drum set.

For amplification, while the 30-watt 1963 JMI Vox AC30/6 Twin Treble amplifiers were still available to Lennon and Harrison, it is more likely that they utilized the newer 50-watt 1963 JMI Vox AC50 Small Box (Mk. I) amplifiers with Vox AC50 cabinets. For bass amplification, McCartney used the 100-watt 1963 Vox AC100 head with a Vox AC100 custom cabinet.

Three takes of the backing track were performed, with take 3 being the best.

Superimposition takes 4 and 5 included Lennon's double-tracked lead vocals, take 5 being the best. With it, work on the song ended for the session.

On June 4th in Studio 2, George Martin added the studio's Steinway "Music Room" Model B Grand Piano to the track in a single superimposition take (take 6).

After completing the performance, remix mono (RM) 1 was created from take 6. RM 1 served as the mono release version of the song.

On June 22nd in a Studio 1 control room remix session, remix stereo (RS) 1 was created from take 6. This version was unreleased contemporary to The Beatles' recording career in the UK, though it did find release on *Something New* in the US market.

Later on the same day in Studio 1, a tape copy of RM 1 was created. This concluded work related to the track.

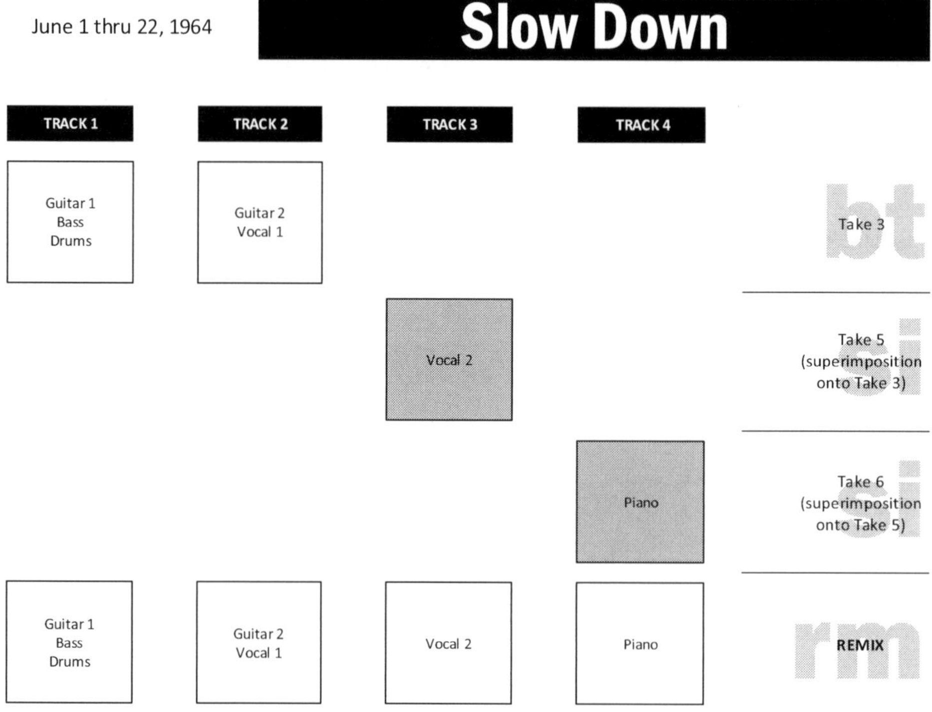

# I'll Be Back

**Sessions**

- June 1, 1964
- June 10, 1964
- June 22, 1964

The final song recorded in the June 1st, 1964 session at EMI Recording Studios, Studio 2, for the *A Hard Day's Night* album was another John Lennon and Paul McCartney original. The ballad *I'll Be Back* was the third song of the night to feature Lennon in the lead vocal role. Once again, the partnership of Lennon and McCartney was on display, as the song's darker verses give way to a soaring middle eight — a hallmark of their collaboration.

The technical team for the session included producer George Martin, balance engineer Norman Smith, and tape operator Ken Scott.

The song was recorded to the four-track Telefunken M10 primary tracking machine.

Surprisingly, initial takes of *I'll Be Back* were not acoustic guitar-based, as was the finished track.

While working out the arrangement and tempo of the tune, Lennon and Harrison both played electric guitars. Available audio evidence through take 3 shows Lennon used his 1964 Rickenbacker 325 Capri electric guitar, while Harrison played his 1963 Rickenbacker 360-12 12-string electric guitar. It is not known at which point in the remaining takes the switch occurred from electric to acoustic guitars, though by take 12 the change of arrangement was in place and the final tempo locked down.

The backing track featured Lennon on Harrison's 1962 Gibson J-160E acoustic guitar and lead vocals, McCartney on his 1962-1963 Hofner 500/1 bass and backing vocals, Harrison on either the Jose Ramirez Guitarra de Estudio or Jose Ramirez A1 Segovia acoustic guitar (both were available), and Starr on his 1964 Ludwig Oyster Black Pearl Super Classic drum set.

For bass amplification, McCartney used the 100-watt 1963 Vox AC100 head with a Vox AC100 custom cabinet.

There were only a handful of completed takes for the track, as Lennon had trouble vocally with the original electric arrangement, and once the acoustic arrangement was in place there were a number of false starts.

Take 16 ended up both being a complete and solid performance of the backing track, and work moved on to superimpositions for the song.

Superimpositions onto take 16 featured Lennon and McCartney's doubled-tracked vocals, with Harrison adding more nylon string acoustic guitar touches. With these additions, work on the track was completed.

On June 10th in a Studio 2 control room session, remix mono (RM) 1 was created from take 16.

On June 22nd in a Studio 1 control room session, two more mono remixes were created from take 16 (RM 2 and 3). RM2 served as the UK release version of the song, while RM3 was destined for the US market.

During the same session, remix stereo (RS) 1 was created from take 16. RS 1 served as the stereo release version of the song.

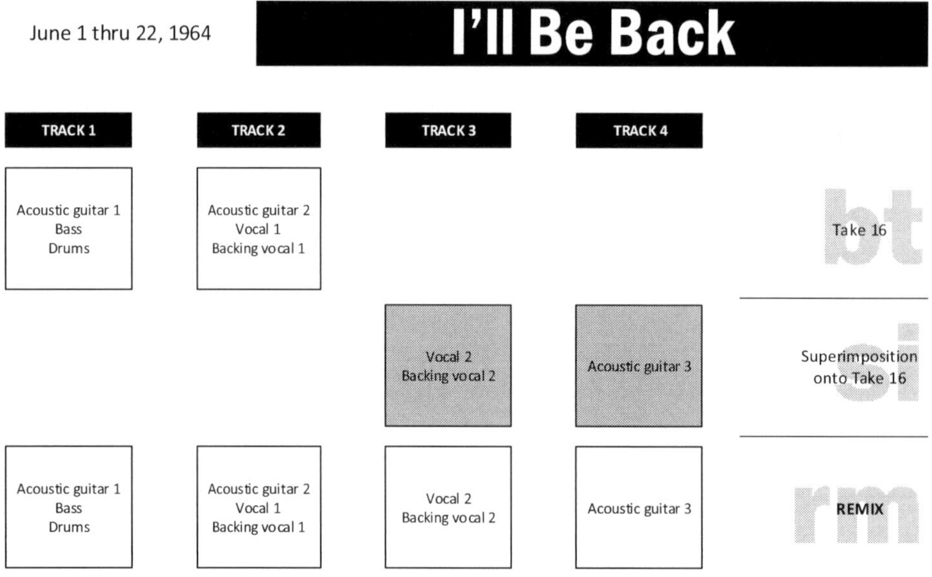

# Any Time At All

**Sessions**

- June 2, 1964
- June 3, 1964
- June 4, 1964
- June 22, 1964

On June 2nd 1964 at EMI Recording Studios, Studio 2, work on the final three songs for the *A Hard Day's Night* album began. The first song of the session, John Lennon and Paul McCartney's *Any Time At All*, once again featured Lennon on lead vocals (Lennon provided the majority of lead vocals for the album, either singing lead or sharing lead vocals with McCartney on nine of the 13 tracks). Martin's work as a producer on the song underscores his sometimes underappreciated skills. In this instance, he identified the two key moments of the song, and enhanced them; Starr's snare shots brought the listener to attention and Lennon's vocal chorus to start the song did the rest of the work.

The technical team for the session included producer George Martin, balance engineer Norman Smith, and tape operator Ken Scott.

The song was recorded to the four-track Telefunken M10 primary tracking machine.

The backing track included Lennon on Harrison's 1962 Gibson J-160E acoustic guitar and lead vocals, McCartney on his 1962-1963 Hofner 500/1 bass and backing vocals, Harrison on his 12-string 1963 Rickenbacker 360-12 electric guitar, and Starr on his 1964 Ludwig Oyster Black Pearl Super Classic drum set.

For amplification, while the 30-watt 1963 JMI Vox AC30/6 Twin Treble amplifiers were still available to Lennon and Harrison, it is more likely that they utilized the newer 50-watt 1963 JMI Vox AC50 Small Box (Mk. I) amplifiers with Vox AC50 cabinets. Lennon's Gibson was also mic'ed acoustically with a Neumann U48 microphone. Engineer Smith blended the acoustic signal with the amplified one to create a unique acoustic guitar tone. For bass amplification, McCartney used the 100-watt 1963 Vox AC100 head with a Vox AC100 custom cabinet.

With seven takes, a solid backing track for this straightforward rocker was completed, take 7 being the best.

Three superimposition takes followed, with Starr reinforcing the snare shots that open the song and precede the last verse, and Harrison adding body to the song with acoustic guitar (takes 8 through 10, with take 10 being the best of these).

The following day in Studio 2, more superimpositions to take 11 included Lennon and McCartney double-tracking their lead and backing vocals and Lennon on Studio 2's Steinway "Music Room" Model B Grand Piano. With these additions, recording on the song was completed.

On June 4th in Studio 2, a push to complete work on the album was in full gear. Along with six other songs, remix mono (RM) 1 was created from take 11. This remix was intended to be the master remix until it was improved upon on June 22nd in a Studio 1 control room session.

During that session, two more mono remixes were created from take 11 (RM 2 and 3). RM 2 served as the UK release version of the song, while RM 3 was destined for the US market. Before work ended, remix stereo (RS) 1 was created from take 11. RS 1 served as the stereo release version of the song.

June 2 thru 22, 1964

# Any Time At All

| TRACK 1 | TRACK 2 | TRACK 3 | TRACK 4 | |
|---|---|---|---|---|
| Acoustic guitar 1<br>Guitar<br>Bass<br>Drums | Vocal 1<br>Backing vocal 1 | | | bt<br>Take 7 |
| | | Snare<br>Acoustic guitar 2 | | si<br>Take 10<br>(superimposition onto Take 7) |
| | | | Vocal 2<br>Backing vocal 2<br>Piano | si<br>Take 11<br>(superimposition onto Take 10) |
| Acoustic guitar 1<br>Guitar<br>Bass<br>Drums | Vocal 1<br>Backing vocal 1 | Snare<br>Acoustic guitar 2 | Vocal 2<br>Backing vocal 2<br>Piano | rm<br>REMIX |

# Things We Said Today

**Sessions**

- June 2, 1964
- June 3, 1964
- June 9, 1964
- June 22, 1964

The June 2nd, 1964 session at EMI Recording Studios, Studio 2, for the final three tunes of the *A Hard Day's Night* album was a compact one, with three songs almost completely tracked before the session ended. The second song of the session, John Lennon and Paul McCartney's *Things We Said Today*, featured McCartney on lead vocals. The song is another advancement in the duo's narrative toolset, as McCartney looks into the future, considering how he and his love will remember the past when they get there.

The technical team for the song's first session included producer George Martin, balance engineer Norman Smith, and tape operator Ken Scott.

The song was recorded to the four-track Telefunken M10 primary tracking machine.

The backing track featured McCartney on his 1962-1963 Hofner 500/1 bass and lead vocals, Lennon on Harrison's 1962 Gibson J-160E acoustic guitar and backing vocals, Harrison on either his 1963 Gretsch PX6122 Chet Atkins Country Gentleman with Gretsch Bigsby B6G vibrato or 1963 Gretsch 6119 Chet Atkins Tennessean with Gretsch Bigsby vibrato electric guitar (both were available to him), and Starr on his 1964 Ludwig Oyster Black Pearl Super Classic drum set.

For amplification, while the 30-watt 1963 JMI Vox AC30/6 Twin Treble amplifier was still available to Harrison, it is more likely that he utilized the newer 50-watt 1963 JMI Vox AC50 Small Box (Mk. I) amplifier with a Vox AC50 cabinet. For bass amplification, McCartney used the 100-watt 1963 Vox AC100 head with a Vox AC100 custom cabinet.

The band made quick work of the tune, with only two takes required to perfect the backing track, take 2 being the best. Superimpositions on the song commenced in the following day's session.

Starr didn't attend the June 3rd session in Studio 2, as he was having his tonsils removed that day. Superimposition take 3 featured McCartney doubling his lead vocal, and adding harmony in select places, while Lennon added the studio's Steinway "Music Room" Model B Grand Piano to the choruses. Finally, McCartney and Harrison added tambourines to the track while Lennon doubled his acoustic guitar strums for the intro, outro, and between verses. With the additions, recording on the song was completed.

The mono remix for the song occurred on June 9th in a Studio 3 control room session. Remix mono (RM) 1 from take 3 served as the mono release version of the song.

On June 22nd in a Studio 1 control room session, remix stereo (RS) 1 was created from take 3. RS 1 served as the stereo release version of the song.

Later the same day in a Studio 2 control room session, a copy was made of RS 1 for unknown use. This completed work on the song.

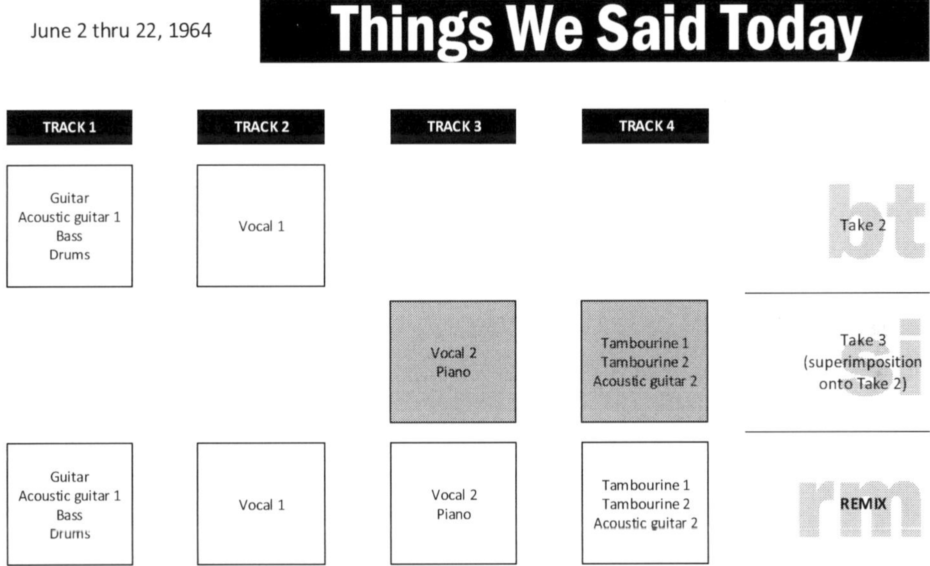

# When I Get Home

**Sessions**

- June 2, 1964
- June 4, 1964
- June 22, 1964

The final track recorded for the *A Hard Day's Night* album on June 2nd, 1964 at EMI Recording Studios, Studio 2, was a straightforward John Lennon and Paul McCartney rocker, *When I Get Home*. Once again, Lennon provided the lead vocals for a song which would have fit just as well on *With The Beatles* as on the upcoming release.

The technical team for the session included producer George Martin, balance engineer Norman Smith, and tape operator Ken Scott..

The song was recorded to the four-track Telefunken M10 primary tracking machine.

The backing track featured Lennon on his 1964 Rickenbacker 325 Capri electric guitar and lead vocals, McCartney on his 1962-1963 Hofner 500/1 bass and backing vocals, Harrison on either his 1963 Gretsch PX6122 Chet Atkins Country Gentleman with Gretsch Bigsby B6G vibrato or 1963 Gretsch 6119 Chet Atkins Tennessean with Gretsch Bigsby vibrato electric guitar (both were available to him) and backing vocals, and Starr on his 1964 Ludwig Oyster Black Pearl Super Classic drum set.

For amplification, while the 30-watt 1963 JMI Vox AC30/6 Twin Treble amplifiers were still available to Lennon and Harrison, it is more likely that they utilized the newer 50-watt 1963 JMI Vox AC50 Small Box (Mk. I) amplifiers with Vox AC50 cabinets. For bass amplification, McCartney used the 100-watt 1963 Vox AC100 head with a Vox AC100 custom cabinet.

It took ten takes to perfect the backing track, take 10 being the best, and then a single superimposition take doubling Lennon's vocals at the middle eight to finish the recording of the song (take 11).

On June 4th in Studio 2, remix mono (RM) 1 was created from take 11. This remix was intended to be the master remix until it was improved upon on June 22nd in a Studio 1 control room session.

During that session, two more mono remixes were created from take 11 (RM 2 and 3). RM 2 served as the UK release version of the song, while RM 3 was destined for the US market, where it was released on *Something New*. During the same session, remix stereo (RS) 1 was created from take 11. RS 1 served as the stereo release version of the song.

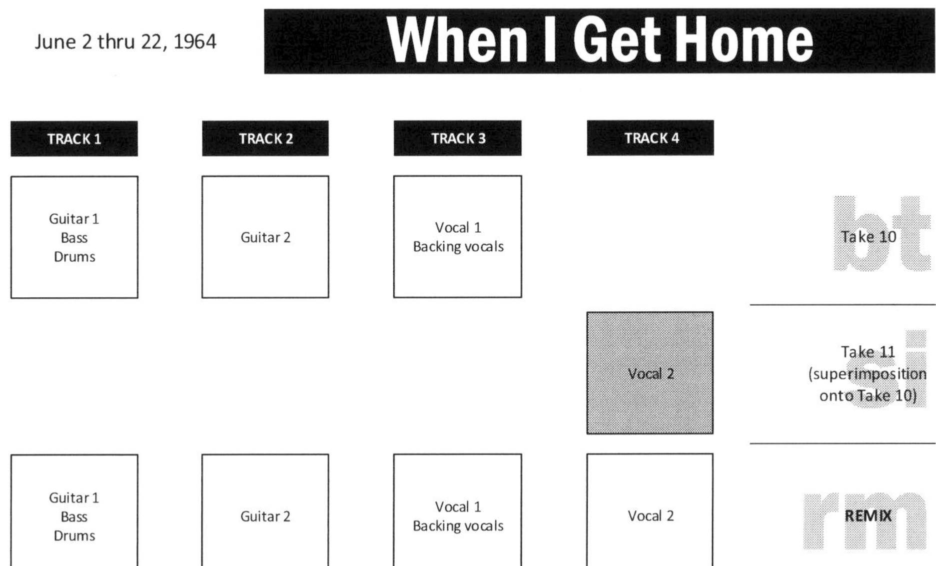

# Demos:

# You Know What To Do, You're My World, and No Reply

**Sessions**

- June 3, 1964

The same June 3rd, 1964 session at EMI Recording Studios, Studio 2, that was devoted to superimposition work on *Any Time At All* and *Things We Said Today* also included preliminary work on two new songs.

The session started off as a rehearsal for The Beatles with drummer Jimmy Nicol, who replaced Ringo Starr (recovering from tonsillitis) at the last minute for upcoming live performances in Denmark, Holland, Hong Kong, Australia and New Zealand (June 3rd through 14th).

After working with Nicol on the live set for an hour, the remaining Beatles returned to demo two additional songs. *You Know What To Do* was a simple sketch of a new Harrison song that never went any further, while *No Reply* would end up as an anchor tune for their next album, *Beatles For Sale.*

The demos were recorded to the four-track Telefunken M10 primary tracking machine.

There is a great mystery and debate as to who the drummer is on the *No Reply* demo. Starr was in the hospital and Nicol was believed to be absent after the hour-long 3PM to 4PM rehearsal. The only unaccounted-for musician, Harrison had never been known to drum on any Beatles track until 1968, when he is believed to have been one of three drummers on *Back In The U.S.S.R.* Winn has speculated Harrison played bass on the tune, leaving the drum chores to McCartney, though to do so, he would have had to quickly figure out how to play McCartney's left-handed Hofner upside down.

While balance engineer Norman Smith was capable of playing drums, the demo contains his voice "slating" the track from the control room ("*No Reply*, take 1."). The most likely scenario is that Nicol wasn't absent at all and is in fact the drummer on the demo.

Besides *No Reply* and *You Know What To Do*, the only other song on this session was not so much a demo as an artifact; McCartney busking a mere 0:30 worth of Cilla Black's current hit, *You're My World.*

With the technical team of producer George Martin, balance engineer Norman Smith, and tape operator Ken Scott, only one take was made of each of the other two songs.

The session featured Lennon on his 1964 Rickenbacker 325 Capri electric guitar, McCartney on his 1962-1963 Hofner 500/1 bass and backing vocals, and Harrison on either his 1963 Gretsch PX6122 Chet Atkins Country Gentleman with Gretsch Bigsby B6G vibrato or 1963 Gretsch 6119 Chet Atkins Tennessean with Gretsch Bigsby vibrato electric guitar (both were available to him).

For *No Reply*, the unknown drummer was likely behind Starr's 1964 Ludwig Oyster Black Pearl Super Classic drum set.

For amplification, while the 30-watt 1963 JMI Vox AC30/6 Twin Treble amplifiers were still available to Lennon and Harrison, it is more likely that they utilized their newer 50-watt 1963 JMI Vox AC50 Small Box (Mk. I) amplifiers with Vox AC50 cabinets. For bass amplification, McCartney used the 100-watt 1963 Vox AC100 head with a Vox AC100 custom cabinet.

The lineups for the demos were simple. For *You Know What To Do*, Harrison played guitar and sang the guide vocal, while Lennon played tambourine and McCartney, bass. For *No Reply*, Lennon played guitar and sang the guide vocal, while McCartney provided bass and backing vocals, all held together by the mystery drummer.

# Beatles For Sale

Spanning 115 days from August 11th through December 4th, 1964, the *Beatles For Sale* era is viewed through the lens of history as a period where the band was at times running on fumes, trying to keep up with demands from their management, label, promoters and fans around the world. This lack of energy is most evident in the album's song selection. For a band building its reputation on Lennon and McCartney as songwriters of the highest calibre, the release was equally weighted with the work of others. Lennon and McCartney had simply reached a point of having spent the catalogue of songs they had available, and with their busy schedules, they hadn't had time to prepare an entirely new batch for the next album and single cycle. The album itself contained only eight new original tunes, while the balance was filled with cover songs, many of which dated back to their Liverpool and Hamburg club sets.

While the era was lacking in the evolution of the band's sound, what did shine through in their original work was a level of refinement and professionalism under duress that paved the way for the groundbreaking music to come.

In addition to thc *Beatles For Sale* album, rclcascs during this era included the single *I Feel Fine* and EPs, *A Hard Day's Night (extracts from the film)* and *A Hard Day's Night (extracts from the album)*.

---

# Baby's in Black

**Sessions**

- August 11, 1964
- August 14, 1964
- October 26, 1964
- November 4, 1964

One short month after the July release of *A Hard Day's Night* on August 11th, 1964, The Beatles were back at EMI Recording Studios, Studio 2, to start work on their follow-up album, *Beatles For Sale*. With days now full of radio, television, live performances, and other appearances, evening sessions were to become more and more common for the band.

The first song recorded for the new album, John Lennon and Paul McCartney's ballad, *Baby's In Black*, includes a middle eight with one of the most transcendent harmonies that Lennon and McCartney ever committed to record, a perfectly matched, soaring vocal: "Oh how long will it take, till she sees the mistake she has made...."

The technical team for the session included producer George Martin, balance engineer Norman Smith, and tape operator, Ron Pender.

The song was recorded to the four-track Telefunken M10 primary tracking machine.

The backing track featured Lennon on Harrison's 1962 Gibson J-160E acoustic guitar and lead vocals (Lennon would finally replace his stolen J-160E the following month), McCartney on his 1962-1963 Hofner 500/1 bass and lead vocals, Harrison on his 1963 Gretsch 6119 Chet Atkins Tennessean electric guitar with Gretsch Bigsby vibrato, and Starr on his 1964 Ludwig Oyster Black Pearl Super Classic drum set.

Amplification had again taken a step up, and now the band not only continued to use the 30-watt 1963 JMI Vox AC30/6 Twin Treble amplifiers, but also the newest offering from Vox, the 100-watt 1964 JMI Vox AC100 Mk I amplifiers with a Vox AC100 cabinet. For bass amplification, McCartney continued to utilize the 100-watt 1963 Vox AC100 with a Vox AC100 custom cabinet.

Fourteen takes were made of the backing track, take 14 being the best.

Superimpositions to take 14 followed, including Lennon and McCartney's double-tracked lead vocals during the middle eight sections, Harrison's guitar solo (also double-tracked), additional acoustic guitar by Lennon, and Starr on tambourine.

Harrison's guitar swells were accomplished by Lennon manually adjusting the volume pot of the guitar as he played.

Next came an edit piece, with 13 attempts made by Harrison to perfect the song's opening guitar lick — none of which were used. With this work, recording on the song was completed.

On August 14th in Studio 2, remix mono (RM) 1 was created from take 14.

On October 26th in a Studio 2 control room session, another pass was made at the mono remix. RM 2 from take 14 served as the mono release version of the song.

On November 4th in another Studio 2 control room session, the stereo remix (RS) took only one take to perfect. RS 1 from take 14 served as the stereo release version of the song.

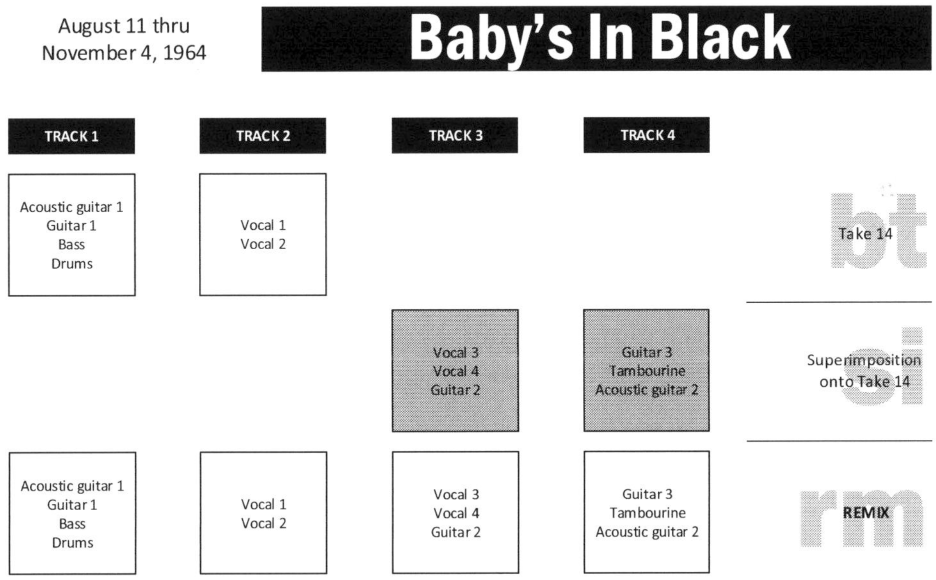

# I'm a Loser

**Sessions**

- August 14, 1964
- October 26, 1964
- November 4, 1964

On August 14th, 1964 at EMI Recording Studios, Studio 2, the second session for the *Beatles For Sale* album began with John Lennon and Paul McCartney's *I'm A Loser*. The track was one of the first of Lennon's primary compositions to depart from the love songs of previous years and focus instead on the inner life of the artist. The first of three tracks started that evening, it was the only original tune of the session.

The technical team for the session included producer George Martin, balance engineer Norman Smith, and tape operator Ron Pender.

The song was recorded to the four-track Telefunken M10 primary tracking machine.

The backing track featured Lennon on his 1964 Framus Hootenanny 5/024 acoustic guitar and lead vocals, McCartney on his 1962-1963 Hofner 500/1 bass and backing vocals, Harrison on his 1963 Gretsch 6119 Chet Atkins Tennessean electric guitar with Gretsch Bigsby vibrato, and Starr on his 1964 Ludwig Oyster Black Pearl Super Classic drum set.

The 12-string 1964 Framus Hootenanny 5/024 is not commonly thought to have become part of The Beatles' instrument complement until the *Help!* sessions in 1965 (primarily due to its appearance in the film), but audio evidence demonstrates Lennon playing the 12-string for this session, nearly six-months before the start of sessions for that album.

For amplification, Harrison used either the 30-watt 1963 JMI Vox AC30/6 Twin Treble amplifier or the 100-watt 1964 JMI Vox AC100 Mk I amplifier with a Vox AC100 cabinet. Lennon's Framus was mic'ed acoustically with a Neumann U48 microphone. For bass amplification, McCartney used the 100-watt 1963 Vox AC100 with a Vox AC100 custom cabinet.

The available audio of the session is revealing as to The Beatles' process in the studio during this period. Take 1 of the song was a false start. Take 2 was more like a rehearsal than a proper take, with McCartney still figuring out his harmony parts. In take 3 the decision was made to begin the song with the chorus' harmony vocals, though the take was still rough around the edges and Harrison's guitar solo had yet to find its place. Take 4 broke down after the first verse.

Take 5 was another breakdown, lasting just a few seconds, while take 6 introduced Lennon's harmonica part and was the first take where Harrison locked in on a solo (it wasn't performed in the backing track, but ended up as a superimposition). By the end of take 6, it was clear that the harmonica wouldn't be a part of the backing track as Lennon exclaimed after fumbling with it, "I'm all wrapped up!"

Take 7 was yet another breakdown, Martin stopping the performance as Lennon "popped" the vocal microphone on the word "appear" and then questioned McCartney about the volume level of his amplifier, which sounded louder suddenly (no George, he didn't turn it up). With take 8, the backing track was finally perfected.

Superimpositions to take 8 followed with Lennon and McCartney double-tracking their vocals, Harrison adding his guitar solo and other touches, Lennon adding his Hohner harmonica, and Starr playing tambourine on the choruses. With these additions, recording on the song was completed.

Before the evening was over, remix mono (RM) 1 was created from take 8. The remix was considered release-ready, though it was improved upon a few months later.

Work on the song recommenced on October 26th in a Studio 2 control room session. A new remix, RM 2, was created from take 8 and served as the mono release version of the song.

On November 4th, the stereo master version of the song was cut, again in a Studio 2 control room session. Remix stereo (RS) 1 from take 8 served as the stereo release version of the song.

August 14 thru
November 4, 1964

# I'm A Loser

| TRACK 1 | TRACK 2 | TRACK 3 | TRACK 4 | |
|---|---|---|---|---|
| Acoustic guitar 1<br>Guitar 1<br>Bass<br>Drums | Vocal 1<br>Vocal 2 | | | bt Take 8 |
| | | Guitar 2<br>Tambourine | Vocal 3<br>Vocal 3<br>Harmonica | si Superimposition onto Take 8 |
| Acoustic guitar 1<br>Guitar 1<br>Bass<br>Drums | Vocal 1<br>Vocal 2 | Guitar 2<br>Tambourine | Vocal 3<br>Vocal 3<br>Harmonica | rm REMIX |

# Mr. Moonlight

**Sessions**

- August 14, 1964
- October 18, 1964
- October 27, 1964
- November 4, 1964

For the second song of the August 14th, 1964 *Beatles For Sale* session at EMI Recording Studios, Studio 2, The Beatles drew on their Hamburg songbook and brought out one of their late night favourites, Roy Lee Johnson's *Mr. Moonlight.* For whatever reason, the song didn't fare well, and is routinely cited among the worst that they ever recorded. Maybe it's the organ?

The technical team for the session included producer George Martin, balance engineer Norman Smith, and tape operator Ron Pender.

The song was recorded to the four-track Telefunken M10 primary tracking machine.

The backing track featured Lennon on his 1964 Rickenbacker 325 Capri electric guitar and lead vocals, McCartney on his 1962-1963 Hofner 500/1 bass and backing vocals, Harrison on his 1963 Gretsch PX6122 Chet Atkins Country Gentleman with Gretsch Bigsby B6G vibrato or 1963 Gretsch 6119 Chet Atkins Tennessean with Gretsch Bigsby vibrato electric guitar (both were available to him), and Starr on congas.

For amplification, Lennon used either the 30-watt 1963 JMI Vox AC30/6 Twin Treble amplifier, or the 100-watt 1964 JMI Vox AC100 Mk I amplifier with a Vox AC100 cabinet. For bass amplification, McCartney used the 100-watt 1963 Vox AC100 with a Vox AC100 custom cabinet.

Takes 1 and 2 broke down as Lennon struggled with the opening solo vocal introduction. Take 3 was also a breakdown, while take 4 was a rough, but complete version of the song. Harrison's guitar solo in this early version was treated with a dominant tremolo effect from the AC30/6 amplifier. Lennon's wonderful vocal introduction to take 4 ended up being edited into the remake of the song from October 18th, though the rest of the performance was abandoned and the song went no further in the session.

On October 18th, a remake of the song began in Studio 2, this time with Geoff Emerick in the tape operator's chair. Four more takes were created of the backing track (takes 5 through 8), with takes 5 and 7 being false starts and take 8 considered the best.

Superimpositions to take 8 followed. Lennon double-tracked his lead vocals, and McCartney double-tracked his backing vocals, as well as adding an organ solo on the studio's Hammond RT3 Organ with Hammond PR-40 tone cabinet. Harrison's contribution consisted of single strikes on an African drum. With these superimpositions, recording on the song was completed.

On October 27th in a Studio 2 control room session, remix mono (RM) 1 and 2 were created from takes 4 and 8 (take 4 being Lennon's vocal introduction only). The remixes were then edited together to create the mono master remix. The edit served as the mono release version of the song.

On November 4th in a Studio 2 control room session, the activity was replicated for the stereo remix of the song. Again, remix stereo (RS) 1 and 2 were created from takes 4 and 8, and these remixes were edited together to form the stereo master. The edit served as the stereo release version of the song.

August 14 thru November 4, 1964

# Mr. Moonlight

| TRACK 1 | TRACK 2 | TRACK 3 | TRACK 4 | |
|---|---|---|---|---|
| | Vocal 1 | | | Take 4 |
| Guitar 1<br>Guitar 2<br>Bass<br>Drums | Vocal 2<br>Vocal 3 | | | Take 8 |
| | | Organ<br>African drum | Vocal 4<br>Vocal 5 | Superimposition onto Take 8 |
| | Vocal 1 | | | **REMIX 1 (from Take 4)** |
| Guitar 1<br>Guitar 2<br>Bass<br>Drums | Vocal 2<br>Vocal 3 | Organ<br>African drum | Vocal 4<br>Vocal 5 | **REMIX 2 (from Take 8)** |
| | | | | **EDIT OF REMIXES** |
| Guitar 1<br>Guitar 2<br>Bass<br>Drums | Vocal 1<br>Vocal 2<br>Vocal 3 | Organ<br>African drum | Vocal 4<br>Vocal 5 | **RELEASE VERSION** |

# Leave My Kitten Alone

**Sessions**

- August 14, 1964

The final song recorded during the August 14th, 1964 session at EMI Recording Studios, Studio 2, for the *Beatles For Sale* album was one that wouldn't see public release until decades after the band officially parted ways. Little Willie John, Titus Turner, and James McDougal's *Leave My Kitten Alone*, a Ray Charles-style rave-up that hit the ground running, was likely a real contender for release at the time. The original version had been a Top 20 hit for Little Willie John in 1959 on the King Records label. The Beatles certainly took their work on it seriously, and it ultimately became a fan favourite of their unreleased material.

The technical team for the session included producer George Martin, balance engineer Norman Smith, and tape operator Ron Pender.

The song was recorded to the four-track Telefunken M10 primary tracking machine.

The backing track featured Lennon on his 1964 Rickenbacker 325 Capri electric guitar and lead vocals, McCartney on his 1962-1963 Hofner 500/1 bass, Harrison on his 1963 Gretsch PX6122 Chet Atkins Country Gentleman with Gretsch Bigsby B6G vibrato or 1963 Gretsch 6119 Chet Atkins Tennessean with Gretsch Bigsby vibrato electric guitar (both were available to him), and Starr on his 1964 Ludwig Oyster Black Pearl Super Classic drum set.

For amplification, Lennon and Harrison used either the 30-watt 1963 JMI Vox AC30/6 Twin Treble amplifiers or the 100-watt 1964 JMI Vox AC100 Mk I amplifiers with Vox AC100 cabinets. For bass amplification, McCartney used the 100-watt 1963 Vox AC100 with a Vox AC100 custom cabinet.

Of the five takes made of the song, only three were complete (takes 2 and 4 were breakdowns), with take 5 being the best.

Superimpositions to take 5 included Lennon's double-tracked lead vocals, Harrison on lead guitar, McCartney on the studio's Steinway "Music Room" Model B Grand Piano, and Starr on tambourine. With these additions, work on the song was completed.

No remix of the song was ever created contemporary to The Beatles' recording career. The song was remixed in stereo and released on *Anthology 1* in 1995.

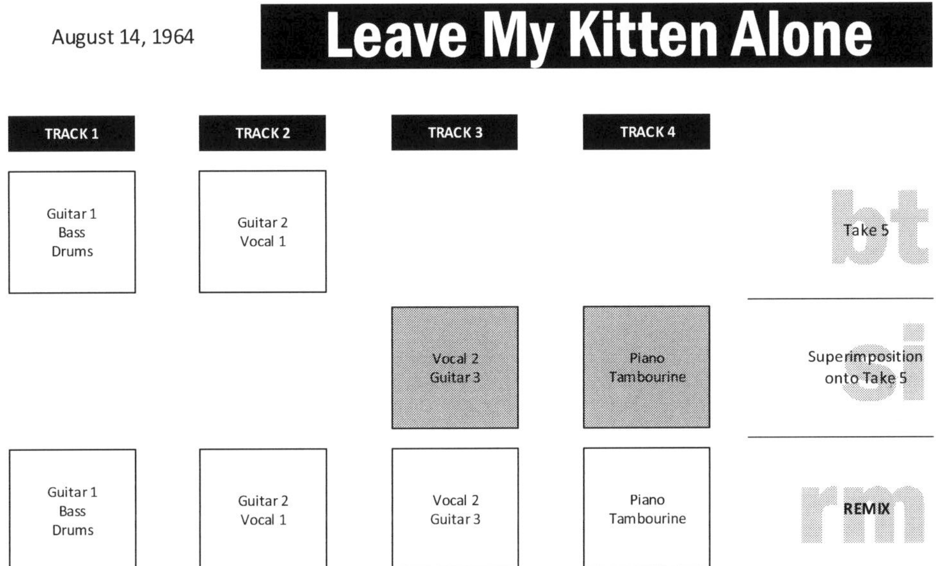

# Every Little Thing

**Sessions**

- September 29, 1964
- September 30, 1964
- October 27, 1964

After August 14th, The Beatles began their 1964 world tour of North America, not returning to EMI Recording Studios until the end of September to continue work on *Beatles For Sale*. The first song recorded upon their return to Studio 2 on September 29th, 1964, was John Lennon and Paul McCartney's *Every Little Thing*. As with a number of tracks on the album, their approach to the drum arrangement and the choice of percussion enhancements were distinctive of this period for the band.

The technical team for the session included producer George Martin, balance engineer Norman Smith, and tape operators Ken Scott and Mike Stone.

The song was recorded to the four-track Telefunken M10 primary tracking machine.

The backing track featured Lennon on his new 1964 Gibson J-160E acoustic guitar and lead vocals, McCartney on his 1962-1963 Hofner 500/1 bass and backing vocals, Harrison on his 1963 Rickenbacker 360-12 (12-string) electric guitar, and Starr on his 1964 Ludwig Oyster Black Pearl Super Classic drum set.

For amplification, Lennon and Harrison used either the 30-watt 1963 JMI Vox AC30/6 Twin Treble amplifiers or the 100-watt 1964 JMI Vox AC100 Mk I amplifiers with Vox AC100 cabinets. For bass amplification, McCartney used the 100-watt 1963 Vox AC100 with a Vox AC100 custom cabinet.

Four takes of the song were made during the first session, with take 4 being considered the best, though it would be improved upon. The song was remade the following day.

The September 30th session in Studio 2 began with another try at the song. This time five takes were created (takes 5 through 9), with take 9 being the best.

To this take, superimpositions were added of Harrison on 12-string guitar, Starr on timpani, and George Martin on the studio's Steinway "Music Room" Model B Grand Piano, completing the recording.

Work ceased on the track until October 27th when remixing for both the mono and stereo versions of the song took place in a Studio 2 control room session. Remix mono (RM) 1 and remix stereo (RS) 1 were both created from take 9 and served as the respective mono and stereo release versions of the song.

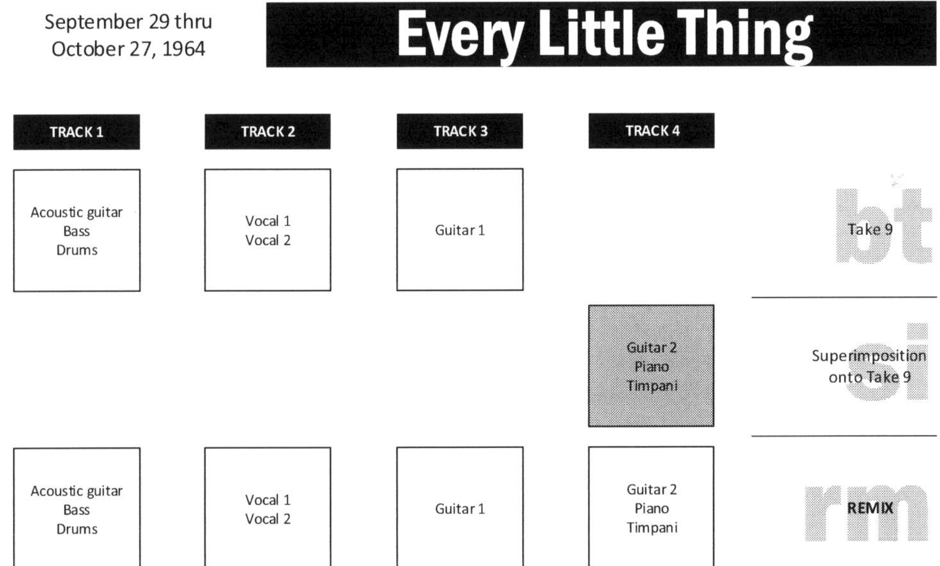

# I Don't Want To Spoil the Party

**Sessions**

- September 29, 1964
- October 26, 1964
- November 4, 1964

The second song recorded on September 29th, 1964, upon The Beatles' return to EMI Recording Studios, Studio 2, following their North American tour was John Lennon and Paul McCartney's *I Don't Want To Spoil The Party*. If there had been any doubts about the duo's ability to continue to create fresh, catchy melodies under the time constraints they faced, the song put those concerns to rest. Drawing on the influence of The Everly Brothers, its dual lead vocal was immediately memorable.

The technical team for the session included producer George Martin, balance engineer Norman Smith, and tape operators Ken Scott and Mike Stone.

The song was recorded to the four-track Telefunken M10 primary tracking machine.

The backing track featured Lennon on his 1964 Gibson J-160E acoustic guitar and lead vocals, McCartney on his 1962-1963 Hofner 500/1 bass and backing vocals, Harrison on his 1963 Gretsch PX6122 Chet Atkins Country Gentleman electric guitar with Gretsch Bigsby B6G vibrato, and Starr on his 1964 Ludwig Oyster Black Pearl Super Classic drum set.

For amplification, Harrison used either the 30-watt 1963 JMI Vox AC30/6 Twin Treble amplifier or the 100-watt 1964 JMI Vox AC100 Mk I amplifier with a Vox AC100 cabinet. For bass amplification, McCartney used the 100-watt 1963 Vox AC100 with a Vox AC100 custom cabinet.

The Beatles made quick work of the song. Nine takes were all that was required to perfect the backing track, take 9 being the best.

Superimpositions to take 9 were equally efficient. Martin's simple brush strokes of Lennon, McCartney, and Harrison on backing vocals, and Starr on tambourine completed the recording.

On October 26th in a Studio 2 control room session, remix mono (RM) 1 was created from take 9. RM 1 served as the mono release version of the song.

On November 4th in a Studio 2 control room session, remix stereo (RS) 1 was created from take 9. RS 1 served as the stereo release version of the song.

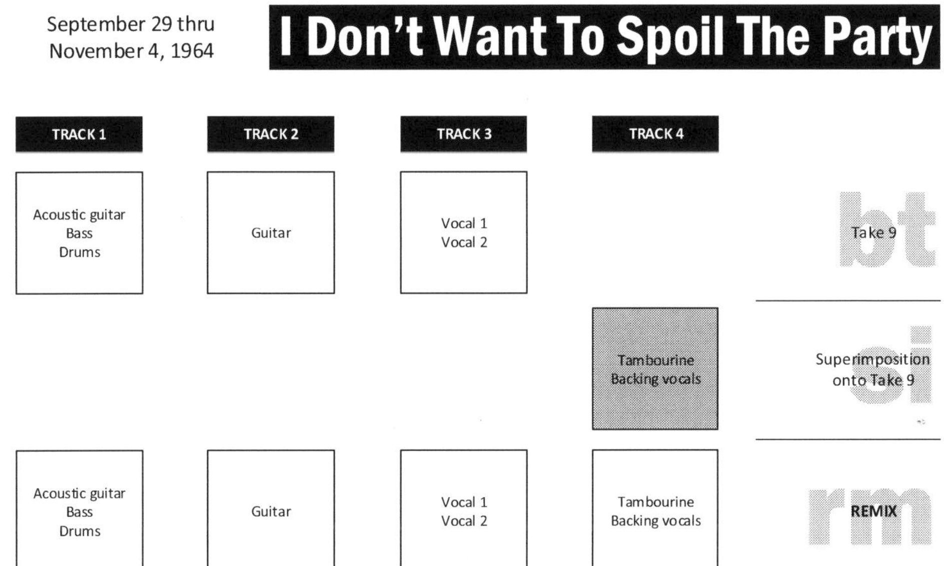

# What You're Doing

**Sessions**

- September 29, 1964
- September 30, 1964
- October 26, 1964
- October 27, 1964

The last of three songs recorded on September 29th, 1964, upon The Beatles' return to EMI Recording Studios, Studio 2, following their North American tour was John Lennon and Paul McCartney's *What You're Doing*. Available studio audio once again demonstrated that Martin and The Beatles took pains to find the right arrangement and tempo for their songs. Three sessions were spent on the backing track, each representing an independent approach to the song.

The technical team for the song's first session included producer George Martin, balance engineer Norman Smith, and tape operators Ken Scott and Mike Stone.

The song was recorded to the four-track Telefunken M10 primary tracking machine.

The backing track featured Lennon on his 1964 Rickenbacker 325-12 electric guitar and lead vocals, McCartney on his 1962-1963 Hofner 500/1 bass and backing vocals, Harrison on his 1963 Rickenbacker 360-12 (12-string) electric guitar, and Starr on his 1964 Ludwig Oyster Black Pearl Super Classic drum set.

For amplification, Lennon and Harrison used either the 30-watt 1963 JMI Vox AC30/6 Twin Treble amplifiers or the 100-watt 1964 JMI Vox AC100 Mk I amplifiers with Vox AC100 cabinets. For bass amplification, McCartney used the 100-watt 1963 Vox AC100 with a Vox AC100 custom cabinet.

The sessions on the 29th and 30th produced 11 takes of the song, the first day's work on the backing track being entirely instrumental (takes 1-7), the following day's adding dual lead vocals along with the instruments (takes 8-11). Lennon played his 12-string Rickenbacker 325-12 for the first and only times during the two days, but despite the fullness of the duelling 12-strings, the track wasn't hitting home.

A remake was in order.

On October 26th, back in Studio 2, the remake got under way, this time with Lennon switching to his 1964 Gibson J-160E acoustic guitar and Harrison adding backing vocals to the backing track. With the change, the entire tune came together into a much smoother version. The Beatles picked up at take 13 (there was no take 12) and perfected the new arrangement in seven takes, take 19 being the best.

Superimpositions onto take 19 included McCartney's double-tracked lead vocals, Lennon on the studio's Steinway "Music Room" Model B Grand Piano, and Harrison's solo guitar.

While George Martin often provided the piano parts on Beatles songs from this period (and Everett makes a detailed case for his work on this session), subjective review of the audio evidence points to Lennon being the piano player on *What You're Doing*. The part shows none of the virtuosity typical in Martin's playing, but does demonstrate the sort of simple, staccato attack that Lennon used on later tracks like *I'm Down*.

The technical team returned the following day for a Studio 2 control room session where both the mono and stereo master remixes were created. Remix mono (RM) 1 and remix stereo (RS) 1, both from take 19, served as the respective mono and stereo release versions of the song.

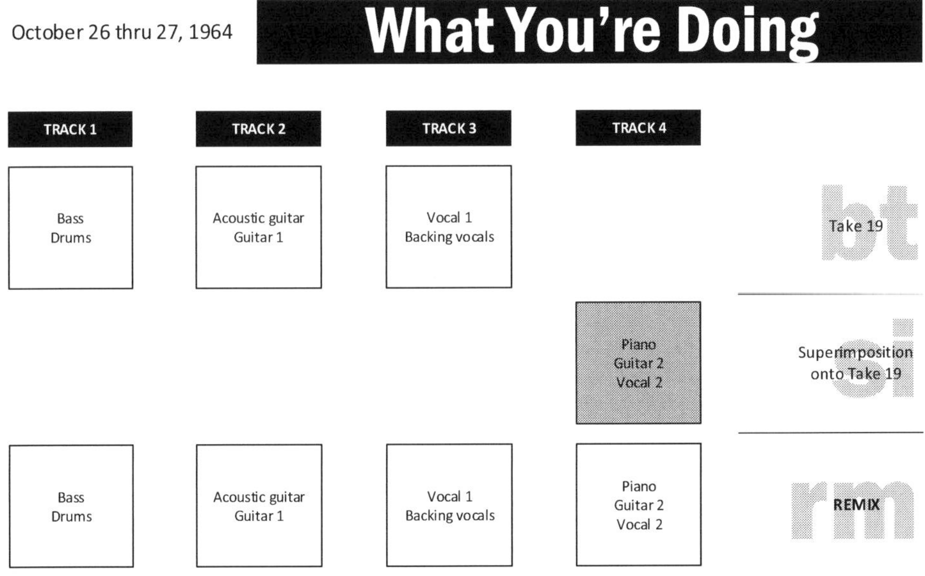

# No Reply

**Sessions**

- September 30, 1964
- October 16, 1964
- November 4, 1964

While work on *No Reply* commenced with a demo of the song created at the end of the *A Hard Day's Night* sessions on June 3rd, 1964, proper recording of the song began nearly four months later on September 30th at EMI Recording Studios, Studio 2, at the tail end of a session that included work on *Every Little Thing* and *What You're Doing*. The song is deceptive in its simplicity, as the arrangement cuts the beat up three different ways between the verse, chorus and bridge. By this device, Martin ensured the listener's interest was held at each juncture, a prelude to techniques that molded the sound of The Beatles in the future.

The technical team for the session included producer George Martin, balance engineer Norman Smith, and tape operators Ken Scott and Mike Stone.

The song was recorded to the four-track Telefunken M10 primary tracking machine.

The backing track featured Lennon on his 1964 Gibson J-160E acoustic guitar and lead vocals, McCartney on his 1962-1963 Hofner 500/1 bass and backing vocals, Harrison on his 1964 Gibson J-160E acoustic guitar, and Starr on his 1964 Ludwig Oyster Black Pearl Super Classic drum set. George Martin joined the band on the studio's Steinway "Music Room" Model B Grand Piano.

For amplification, Lennon and Harrison used either the 30-watt 1963 JMI Vox AC30/6 Twin Treble amplifiers or the 100-watt 1964 JMI Vox AC100 Mk I amplifiers with Vox AC100 cabinets. The Gibsons were also mic'ed acoustically with Neumann U48 microphones. For bass amplification, McCartney used the 100-watt 1963 Vox AC100 with a Vox AC100 custom cabinet.

Of the eight takes of the backing track, three were false starts, or partial performances (takes 1, 3 and 6), while take 5 was an attempt to extend the song by nearly a minute. In the end, the more compact take 8 (at 2:14) was considered the best version.

As a view into The Beatles' process in the studio, take 2 is informative. The early takes of the song included George Martin on piano throughout the entire song, as well as McCartney doubling Lennon's lead vocal during the verse. It's clear that the song's arrangement was being settled upon during these early stages. Once set, Martin determined which aspects of the arrangement were recorded as part of the backing track, and which would be reserved for superimpositions.

After the completion of the backing track, multiple superimpositions were made to take 8 including Martin's piano (now reserved to reinforce the "I saw the light", "I nearly died" and middle eight sections), Lennon double-tracking his lead vocals, McCartney double-tracking his backing vocals (but leaving the verses to Lennon), handclaps for the middle eight, and Starr overdubbing bass drum and crash cymbal. With these additions, recording on the track was completed.

On October 16th in a Studio 1 control room session, remix mono (RM) 1 and 2 were created from take 8. RM 2 was the best of these remixes and served as the mono release version of the song.

On November 4th in a Studio 2 control room session, remix stereo (RS) 1 was created from take 8. RS 1 served as the stereo release version of the song.

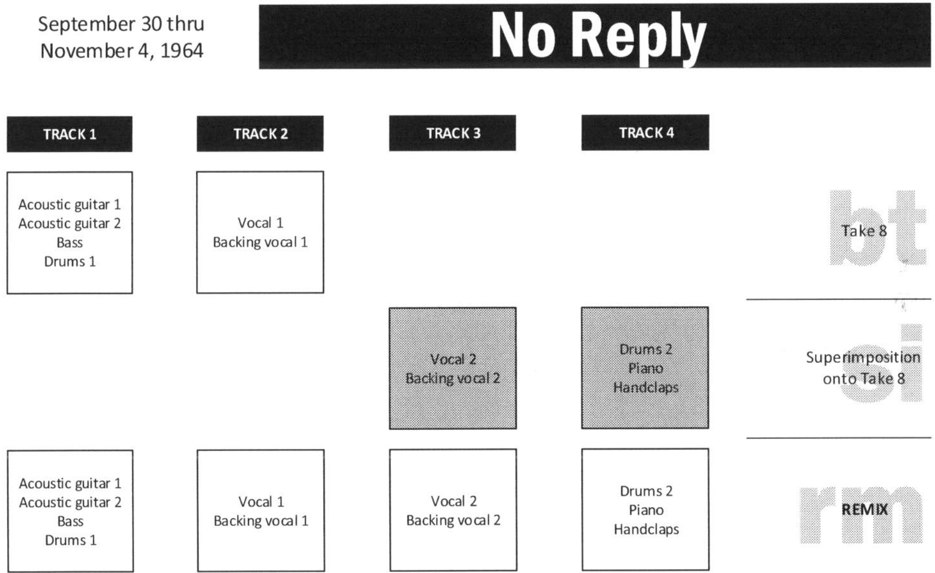

# Eight Days A Week

**Sessions**

- October 6, 1964
- October 12, 1964
- October 18, 1964
- October 27, 1964

*Eight Days A Week* was one of The Beatles' all-time classic hits (though not released as a single in the UK, it reached #1 on the US singles chart in 1965). The first session of the new month at EMI Recording Studios, Studio 2, on October 6th, 1964, was solely dedicated to the John Lennon and Paul McCartney song. Martin earned his keep in helping refine the initially awkward introduction, exchanging a marginal vocal passage for a ringing guitar introduction that broke upon the shore of the opening verse.

The technical team for the song's first session included producer George Martin, balance engineer Norman Smith, and tape operators Ken Scott and Mike Stone.

The song was recorded to the four-track Telefunken M10 primary tracking machine.

The backing track featured Lennon on his 1964 Gibson J-160E acoustic guitar and lead vocals, McCartney on his 1962-1963 Hofner 500/1 bass and lead vocals, Harrison on his 1963 Gretsch PX6122 Chet Atkins Country Gentleman with Gretsch Bigsby B6G vibrato or 1963 Gretsch 6119 Chet Atkins Tennessean with Gretsch Bigsby vibrato electric guitar (both were available), and Starr on his 1964 Ludwig Oyster Black Pearl Super Classic drum set.

For amplification, Lennon and Harrison used either the 30-watt 1963 JMI Vox AC30/6 Twin Treble amplifiers or the 100-watt 1964 JMI Vox AC100 Mk I amplifiers with Vox AC100 cabinets. Lennon's Gibson was also mic'ed acoustically with a Neumann U48 microphone. For bass amplification, McCartney used the 100-watt 1963 Vox AC100 with a Vox AC100 custom cabinet.

Through at least take 5, Lennon and McCartney began early versions of the song with harmony "Oooo's" on top of Lennon's acoustic guitar for the five bars at the top of the song. Harrison's volume pedal swells through the "Hold me, love me" section were particularly dominant in the early takes. It was eventually decided at some point to start the song with the fade-in of guitars (accomplished during the remixing phase).

The majority of the 13 takes of the backing tracks were complete takes, with take 13 being the best of these.

Superimpositions to take 13 included Harrison on guitar, Lennon's double-tracked lead vocals, McCartney's backing vocals, and group handclaps.

In an October 12th control room session in Studio 2, the first try at remixing the song occurred. During the session, remix mono (RM) 1 was created from take 13, but Martin must have felt something was missing from the track.

On October 18th, the band returned to Studio 2 to create an edit piece with Starr on drums and Harrison on his 1963 Rickenbacker 360-12 (12-string) electric guitar. Both the introduction (take 14) and ending of the song (take 15) were attempted, though in the end, only the ending edit piece was used (it can be heard in the right channel of the stereo remix at around 2:33).

An October 27th control room session in Studio 2 saw the remixing of both the primary track and edit piece and their assembly into the finished track. RM 2 and 3 were created from takes 13 and 15 and edited together to create the mono release version of the song.

Before work ended for the session, remix stereo (RS) 1 and 2 were created from takes 13 and 15 and edited together to create the stereo release version of the song.

October 6 thru 27, 1964

# Eight Days A Week

| TRACK 1 | TRACK 2 | TRACK 3 | TRACK 4 | |
|---|---|---|---|---|
| Acoustic guitar<br>Guitar 1<br>Bass<br>Drums 1 | Vocal 1<br>Vocal 2 | | | bt Take 13 |
| | | Vocal 3<br>Vocal 4<br>Handclaps | Guitar 2 | si Superimposition onto Take 13 |
| | | | Guitar 3<br>Drums 2 | ep Edit piece Take 15 |
| Acoustic guitar<br>Guitar 1<br>Bass<br>Drums 1 | Vocal 1<br>Vocal 2 | Vocal 3<br>Vocal 4<br>Handclaps | Guitar 2 | rm REMIX OF TAKE 13 |
| | | | Guitar 2<br>Guitar 3<br>Drums 2 | rm REMIX OF TAKE 15 |
| | | | | EDIT OF REMIXES |
| Acoustic guitar<br>Guitar 1<br>Bass<br>Drums 1 | Vocal 1<br>Vocal 2 | Vocal 3<br>Vocal 4<br>Handclaps | Guitar 2<br>Guitar 3<br>Drums 2 | rv RELEASE VERSION |

# She's A Woman

**Sessions**

- October 8, 1964
- October 12, 1964
- October 21, 1964

The Beatles were not only working on their next album in the fall of 1964, they also had a commitment to deliver a new single. On October 8th, 1964, work began at EMI Recording Studios, Studio 2, for the autumn single release in a session for *She's A Woman*, a John Lennon and Paul McCartney rocker featuring McCartney in full Little Richard mode.

The technical for the session team included producer George Martin, balance engineer Norman Smith, and tape operators Ken Scott and Mike Stone.

The song was recorded to the four-track Telefunken M10 primary tracking machine.

The backing track featured McCartney on his 1962-1963 Hofner 500/1 bass and lead vocals, Lennon on his 1964 Rickenbacker 325 Capri electric guitar, and Starr on his 1964 Ludwig Oyster Black Pearl Super Classic drum set.

For amplification, Lennon used either the 30-watt 1963 JMI Vox AC30/6 Twin Treble amplifier or the 100-watt 1964 JMI Vox AC100 Mk I amplifier with a Vox AC100 cabinet. For bass amplification, McCartney used the 100-watt 1963 Vox AC100 with a Vox AC100 custom cabinet.

Takes 1 through 6 of the backing track were great three-piece versions, omitting Harrison, and with Lennon stabbing the song's chords behind McCartney's gravel-voiced vocal.

Takes 1 and 2 found the trio getting a feel for the track, and a false start on take 3 led directly into take 4's complete, but sloppy version. Take 5 (or was it 7? Martin wasn't sure in the slating of the song) was also sloppy from the outset, though the trio worked it to the end regardless, a chaotic Lennon leading the charge into the song's long outro jam. Lasting nearly three minutes, Starr commented, "We got a song and an instrumental there."

Take 6 finally gave Martin the backing track he needed.

Superimpositions to take 6 included McCartney on the studio's Steinway "Music Room" Model B Grand Piano and double-tracked vocals, Harrison's double-tracked guitar solo (Harrison on his 1963 Gretsch PX6122 Chet Atkins Country Gentleman with Gretsch Bigsby B6G vibrato or 1963 Gretsch 6119 Chet Atkins Tennessean with Gretsch Bigsby vibrato electric guitar [both were available] and using the same amplification options as Lennon), and Starr on chocalho (a Portuguese percussion instrument similar to a tambourine in effect).

On October 12th in a Studio 2 control room session, mono and stereo remixes (RM 1 and RS 1) were created from take 6. RM 1 and RS 1 served as the respective mono release and stereo versions of the song. The stereo version of the song was unreleased contemporary to The Beatles' recording career.

More work occurred on the track on October 21st when a new mono remix (RM 2) was created for the US market in a remixing session in Room 65, a small remix-only room on the EMI Recording Studios grounds located in a row of buildings next to the main studios. The song was released in the US as a single and on *Beatles '65*.

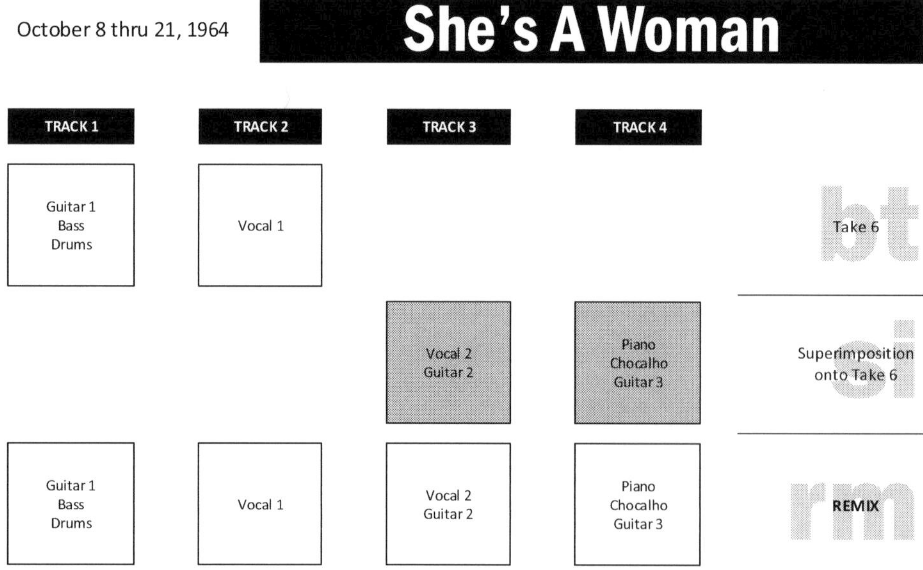

# Kansas City/Hey-Hey-Hey-Hey!

**Sessions**

- October 18, 1964
- October 26, 1964

Work on the *Beatles For Sale* album kicked into high gear on October 18$^{th}$, 1964, when eight songs (seven of them new) were tracked by The Beatles at EMI Recording Studios, Studio 2. One of five classic rockers recorded in the session, Jerry Leiber and Mike Stoller's *Kansas City* combined with (Little) Richard Penniman's *Hey-Hey-Hey-Hey!* was a standout, completed in just two takes, with the addition of some simple superimpositions.

The technical team for the session included producer George Martin, balance engineer Norman Smith, and tape operator Geoff Emerick.

The song was recorded to the four-track Telefunken M10 primary tracking machine.

The backing track featured McCartney on his 1962-1963 Hofner 500/1 bass and lead vocals, Lennon on his 1964 Rickenbacker 325 Capri electric guitar, Harrison on his 1963 Gretsch PX6122 Chet Atkins Country Gentleman with Gretsch Bigsby B6G vibrato or 1963 Gretsch 6119 Chet Atkins Tennessean with Gretsch Bigsby vibrato electric guitar (both were available), and Starr on his 1964 Ludwig Oyster Black Pearl Super Classic drum set.

For amplification, Lennon and Harrison used either the 30-watt 1963 JMI Vox AC30/6 Twin Treble amplifiers or the 100-watt 1964 JMI Vox AC100 Mk I amplifiers with Vox AC100 cabinets. For bass amplification, McCartney used the 100-watt 1963 Vox AC100 with a Vox AC100 custom cabinet.

Martin could have stopped with take 1, which ended up as the best backing track, but he had the band record one more take before moving on to superimpositions. It's clear he wasn't sure which of the two takes he preferred, as both takes 1 and 2 received superimpositions of Lennon, McCartney, and Harrison on backing vocals and handclaps.

By the time Martin added his performance on the Steinway "Music Room" Model B Grand Piano he had settled on take 1 as the best version of the song. With the vocal and piano additions in place, recording on the song was completed.

On October 26th in a Studio 2 control room session, remix mono (RM) 1 and remix stereo (RS) 1 were created from take 1. RM 1 and RS 1 served as the respective mono and stereo release versions of the song.

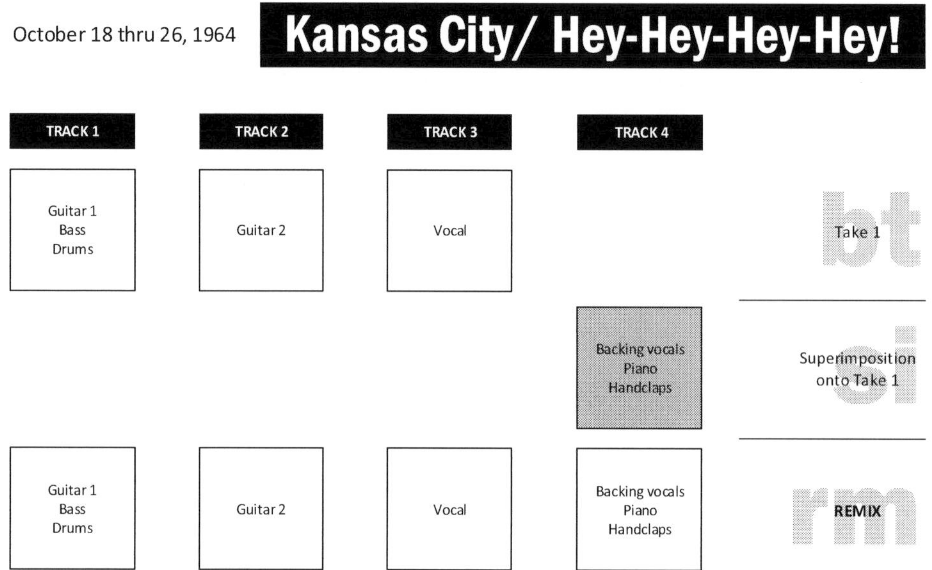

# I Feel Fine

**Sessions**

- October 18, 1964
- October 21, 1964
- October 22, 1964
- November 4, 1964

*She's A Woman* was certainly slated for a role in the next Beatles single, but as soon as John Lennon and Paul McCartney's *I Feel Fine* came to light during the October 18th, 1964 session at EMI Recording Studios, Studio 2, it was clear that its place was on the single's B-side. *I Feel Fine* had all the hallmarks of a great single — a compact melody, hooks galore and an opening note, the likes of which had never been heard; arguably the first recorded instance of feedback distortion. Martin knew a gold record when he heard it.

The technical team for the session included producer George Martin, balance engineer Norman Smith, and tape operator Geoff Emerick.

The song was recorded to the four-track Telefunken M10 primary tracking machine.

The backing track featured Lennon on his 1964 Gibson J-160E acoustic guitar, McCartney on his 1962-1963 Hofner 500/1 bass, Harrison on his 1963 Gretsch 6119 Chet Atkins Tennessean electric guitar with Gretsch Bigsby vibrato, and Starr on his 1964 Ludwig Oyster Black Pearl Super Classic drum set.

For amplification, Lennon and Harrison used either the 30-watt 1963 JMI Vox AC30/6 Twin Treble amplifiers or the 100-watt 1964 JMI Vox AC100 Mk I amplifiers with Vox AC100 cabinets. Lennon's Gibson was also mic'ed acoustically with a Neumann U48 microphone. For bass amplification, McCartney used the 100-watt 1963 Vox AC100 with a Vox AC100 custom cabinet.

Nine takes were created of the backing track, with the feedback distortion introduction in place from take 1. Lennon recalled in an interview, "That's me completely. Including the electric guitar lick and the record with the first feedback anywhere." Harrison doubles Lennon's part after a few bars for the majority of the song.

It wasn't until take 5 that a complete pass at the song was made. Only three complete passes were made throughout the nine takes recorded (takes 5, 6 and 9). By take 6, Lennon gave up trying to sing the lead vocal along with the track. Vocals were left for the superimpositions. Take 9 was considered the best of the completed takes.

Superimpositions to take 9 included Lennon's double-tracked lead vocals, Lennon, McCartney, and Harrison on backing vocals, and Harrison's solo guitar. With these additions, recording on the song was completed.

On October 21st in Room 65, a small remix-only room on the EMI Recording Studios grounds in a row of buildings next to the main studios, remix mono (RM) 1 through 4 were created from take 9. Of these, RM 3 was considered the best and served as the mono release version of the song (RM 4 was the version used in the US market, released as a single).

On October 22nd in a Studio 1 control room session, another mono remix (RM 5) was created from take 9. RM 5 is not known to have been used in any release version of the song.

On November 4th in a Studio 2 control room session, remix stereo (RS) 1 was created from take 9. RS 1 served as the stereo release version of the song.

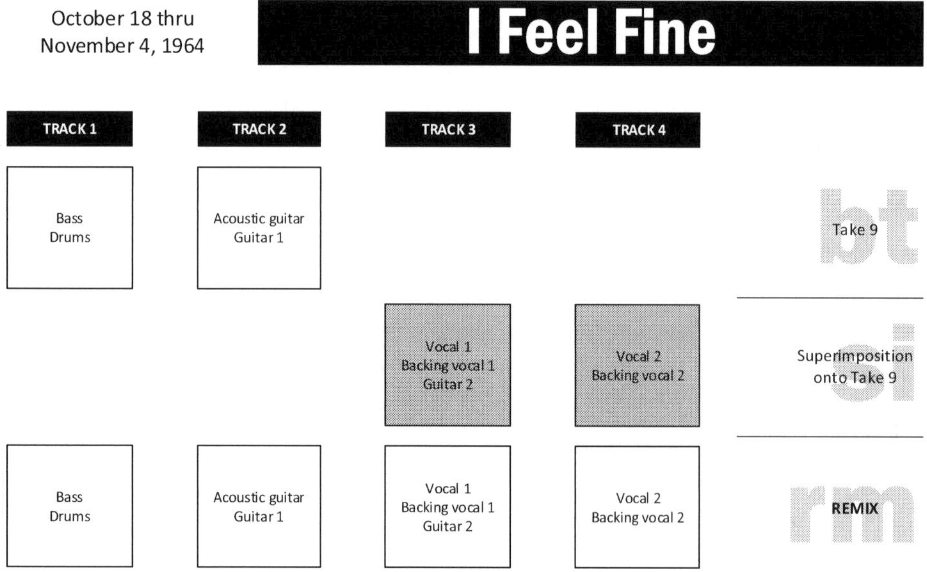

# I'll Follow The Sun

**Sessions**

- October 18, 1964
- October 21, 1964
- November 4, 1964

The busy October 18th, 1964 session at EMI Recording Studios, Studio 2, for the *Beatles For Sale* album featured one of the earliest songs written by John Lennon and Paul McCartney; *I'll Follow The Sun.* Composed almost six years prior to its recording, the straightforward ballad was quickly tracked; one of only three originals in a remarkable session that included work on eight total songs.

The technical team for the session included producer George Martin, balance engineer Norman Smith, and tape operator Geoff Emerick.

The song was recorded to the four-track Telefunken M10 primary tracking machine.

The backing track featured McCartney on his 1962-1963 Hofner 500/1 bass and lead vocals, Lennon on his 1964 Gibson J-160E acoustic guitar and backing vocals, Harrison on his 1963 Gretsch PX6122 Chet Atkins Country Gentleman with Gretsch Bigsby B6G vibrato or 1963 Gretsch 6119 Chet Atkins Tennessean with Gretsch Bigsby vibrato electric guitar (both were available), and Starr hand-drumming a simple back beat on an undetermined percussion instrument.

For amplification, Harrison used either the 30-watt 1963 JMI Vox AC30/6 Twin Treble amplifier or the 100-watt 1964 JMI Vox AC100 Mk I amplifier with a Vox AC100 cabinet. For bass amplification, McCartney used the 100-watt 1963 Vox AC100 with a Vox AC100 custom cabinet.

Of the eight takes made of the song, only takes 7 and 8 were complete. Takes 1 through 6 were all either false starts or breakdowns. Take 8 was considered the best and a simple superimposition of Harrison's guitar solo was added to it, completing recording work on the track.

On October 21st in Room 65, remix mono (RM) 1 was created from take 8. RM 1 served as the mono release version of the song.

On November 4th in a Studio 2 control room session, remix stereo (RS) 1 was created from take 8. RS 1 served as the stereo release version of the song.

October 18 thru
November 4, 1964

# I'll Follow The Sun

| TRACK 1 | TRACK 2 | TRACK 3 | TRACK 4 | |
|---|---|---|---|---|
| Acoustic guitar<br>Bass<br>Drums | Guitar 1 | Vocal<br>Backing vocals | | bt Take 8 |
| | | | Guitar 2 | si Superimposition onto Take 8 |
| Acoustic guitar<br>Bass<br>Drums | Guitar 1 | Vocal<br>Backing vocals | Guitar 2 | rm REMIX |

# Everybody's Trying To Be My Baby

**Sessions**

- October 18, 1964
- October 21, 1964
- November 4, 1964

The October 18th, 1964, session at EMI Recording Studios, Studio 2, for the *Beatles For Sale* album featured work on a number of cover songs, including *Mr. Moonlight*, *Kansas City/ Hey-Hey-Hey-Hey!*, *Words Of Love* and Carl Perkins' *Everybody's Trying To Be My Baby*. Harrison's featured track for the new release wouldn't take long to perfect. The song was originally released by Perkins on the *Dance Album Of...Carl Perkins* in 1957 on the Sun label.

The technical team for the session included producer George Martin, balance engineer Norman Smith, and tape operator Geoff Emerick.

The song was recorded to the four-track Telefunken M10 primary tracking machine.

The backing track featured Harrison on his 1963 Gretsch PX6122 Chet Atkins Country Gentleman with Gretsch Bigsby B6G vibrato or 1963 Gretsch 6119 Chet Atkins Tennessean with Gretsch Bigsby vibrato electric guitar (both were available) and lead vocals (heavily washed with repeat echo), Lennon on his 1964 Gibson J-160E acoustic guitar, McCartney on his 1962-1963 Hofner 500/1 bass, and Starr his 1964 Ludwig Oyster Black Pearl Super Classic drum set.

For amplification, Harrison used either the 30-watt 1963 JMI Vox AC30/6 Twin Treble amplifier or the 100-watt 1964 JMI Vox AC100 Mk I amplifier with a Vox AC100 cabinet. For bass amplification, McCartney used the 100-watt 1963 Vox AC100 with a Vox AC100 custom cabinet.

One take of the backing track was all that it took for the band, as Harrison's confidence with anything Carl Perkins was always strong, and the slapback (repeat) echo only added to the atmosphere of the track.

A simple superimposition to take 1 included Starr on tambourine and Harrison's double-tracked lead vocals for the choruses. With these additions, recording on the song was completed.

On October 21st in Room 65, remix mono (RM) 1 was created from take 1. RM 1 served as the mono release version of the song.

On November 4th in a Studio 2 control room session, remix stereo (RS) 1 was created from take 1. RS 1 served as the stereo release version of the song.

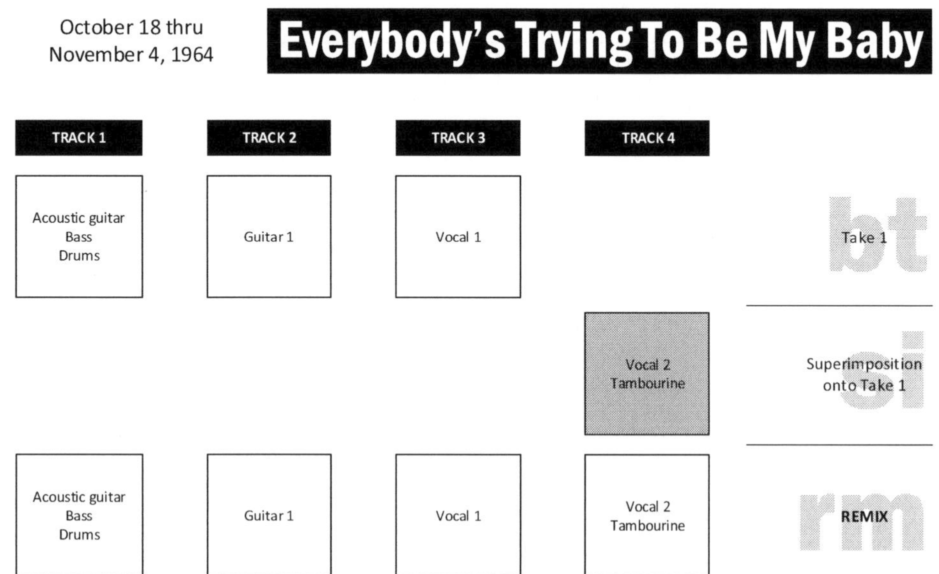

# Rock And Roll Music

**Sessions**

- October 18, 1964
- October 26, 1964
- November 4, 1964

Ask John Lennon, and he likely would have cited Chuck Berry as one of the artists who inspired him to a life in rock-and-roll in the first place. At least 15 of Berry's tunes had been part of The Beatles' live repertoire since 1957. *Rock And Roll Music*, the song they recorded in a single take on October 18th, 1964, at EMI Recording Studios, Studio 2, for the *Beatles For Sale* album had been featured in their shows since 1959. The song was a Top 10 hit in the US for Berry in 1957 on the Chess label.

The technical team for the session included producer George Martin, balance engineer Norman Smith, and tape operator Geoff Emerick.

The song was recorded to the four-track Telefunken M10 primary tracking machine.

The backing track featured Lennon on his 1964 Rickenbacker 325 Capri electric guitar and lead vocals (with a heavy application of repeat echo), McCartney on his 1962-1963 Hofner 500/1 bass, Harrison on his 1962 Gibson J-160E acoustic guitar, and Starr on his 1964 Ludwig Oyster Black Pearl Super Classic drum set.

Producer Martin also sat in on the track, displaying his skills as a rock-and-roll pianist. He played the studio's Steinway "Music Room" Model B Grand Piano for the track.

For amplification, Lennon and Harrison used either the 30-watt 1963 JMI Vox AC30/6 Twin Treble amplifiers or the 100-watt 1964 JMI Vox AC100 Mk I amplifiers with Vox AC100 cabinets. Harrison's Gibson was also mic'ed acoustically with a Neumann U48. For bass amplification, McCartney used the 100-watt 1963 Vox AC100 with a Vox AC100 custom cabinet.

In one magnificent take, the song was complete. No superimpositions were required. With the performance, the song joined just two other Beatles rockers to date that had achieved such immediacy of impact — *Boys* and *Long Tall Sally*.

On October 26th in a Studio 2 control room session, remix mono (RM) 1 was created from take 1. This remix served as the mono release version of the song.

On November 4th in a Studio 2 control room session, remix stereo (RS) 1 was created from take 1. RS 1 served as the stereo release version of the song.

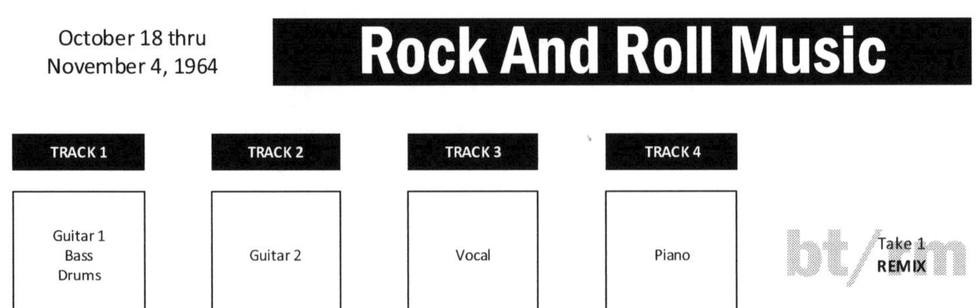

# Words Of Love

**Sessions**

- October 18, 1964
- October 26, 1964
- November 4, 1964

Another huge influence on The Beatles was US rocker Buddy Holly. The myopic Lennon even wore black horn-rimmed glasses during this period that mirrored the Texan's trademark look. As the band mined their back catalogue of cover tunes during the productive October 18th, 1964, session at EMI Recording Studios, Studio 2, the last song recorded was Buddy Holly's *Words Of Love*. Originally released by Holly in 1957 on the Coral label, it was never a hit for the artist, but The Beatles' cover song choices were rarely the popular songs to which other artists gravitated.

The technical team for the session included producer George Martin, balance engineer Norman Smith, and tape operator Geoff Emerick.

The song was recorded to the four-track Telefunken M10 primary tracking machine.

The backing track featured Lennon on his 1964 Rickenbacker 325 Capri electric guitar, McCartney on his 1962-1963 Hofner 500/1 bass, Harrison on his1963 Gretsch 6119 Chet Atkins Tennessean electric guitar with Gretsch Bigsby vibrato, and Starr on his 1964 Ludwig Oyster Black Pearl Super Classic drum set.

For amplification, Lennon and Harrison used either the 30-watt 1963 JMI Vox AC30/6 Twin Treble amplifiers or the 100-watt 1964 JMI Vox AC100 Mk I amplifiers with Vox AC100 cabinets. For bass amplification, McCartney used the 100-watt 1963 Vox AC100 with a Vox AC100 custom cabinet.

It only took three takes to perfect the backing track, take 3 being the best.

Superimpositions onto take 3 followed, with Harrison on double-tracked lead guitar, and Lennon, McCartney, and Harrison on double-tracked vocals with handclaps. Emerick recalls that Lennon, McCartney, and Harrison sang the lead vocals for the song together into the same microphone.

On October 26th in a Studio 2 control room session, remix mono (RM) 1 was created from take 3. RM 1 served as the mono release version of the song.

On November 4th in a Studio 2 control room session, remix stereo (RS) 1 was created from take 3. RS 1 served as the stereo release version of the song.

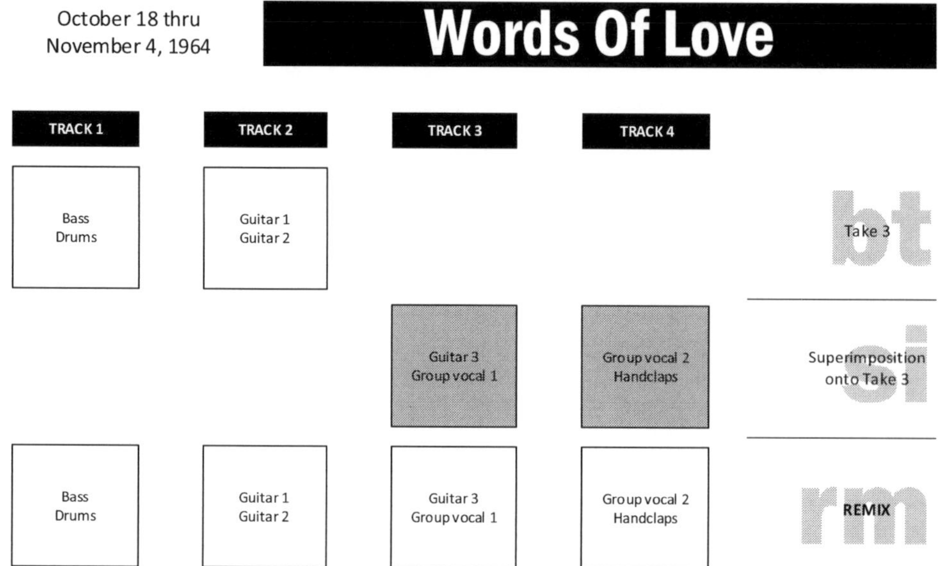

# Honey Don't

**Sessions**

- October 26, 1964
- October 27, 1964

October 26th, 1964, was the final date slated for recording new material for the *Beatles For Sale* album. The session at EMI Recording Studios, Studio 2, included Starr's feature track as the first order of business — another Carl Perkins song, *Honey Don't.* A good choice for Starr's limited vocal range, it was in keeping with the overall flavour of the cover tunes that comprised half the album's tracks. The song was originally released by Perkins as the B-side to his hit, *Blue Suede Shoes* in 1956 on the Sun label.

The technical team for the session included producer George Martin, balance engineer Norman Smith, and tape operators Tony Clark and Anthony (Tony) Bridge.

The song was recorded to the four-track Telefunken M10 primary tracking machine.

The backing track featured Starr on his 1964 Ludwig Oyster Black Pearl Super Classic drum set and lead vocals, Lennon on his 1964 Framus Hootenanny 5/024 (12-string) acoustic guitar, McCartney on his 1962-1963 Hofner 500/1 bass, and Harrison on his1963 Gretsch 6119 Chet Atkins Tennessean electric guitar with Gretsch Bigsby vibrato.

For amplification, Harrison used either the 30-watt 1963 JMI Vox AC30/6 Twin Treble amplifier or the 100-watt 1964 JMI Vox AC100 Mk I amplifier with a Vox AC100 cabinet. For bass amplification, McCartney used the 100-watt 1963 Vox AC100 with a Vox AC100 custom cabinet.

Starr was the consummate professional. Of the five takes recorded for the song, four were complete; only take 2 was a false start. Take 5 was considered the best, and with a quick superimposition of tambourine on the track by Starr, recording of the song was completed.

On October 27th in a busy Studio 2 control room session, both remix mono (RM) 1 and stereo (RS) 1 were created from take 5. RM 1 and RS 1 served as the respective mono and stereo release versions of the song.

October 26 thru 27, 1964

# Honey Don't

| TRACK 1 | TRACK 2 | TRACK 3 | TRACK 4 | |
|---|---|---|---|---|
| Bass<br>Drums | Guitar<br>Acoustic guitar | Vocal | | bt Take 5 |
| | | | Tambourine | si Superimposition onto Take 5 |
| Bass<br>Drums | Guitar<br>Acoustic guitar | Vocal | Tambourine | rm REMIX |

# Appendix 1

## Recording session technical equipment assignments and assumptions

The information collected and presented for each recording session includes:

- Session location, date, and time
- Recording activity
- Studio name and room
- Songs recorded (including their composer and what activities took place in relation to them)
- Songs mixed (including which version (mono or stereo) and from what take(s) they were created)
- Studio personnel (producers, balance engineers, and tape operators)
- Musicians (and what instruments they played)
- Instruments used on the sessions (electric guitars, acoustic guitars, bass guitars, drums, percussion, pianos and keyboards, and other instruments)
- Amplifiers used on the session (guitar, bass and other amplification)
- Recording equipment used on the session (recording consoles, primary tracking machines, mixdown machines, outboard gear, effects, and monitors for both studios and control rooms)
- Microphones used on the session (for vocals, electric guitar amplifiers, acoustic guitars, bass guitar amplifiers, drums, pianos, and other instruments)
- Additional session information (where available)

**Studio equipment assignments and assumptions**

For each year's activity, I provide information on the known range of studio equipment options The Beatles worked with during the sessions in question.

Core recording and outboard equipment assigned for each session represents the tools available to studio engineers during that period, and within the particular studio where the work took place.

The assignments of EMI Recording Studio equipment for each studio are based on when a particular piece of equipment was acquired and in use in a particular studio or room. Some studio features and equipment such as recording consoles and echo chambers (of which the studio had three) could be accessed from any studio or room via an internal Siemens wiring and signal routing system.

The inclusion of outboard equipment at a session does not equate the use of the equipment during the session, only that it can be assumed to have been at hand for the work of the day.

Numerous studio equipment assignments have been made based on the known preferences of personnel who worked on a specific session. For example: In recording electric guitar amplifiers, Norman Smith-engineered sessions in 1962-63 commonly (though not always) utilized a combination of a Neumann U47 on one amplifier and a Neumann KM54 on the second amplifier (typically Lennon's). For sessions engineered by Smith, it is assumed this combination was in use. Post-1963, it is assumed that the U48, U47/48 (U47/8) replaced the U47 in this configuration.

Whether as in this example a U47, KM 54, or a combination of both was used is generally unknowable.

Further to the studio setups assigned: My interview with EMI engineer Richard Langham made it clear that EMI Recording Studios were in the business of making hit recordings; reliably, predictably. You can think of it as a kind of "factory" in that aspect. Just like in a factory, when you find a process that works, you don't change it — and EMI Recording Studios in the 1960s had their processes down to a science.

To correlate that approach with the work presented here, I again employed the assumption that when sessions are either in close proximity (day after day in the same studio), and/or utilizing the identical production team to record common elements within a similar production period, the setups assigned will be similar. Where there is direct documentation or evidence to the contrary, these facts are reflected in the session notes.

All known technical options in use for a production year are presented in a summary at the start of each year's activity.

**Instrument and performance assignments**

For each year's activity I provide a summary of the known instruments The Beatles worked with during the sessions within that period.

In my research, I have come across many sources which claim with confidence "who-played-what"; but few that articulate how they came upon their conclusions. This sort of misinformation unfortunately can become gospel when republished enough times.

Where previous authors have not justified their performance assignments, I have ignored them, and relied on my own thorough examination of the facts at hand. Where there is honest debate on who performed certain parts on a song from credible sources, I noted it whenever possible along with my own conclusions regarding the debate.

On a session-by-session basis, I have taken some editorial liberty in situations regarding the assignment of undocumented instruments or performances by making logical assumptions from The Beatles' known history of ownership and in-studio use, the nature of work being recorded, the known work of other Beatles on the same track, as well as other documentary evidence. While a number of the instrument and performance assignments are admittedly speculative, they are fully researched and logically applied based on the best evidence available, as well as an understanding from those who participated in the sessions of the mindset associated with the "work" of recording as it related to The Beatles.

In many cases, the record is unclear, or it is impossible to know who played what, or certain other details regarding these sessions. Where this is the situation, you will find either an end note to that effect; performances noted, but unaccredited; or the word "unknown" as a value for a particular category of information.

In situations where the instrument, amplification or other usage cannot be identified with confidence, all options available for use are presented. This is not an unusual situation in relation to The Beatles who, particularly in their post-touring "studio" years would freely jump between instruments and amplifiers to find just the right sound they were looking for. Photographic evidence from a number of sessions reveal multiple guitars, amplifiers and keyboards at the ready for their use and experimentation.

The inclusion of instruments and amplification at a session does not equate the use of the equipment during the session; simply its availability.

**Determining backing tracks and superimpositions**

In determining the composition of backing tracks and overdubs, known as "superimpositions" in the era of The Beatles, I have utilized the following methodology:

The first step is to determine what recording activity took place on a certain day. Early song takes, session and other documentary evidence point to the makeup of the basic, or "backing" track for each song. In some cases, determining the backing track is a subtractive process: Knowing what superimpositions were later performed on a track makes it possible to reconstruct the backing track for a song.

In the case of complex recordings (those with multiple superimpositions, or that span many sessions), Lewisohn, Winn, and Ryan and Kehew (working from EMI artifacts including Barrett's tape logs and Martin's notes) have in many instances documented superimpositions that were performed in a particular session.

Where backing tracks or superimpositions were noted by those authors, the next step is to listen to corresponding takes or remixes of the track (if they are available), as well as to the track in its various stereo mixes. This is done in order to verify the accuracy of previously documented information, as well as attempt to identify the performance, part, or player if not specifically identified. In many cases, an A/B comparison of the work from one session to the next reveals what was recorded.

Across the span of my research on all Beatles recordings, I have referenced close to 5,400 audio files in multiple formats in the effort to identify the backing tracks and superimpositions that were the building blocks of the songs we all love.

Additional assistance in this detective work comes from the known technical restrictions built into EMI Recording Studios' REDD mixing consoles. Up until 1967, recording and remixing practises with the REDD consoles witnessed fixed stereo pans for input channels 1 and 2 (and correspondingly, channels 7 and 8). Channel 1 was fix-panned left and channel 2 was panned right. Only the relative "width" of the audio signal could be affected on these channels.

EMI engineers used a standard assignment of tracks that corresponded to the board channels. Backing tracks were almost always sent to track one of the audio tape (via channel one - its fixed-pan being left). When a larger backing track was recorded, or some isolation within the backing track desired, it was spread over two tracks (one and two, with two panned right).

With nearly all four-track recordings made during this period, backing instrumental tracks were sent to the left, or left and right channels (channels one and two). Channels three and four had the ability to be variably panned from left to right, but in the stereo remixes were usually sent up the middle, or just slightly off centre, and were primarily used for superimpositions.

Lead vocals were commonly sent to channel three and additional superimpositions to channel four. If channel two wasn't utilized for a backing track along with channel one, it was used for superimpositions. By careful listening to the progressive versions of the tracks in conjunction with the written record, superimpositions can be readily identified.

In 1967, engineers began using channels 3-6 to route signals for remixing. That meant they had full control of the stereo pan with any channel, as opposed to the fixed L-R (with some "spreading" capability) when using channels 1-2, or 7-8 as was the previous practise.

A diagram of each song was then generated to account for each sound source and assigning each source to an audio track. This aided in tracing each song from first take to final remix.

While admittedly subjective, an understanding of the activity on a song, the capabilities of the EMI equipment, and the assignment of tracks by EMI engineers, it is possible to isolate performances and identify superimpositions with some measure of confidence.

**Remixes, mono and stereo masters**

Remixing of Beatles tracks for mono and stereo often occurred in close proximity to the completion of tracking for the songs.

Where a remix resulted in either a mono or stereo master for disc cutting and release, the song and remix number are noted in the related session. A list of all master mono and stereo remixes is included in Appendix 3 to the main text.

**Notes**

Some sessions include notes with further details on "backing tracks", "edit pieces", "superimpositions" (overdubs), and other particulars of the session. These are included to assist the reader in understanding what work was completed on which songs, particularly on days where multiple songs were worked upon.

This additional session information is as complete as the record allows, and is only included where it has previously been made available from recognized, reliable sources, or where evidenced from my own examination of session recordings (takes), numbered remixes, photographic, film or video records of the events, or interviews with participants. If available additional information could not be reasonably verified for accuracy, it has not been included.

Notes also make mention of situations where the record is in conflict as to exactly what occurred during a session, or the technical details presented. I have made every attempt to document and reconcile these discrepancies and provide well-considered justification whenever my own interpretation is included.

## Additional sources

In addition to my own original research, I have scoured the published record of books, magazines, photographs, audio, film and video relating to The Beatles' recording sessions to assist in generating the most accurate picture of the sessions that follow. This includes dozens of books and magazine articles, many hours of archival video, hundreds of photographs and thousands of both official releases and unauthorized audio tracks.

Through this research, I determined that aside from works that contain information gained from period-specific documentary sources (such as archives, audio, photo or film) or personal interviews, vetted for accuracy, there are few reliable sources for the information presented here prior to 1988.

Beyond the previously stated, none of the works prior to that year had the benefit of Lewisohn's documentation from actual EMI archives, or Barrett's log books. This makes the conclusions reached by those authors highly subjective and suspect. So, while many fan-favourite books regarding this subject matter were parsed, only a select few were found reliable or relevant in the development of this book.

Applicable additional sources are noted at the end of each session, and a complete list is found in the Bibliography.

## Diagrams

This book includes diagrams that provide a graphic illustration of the recording process for each song documented. The diagrams represent the tracks of audio tape (one, two, or four tracks) and how performances were allocated to the tracks at each milestone of recording in order to create the songs as you hear them.

While the groupings of performances are as accurate as the historical record allows, the assignment of a performance or group of performances to a specific track is not possible in most cases (e.g. placing Starr's drums on track one versus track four of a song's backing track). This is due to the fact that I had no access to original audio tapes in the course of my research. Where the performance and track assignments are accurate, it is due to artifacts such as notes on audio tape boxes, EMI Recording Sheets, or George Martin's own notes on which track was used for a particular performance.

# Appendix 2

# Studios and sessions

---

# 1961-1963

# Recording Studios

---

## EMI Recording Studios

### Location

London, England
3 Abbey Road
London NW8 9AY

### Studio name and room(s)

EMI Recording Studios

- Studio 1
- Studio 2
- Studio 3

### Studio Personnel

- Producer: George Martin
- Balance engineer: Norman Smith
- Tape operators: Richard Langham, Chris Neal, Geoff Emerick, Anthony (Tony) Bridge

### Studio instrumentation

*Percussion*

- Doumbek
- Ludwig Timpani
- Maracas
- Premier bongos
- Tambourine (Olympic or Ludwig)
- Wood Block

*Pianos and keyboards*

- Celeste (Schiedmayer (unknown year) or Mustel (1953))
- Steinway "Music Room" Model B Grand Piano (circa 1880s)
- 1905 Steinway Vertegrand (the "Mrs. Mills" upright piano) (#115519)
- Hammond RT3 Organ (circa 1954-1962)

*Other instrumentation*

- Hammond PR-40 tone cabinet

### Recording equipment

*Recording console*

- Studio 1 - REDD.37
- Studio 2 - REDD.37
- Studio 3 - REDD.51

*Primary tracking machines*

- MONO: 1/4" EMI BTR2
- TWIN-TRACK: 1/4" EMI BTR3
- FOUR-TRACK: 1" Telefunken T9u and 1" Telefunken M10 (after October 17 1963)

*Mixdown machines*

- MONO: 1/4" EMI BTR2
- STEREO: 1/4" EMI BTR3
- MONO Tape Copying: 1/4" Lyrec TR4

*Outboard signal processors*

- EMI RS114 Limiter
- EMI RS124 Altec Compressor
- EMI RS127 Presence Box
- EMI RS144 4-Way Mixer/Premix
- EMI RS158 Fairchild 666 Compressor
- EMI RS92 Neumann Mic Equaliser
- Plug-in EQ Boxes

*Effects*

- Echo chamber (includes RS61 Low Level Amplifier with RS62 Power Supply and RS106A Echo Control Unit – Band Pass Filter)
- Half-speed recording
- STEED (send tape echo/echo delay)
- Tape echo/ repeat echo

*Monitors*

Control room

- Altec 605A (Altec 612 Cabinet) with EMI RS141 Leak TL/25 Plus Amplifier

Studio

- RLS10 - "White Elephant"

*Microphones*

Vocals

- Neumann U47, U48 or U47/48 (U47/8)

Electric guitar amplifiers

- Neumann U47, U48, U47/48 (U47/8)
- Neumann KM54

Acoustic guitars

- Neumann U47, U48 or U47/48 (U47/8)

Bass amplifier

- STC 4033-A

Drums

- Overhead - STC 4038
- Bass drum - STC 4033-A or AKG D20

Piano

- Neumann U47, U48 or U47/48 (U47/8)

Other

- Neumann U47, U48, U47/48 (U47/8)
- STC 4038

## Notes on studio equipment background, assignments, and applications

The first Beatles recordings for Parlophone at EMI Recording Studios were made on mono or twin-track British Tape Recorders (the mono BTR2 and twin-track BTR3 primary tracking machines). Their early success resulted in a move to the four-track Telefunken M10 machines in October 1963. Up until that point, multi-tracks had been the domain of classical music recordings, not pop records.

According to an author interview with EMI engineer Richard Langham another available four-track, the Telefunken T9u, was not used for primary tracking within the studio. It was instead used for remote sessions. A T9u installed within the studio was likely used for playback of these remote sessions. This unit moved to the Studio's Room 65 in mid-1965, where it remained until 1967, when it was replaced by a Studer J-37 four-track.

EMI Recording Studios' Record Engineering and Development Department (REDD) consoles were beautiful sounding, vacuum tube-based units. Technologically limited, they employed both fixed and variable-pan channels and limited desk inputs (10) and outputs (4) supplemented on the input side by EMI RS144 4-Way Mixer/Premix units. These consoles (in two iterations, the REDD.37 and REDD.51) served The Beatles for their entire career at EMI Recording Studios.

The EMI RS158 Fairchild 666 Compressor was available to engineers as of 1963. There is no direct evidence of their use on Beatles sessions during this period

The EMI RS92 Neumann Mic Equaliser was used specifically with Neumann U47, U49 and U50 microphones to cut or boost certain frequencies. This capability was also found to be very useful by EMI engineers with the studio's echo chambers and EMT plate reverbs. It is included in listings whenever those specific microphones are in use, as well as when echo chambers or the EMT reverbs are in use.

Plug-in EQ Boxes were available to engineers at all EMI Recording Studios sessions, though specific boxes cannot be accurately assigned to any one session. Because of this, they are omitted from specific session listings.

The assignment of STEED (send tape echo/echo delay) occurs whenever an echo chamber is in use. According to Ryan and Kehew, the effect was commonly used to thicken the echo produced.

There were three echo chambers at EMI, two within the studios (Chamber 1, which was created for use with Studio 3, Chamber 2, which was used with Studio 2), and one chamber on the roof of the facility (Chamber 3, which was used with Studio 1). While designed with the needs of a certain studio in mind, any of the chambers could be used with any of the studios through the Siemens patch bay system. Therefore, echo chamber numbers are not specifically assigned to sessions in specific studios.

Other than the use of the echo chamber (which during this period was typically recorded to tape with the original performance), The Beatles utilized half-speed recording effects early on. With this technique, the primary tape machine records the audio at half the normal playback speed, allowing for either complicated parts to be more easily executed, and/or for the pitch of an instrument to be changed by an octave.

EMI Recording Studios had a number of Neumann U47 and U48 microphones when The Beatles began to record in 1962. The microphones were primarily used in Beatles sessions to capture vocals and amplifiers during this period. The primary difference between the two microphones was their switchable patterns. The U47 switched between omni (which means it could accept a signal addressed from any direction) to cardioid (primarily addressed from the front of the mic, rejecting sound from the back of the mic), while the U48 switched from cardioid to figure-8 (addressed from front and back, but rejecting sound at the sides). In 1963, EMI decided the omni pattern of the U47 was not of as much use to them as the figure-8 of the U48, and had Neumann modify a number of the microphones (coming back numbered U47/48 or U47/8).

While unaltered U47's undoubtedly remained at EMI, for purposes of Beatles sessions from 1963 forward, the U47 will not be listed. Additionally, while multiple designations are utilized for the U48 (U48, U47/48 or U47/8), for the purposes of recording, they can all be thought of as U48's, as they share reception pattern characteristics.

In recording electric guitar amplifiers, Norman Smith-engineered sessions in 1962-63 commonly (though not always) utilized a combination of a Neumann U47 on one amplifier and a Neumann KM54 on the second amplifier (typically Lennon's). For sessions engineered by Smith, it is assumed this combination was in use. Post 1963, it is assumed that the U48, U47/48 (U47/8) replaced the U47 in this configuration.

In mic'ing drums, Smith utilized a standard combination of an STC 4038 for the overhead microphone, and STC 4033-A placed in front of the bass drum. An optional bass drum microphone was the AKG D20 (though it was only known to have been used on the *From Me To You* session)

The Neumann U47, U48, U47/48 (U47/8) microphones' primary application in the context of The Beatles' recordings were for vocals, amplifiers, and acoustic guitars; though along with the STC 4038 they were also studio workhorses employed for everything from capturing percussion to keyboard cabinets (like the Hammond PR-40 tone cabinet or Leslie speaker cabinets).

A key element of The Beatles' sound during this period was Smith's use of ambient microphones during their sessions. He often placed a "room" microphone (typically a Neumann U47 or U48) up to 20 feet away from the amplifiers to capture the live sound of the session.

Among studio instrumentation that included numerous keyboards and percussion options, the Steinway "Music Room" Model B Grand Piano (one in both Studio 2 and 3) and Studio 2's Hammond RT3 Organ played the largest roles in The Beatles' recording career, finding a place on virtually every album they recorded.

A complete list of all sources utilized for the identification and assignment of studio equipment is available in the Bibliography.

---

# Decca Recording Studios

**Location**

London, England
Broadhurst Gardens
West Hampstead,
North London

**Studio name and room**

Decca Recording Studios

**Studio Personnel**

- Producer: Tony Meehan

**Recording equipment**

*Recording console*

- Decca custom console (10-input)

*Primary tracking machine*

- MONO: 1/4" EMI BTR2
- TWIN-TRACK: 1/4" EMI TR90

*Mixdown machines*

- MONO: 1/4" EMI BTR2
- STEREO: 1/4" EMI TR90

*Outboard signal processors*

- Decca compressor/limiter

*Effects*

- EMT 140 plate reverb

*Monitors*

Control room

- Tannoy "Red" 15" (Lockwood cabinets)

Studio

- Unknown

*Microphones*

Vocals

- Unknown

Electric guitar amplifiers

- Unknown

Bass amplifier

- Unknown

Drums

- Unknown

Other

- AKG C12
- AKG C28
- AKG D19
- Neumann KM53
- Neumann KM56
- Neumann M49
- Neumann M50
- Neumann U47
- RCA 77DX
- STC 4038
- Telefunken ELA M251

---

## Other Studios

The Beatles recorded at three other locations between 1960 and 1963.

In 1960, Lennon, McCartney, and Harrison were booked for a recording session with Rory Storm and The Hurricanes (with Ringo Starr) in Hamburg at Akustik Studios, on the 5th floor of the Klockmann-Haus building. They recorded three songs during the session: Eddie Cooley and John Davenport's *Fever*, Kurt Weill and Maxwell Anderson's *September Song*, and George Gershwin's *Summertime.* Session and studio details for this work are unknown.

Friedrich-Ebert-Halle, located in Hamburg, Germany at Alter Postweg 30 – 38 was not a studio in the proper sense, but instead, a public school gymnasium in Hamburg that was used by German labels Polydor and Philips for recording sessions due to its excellent acoustics. It is assumed that remote recording equipment was utilized for the Beatles session at the venue.

Studio Rahlstedt, located in Hamburg-Tonndorf at Gebäude M1, Rahlau 128 was a proper recording studio though no details of its technical equipment remain.

# 1961-1963

# Instruments and amplification

---

### Instruments

### Electric guitars

*Lennon*

- 1958 Rickenbacker 325 Capri with Bigsby B5 vibrato (first model – natural finish – repainted black after September 11, 1962) Note: Kaufmann vibrato in use until August 1961

*Harrison*

- 1958/1959 Resonet Futurama
- 1957 Gretsch PX6128 Duo Jet with Gretsch Bigsby vibrato
- 1962 Gretsch 6122 Chet Atkins Country Gentleman with Gretsch Bigsby B6G vibrato
- 1962 Rickenbacker 425
- 1963 Gretsch PX6122 Chet Atkins Country Gentleman with Gretsch Bigsby B6G vibrato
- 1963 Gretsch 6119 Chet Atkins Tennessean with Gretsch Bigsby vibrato

### Acoustic guitars

*Lennon*

- 1962 Gibson J-160E

*Harrison*

- 1962 Gibson J-160E

### Bass guitars

*McCartney*

- 1961 Hofner 500/1
- 1962-1963 Hofner 500/1

### Drums

*Starr*

- 1960 Premier 58 Mahogany Duroplastic (20" bass drum/ 12" rack tom/ 16" floor tom/ 14"X4" "Royal Ace" snare); Ajax, Paiste Stambul or Kurts cymbals (20" ride/ 18" crash/ 14" hi-hats) (through June 1963)
- 1963 Ludwig Oyster Black Pearl Downbeat (14" X 20" bass drum/ 8" X 12" rack tom/ 14" X 14" floor tom/ 14" X 5.5" Jazz Festival snare); Paiste, Zyn, Zildjian cymbals (20" ride/ 20" ride with 4-rivet "sizzle"/ 18" crash) Zildjian cymbals (14" model A hi-hats) (Ludwig Set 1) (from July 1963)

*Pete Best*

- 1960 Premier 54 Marine Pearl (14" X 22" bass drum/ 8" X 12" rack tom/ 16" X 16" floor tom/ 14" X 5.5" "Super Ace" snare) Zyn cymbals (16" crash / 18" custom "sizzle" ride), Zildjian cymbals (18" crash/ 14" hi-hats)

*Andy White*

- 1956 Ludwig Black Diamond Pearl Buddy Rich Super Classic (14" X 22" bass drum/ 9" X 13" rack tom/ 16" X 16" floor tom/ 14" X 5.5" snare); Unknown cymbals (20" ride/ 18" crash/ 14" hi-hats)

**Percussion**

- Doumbek
- Ludwig Timpani
- Maracas
- Premier bongos
- Tambourine (Olympic or Ludwig)
- Wood Block

**Other**

- Hohner harmonica (Echo Vamper or Super Chromonica)

## Amplifiers

**Guitar**

*Lennon*

- 1960 Fender Narrow Panel Deluxe (Tweed) 15W with one 12" Jensen P12R or Jensen P12Q speaker (pre-EMI Recording Studios era)

*Harrison*

- 1960 Gibson GA-40T, 16W with one 12" Jensen P12Q speaker (pre-EMI Recording Studios era)

*Lennon/Harrison*

- 1962 JMI Vox AC30/6 Twin (original fawn colour) with "Top Boost" circuit, 30W with two 12" Vox Celestion Alinco Blue G12 T530 speakers
- 1962 JMI Vox AC30/6 Twin (re-covered black) with "Top Boost" circuit, 30W with two 12" Vox Celestion Alinco Blue G12 T530 speakers
- 1963 JMI Vox AC30/6 Twin Treble with "Top Boost" circuit, 30W with two 12" Vox Celestion Alnico Gray G12 T530 speakers

**Bass**

*McCartney*

- 1960 Selmer Truvoice Stadium, 15W head with one 10" speaker (pre-EMI Recording Studios era)
- 1960 Selmer Truvoice Stadium, 15W head with 1961 Barber "Coffin" cabinet, with one 15" speaker (pre-EMI Recording Studios era)
- Quad II/22 (circa 1959-61), 15W (modified to 40W with Quad model 22 preamplifier) head with 1961 Barber "Coffin" cabinet, with one 15" speaker (first EMI Recording Studios sessions)
- Leak Point One preamplifier and Leak TL-12 Plus amplifier with Tannoy

Dual Concentric 15" speaker and cabinet

- 1963 Vox T60 head, 60W with Vox T60 speaker cabinet, with one 12", and one 15" Vox Celestion Alinco Blue speakers
- 1963 Vox AC30 head, 30W with Vox T60 speaker cabinet, with one 12", and one 15" Vox Celestion Alinco Blue speakers

**Notes on instrument and amplification background, assignments and applications**

Lennon played his 1958 Rickenbacker 325 electric guitar exclusively for recordings during this period.

For acoustic work, Lennon and Harrison played matching 1962 Gibson J-160E acoustic guitars. Lennon's instrument was lost on November 25, 1963. Until its replacement in September of 1964, he borrowed Harrison's J-160E for any recording sessions where he played acoustic guitar.

Harrison played his 1957 Gretsch PX6128 Duo Jet guitar with Gretsch Bigsby vibrato through June of 1963, when it was joined by a 1962 Gretsch 6122 Chet Atkins Country Gentleman with Gretsch Bigsby B6G vibrato.

In September of the same year, Harrison acquired a 1962 Rickenbacker 425. Though he toured with it through Scandinavia, the only session where it was known to have been used was the October 17 session for *I Want To Hold Your Hand* and *This Boy*.

November saw the addition to the arsenal of guitars Harrison had to choose from of a 1963 Gretsch PX6122 Chet Atkins Country Gentleman with Gretsch Bigsby B6G vibrato, and in late December, a 1963 Gretsch 6119 Chet Atkins Tennessean with Gretsch Bigsby vibrato.

Beatles scholars may note that Harrison's two Gretsch 6122's, while identical save for their year of manufacture, have different model numbers. There is an explanation for this: The PX prefix on some Gretsch models was required to do business in the catalog industry, a significant aspect of USA retailing for the Gretsch company going back to the 1920s. The prefix meant the model was one available to be sold through this distribution channel (though this does not imply Harrison obtained his PX-designated guitars in that manner).

Guitar amplification was still primitive for The Beatles before July of 1962. When recording with Tony Sheridan, producer Bert Kaempfert provided the amplifiers. Decca thought so little of The Beatles' amplifiers that they were not permitted to use any of them in their audition for the label.

During this early period Lennon used his 15-watt 1960 Fender Narrow Panel Deluxe amplifier, while Harrison played through a 16-watt 1960 Gibson GA-40T amplifier.

By their September EMI session for *How Do You Do It*, both Lennon and Harrison had moved on to proper 30-watt 1962 JMI Vox AC30/6 Twin amplifiers. These remained their primary amplifiers through July of 1963 when they were supplemented with the 1963 update of the same model.

McCartney played two Hofner 500/1 violin basses during this period. The 1961 model was used for the earliest recordings until it was replaced in October, 1963 by a 1962-1963 model.

McCartney's initial bass amplification was highly unsuited for recording. His rig at the time of the first Sheridan session consisted of a road-weary 15-watt 1960 Selmer Truvoice Stadium amplifier, with one 10" speaker. By the date of the Decca audition, the same Selmer amplifier drove a 1961 Barber "Coffin" cabinet. Decca would have none of it (providing their own amplifier and cabinet), and neither would EMI when the time came.

McCartney's first recordings at EMI were facilitated with the studio's own Leak Point One preamplifier and Leak TL-12 Plus amplifier with a Tannoy Dual Concentric 15" speaker and cabinet (the speaker being borrowed from the studio's echo chamber one).

As with Lennon and Harrison, by the end of 1963, McCartney had moved up to fully professional gear: Both a 60-watt 1963 Vox T60 with Vox T60 speaker cabinet and a 30-watt 1963 Vox AC30 using the same T60 cabinet accompanied him to finish out the year's work.

Lennon and Harrison often (though not always) recorded their Gibson J-160E acoustic guitars through an amplifier during this period, though specifically for which performances is unknown. When an amplifier was utilized, an unamplified signal from the acoustic was blended with it. McCartney recalled, "They only used a tiny bit of electric, just for colour. If you turned it up too much, you don't get any string noise, so the engineers and George Martin used to strike a balance between the colour of the electric thing and the natural acoustic." Whenever a Gibson J-160E acoustic guitar is assigned in this period, amplification is also assigned.

Pete Best got the short end of the stick when it came to recording. His 1960 Premier Marine Pearl 54 set mostly sat idle, as Kaempfert thought so little of his time keeping during their recordings that he was limited to playing only part of his kit in the initial session. By the second Hamburg recording session, he was only allowed to play his snare drum.

Starr started his work with The Beatles on his 1960 Premier 58 Mahogany Duroplastic set. He continued to use the set until July of 1963 when he replaced it with a new 1963 Ludwig Oyster Black Pearl Downbeat kit (Ludwig Set 1).

A complete list of all sources utilized for the identification, specification and assignments of instruments and amplification is available in the Bibliography.

# Sessions

---

# 1961

# Early sessions

---

## June 22 (or 22 and 23), 1961

**Time**
Unknown

**Studio name and room**
Friedrich-Ebert-Halle

**Studio Personnel**

- Producer: Bert Kaempfert
- Balance engineer: Karl Hinze

**Songs recorded (composer) (activities)**

- *My Bonnie* (traditional, arranged by Tony Sheridan)
    - unnumbered takes
- *The Saints* (Black and Purvis)
    - unnumbered takes
- *Why* (Crompton and Sheridan)
    - unnumbered takes
- *Beatle Bop* (*Cry For A Shadow*) (Lennon and Harrison)
    - unnumbered takes
- *Nobody's Child* (Coben and Foree)
    - unnumbered takes
- *Take Out Some Insurance On Me Baby* (Stone)
    - unnumbered takes
- *Ain't She Sweet* (Ager and Yellen)
    - unnumbered takes

**Musicians (instruments played)**

- Tony Sheridan (guitar, vocals)
- John Lennon (guitar, vocals)
- Paul McCartney (bass, vocals)
- George Harrison (guitar, vocals)
- Pete Best (drums)

**Instruments**

**Electric guitars**

*Sheridan*

- 1959 Gibson ES-175 (single pickup) with Selmer Bigsby B7 vibrato

*Lennon*

- 1958 Rickenbacker 325 Capri with Kaufmann vibrato (first model – Natural finish)

*Harrison*

- 1957 Gretsch PX6128 Duo Jet with Gretsch Bigsby vibrato

**Bass guitars**

*McCartney*

- 1961 Hofner 500/1

**Drums**

*Best*

- 1960 Premier Marine Pearl 54 (8" X 12" rack tom/ 16" X 20" floor tom/ 14" X 5.5" Super Ace snare) Zyn cymbals (18" custom "sizzle" ride), Zildjian cymbals (20" crash/ 14" hi-hats)

## Amplifiers

**Guitar**

- Unknown

**Bass**

- Unknown

## Recording equipment

*Recording console*

- Unknown

*Primary tracking machine*

- Unknown

*Outboard signal processors*

- Unknown

*Effects*

- Unknown

*Monitors*

Control room

- Unknown

Studio

- Unknown

*Microphones*

Vocals

- Unknown

Electric guitar amplifiers

- Unknown

Bass amplifier

- Unknown

Drums

- Unknown

Piano

- Unknown

Other

- Unknown

**Backing Tracks**

- *My Bonnie* - backing track included Tony Sheridan on guitar and lead vocals; Lennon on guitar; McCartney

on bass; Harrison on guitar; Best on drums
- *The Saints* - backing track included Tony Sheridan on guitar and lead vocals; Lennon on guitar; McCartney on bass; Harrison on guitar; Best on drums
- *Why* - backing track included Tony Sheridan lead vocals; Lennon on guitar; McCartney on bass; Harrison on guitar; Best on drums
- *Beatle Bop (Cry For A Shadow)* - backing track included Lennon on guitar; McCartney on bass; Harrison on guitar; Best on drums
- *Nobody's Child* - backing track included Tony Sheridan on guitar and lead vocals; McCartney on bass; Best on drums
- *Take Out Some Insurance On Me Baby* - backing track included Tony Sheridan on guitar and lead vocals; McCartney on bass; Harrison on guitar; Best on drums
- *Ain't She Sweet* - backing track included Lennon on guitar and lead vocals; McCartney on bass; Harrison on guitar; Best on drums

### Superimpositions

- *My Bonnie* - superimpositions included Lennon and McCartney on backing vocals and handclaps
- *Why* - superimpositions included Lennon, McCartney, and Harrison on backing vocals and handclaps

### Notes

Lewisohn noted these sessions were recorded and remixed live to two-track stereo. Audio examination of these sessions indicate that while a number of songs were indeed recorded live, some backing vocal performances were recorded as superimpositions.

According to Lewisohn, Kaempfert provided the amplifiers for this session. Best was only allowed to play part of his kit (no kick drum) because of tempo issues.

It is not definitive whether this session occurred on June 22nd or on both the 22nd and 23rd.

**Sources -** Lewisohn, Mark (2). p. 42. / Lewisohn, Mark (3). pp.446, 447. / The Beatles with Tony Sheridan. *The Early Tapes of The Beatles – The Beatles with Tony Sheridan – Tony Sheridan and the Beat Brothers*. Polydor. 1984. CD.

# 1962

## January 1, 1962

**Time**
Unknown

**Studio name and room**
Decca Recording Studios
Studio 2

**Songs recorded (composer) (activities)**

- *Like Dreamers Do* (Lennon and McCartney)
    - unnumbered takes
- *Money (That's What I Want)* (Gordy and Bradford)
    - unnumbered takes
- *Till There Was You* (Meredith Willson)
    - unnumbered takes
- *The Sheik Of Araby* (Smith, Wheeler and Snyder)
    - unnumbered takes
- *To Know Her Is To Love Her* (Phil Spector)
    - unnumbered takes
- *Take Good Care Of My Baby* (King and Goffin)
    - unnumbered takes
- *Memphis, Tennessee* (Chuck Berry)
    - unnumbered takes
- *Sure To Fall (In Love With You)* (Cantrell, Claunch and Perkins)
    - unnumbered takes
- *Hello Little Girl* (Lennon and McCartney)
    - unnumbered takes
- *Three Cool Cats* (Leiber and Stoller)
    - unnumbered takes
- *Crying, Waiting, Hoping* (Holly)
    - unnumbered takes
- *Love Of The Loved* (Lennon and McCartney)
    - unnumbered takes
- *September In The Rain* (Warren and Dubin)
    - unnumbered takes
- *Bésame Mucho* (Velázquez)
    - unnumbered takes
- *Searchin'* (Leiber and Stoller)
    - unnumbered takes

**Studio Personnel**

- Producer: Tony Meehan
- Balance engineer: Unknown
- Tape operator(s): Unknown

**Musicians (instruments played)**

- John Lennon (guitar, vocals)
- Paul McCartney (bass, vocals)
- George Harrison (guitar, vocals)
- Pete Best (drums)

**Instruments**

**Electric guitars**

*Lennon*

- 1958 Rickenbacker 325 Capri with Bigsby B5 vibrato (first model – Natural finish)

*Harrison*

- 1957 Gretsch PX6128 Duo Jet with Gretsch Bigsby vibrato

**Bass guitars**

*McCartney*

- 1961 Hofner 500/1

**Drums**

*Best*

- 1960 Premier 54 Marine Pearl (14" X 22" bass drum/ 8" X 12" rack tom/ 16" X 16" floor tom/ 14" X 5.5" "Super Ace" snare) Zyn cymbals (16" crash / 18" custom "sizzle" ride), Zildjian cymbals (18" crash/ 14" hi-hats)

## Amplifiers

**Guitar**

- Unknown

**Bass**

- Unknown

## Recording equipment

*Recording console*

- Decca custom console (10-input)

*Primary tracking machine*

- MONO: 1/4" EMI BTR2
- TWIN-TRACK: 1/4" EMI TR90

*Mixdown machines*

- MONO: 1/4" EMI BTR2
- STEREO: 1/4" EMI TR90

*Outboard signal processors*

- Decca compressor/limiter

*Effects*

- EMT 140 plate reverb

*Monitors*

Control room

- Tannoy "Red" 15" (Lockwood cabinets)

Studio

- Unknown

*Microphones*

Vocals

- Unknown

Electric guitar amplifiers

- Unknown

Bass amplifier

- Unknown

Drums

- Unknown

Other

- AKG C12
- AKG C28
- AKG D19
- Neumann KM53
- Neumann KM56
- Neumann M49
- Neumann M50
- Neumann U47
- RCA 77DX
- STC 4038
- Telefunken ELA M251

**Backing Tracks**

- *Like Dreamers Do* - backing track included McCartney on bass and lead vocals; Lennon on guitar; Harrison on guitar; Best on drums;
- *Money (That's What I Want)* - backing track included Lennon on guitar and lead vocals; McCartney on bass and backing vocals; Harrison on guitar and backing vocals; Best on drums
- *Till There Was You* - backing track included McCartney on bass and lead vocals; Lennon on guitar; Harrison on guitar; Best on drums
- *The Sheik Of Araby* - backing track included Harrison on guitar and lead vocals; Lennon on guitar; McCartney on bass; Best on drums
- *To Know Her Is To Love Her* - backing track included Lennon on guitar and lead vocals; McCartney on bass and backing vocals; Harrison on guitar and backing vocals; Best on drums
- *Take Good Care Of My Baby* - backing track included Harrison on guitar and lead vocals; Lennon on guitar; McCartney on bass and backing vocals; Best on drums
- *Memphis, Tennessee* - backing track included Lennon on guitar and lead vocals; McCartney on bass; Harrison on guitar; Best on drums
- *Sure To Fall (In Love With You)* - backing track included Lennon on guitar and lead vocals; McCartney on bass and lead vocals; Harrison on guitar; Best on drums
- *Hello Little Girl* - backing track included Lennon on guitar and lead vocals; McCartney on bass and lead vocals; Harrison on guitar and backing vocals; Best on drums
- *Three Cool Cats* - backing track included Harrison on guitar and lead vocals; Lennon on guitar and backing vocals; McCartney on bass and backing vocals; Best on drums
- *Crying, Waiting, Hoping* - backing track included Harrison on guitar and lead vocals; Lennon on guitar and backing vocals; McCartney on bass and backing vocals; Best on drums
- *Love Of The Loved* - backing track included McCartney on bass and lead vocals; Lennon on guitar and backing vocals; Harrison on guitar and backing vocals; Best on drums
- *September In The Rain* - backing track included McCartney on bass and lead vocals; Lennon on guitar; Harrison on guitar; Best on drums
- *Bésame Mucho* - backing track included McCartney on bass and lead vocals; Lennon on guitar and backing vocals; Harrison on guitar and backing vocals; Best on drums
- *Searchin'* - backing track included McCartney on bass and lead vocals; Lennon on guitar and backing vocals; Harrison on guitar and backing vocals; Best on drums

**Notes**

The Beatles were not allowed to use their own amps for this audition by the Decca engineers. All of the songs tracked during the session were recorded live with no superimpositions.

**Sources -** Babiuk, Andy (1). p. 61. / Lewisohn, Mark (2). p. 63. / Lewisohn, Mark (3). pp. 539, 540. / The Beatles. "*Bésame Mucho*". Rec.1 January 1962. The Beatles. FLAC audio file. / The Beatles. "*Crying, Waiting, Hoping*". Rec.1 January 1962. The Beatles. FLAC audio file. / The Beatles. *"Hello Little Girl". Anthology*. George Martin, 1995. CD. / The Beatles. *"Like Dreamers Do". Anthology*. George Martin, 1995. CD. / The Beatles. "*Love Of The Loved*". Rec.1 January 1962. The Beatles. FLAC audio file. / The Beatles. "*Memphis, Tennessee*". Rec.1 January 1962. The Beatles. FLAC audio file. / The Beatles. "*Money (That's What I Want)*". Rec.1 January 1962. The Beatles. FLAC audio file. / The Beatles. *"Searchin'". Anthology*. George Martin, 1995. CD. / The Beatles. "*September In The Rain*". Rec.1 January 1962. The Beatles. FLAC audio file. / The Beatles. "*Take Good Care Of My Baby*". Rec.1 January 1962. The Beatles. FLAC audio file. / The Beatles. *"The Sheik of Araby". Anthology*. George Martin, 1995. CD. / The Beatles. *"Three Cool Cats". Anthology*. George Martin, 1995. CD. / The Beatles. "*Till There Was You*". Rec.1 January 1962. The Beatles. FLAC audio file. / The Beatles. "*To Know Her Is To Love Her*". Rec.1 January 1962. The Beatles. FLAC audio file.

# May 24, 1962

**Time**
Unknown

**Studio name and room**
Studio Rahlstedt

**Songs recorded (composer) (activities)**

- *Swanee River* (Foster)
    - unnumbered takes
- *Sweet Georgia Brown* (Bernie, Pinkard, Casey)
    - unnumbered takes

**Studio Personnel**

- Producer: Bert Kaempfert
- Balance engineer: Karl Hinze

**Musicians (instruments played)**

- Tony Sheridan (guitar, vocals)
- John Lennon (guitar)
- Paul McCartney (bass, vocals)
- George Harrison (vocals)
- Pete Best (drums)

**Other musicians (instruments played)**

- Roy Young (piano)

**Instruments**

**Electric guitars**

*Sheridan*

- 1959 Gibson ES-175 (single pickup) with Selmer Bigsby B7 vibrato

*Lennon*

- 1958 Rickenbacker 325 Capri with Bigsby B5 vibrato (first model – Natural finish)

**Bass guitars**

*McCartney*

- 1961 Hofner 500/1

**Drums**

*Best*

- 1960 Premier Marine Pearl 54 (14" X 5.5" Super Ace snare)

**Pianos and keyboards**

- Unknown

**Amplifiers**

**Guitar**

- Unknown

**Bass**

- Unknown

**Recording equipment**

*Recording console*

- Unknown

*Primary tracking machine*

- Unknown

*Outboard signal processors*

- Unknown

*Effects*

- Unknown

*Monitors*

Control room

- Unknown

Studio

- Unknown

*Microphones*

Vocals

- Unknown

Electric guitar amplifiers

- Unknown

Bass amplifier

- Unknown

Drums

- Unknown

Piano

- Unknown

Other

- Unknown

**Backing tracks**

- *Swanee River* – unknown backing track. Released version included Tony Sheridan on guitar and lead vocals;

unknown on guitar, bass, drums, piano and saxophone

- *Sweet Georgia Brown* – backing tracks included Tony Sheridan on guitar and lead vocals; Lennon on guitar; McCartney on bass and backing vocals; Harrison on backing vocals; Best on drums; Roy Young on piano

**Notes**

These sessions were most likely recorded live to twin-track. As with the previous Hamburg session, it is assumed that Kaempfert provided the amplifiers. According to Lewisohn, Best was only allowed to play his snare drum and ride cymbal in this session. Harrison did not play, but along with McCartney, provided backing vocals.

It is unlikely that the version of *Swanee River* recorded with The Beatles during the session is the release version of the song. An examination of the single release indicates a backing band that included a full drum kit (as opposed to the snare-only work of Best on *Sweet Georgia Brown*) as well as a saxophone player. Additionally, the production of the sessions differs dramatically.

On December 21st, 1961, Sheridan is known to have recorded an additional ten songs for Kaempfert in Hamburg. The Beatles were in Liverpool on that day, playing a lunchtime session at The Cavern Club. According to Gottfridsson, on the date, Sheridan recorded in a session with Roy Young on piano, Colin Melander on bass, Ricki Barnes on saxophone, and either Jimmy Doyle or Johnny Watson on drums. It is likely that this lineup recorded *Swanee River* on this date and are the musicians that appear on the release version of the song.

**Sources -** Gottfridsson, Hans Olof. p. 94. / Lewisohn, Mark (2) p. 51. / Lewisohn, Mark (3). pp.629, 630. / The Beatles with Tony Sheridan. *The Early Tapes of The Beatles – The Beatles with Tony Sheridan – Tony Sheridan and the Beat Brothers*. Polydor. 1984. CD. / Tony Sheridan and The Beat Brothers. *You Are My Sunshine b/w Swanee River*. Polydor. 1962. Vinyl, FLAC audio file.

# Initial EMI sessions

---

## June 6, 1962

**Time**
6PM - 8PM

**Studio name and room**
EMI Recording Studios
Studio 2

**Songs recorded (composer) (activities)**

- *Bésame Mucho* (Velázquez)
    - takes 1-4
- *Love Me Do* (McCartney/Lennon)
    - takes 1-5
- *P.S. I Love You* (McCartney/Lennon)
    - takes 1-3
- *Ask Me Why* (McCartney/Lennon)
    - take 1

**Studio Personnel**

- Producer: Ron Richards and George Martin
- Balance engineer: Norman Smith
- Tape operator: Chris Neal

**Musicians (instruments played)**

- John Lennon (guitar, harmonica, vocals)
- Paul McCartney (bass, vocals)
- George Harrison (guitar, vocals)
- Pete Best (drums)

### Instruments

**Electric guitars**

*Lennon*

- 1958 Rickenbacker 325 Capri with Bigsby B5 vibrato (first model – Natural finish)

*Harrison*

- 1957 Gretsch PX6128 Duo Jet with Gretsch Bigsby vibrato

**Bass guitars**

*McCartney*

- 1961 Hofner 500/1

**Drums**

*Best*

- 1960 Premier 54 Marine Pearl (14" X 22" bass drum/ 8" X 12" rack tom/ 16" X 16" floor tom/ 14" X 5.5" "Super Ace" snare) Zyn cymbals (16" crash / 18" custom "sizzle" ride), Zildjian cymbals (18" crash/ 14" hi-hats)

**Other**

- Hohner harmonica (Echo Vamper or Super Chromonica)

### Amplifiers

**Guitar**

*Lennon*

- 1960 Fender Narrow Panel Deluxe 15W with 1X12 Jensen P12R or Jensen P12Q speaker

*Harrison*

- 1960 Gibson GA-40T, 16W with one 12" Jensen speaker

**Bass**

*McCartney*

- Quad II/22 (circa 1959-61), 15W (modified to 40W with Quad model 22 preamplifier) head with 1961 Barber "Coffin" cabinet, with one 15" speaker
- Leak Point One preamplifier and Leak TL-12 Plus amplifier with Tannoy Dual Concentric 15" speaker and cabinet

## Recording equipment

*Recording console*

- REDD.37

*Primary tracking machine*

- MONO: 1/4" EMI BTR2
- TWIN-TRACK: 1/4" EMI BTR3

*Mixdown machine*

- MONO: 1/4" EMI BTR2

*Outboard signal processors*

- EMI RS114 Limiter
- EMI RS124 Altec Compressor
- EMI RS127 Presence Box
- EMI RS144 4-Way Mixer/Premix
- EMI RS92 Neumann Mic Equaliser

*Effects*

- Echo chamber (includes RS61 Low Level Amplifier with RS62 Power Supply and RS106A Echo Control Unit – Band Pass Filter)
- STEED (send tape echo/echo delay)

*Monitors*

Control room

- Altec 605A (Altec 612 Cabinet) with EMI RS141 Leak TL/25 Plus Amplifier

Studio

- RLS10 - "White Elephant"

*Microphones*

Vocals

- Neumann U47 or U48

Electric guitar amplifiers

- Neumann U47
- Neumann KM54

Acoustic guitars

- Neumann U47 or U48

Bass amplifier

- STC 4033-A

Drums

- Overhead - STC 4038
- Bass drum - STC 4033-A

Other

- Neumann U47, U48
- STC 4038

**Backing Tracks**

- *Bésame Mucho* – backing track included McCartney on bass and vocals; Lennon on guitar and vocals; Harrison on guitar; and Best on drums.
- *Love Me Do* – backing track included Lennon on guitar, harmonica and vocals; McCartney on bass and vocals; Harrison on guitar and vocals; and Best on drums.
- *P.S. I Love You* – backing track included Lennon on guitar and vocals;

McCartney on bass and vocals; Harrison on guitar and vocals; and Best on drums.
- *Ask Me Why* – backing track included Lennon on guitar and vocals; McCartney on bass and vocals; Harrison on guitar and vocals; and Best on drums.

**Notes**
All of the songs tracked this day were recorded live, with no superimpositions.

McCartney's Quad II/22 with "Coffin" cabinet was initially mic'ed, but immediately considered unsuitable for recording and replaced by studio engineer Ken Townsend with a Leak Point One preamplifier and Leak TL-12 Plus amplifier with Tannoy Dual Concentric 15" speaker and cabinet from echo chamber one. This combination continued to be used in the studio for bass amplification until McCartney improved his bass rig in March of 1963.

At times during this period, tracks were simultaneously recorded to both twin-track and mono. For this purpose, inputs to the REDD console were split-routed to a "Delta-Mono" control bay that allowed an alternative mix to be created. For such sessions the BTR2 and BTR3 are both considered to be primary tracking machines, though it is not believed any of the direct-to-mono mixes were ever used.

After Geoff Emerick's passing in 2018, his estate discovered that he had in his possession the original master tape from the June 6th session. There is an ongoing dispute as to whether he rightfully possessed the work, which was slated for destruction in the 60s. Examined by producer Ben Rowling in 2020, the original tape box noted four takes of *Bésame Mucho*, with take 4 being the best; five takes of *Love Me Do*, with take 5 being the best; three takes of *P.S. I Love You*, with take 2 being the best; and one take of *Ask Me Why*.

The reel is about 18 minutes in duration.

**Sources -** Dowlding, William J. p. 31. / Lewisohn, Mark (1). pp. 16: 25-27. / Rowling, Ben. Author interview, October 2020. Via email. / Ryan, Kevin and Brian Kehew. pp.102, 348-350; 358, 368.

# September 4, 1962

**Time**
7PM - 10PM

**Studio name and room**
EMI Recording Studios
Studio 2

**Songs recorded (composer) (activities)**

- *How Do You Do It* (Murray)
    - unnumbered takes
    - unnumbered superimpositions
- *Love Me Do* (Lennon and McCartney)
    - takes 1-15+
    - unnumbered superimpositions

**Songs mixed (version) (remix number and take)**

- *How Do You Do It* (mono)
    - unnumbered remix (RM) from take 2
- *Love Me Do* (mono)
    - unnumbered remix (RM) from unnumbered take

**Studio Personnel**

- Producer: George Martin
- Balance engineer: Norman Smith
- Tape operator: Unknown

**Musicians (instruments played)**

- John Lennon (guitar, harmonica, vocals)
- Paul McCartney (bass, vocals)
- George Harrison (guitar, vocals)
- Ringo Starr (drums)

**Instruments**

**Electric guitars**

*Lennon*

- 1958 Rickenbacker 325 Capri with Bigsby B5 vibrato (first model – Natural finish)

*Harrison*

- 1957 Gretsch PX6128 Duo Jet with Gretsch Bigsby vibrato

**Acoustic guitars**

*Lennon*

- Unknown

**Bass guitars**

*McCartney*

- 1961 Hofner 500/1

**Drums**

*Starr*

- 1960 Premier 58 Mahogany Duroplastic (20" bass drum/ 12" rack tom/ 16" floor tom/ 14"X4" "Royal Ace" snare); Ajax, Paiste Stambul or Kurts cymbals (20" ride/ 18" crash/ 14" hi-hats)

**Percussion**

- Handclaps

**Other**

- Hohner harmonica (Echo Vamper or Super Chromonica)

**Amplifiers**

**Guitar**

*Lennon/Harrison*

- 1962 JMI Vox AC30/6 Twin (original fawn colour) with "Top Boost" circuit, 30W with two 12" Vox

Celestion Alinco Blue G12 T530 speakers

**Bass**

*McCartney*

- Leak Point One preamplifier and Leak TL-12 Plus amplifier with Tannoy Dual Concentric 15" speaker and cabinet

## Recording equipment

*Recording console*

- REDD.37

*Primary tracking machine*

- MONO: 1/4" EMI BTR2

*Mixdown machine*

- MONO: 1/4" EMI BTR2

*Outboard signal processors*

- EMI RS114 Limiter
- EMI RS124 Altec Compressor
- EMI RS127 Presence Box
- EMI RS144 4-Way Mixer/Premix
- EMI RS92 Neumann Mic Equaliser

*Effects*

- Echo chamber (includes RS61 Low Level Amplifier with RS62 Power Supply and RS106A Echo Control Unit – Band Pass Filter)
- Tape echo/ repeat echo (STEED – send tape echo/echo delay

*Monitors*

Control room

- Altec 605A (Altec 612 Cabinet) with EMI RS141 Leak TL/25 Plus Amplifier

Studio

- RLS10 - "White Elephant"

*Microphones*

Vocals

- Neumann U47 or U48

Electric guitar amplifiers

- Neumann U47
- Neumann KM54

Acoustic guitars

- Neumann U47 or U48

Bass amplifier

- STC 4033-A

Drums

- Overhead - STC 4038
- Bass drum - STC 4033-A

Other

- Neumann U47
- Neumann U48
- STC 4038

**Backing tracks:**

- *How Do You Do It* – backing track included Lennon on acoustic guitar; Harrison on guitar; McCartney on bass; Starr on drums
- *Love Me Do* – backing track included Lennon on guitar and harmonica; Harrison on acoustic guitar; McCartney on bass; Starr on drums

**Superimpositions**

- *How Do You Do It* – superimpositions included Lennon and McCartney on vocals and handclaps
- *Love Me Do* – superimpositions included Lennon and McCartney on vocals and handclaps

**Remixes**

Mono master remixes

- *How Do You Do It* (mono) (unnumbered remix (RM) from take 2)

**Notes**

Mono to mono superimpositions during this period were accomplished by recording a backing track onto a BTR2 mono machine, then sending that track to another BTR2 while simultaneously recording the superimposition.

*How Do You Do It* (mono), unnumbered remix (RM) from take 2 represents the release-ready version of the song, though it was replaced by *P.S. I Love You* for the *Love Me Do* single.

**Sources** - Dowlding, William J. p. 31. / Forte, Dan (1). / Lewisohn, Mark (1). p.18. / Lewisohn, Mark (3). p. 697. / Ryan, Kevin and Brian Kehew. p.350. / The Beatles. "*How Do You Do It*". Rec.4 September 1962. The Beatles. FLAC audio file. / The Beatles. "*Love Me Do*". Rec.4 September 1962. The Beatles. FLAC audio file.

# September 11, 1962

**Time**
10AM - 1PM

**Studio name and room**
EMI Recording Studios
Studio 2

**Songs recorded (composer) (activities)**

- *P.S. I Love You* (McCartney/Lennon)
  - takes 1-10 including superimpositions
- *Please Please Me* (McCartney/Lennon)
  - unnumbered takes
- *Love Me Do* (McCartney/Lennon)
  - takes 1-18 takes including superimpositions

**Songs mixed (version) (remix number and take)**

- *P.S. I Love You* (mono)
  - unnumbered remix (RM) from take 10
- *Please Please Me* (mono)
  - unnumbered remix (RM) from unknown take
- *Love Me Do* (mono) (remake)
  - unnumbered remix (RM) from take 18

**Studio Personnel**

- Producer: Ron Richards
- Balance engineer: Norman Smith

- Tape operator: Unknown

**Musicians (instruments played)**

- John Lennon (guitar, harmonica, vocals)
- Paul McCartney (bass, vocals)
- George Harrison (guitar, vocals)
- Ringo Starr (percussion)

**Other musicians (instruments played)**

- Andy White (drums)

**Instruments**

**Electric guitars**

*Lennon*

- 1958 Rickenbacker 325 Capri with Bigsby B5 vibrato (first model – Natural finish)

*Harrison*

- 1957 Gretsch PX6128 Duo Jet with Gretsch Bigsby vibrato
- 1962 Rickenbacker 425

**Acoustic guitars**

*Lennon/Harrison*

- 1962 Gibson J-160E

**Bass guitars**

*McCartney*

- 1961 Hofner 500/1

**Drums**

- 1956 Ludwig Black Diamond Pearl Buddy Rich Super Classic (14" X 22" bass drum/ 9" X 13" rack tom/ 16" X 16" floor tom/ 14" X 5.5" snare); Unknown cymbals (20" ride/ 18" crash/ 14" hi-hats)

**Percussion**

- Maracas
- Tambourine (Olympic or Ludwig)

**Other**

- Hohner harmonica (Echo Vamper or Super Chromonica)

**Amplifiers**

**Guitar**

*Lennon/Harrison*

- 1962 JMI Vox AC30/6 Twin (original fawn colour) with "Top Boost" circuit, 30W with two 12" Vox Celestion Alinco Blue G12 T530 speakers

**Bass**

McCartney

- Leak Point One preamplifier and Leak TL-12 Plus amplifier with Tannoy Dual Concentric 15" speaker and cabinet

## Recording equipment

*Recording console*

- REDD.37

*Primary tracking machine*

- MONO: 1/4" EMI BTR2

*Mixdown machine*

- MONO: 1/4" EMI BTR2

*Outboard signal processors*

- EMI RS114 Limiter
- EMI RS124 Altec Compressor
- EMI RS127 Presence Box
- EMI RS144 4-Way Mixer/Premix
- EMI RS92 Neumann Mic Equaliser

*Effects*

- Echo chamber (includes RS61 Low Level Amplifier with RS62 Power Supply and RS106A Echo Control Unit – Band Pass Filter)
- STEED (send tape echo/echo delay)

*Monitors*

Control room

- Altec 605A (Altec 612 Cabinet) with EMI RS141 Leak TL/25 Plus Amplifier

Studio

- RLS10 - "White Elephant"

*Microphones*

Vocals

- Neumann U47 or U48

Electric guitar amplifiers

- Neumann U47
- Neumann KM54

Acoustic guitars

- Neumann U47 or U48

Bass amplifier

- STC 4033-A

Drums

- Overhead - STC 4038
- Bass drum - STC 4033-A

Other

- Neumann U47
- Neumann U48
- STC 4038

## Backing Tracks

- *P.S. I Love You* – backing track included Lennon and Harrison on guitars; McCartney on bass; Andy White on drums; Starr on maracas
- *Love Me Do (remake)* – backing track included Lennon on guitar and

harmonica; Harrison on acoustic guitar; McCartney on bass; Andy White on drums; Starr on tambourine
- *Please Please Me* – backing track included Lennon and Harrison on guitars; McCartney on bass; Andy White on drums

**Superimpositions**

- *P.S. I Love You* – superimpositions included McCartney on lead vocals; Lennon and Harrison on backing vocals
- *Love Me Do (remake)* – superimpositions included Lennon and McCartney on vocals and handclaps
- *Please Please Me* – superimpositions included Lennon and McCartney on vocals; Harrison on backing vocals

**Remixes**

Mono master remixes

- *P.S. I Love You* (mono) (unnumbered remix (RM) from take 10)
- *Love Me Do* (mono) (remake) (unnumbered remix (RM) from take 18)

**Notes**
A 1987 article in *Guitar Player* magazine drawn from photographic evidence found in the monthly fan magazine, *Beatles Book*, indicates that the Gibson J-160E acoustics were run through the Vox amplifiers for the recording of *P.S. I Love You.*

Mono to mono superimpositions during this period were accomplished by recording a backing track onto a BTR2 mono machine, then sending that track to another BTR2 while simultaneously recording the superimposition.

**Sources -** Everett, Walter (1). pp. 126, 128, 134. / Lewisohn, Mark (1) p. 20. / Mytkowicz, Bob. / Ryan, Kevin and Brian Kehew. p. 350. / The Beatles. "*Love Me Do*". Rec.11 September 1962. The Beatles. FLAC audio file. The Beatles. "*P.S. I Love You*". Rec.11 September 1962. The Beatles. FLAC audio file. / The Beatles. "*Please Please Me*". Rec.11 September 1962. The Beatles. FLAC audio file. / Winn, John C. (3). p. 2.

# November 26, 1962

**Time**
7PM - 10PM

**Studio name and room**
EMI Recording Studios
Studio 2

**Songs recorded (composer) (activities)**

- *Please Please Me* (remake) (Lennon and McCartney)
  - takes 1-18 including superimpositions
  - unnumbered edit pieces
- *Ask Me Why* (remake) (Lennon and McCartney)
  - takes 1-6

**Studio Personnel**

- Producer: George Martin
- Balance engineer: Norman Smith
- Tape operator: Unknown

**Musicians (instruments played)**

- John Lennon (guitar, harmonica, vocals)
- Paul McCartney (bass, vocals)
- George Harrison (guitar, vocals)
- Ringo Starr (drums)

## Instruments

**Electric guitars**

*Lennon*

- 1958 Rickenbacker 325 Capri with Bigsby B5 vibrato (first model – repainted black)

*Harrison*

- 1957 Gretsch PX6128 Duo Jet with Gretsch Bigsby vibrato

**Acoustic guitars**

*Lennon/Harrison*

- 1962 Gibson J-160E

**Bass guitars**

*McCartney*

- 1961 Hofner 500/1

**Drums**

*Starr*

- 1960 Premier 58 Mahogany Duroplastic (20" bass drum/ 12" rack tom/ 16" floor tom/ 14"X4" "Royal Ace" snare); Ajax, Paiste Stambul or Kurts cymbals (20" ride/ 18" crash/ 14" hi-hats)

**Other**

- Hohner harmonica (Echo Vamper or Super Chromonica)

## Amplifiers

**Guitar**

*Lennon/Harrison*

- 1962 JMI Vox AC30/6 Twin (original fawn colour) with "Top Boost" circuit, 30W with two 12" Vox Celestion Alinco Blue G12 T530 speakers

**Bass**

*McCartney*

- Leak Point One preamplifier and Leak TL-12 Plus amplifier with Tannoy Dual Concentric 15" speaker and cabinet

## Recording equipment

*Recording console*

- REDD.37

*Primary tracking machine*

- TWIN-TRACK: 1/4" EMI BTR3
- MONO: 1/4" EMI BTR2

*Outboard signal processors*

- EMI RS114 Limiter
- EMI RS124 Altec Compressor
- EMI RS127 Presence Box
- EMI RS144 4-Way Mixer/Premix
- EMI RS92 Neumann Mic Equaliser

*Monitors*

Control room

- Altec 605A (Altec 612 Cabinet) with EMI RS141 Leak TL/25 Plus Amplifier

Studio

- RLS10 - "White Elephant"

*Microphones*

Vocals

- Neumann U47 or U48

Electric guitar amplifiers

- Neumann U47
- Neumann KM54

Acoustic guitars

- Neumann U47 or U48

Bass amplifier

- STC 4033-A

Drums

- Overhead - STC 4038
- Bass drum - STC 4033-A

Other

- Neumann U47
  Neumann U48
- STC 4038

**Backing Tracks**

- *Please Please Me (remake)* – backing track included Lennon on guitar and vocals; McCartney on bass and vocals; Harrison on guitar; Starr on drums
- *Ask Me Why (remake)* – backing track included Lennon on acoustic guitar and vocals; McCartney on bass and backing vocals; Harrison on guitar and backing vocals; Starr on drums

**Superimpositions**

- *Please Please Me (remake)* – superimpositions included Lennon and McCartney on vocals; McCartney and Harrison on backing vocals; Lennon on harmonica

**Edit Pieces**

- *Please Please Me (remake)* – edit piece included ending of the song

**Notes**

Superimpositions during this period were accomplished by recording a backing track onto a BTR2 mono machine or BTR3 twin-track, then sending that track to another BTR3 twin-track while simultaneously recording the superimposition.

At times during this period, tracks were simultaneously recorded to both twin-track and mono. For this purpose, inputs to the REDD console were split-routed to a "Delta-Mono" control bay that allowed an alternative mix to be created. For such sessions the BTR2 and BTR3 are both considered to be primary tracking machines, though it is not believed any of the direct-to-mono mixes were ever used.

The edit piece comprising the last 0:18 of the ending for *Please Please Me* can be heard as a slight drop out and in of the audio in the contemporary mono release version and as partially out of sync with the main track in the contemporary stereo release of the song. The 2009 remasters of the track corrected these flaws.

**Sources -** Dowlding, William J. p. 29. / Everett, Walter (1). p. 127. / Lewisohn, Mark (1). p. 23. / Ryan, Kevin and Brian Kehew. pp. 102, 358, 368. / The Beatles. "*Ask Me Why (take 6)*". Rec.11 September 1962. The Beatles. FLAC audio file. / The Beatles. "*Please Please Me (takes 16, 17, 18, plus edit piece)*". Rec.26 September 1962. The Beatles. FLAC audio file. / Winn, John C. (3). p. 2.

# November 30, 1962

**Time**
Unknown

**Studio name and room**
EMI Recording Studios
Studio 2 (control room)

**Songs mixed (version) (remix number and take)**

- *Please Please Me* (mono)
    - unnumbered remix (RM) from unknown take
- *Ask Me Why* (mono)
    - unnumbered remix (RM) from take 6

**Studio Personnel**

- Producer: George Martin
- Balance engineer: Norman Smith
- Tape operator: Unknown

**Recording equipment**

*Recording console*

- REDD.37

*Primary tracking machine*

- MONO: 1/4" EMI BTR2
- TWIN-TRACK: 1/4" EMI BTR3

*Mixdown machine*

- MONO: 1/4" EMI BTR2

*Outboard signal processors*

- EMI RS114 Limiter
- EMI RS124 Altec Compressor
- EMI RS127 Presence Box
- EMI RS144 4-Way Mixer/Premix
- EMI RS92 Neumann Mic Equaliser

*Monitors*

Control room

- Altec 605A (Altec 612 Cabinet) with EMI RS141 Leak TL/25 Plus Amplifier

**Remixes**

Mono master remixes

- *Please Please Me* (mono) (unnumbered remix (RM) from unknown take)
- *Ask Me Why* (mono) (unnumbered remix (RM) from take 6)

**Notes**

Winn notes that echo was not present in the single release versions of these songs, though it was later added to both songs as released in album form.

**Sources** - Lewisohn, Mark (1). p. 23. / Winn, John C. (3). p. 3

# 1963

# *Please Please Me* sessions

---

## February 11, 1963

**Time**
10AM - 1045PM

**Studio name and room**
EMI Recording Studios
Studio 2

- 10AM – 1PM
- 230PM – 630PM
- 730PM – 1045PM

**Songs recorded (composer) (activities)**

- *There's A Place* (Lennon and McCartney)
    - takes 1-10
    - superimposition takes 11-13
- *Seventeen (I Saw Her Standing There)* (Lennon and McCartney)
    - takes 1-2
    - edit piece takes 3-5
    - take 6-9
    - superimposition takes 10-12
- *A Taste Of Honey* (Scott and Marlow)
    - takes 1-5
    - superimposition takes 6-7

- *Do You Want To Know A Secret* (Lennon and McCartney)
  - takes 1-6
  - superimposition takes 7,8
- *Misery* (Lennon and McCartney)
  - takes 1-11
- *Hold Me Tight* (Lennon and McCartney)
  - takes 1-9
  - edit piece takes 10-13
  - edit of takes 9 and 13
- *Anna (Go To Him)* (Alexander)
  - takes 1-3
- *Boys* (Dixon and Farrell)
  - take 1
- *Chains* (Goffin and King)
  - takes 1-4
- *Baby It's You* (David, Bacharach, Williams)
  - takes 1-3
- *Twist And Shout* (Medley and Burns)
  - takes 1 and 2

**Songs mixed (version) (remix number and take)**

- *Twist And Shout* (mono)
  - unnumbered rough remix (RM)

**Studio Personnel**

- Producer: George Martin
- Balance engineer: Norman Smith
- Tape operator: Richard Langham

**Musicians (instruments played)**

- John Lennon (guitar, harmonica, percussion, vocals)
- Paul McCartney (bass, percussion, vocals)
- George Harrison (guitar, vocals)
- Ringo Starr (drums, percussion, vocals)

**Instruments**

**Electric guitars**

*Lennon*

- 1958 Rickenbacker 325 Capri with Bigsby B5 vibrato (first model – repainted black)

*Harrison*

- 1957 Gretsch PX6128 Duo Jet with Gretsch Bigsby vibrato

**Acoustic guitars**

*Lennon/Harrison*

- 1962 Gibson J-160E

**Bass guitars**

*McCartney*

- 1961 Hofner 500/1

**Drums**

*Starr*

- 1960 Premier 58 Mahogany Duroplastic (20" bass drum/ 12" rack tom/ 16" floor tom/ 14"X4" "Royal Ace" snare); Ajax, Paiste Stambul or Kurts cymbals (20" ride/ 18" crash/ 14" hi-hats)

**Percussion**

- Drumsticks
- Wood Block
- Tambourine (Olympic or Ludwig)
- Handclaps

**Other**

- Hohner harmonica (Echo Vamper or Super Chromonica)

## Amplifiers

**Guitar**

*Lennon/Harrison*

- 1962 JMI Vox AC30/6 Twin (original fawn colour) with "Top Boost" circuit, 30W with two 12" Vox Celestion Alinco Blue G12 T530 speakers

**Bass**

- Leak Point One preamplifier and Leak TL-12 Plus amplifier with Tannoy Dual Concentric 15" speaker and cabinet

## Recording equipment

*Recording console*

- REDD.37

*Primary tracking machine*

- TWIN-TRACK: 1/4" EMI BTR3
- MONO: 1/4" EMI BTR2

*Mixdown machine*

- MONO: 1/4" EMI BTR2

*Outboard signal processors*

- EMI RS114 Limiter
- EMI RS124 Altec Compressor
- EMI RS127 Presence Box
- EMI RS144 4-Way Mixer/Premix
- EMI RS92 Neumann Mic Equaliser

*Effects*

- Double-tracking
- Echo chamber (includes RS61 Low Level Amplifier with RS62 Power Supply and RS106A Echo Control Unit – Band Pass Filter)
- Half-speed recording
- STEED (send tape echo/echo delay)

*Monitors*

Control room

- Altec 605A (Altec 612 Cabinet) with EMI RS141 Leak TL/25 Plus Amplifier

Studio

- RLS10 - "White Elephant"

*Microphones*

Vocals

- Neumann U48 or U47/48 (U47/8)

Electric guitar amplifiers

- Neumann U48, U47/48 (U47/8)
- Neumann KM54

Acoustic guitars

- Neumann U48 or U47/48 (U47/8)

Bass amplifier

- STC 4033-A

Drums

- Overhead - STC 4038
- Bass drum - STC 4033-A

Other

- Neumann U48, U47/48 (U47/8)
- STC 4038

**Backing Tracks**

- *There's A Place* – backing track included Lennon on guitar and vocals; Harrison on guitar and backing vocals; McCartney on bass and vocals; Starr on drums
- *Seventeen (I Saw Her Standing There)* – backing track included Lennon on guitar and backing vocals; Harrison on guitar; McCartney on bass and lead vocals; Starr on drums
- *A Taste Of Honey* – backing track included Lennon on acoustic guitar and backing vocals; Harrison on guitar and backing vocals; McCartney on bass and lead vocals; Starr on drums
- *Do You Want To Know A Secret* – backing track included Lennon on guitar; Harrison on guitar and lead vocals; McCartney on bass; Starr on drums
- *Misery* – backing track included Lennon on guitar and vocals; Harrison on guitar; McCartney on bass and vocals; Starr on drums
- *Hold Me Tight* – backing track included Lennon on guitar and backing vocals; Harrison on guitar; McCartney on bass and lead vocals; Starr on drums
- *Anna (Go To Him)* – backing track included Lennon on acoustic guitar and lead vocals; Harrison on guitar and backing vocals; McCartney on bass and backing vocals; Starr on drums
- *Boys* – backing track included Lennon on guitar; Harrison on guitar and backing vocals; McCartney on bass and backing vocals; Starr on drums and lead vocals
- *Chains* – backing track included Lennon on guitar, harmonica and backing vocals; Harrison on guitar and lead vocals; McCartney on bass and backing vocals; Starr on drums
- *Baby It's You* – backing track included Lennon on guitar and lead vocals; Harrison on guitar and backing vocals; McCartney on bass and backing vocals; Starr on drums
- *Twist And Shout* – backing track included Lennon on guitar and lead vocals; Harrison on guitar and backing vocals; McCartney on bass and backing vocals; Starr on drums

**Superimpositions**

- *A Taste Of Honey* – superimposition included McCartney on doubled-tracked lead vocals

- *Do You Want To Know A Secret* – superimposition included Lennon, McCartney, Harrison on harmony vocals; Starr on drumsticks used as percussion
- *There's A Place* – superimposition included Lennon on harmonica
- *Seventeen (I Saw Her Standing There)* – superimposition included handclaps

**Edit Pieces**

- *Seventeen (I Saw Her Standing There)* – edit piece included entire band for solo section of the song
- *Hold Me Tight* – unknown edit piece

**Notes**

The pace at which the *Please Please Me* album sessions were recorded is illustrated with the song *Chains*. In it, distortion and crackling are present in Lennon's guitar part (starting at around the 1:02 mark), likely caused by a loose guitar connection to his amplifier. This flaw isn't evident in the mono remix of the song, but stands out in the left channel of the stereo version.

Superimpositions during this period were accomplished by recording a backing track onto a BTR2 mono machine or BTR3 twin-track, then sending that track to another BTR3 twin-track while simultaneously recording the superimposition.

At times during this period, tracks were simultaneously recorded to both twin-track and mono. For this purpose, inputs to the REDD console were split-routed to a "Delta-Mono" control bay that allowed an alternative mix to be created. For such sessions the BTR2 and BTR3 are both considered to be primary tracking machines, though it is not believed any of the direct-to-mono mixes were ever used.

With few exceptions, the balance of The Beatles' recordings from this date until the introduction of the Telefunken T9u and M10 four-track machines utilized the BTR3 twin-tracks.

**Sources -** Dowlding, William J. pp. 23, 25, 38, 39. / Everett, Walter (1). pp. 142, 155. / Lewisohn, Mark (1). pp. 24, 25-27. / Ryan, Kevin and Brian Kehew. pp. 102, 358, 368. / The Beatles. "*Chains*". *Please Please Me.* The Beatles. Vinyl record, FLAC audio file. / The Beatles. "*A Taste Of Honey (take 6)*". Rec.11 February 1963. The Beatles. FLAC audio file. / The Beatles. "*A Taste Of Honey (take 7)*". Rec.11 February 1963. The Beatles. FLAC audio file. / The Beatles. "*Do You Want To Know A secret (take 7)*". Rec.11 February 1963. The Beatles. FLAC audio file. / The Beatles. "*Do You Want To Know A secret (take 8)*". Rec.11 February 1963. The Beatles. FLAC audio file. / The Beatles. "*I Saw Her Standing There (take 1)*". Rec.11 February 1963. The Beatles. FLAC audio file. / The Beatles. "*I Saw Her Standing There (take 10)*". Rec.11 February 1963. The Beatles. FLAC audio file. / The Beatles. "*I Saw Her Standing There (take 11)*". Rec.11 February 1963. The Beatles. FLAC audio file. / The Beatles. "*I Saw Her Standing There (take 12)*". Rec.11 February 1963. The Beatles. FLAC audio file. / The Beatles. "*I Saw Her Standing There (take 2)*". Rec.11 February 1963. The Beatles. FLAC audio file. / The Beatles. "*I Saw Her Standing There (take 3)*". Rec.11 February 1963. The Beatles. FLAC audio file. / The Beatles. "*I Saw Her Standing There (take 4)*". Rec.11 February 1963. The Beatles. FLAC audio file. / The Beatles. "*I Saw Her Standing There (take 5)*". Rec.11 February 1963. The Beatles. FLAC audio file. / The Beatles. "*I Saw Her Standing There (take 6)*". Rec.11 February 1963. The Beatles. FLAC audio file. / The Beatles. "*I Saw Her Standing There (take 7)*". Rec.11 February 1963. The Beatles. FLAC audio file. / The Beatles. "*I Saw Her Standing There (take 8)*". Rec.11 February 1963. The Beatles. FLAC audio file. / The Beatles. "*I Saw Her Standing There (take 9)*". Rec.11 February 1963. The Beatles. FLAC audio file. / The Beatles. "*Misery (take 1)*". Rec.11 February 1963. The

Beatles. FLAC audio file. / The Beatles. "*Misery (take 2)*". Rec.11 February 1963. The Beatles. FLAC audio file. / The Beatles. "*Misery (take 3)*". Rec.11 February 1963. The Beatles. FLAC audio file. / The Beatles. "*Misery (take 4)*". Rec.11 February 1963. The Beatles. FLAC audio file. / The Beatles. "*Misery (take 5)*". Rec.11 February 1963. The Beatles. FLAC audio file. / The Beatles. "*Misery (take 6)*". Rec.11 February 1963. The Beatles. FLAC audio file. / The Beatles. "*Misery (take 7)*". Rec.11 February 1963. The Beatles. FLAC audio file. / The Beatles. "*Misery (take 8)*". Rec.11 February 1963. The Beatles. FLAC audio file. / The Beatles. "*There's A Place (take 1)*". Rec.11 February 1963. The Beatles. FLAC audio file. / The Beatles. "*There's A Place (take 10)*". Rec.11 February 1963. The Beatles. FLAC audio file. / The Beatles. "*There's A Place (take 11)*". Rec.11 February 1963. The Beatles. FLAC audio file. / The Beatles. "*There's A Place (take 12)*". Rec.11 February 1963. The Beatles. FLAC audio file. / The Beatles. "*There's A Place (take 13)*". Rec.11 February 1963. The Beatles. FLAC audio file. / The Beatles. "*There's A Place (take 2)*". Rec.11 February 1963. The Beatles. FLAC audio file. / The Beatles. "*There's A Place (take 3)*". Rec.11 February 1963. The Beatles. FLAC audio file. / The Beatles. "*There's A Place (take 4)*". Rec.11 February 1963. The Beatles. FLAC audio file. / The Beatles. "*There's A Place (take 5)*". Rec.11 February 1963. The Beatles. FLAC audio file. / The Beatles. "*There's A Place (take 6)*". Rec.11 February 1963. The Beatles. FLAC audio file. / The Beatles. "*There's A Place (take 7)*". Rec.11 February 1963. The Beatles. FLAC audio file. / The Beatles. "*There's A Place (take 8)*". Rec.11 February 1963. The Beatles. FLAC audio file. / The Beatles. "*There's A Place (take 9)*". Rec.11 February 1963. The Beatles. FLAC audio file. / The Beatles. *Please Please Me*. George Martin, 1963. FLAC audio. / Winn, John C. (3). pp. 3-5.

# February 20, 1963

### Time

1030AM - 1PM

### Studio name and room

EMI Recording Studios
Studio 1

### Songs recorded (composer) (activities)

- *Misery* (Lennon and McCartney)
    - superimposition takes 12-16
- *Baby It's You* (Lennon and McCartney)
    - superimposition takes 4-6

### Studio Personnel

- Producer: George Martin
- Balance engineer: Stuart Eltham
- Tape operator: Geoff Emerick

### Musicians (instruments played)

- George Martin (piano, celeste)

### Instruments

### Pianos and keyboards

- Steinway "Music Room" Model B Grand Piano (circa 1880s)
- Schiedmayer celeste (unknown year)

### Recording equipment

*Recording console*

- REDD.37

*Primary tracking machine*

- TWIN-TRACK: 1/4" EMI BTR3

*Outboard signal processors*

- EMI RS114 Limiter
- EMI RS124 Altec Compressor
- EMI RS127 Presence Box
- EMI RS144 4-Way Mixer/Premix
- EMI RS92 Neumann Mic Equaliser

*Effects*

- Double-tracking
- Echo chamber (includes RS61 Low Level Amplifier with RS62 Power Supply and RS106A Echo Control Unit – Band Pass Filter)
- Half-speed recording
- STEED (send tape echo/echo delay)

*Monitors*

Control room

- Altec 605A (Altec 612 Cabinet) with EMI RS141 Leak TL/25 Plus Amplifier

Studio

- RLS10 - "White Elephant"

*Microphones*

Piano

- Neumann U48 or U47/48 (U47/8)

Other

- Neumann U48, U47/48 (U47/8)
- STC 4038

**Superimpositions**

- *Misery* – superimposition included George Martin on piano
- *Baby It's You* – superimposition included George Martin on piano and celeste

**Notes**

Take 5 of *Baby It's You* contained George Martin's celeste superimposition, while take 6 contained his piano work. The piano contribution to *Baby It's You* did not appear on the final remix of the song.

**Sources -** Dowlding, William J. pp. 24, 36. / Emerick, Geoff. p. 60. / Lewisohn, Mark (1). p. 28. /Winn, John C. (3). p. 6.

# February 25, 1963

**Time**
10AM - 1PM

**Studio name and room**
EMI Recording Studios
Studio 1 (control room)

**Songs recorded (composer) (activities)**

- *Seventeen (I Saw Her Standing There)* (Lennon and McCartney)
    - edit of takes 9 and 12

### Songs mixed (version) (remix number and take)

- *Anna (Go To Him)* (mono)
  - unnumbered remix (RM) from take 3
- *Boys* (mono)
  - unnumbered remix (RM) from take 1
- *Chains* (mono)
  - unnumbered remix (RM) from take 1
- *Misery* (mono)
  - unnumbered remix (RM) from take 16
- *Do You Want To Know A Secret* (mono)
  - unnumbered remix (RM) from take 8
- *There's A Place* (mono)
  - unnumbered remix (RM) from take 13
- *Seventeen (I Saw Her Standing There)* (mono)
  - unnumbered remix (RM) from edit of takes 10 and 12
- *Twist And Shout* (mono)
  - unnumbered remix (RM) from take 1
- *A Taste Of Honey* (mono)
  - unnumbered remix (RM) from take 7
- *Anna (Go To Him)* (stereo)
  - unnumbered remix (RS) from take 3
- *Boys* (stereo)
  - unnumbered remix (RS) from take 1
- *Chains* (stereo)
  - unnumbered remix (RS) from take 1
- *Misery* (stereo)
  - unnumbered remix (RS) from take 16
- *Baby It's You* (stereo)
  - unnumbered remix (RS) from take 5
- *Do You Want To Know A Secret* (stereo)
  - unnumbered remix (RS) from take 8
- *There's A Place* (stereo)
  - unnumbered remix (RS) from take 13
- *Seventeen (I Saw Her Standing There)* (stereo)
  - unnumbered remix (RS) from edit of takes 9 and 12
- *Twist And Shout* (stereo)
  - unnumbered remix (RS) from take 1
- *A Taste Of Honey (*stereo)
  - unnumbered remix (RS) from take 7

### Studio Personnel

- Producer: George Martin
- Balance engineer: Norman Smith
- Tape operator: Anthony (Tony) Bridge

### Recording equipment

*Recording console*

- REDD.37

*Primary tracking machine*

- TWIN-TRACK: 1/4" EMI BTR3
- MONO: 1/4" EMI BTR2

*Mixdown machine*

- MONO: 1/4" EMI BTR2
- STEREO: 1/4" EMI BTR3

*Outboard signal processors*

- EMI RS114 Limiter
- EMI RS124 Altec Compressor
- EMI RS127 Presence Box
- EMI RS144 4-Way Mixer/Premix
- EMI RS92 Neumann Mic Equaliser

*Effects*

- Echo chamber (includes RS61 Low Level Amplifier with RS62 Power Supply and RS106A Echo Control Unit – Band Pass Filter)
- STEED (send tape echo/echo delay)

*Monitors*

Control room

- Altec 605A (Altec 612 Cabinet) with EMI RS141 Leak TL/25 Plus Amplifier

**Remixes**

Mono master remixes

- *Anna (Go To Him)* (mono) (unnumbered remix (RM) from take 3)
- *Boys* (mono) (unnumbered remix (RM) from take 1)
- *Chains* (mono) (unnumbered remix (RM) from take 1)
- *Misery* (mono) (unnumbered remix (RM) from take 16)
- *Do You Want To Know A Secret* (mono) (unnumbered remix (RM) from take 8)
- *There's A Place* (mono) (unnumbered remix (RM) from take 13)
- *Seventeen (I Saw Her Standing There)* (mono) (unnumbered remix (RM) from edit of takes 9 and 12)
- *Twist And Shout* (mono) (unnumbered remix (RM) from take 1)
- *A Taste Of Honey* (mono) (unnumbered remix (RM) from take 7)

Stereo master remixes (direct copies from twin-track masters)

- *Anna (Go To Him)* (stereo) (unnumbered remix (RS) from take 3)
- *Boys* (stereo) (unnumbered remix (RS) from take 1)
- *Chains* (stereo) (unnumbered remix (RS) from take 1)
- *Misery* (stereo) (unnumbered remix (RS) from take 16)
- *Baby It's You* (stereo) (unnumbered remix (RS) from take 5)
- *Do You Want To Know A Secret* (stereo) (unnumbered remix (RS) from take 8)
- *There's A Place* (stereo) (unnumbered remix (RS) from take 13)
- *Seventeen (I Saw Her Standing There)* (stereo) (unnumbered remix (RS) from edit of takes 9 and 12)
- *Twist And Shout* (stereo) (unnumbered remix (RS) from take 1)
- *A Taste Of Honey* (stereo) (unnumbered remix (RS) from take 7)

**Notes**

This was the first of two editing and remixing sessions on the same day. The second session was in Studio 1.

**Sources -** Lewisohn, Mark (1). pp 28. / Winn, John C. (3). pp. 6,7.

# February 25, 1963

**Time**
230PM - 545PM

**Studio name and room**
EMI Recording Studios
Studio 1 (control room)

**Songs recorded (composer) (activities)**

- *Please Please Me* (Lennon and McCartney)
  - edit of takes 16, 17, 18

**Songs mixed (version) (remix number and take)**

- *Ask Me Why* (mono)
  - unnumbered remix (RM) from take 6
- *Misery* (mono)
  - unnumbered remix (RM) from take 16
- *Baby It's You* (mono)
  - unnumbered remix (RM) from take 5
- *Ask Me Why* (stereo)
  - unnumbered remix (RS) from take 6
- *Please Please Me* (stereo)
  - unnumbered remix (RS) from edit of takes 16, 17, 18
- *Love Me Do* (stereo)
  - unnumbered remix (RS) from take 18 from 09/11/1962 session
- *P.S. I Love You* (stereo)
  - unnumbered remix (RS) from take 10 from 09/11/1962 session
- *Misery* (stereo)
  - unnumbered remix (RS) from take 16

**Studio Personnel**

- Producer: George Martin
- Balance engineer: Norman Smith
- Tape operator: Anthony (Tony) Bridge

**Recording equipment**

*Recording console*

- REDD.37

*Primary tracking machine*

- TWIN-TRACK: 1/4" EMI BTR3
- MONO: 1/4" EMI BTR2

*Mixdown machine*

- MONO: 1/4" EMI BTR2
- STEREO: 1/4" EMI BTR3

*Outboard signal processors*

- EMI RS114 Limiter
- EMI RS124 Altec Compressor
- EMI RS127 Presence Box
- EMI RS144 4-Way Mixer/Premix
- EMI RS92 Neumann Mic Equaliser

*Effects*

- Echo chamber (includes RS61 Low Level Amplifier with RS62 Power Supply and RS106A Echo Control Unit – Band Pass Filter)
- STEED (send tape echo/echo delay)

*Monitors*

Control room

- Altec 605A (Altec 612 Cabinet) with EMI RS141 Leak TL/25 Plus Amplifier

**Remixes**

Mono master remixes

- *Baby It's You* (mono) (unnumbered remix (RM) from take 5)
- *Ask Me Why* (mono) (unnumbered remix (RM) from take 6)

Stereo master remixes (direct copies from twin-track masters)

- *Ask Me Why* (stereo) (unnumbered remix (RS) from take 6)
- *Please Please Me* (stereo) (unnumbered remix (RS) from edit of takes 16, 17, 18)
- *Love Me Do* (stereo) (unnumbered remix (RS) from 09/11/1962 session)
- *P.S. I Love You* (stereo) (unnumbered remix (RS) from take 10)
- *Misery* (stereo) (unnumbered remix (RS) from take 16)

**Notes**

This was the second of two editing and remixing sessions on the same day. The first session was in Studio 2.

**Sources** - Lewisohn, Mark (1). p. 28. / Winn, John C. (3). pp. 6,7.

# March 5, 1963

**Time**
230PM - 530PM

**Studio name and room**
EMI Recording Studios
Studio 2

**Songs recorded (composer) (activities)**

- *From Me To You* (Lennon and McCartney)
  - takes 1-7
  - edit pieces, takes 8-13
  - edit of takes 12, 8,9 and 10
- *Thank You Little Girl (Thank You Girl)* (Lennon and McCartney)
  - takes 1-6
  - edit pieces, takes 7-13
- *The One After 909* (Lennon and McCartney)
  - takes 1-4
  - edit piece, take 5

**Studio Personnel**

- Producer: George Martin
- Balance engineer: Norman Smith
- Tape operator: Richard Langham

**Musicians (instruments played)**

- John Lennon (guitar, harmonica, vocals)
- Paul McCartney (bass, vocals)
- George Harrison (guitar, vocals)
- Ringo Starr (drums)

## Instruments

### Electric guitars

*Lennon*

- 1958 Rickenbacker 325 Capri with Bigsby B5 vibrato (first model – repainted black)

*Harrison*

- 1957 Gretsch PX6128 Duo Jet with Gretsch Bigsby vibrato
- 1962 Rickenbacker 425

### Acoustic guitars

*Lennon/Harrison*

- 1962 Gibson J-160E

### Bass guitars

- 1961 Hofner 500/1

### Drums

- 1960 Premier 58 Mahogany Duroplastic (20" bass drum/ 12" rack tom/ 16" floor tom/ 14"X4" "Royal Ace" snare); Ajax, Paiste Stambul or Kurts cymbals (20" ride/ 18" crash/ 14" hi-hats)

### Other

- Hohner harmonica (Echo Vamper or Super Chromonica)

## Amplifiers

### Guitar

*Lennon/Harrison*

- 1962 JMI Vox AC30/6 Twin (re-covered black) with "Top Boost" circuit, 30W with two 12" Vox Celestion Alinco Blue G12 T530 speakers

### Bass

*McCartney*

- Leak Point One preamplifier and Leak TL-12 Plus amplifier with Tannoy Dual Concentric 15" speaker and cabinet

## Recording equipment

*Recording console*

- REDD.37

*Primary tracking machine*

- TWIN-TRACK: 1/4" EMI BTR3
- MONO: 1/4" EMI BTR2

*Outboard signal processors*

- EMI RS114 Limiter
- EMI RS124 Altec Compressor
- EMI RS127 Presence Box
- EMI RS144 4-Way Mixer/Premix
- EMI RS92 Neumann Mic Equaliser

*Effects*

- Echo chamber (includes RS61 Low Level Amplifier with RS62 Power Supply and RS106A Echo Control Unit – Band Pass Filter)
- STEED (send tape echo/echo delay)

*Monitors*

Control room

- Altec 605A (Altec 612 Cabinet) with EMI RS141 Leak TL/25 Plus Amplifier

Studio

- RLS10 - "White Elephant"

*Microphones*

Vocals

- Neumann U48 or U47/48 (U47/8)

Electric guitar amplifiers

- Neumann U48, U47/48 (U47/8)
- Neumann KM54

Acoustic guitars

- Neumann U47, U48 or U47/48 (U47/8)

Bass amplifier

- STC 4033-A

Drums

- Overhead - STC 4038
- Bass drum - AKG D20

Other

- Neumann U47/48 (U47/8)
- Neumann U48
- STC 4038

**Backing Tracks**

- *From Me To You* – backing track included Lennon on acoustic guitar and lead vocals; McCartney on bass and backing vocals; Harrison on guitar; Starr on drums
- *Thank You Little Girl (Thank You Girl)* – backing track included Lennon on acoustic guitar and lead vocals; McCartney on bass and lead vocals; Harrison on acoustic guitar; Starr on drums
- *The One after 909* – backing track included Lennon on acoustic guitar and lead vocals; McCartney on bass and lead vocals; Harrison on guitar; Starr on drums

**Edit Pieces**

- *From Me To You* – edit pieces included harmonica; guitar solo; Lennon and McCartney vocal harmony introduction
- *Thank You Little Girl (Thank You Girl)* – edit piece included end of song; Lennon and McCartney vocals
- *The One After 909* – edit piece included middle eight guitar solo, through end of song

**Sources** - Everett, Walter (1). p. 162. / Lewisohn, Mark (1). pp. 28, 29. / Ryan, Kevin and Brian Kehew. pp. 363, 444. / The Beatles. "*From Me To You (edit of takes 12, 8, 9 and 10)*". Rec.5 March 1963. The Beatles. FLAC audio file. / The Beatles. "*From Me To You (edit of takes 8, 9 and 10)*". Rec.5 March 1963. The Beatles. FLAC audio file. / The Beatles. "*From Me To You (final edit)*". Rec.5 March 1963. The Beatles. FLAC audio file. / The Beatles. "*From Me To You (take 1)*". Rec.5 March 1963. The Beatles. FLAC audio file. / The Beatles. "*From Me To You (take 10)*". Rec.5 March 1963. The Beatles. FLAC audio file. / The Beatles. "*From Me To You (take 11)*". Rec.5 March 1963. The Beatles. FLAC audio file. / The Beatles. "*From Me To You (take 12)*". Rec.5 March 1963. The Beatles. FLAC audio file. / The Beatles. "*From Me To You (take 13)*". Rec.5 March 1963. The Beatles. FLAC audio file. / The Beatles. "*From Me To You (take 2)*". Rec.5 March 1963. The Beatles. FLAC audio file. / The Beatles. "*From Me To You (take 3)*". Rec.5 March 1963. The Beatles. FLAC audio file. / The Beatles. "*From Me To You (take 4)*". Rec.5 March 1963. The Beatles. FLAC audio file. / The Beatles. "*From Me To You (take 5)*". Rec.5 March 1963. The Beatles. FLAC audio file. / The Beatles. "*From Me To You (take 6)*". Rec.5 March 1963. The Beatles. FLAC audio file. / The Beatles. "*From Me To You (take 7)*". Rec.5 March 1963. The Beatles. FLAC audio file. / The Beatles. "*From Me To You (take 8)*". Rec.5 March 1963. The Beatles. FLAC audio file. / The Beatles. "*From Me To You (take 9)*". Rec.5 March 1963. The Beatles. FLAC audio file. / The Beatles. "*From Me To You*". Rec.5 March 1963. The Beatles. FLAC audio file. / The Beatles. "*Thank You Girl (take 1)*". Rec.5 March 1963. The Beatles. FLAC audio file. / The Beatles. "*Thank You Girl (take 10)*". Rec.5 March 1963. The Beatles. FLAC audio file. / The Beatles. "*Thank You Girl (take 11)*". Rec.5 March 1963. The Beatles. FLAC audio file. / The Beatles. "*Thank You Girl (take 12)*". Rec.5 March 1963. The Beatles. FLAC audio file. / The Beatles. "*Thank You Girl (take 13)*". Rec.5 March 1963. The Beatles. FLAC audio file. / The Beatles. "*Thank You Girl (take 2)*". Rec.5 March 1963. The Beatles. FLAC audio file. / The Beatles. "*Thank You Girl (take 3)*". Rec.5 March 1963. The Beatles. FLAC audio file. / The Beatles. "*Thank You Girl (take 4)*". Rec.5 March 1963. The Beatles. FLAC audio file. / The Beatles. "*Thank You Girl (take 5)*". Rec.5 March 1963. The Beatles. FLAC audio file. / The Beatles. "*Thank You Girl (take 6)*". Rec.5 March 1963. The Beatles. FLAC audio file. / The Beatles. "*Thank You Girl (take 7)*". Rec.5 March 1963. The Beatles. FLAC audio file. / The Beatles. "*Thank You Girl (take 8)*". Rec.5 March 1963. The Beatles. FLAC audio file. / The Beatles. "*Thank You Girl (take 9)*". Rec.5 March 1963. The Beatles. FLAC audio file. / The Beatles. "*Thank You Girl*". Rec.5 March 1963. The Beatles. FLAC audio file. / The Beatles. "*The One After 909 (take 1)*". Rec.5 March 1963. The Beatles. FLAC audio file. / The Beatles. "*The One After 909 (take 2)*". Rec.5 March 1963. The Beatles. FLAC audio file. / The Beatles. "*The One After 909 (take 3)*". Rec.5 March 1963. The Beatles. FLAC audio file. / The Beatles. "*The One After 909 (take 4)*". Rec.5 March 1963. The Beatles. FLAC audio file. / The Beatles. "*The One After 909 (take 5)*". Rec.5 March 1963. The Beatles. FLAC audio file. / The Beatles. *The One After 909*. *Anthology*. George Martin, 1995. CD.

# March 13, 1963

### Time

10AM - 1PM

### Studio name and room

EMI Recording Studios
Studio 2

### Songs recorded (composer) (activities)

- *Thank You Little Girl (Thank You Girl)* (Lennon and McCartney)
  - superimposition takes 14-28
  - edit of takes 6, 13, 17, 20, 21, and 23, called take 30

### Songs mixed (version) (remix number and take)

- *Thank You Little Girl (Thank You Girl)* (mono)
  - unnumbered remix (RM) from edit of takes 6, 13, 17, 20, 21, and 23
- *Thank You Little Girl (Thank You Girl)* (stereo)
  - unnumbered remix (RS) from edit of takes 6, 13, 17, 20, 21, and 23

**Studio Personnel**

- Producer: George Martin
- Balance engineer: Norman Smith
- Tape operator: Geoff Emerick

**Musicians (instruments played)**

- John Lennon (harmonica)

**Instruments**

**Other**

- Hohner harmonica (Echo Vamper or Super Chromonica)

**Recording equipment**

*Recording console*

- REDD.37

*Primary tracking machine*

- TWIN-TRACK: 1/4" EMI BTR3
- MONO: 1/4" EMI BTR2

*Mixdown machine*

- MONO: 1/4" EMI BTR2
- STEREO: 1/4" EMI BTR3

*Outboard signal processors*

- EMI RS114 Limiter
- EMI RS124 Altec Compressor
- EMI RS127 Presence Box
- EMI RS144 4-Way Mixer/Premix
- EMI RS92 Neumann Mic Equaliser

*Effects*

- Echo chamber (includes RS61 Low Level Amplifier with RS62 Power Supply and RS106A Echo Control Unit – Band Pass Filter)
- STEED (send tape echo/echo delay)

*Monitors*

Control room

- Altec 605A (Altec 612 Cabinet) with EMI RS141 Leak TL/25 Plus Amplifier

Studio

- RLS10 - "White Elephant"

*Microphones*

Other

- Neumann U48, U47/48 (U47/8)

**Superimpositions**

- *Thank You Little Girl (Thank You Girl)* – superimposition included Lennon on harmonica

**Remixes**

Mono master remixes

- *Thank You Little Girl (Thank You Girl)* (mono) (unnumbered remix (RM) from edit of takes 6, 13, 17, 20, 21, and 23)

Stereo master remixes

- *Thank You Little Girl (Thank You Girl)* (stereo) (unnumbered remix (RS) from edit of takes 6, 13, 17, 20, 21, and 23)

**Sources -** Emerick, Geoff. p. 61. / Lewisohn, Mark (1). p. 31. / Winn, John C. (3). p. 9. /The Beatles. "*Thank You Girl (take 14)*". Rec.13 March 1963. The Beatles. FLAC audio file.

# March 14, 1963

**Time**
10AM - 1PM

**Studio name and room**
EMI Recording Studios
Studio 2 (control room)

**Songs mixed (version) (remix number and take)**

- *From Me To You* (mono)
    - unnumbered remix (RM) from edit of takes 12, 8, 9 and 10, synced with take 8
- *From Me To You* (stereo)
    - unnumbered remix (RS) from edit of takes 12, 8, 9 and 10

**Studio Personnel**

- Producer: George Martin
- Balance engineer: Unknown
- Tape operator: Unknown

**Recording equipment**

*Recording console*

- REDD.37

*Primary tracking machine*

- TWIN-TRACK: 1/4" EMI BTR3

*Mixdown machine*

- MONO: 1/4" EMI BTR2
- STEREO: 1/4" EMI BTR3

*Outboard signal processors*

- EMI RS114 Limiter
- EMI RS124 Altec Compressor
- EMI RS127 Presence Box
- EMI RS144 4-Way Mixer/Premix
- EMI RS92 Neumann Mic Equaliser

*Effects*

- Echo chamber (includes RS61 Low Level Amplifier with RS62 Power Supply and RS106A Echo Control Unit – Band Pass Filter)
- STEED (send tape echo/echo delay)

*Monitors*

Control room

- Altec 605A (Altec 612 Cabinet) with EMI RS141 Leak TL/25 Plus Amplifier

**Remixes**

Mono master remixes

- *From Me To You* (mono) (unnumbered remix (RM) from edit of takes 8, 9, 10, and 12)

Stereo master remixes

- *From Me To You* (stereo) (unnumbered remix (RS) from edit of takes 8, 9, 10, and 12)

**Sources -** Lewisohn, Mark (1). p. 31. / Ryan, Kevin and Brian Kehew. p. 363. / Winn, John C. (3). p. 8.

# *With The Beatles* sessions

---

## July 1, 1963

**Time**
230PM - 530PM

**Studio name and room**
EMI Recording Studios
Studio 2

**Songs recorded (composer) (activities)**

- *She Loves You* (Lennon and McCartney)
    - unnumbered takes including superimpositions
- *Get You In The End (I'll Get You)* (Lennon and McCartney)
    - unnumbered takes including superimpositions

**Studio Personnel**

- Producer: George Martin
- Balance engineer: Norman Smith
- Tape operator: Geoff Emerick

**Musicians (instruments played)**

- John Lennon (guitar, harmonica, vocals)
- Paul McCartney (bass, vocals)
- George Harrison (guitar, vocals)
- Ringo Starr (drums)

## Instruments

### Electric guitars

*Lennon*

- 1958 Rickenbacker 325 Capri with Bigsby B5 vibrato (first model – repainted black)

*Harrison*

- 1962 Gretsch 6122 Chet Atkins Country Gentleman with Gretsch Bigsby B6G vibrato

### Acoustic guitars

*Lennon*

- 1962 Gibson J-160E

### Bass guitars

*McCartney*

- 1961 Hofner 500/1

### Drums

*Starr*

- 1963 Ludwig Oyster Black Pearl Downbeat (14" X 20" bass drum/ 8" X 12" rack tom/ 14" X 14" floor tom/ 14" X 5.5" Jazz Festival snare); Paiste, Zyn, Zildjian cymbals (20" ride/ 20" ride with 4-rivet "sizzle"/ 18" crash) Zildjian cymbals (14" model A hi-hats) (Ludwig Set 1)

### Percussion

- Handclaps

### Other

- Hohner harmonica (Echo Vamper or Super Chromonica)

## Amplifiers

### Guitar

*Lennon/Harrison*

- 1962 JMI Vox AC30/6 Twin (re-covered black) with "Top Boost" circuit, 30W with two 12" Vox Celestion Alinco Blue G12 T530 speakers

### Bass

*McCartney*

- 1963 Vox T60 head, 60W with Vox T60 speaker cabinet, with one 12", and one 15" Vox Celestion Alinco Blue speakers

## Recording equipment

*Recording console*

- REDD.37

*Primary tracking machine*

- TWIN-TRACK: 1/4" EMI BTR3

*Outboard signal processors*

- EMI RS114 Limiter
- EMI RS124 Altec Compressor
- EMI RS127 Presence Box
- EMI RS144 4-Way Mixer/Premix
- EMI RS92 Neumann Mic Equaliser

*Effects*

- Double tracking
- Echo chamber (includes RS61 Low Level Amplifier with RS62 Power Supply and RS106A Echo Control Unit – Band Pass Filter)
- STEED (send tape echo/echo delay)

*Monitors*

Control room

- Altec 605A (Altec 612 Cabinet) with EMI RS141 Leak TL/25 Plus Amplifier

Studio

- RLS10 - "White Elephant"

*Microphones*

Vocals

- Neumann U48 or U47/48 (U47/8)

*Electric guitar amplifiers*

- Neumann U48, U47/48 (U47/8)
- Neumann KM54

Acoustic guitars

- Neumann U48 or U47/48 (U47/8)

Bass amplifier

- STC 4033-A

*Drums*

- Overhead - STC 4038
- Bass drum - STC 4033-A

*Other*

- Neumann U48, U47/48 (U47/8)
- STC 4038

**Backing Tracks**

- *She Loves You* – backing track included Lennon on acoustic guitar and lead vocals; McCartney on bass and lead vocals; Harrison on guitar and backing vocals; Starr on drums
- *Get You In The End (I'll Get You)* – backing track included Lennon on guitar and lead vocals; McCartney on bass and lead vocals; Harrison on guitar; Starr on drums

**Superimpositions**

- *She Loves You* – superimposition of Harrison on guitar
- *Get You In The End (I'll Get You)* – superimposition of Lennon on harmonica; McCartney and Harrison on handclaps

**Notes**

A 1987 article in *Guitar Player* magazine drawn

from photographic evidence found in the monthly fan magazine, *Beatles Book*, noted Harrison played the 1963 Gretsch PX6122 Chet Atkins Country Gentleman with Gretsch Bigsby B6G vibrato on *She Loves You.* However, that guitar did not come into his possession until early November of 1963, making it unavailable for this session. He did possess the 1962 Gretsch 6122 Chet Atkins Country Gentleman with Gretsch Bigsby B6G vibrato at the time of the session which, being virtually identical, is likely the guitar used.

**Sources -** Babiuk, Andy (1). pp. 91, 92. / Dowlding, William J. p. 46. / Lewisohn, Mark (1). p. 32. / Mytkowicz, Bob. / The Beatles. "*I'll Get You*". Rec.1 July 1963. The Beatles. FLAC audio file. / The Beatles. "*She Loves You (RS2)*". Rec.1 July 1963. The Beatles. FLAC audio file.

# July 4, 1963

**Time**
10AM - 1PM

**Studio name and room**
EMI Recording Studios
Studio 2 (control room)

**Songs recorded (composer) (activities)**

- *She Loves You* (Lennon and McCartney)
    - edit of unknown take numbers

**Songs mixed (version) (remix number and take)**

- *She Loves You* (mono)
    - unnumbered remix (RM) from edit of unknown take numbers
- *Get You In The End (I'll Get You)* (mono)
    - unnumbered remix (RM) from unknown take number

**Studio Personnel**

- Producer: George Martin
- Balance engineer: Unknown
- Tape operator: Unknown

**Recording equipment**

*Recording console*

- REDD.37

*Primary tracking machine*

- TWIN-TRACK: 1/4" EMI BTR3

*Mixdown machine*

- MONO: 1/4" EMI BTR2

*Outboard signal processors*

- EMI RS114 Limiter
- EMI RS124 Altec Compressor
- EMI RS127 Presence Box
- EMI RS144 4-Way Mixer/Premix
- EMI RS92 Neumann Mic Equaliser

*Effects*

- Echo chamber (includes RS61 Low Level Amplifier with RS62 Power Supply and RS106A Echo Control Unit – Band Pass Filter)
- STEED (send tape echo/echo delay)

*Monitors*

Control room

- Altec 605A (Altec 612 Cabinet) with EMI RS141 Leak TL/25 Plus Amplifier

**Remixes**

Mono master remixes

- *She Loves You* (mono) (unnumbered remix (RM) from edit of unknown take numbers)
- *Get You In The End (I'll Get You)* (mono) (unnumbered remix (RM) from unknown take number)

**Sources -** Lewisohn, Mark (1). p. 32. / Winn, John C. (3). p. 11.

# July 18, 1963

**Time**
7PM - 1045PM

**Studio name and room**
EMI Recording Studios
Studio 2

**Songs recorded (composer) (activities)**

- *You Really Got A Hold On Me* (Robinson)
    - takes 1-5, including superimpositions (see Notes)
    - superimposition takes 6,7
    - edit piece takes 8-11
- *Money (That's What I Want)* (Bradford and Gordy)
    - takes 1-5
    - edit piece take 6
    - superimposition take 7
- *Devil In Her Heart* (Drapkin)
    - takes 1-3
    - superimposition takes 4-6
- *Till There Was You* (Willson)
    - takes 1-3

**Studio Personnel**

- Producer: George Martin
- Balance engineer: Norman Smith
- Tape operator: Richard Langham

**Musicians (instruments played)**

- John Lennon (guitar, vocals)
- Paul McCartney (bass, vocals)
- George Harrison (guitar, vocals)
- Ringo Starr (drums, percussion)

### Other musicians (instruments played)

- George Martin (piano)

## Instruments

### Electric guitars

*Lennon*

- 1958 Rickenbacker 325 Capri with Bigsby B5 vibrato (first model – repainted black)

*Harrison*

- 1962 Gretsch 6122 Chet Atkins Country Gentleman with Gretsch Bigsby B6G vibrato

### Acoustic guitars

*Lennon/Harrison*

- 1962 Gibson J-160E

*Harrison*

- Jose Ramirez Guitarra de Estudio (nylon string)

### Bass guitars

*McCartney*

- 1961 Hofner 500/1

### Drums

*Starr*

- 1963 Ludwig Oyster Black Pearl Downbeat (14" X 20" bass drum/ 8" X 12" rack tom/ 14" X 14" floor tom/ 14" X 5.5" Jazz Festival snare); Paiste, Zyn, Zildjian cymbals (20" ride/ 20" ride with 4-rivet "sizzle"/ 18" crash) Zildjian cymbals (14" model A hi-hats) (Ludwig Set 1)

### Percussion

- Premier bongos
- Maracas
- Handclaps

### Pianos and keyboards

- Steinway "Music Room" Model B Grand Piano (circa 1880s)

## Amplifiers

### Guitar

*Lennon/Harrison*

- 1963 JMI Vox AC30/6 Twin Treble with "Top Boost" circuit, 30W with two 12" Vox Celestion Alnico Gray G12 T530 speakers

### Bass

*McCartney*

- 1963 Vox AC30 head, 30W with Vox T60 speaker cabinet, with one 12", and one 15" Vox Celestion Alinco Blue speakers

## Recording equipment

*Recording console*

- REDD.37

*Primary tracking machine*

- TWIN-TRACK: 1/4" EMI BTR3

*Outboard signal processors*

- EMI RS114 Limiter
- EMI RS124 Altec Compressor
- EMI RS127 Presence Box
- EMI RS144 4-Way Mixer/Premix
- EMI RS92 Neumann Mic Equaliser

*Effects*

- Echo chamber (includes RS61 Low Level Amplifier with RS62 Power Supply and RS106A Echo Control Unit – Band Pass Filter)
- STEED (send tape echo/echo delay)

*Monitors*

Control room

- Altec 605A (Altec 612 Cabinet) with EMI RS141 Leak TL/25 Plus Amplifier

Studio

- RLS10 - "White Elephant"

*Microphones*

Vocals

- Neumann U48 or U47/48 (U47/8)

Electric guitar amplifiers

- Neumann U48, U47/48 (U47/8)
- Neumann KM54

Acoustic guitars

- Neumann U48 or U47/48 (U47/8)

Bass amplifier

- STC 4033-A

Drums

- Overhead - STC 4038
- Bass drum - STC 4033-A

Piano

- Neumann U48 or U47/48 (U47/8)

Other

- Neumann U48, U47/48 (U47/8)
- STC 4038

**Backing Tracks**

- *You Really Got A Hold On Me* – backing track included Lennon on acoustic guitar and lead vocals; McCartney on bass and backing vocals; Harrison on guitar and backing vocals; Starr on drums

- *Money (That's What I Want)* – backing track included Lennon on guitar and lead vocals; Harrison on guitar and backing vocals; McCartney on bass and backing vocals; Starr on drums
- *Devil In Her Heart* – backing track included Harrison on guitar and lead vocals; Lennon on guitar and backing vocals; McCartney on bass and backing vocals; Starr on drums
- *Till There Was You* – unknown backing track (likely McCartney on bass; Lennon on acoustic guitar; Harrison on nylon string acoustic guitar; Starr on bongos)

**Superimpositions**

- *You Really Got A Hold On Me* – superimpositions included Lennon on lead vocals; McCartney on backing vocals; Harrison on guitar and backing vocals; George Martin on piano
- *Money (That's What I Want)* – superimpositions included George Martin on piano; Lennon, McCartney, and Harrison on backing vocals and handclaps
- *Devil In Her Heart* – superimpositions included on Harrison on lead vocals; Starr on maracas

**Edit pieces**

- *You Really Got A Hold On Me* – edit piece included McCartney on backing vocals; George Martin on piano
- *Money (That's What I Want)* – edit piece included George Martin on piano introduction; Starr on drumsticks

**Notes**

Superimpositions to take 5 of *You Really Got A Hold On Me* (the "best" backing track) included both lead and backing vocals, and some touches of lead guitar by Harrison.

**Sources -** Everett, Walter (1). p. 184. / Lewisohn, Mark (1). p. 34. / Ryan, Kevin and Brian Kehew. p. 360. / The Beatles. "*Devil In Her Heart*". Rec.18 July 1963. The Beatles. FLAC audio file. / The Beatles. "*Money (That's What I Want)*". Rec.18 July 1963. The Beatles. FLAC audio file. / Winn, John C. (3). pp. 11, 12

# July 30, 1963

**Time**
10AM - 11PM

**Studio name and room**
EMI Recording Studios
Studio 2

- 10AM – 130PM
- 5PM – 11PM

**Songs recorded (composer) (activities)**

- *Please Mister Postman* (Dobbins, Garrett, Gorman, Holland & Bateman)
  - takes 1 and 2
  - superimposition take 3
  - takes 4-7
  - superimposition takes 8 and 9
- *It Won't Be Long* (Lennon and McCartney)
  - takes 1-10
  - superimposition takes 11-17
  - edit pieces takes 18-23
- *Money (That's What I Want)* (Bradford and Gordy)
  - piano test takes 8-14

- *Till There Was You* (remake) (Willson)
    - takes 4-8
- *Roll Over Beethoven* (Berry)
    - takes 1-5
    - superimposition takes 6 and 7
    - edit piece, take 8
- *All My Loving* (Lennon and McCartney)
    - takes 1-4
    - takes 6-11
    - superimposition takes 12-14

**Studio Personnel**

- Producer: George Martin
- Balance engineer: Norman Smith
- Tape operator: Richard Langham

**Musicians (instruments played)**

- John Lennon (guitar, vocals)
- Paul McCartney (bass, vocals)
- George Harrison (guitar, vocals)
- Ringo Starr (drums, bongos)

**Other musicians (instruments played)**

- George Martin (piano)

**Instruments**

**Electric guitars**

*Lennon*

- 1958 Rickenbacker 325 Capri with Bigsby B5 vibrato (first model – repainted black)

*Harrison*

- 1962 Gretsch 6122 Chet Atkins Country Gentleman with Gretsch Bigsby B6G vibrato

**Acoustic guitars**

*Lennon/Harrison*

- 1962 Gibson J-160E

**Bass guitars**

*McCartney*

- 1961 Hofner 500/1

**Drums**

*Starr*

- 1963 Ludwig Oyster Black Pearl Downbeat (14" X 20" bass drum/ 8" X 12" rack tom/ 14" X 14" floor tom/ 14" X 5.5" Jazz Festival snare); Paiste, Zyn, Zildjian cymbals (20" ride/ 20" ride with 4-rivet "sizzle"/ 18" crash) Zildjian cymbals (14" model A hi-hats) (Ludwig Set 1)

**Percussion**

- Premier bongos

**Pianos and keyboards**

- Steinway "Music Room" Model B Grand Piano (circa 1880s)

## Amplifiers

### Guitar

*Lennon/Harrison*

- 1963 JMI Vox AC30/6 Twin Treble with "Top Boost" circuit, 30W with two 12" Vox Celestion Alnico Gray G12 T530 speakers

### Bass

*McCartney*

- 1963 Vox AC30 head, 30W with Vox T60 speaker cabinet, with one 12", and one 15" Vox Celestion Alinco Blue speakers

## Recording equipment

*Recording console*

- REDD.37

*Primary tracking machine*

- TWIN-TRACK: 1/4" EMI BTR3

*Outboard signal processors*

- EMI RS114 Limiter
- EMI RS124 Altec Compressor
- EMI RS127 Presence Box
- EMI RS144 4-Way Mixer/Premix
- EMI RS92 Neumann Mic Equaliser

*Effects*

- Echo chamber (includes RS61 Low Level Amplifier with RS62 Power Supply and RS106A Echo Control Unit – Band Pass Filter)
- STEED (send tape echo/echo delay)

*Monitors*

Control room

- Altec 605A (Altec 612 Cabinet) with EMI RS141 Leak TL/25 Plus Amplifier

Studio

- RLS10 - "White Elephant"

*Microphones*

Vocals

- Neumann U48 or U47/48 (U47/8)

Electric guitar amplifiers

- Neumann U48, U47/48 (U47/8)
- Neumann KM54

Acoustic guitars

- Neumann U48 or U47/48 (U47/8)

Bass amplifier

- STC 4033-A

Drums

- Overhead - STC 4038
- Bass drum - STC 4033-A

Piano

- Neumann U48 or U47/48 (U47/8)

Other

- Neumann U48, U47/48 (U47/8)

**Backing Tracks**

- *Please Mister Postman*– backing track included Lennon on guitar and lead vocals; McCartney on bass and backing vocals; Harrison on guitar and backing vocals; Starr on drums
- *It Won't Be Long* – backing track included Lennon on guitar and lead vocals; McCartney on bass and backing vocals; Harrison on guitar and backing vocals; Starr on drums
- *Till There Was You* – backing track included Lennon on acoustic guitar; McCartney on bass and lead vocals; Harrison on nylon string acoustic guitar; Starr on bongos
- *Roll Over Beethoven* – backing track included Lennon on guitar; McCartney on bass; Harrison on guitar and lead vocals; Starr on drums
- *All My Loving* – backing track included Lennon on guitar and backing vocals; McCartney on bass and lead vocals; Harrison on guitar and backing vocals; Starr on drums

**Superimpositions**

- *Please Mister Postman*– superimpositions included Lennon on double-tracked lead vocals; McCartney and Harrison on double-tracked backing vocals and handclaps
- *It Won't Be Long* – superimposition included Lennon on double-tracked lead vocals; Harrison on guitar

- *Roll Over Beethoven* – superimpositions included Harrison on double-tracked lead vocals; Harrison on lead guitar; handclaps
- *All My Loving* – superimpositions included McCartney double tracked-lead vocals

**Edit Pieces**

- *Money (That's What I Want)* – edit piece included George Martin on piano (test only)
- *It Won't Be Long* – edit piece included the entire band playing the ending of the song
- *Roll Over Beethoven* - edit piece included ending guitar part

**Sources -** Lewisohn, Mark (1). p. 34. / Dowlding, William J. pp. 48, 52. / The Beatles. "*Please Mister Postman*". Rec.30 July 1963. The Beatles. FLAC audio file. / The Beatles. "*It Won't Be Long*". Rec.30 July 1963. The Beatles. FLAC audio file. / The Beatles. "*It Won't Be Long (take 7)*". Rec.30 July 1963. The Beatles. FLAC audio file. / The Beatles. "*It Won't Be Long (take 10)*". Rec.30 July 1963. The Beatles. FLAC audio file. / The Beatles. "*Roll Over Beethoven*". Rec.30 July 1963. The Beatles. FLAC audio file. / The Beatles. "*All My Loving*". Rec.30 July 1963. The Beatles. FLAC audio file. / Winn, John C. (3). pp. 12-14.

# August 21, 1963

**Time**
10AM - 530PM

**Studio name and room**
EMI Recording Studios
Studio 3 (control room)

- 10AM – 1PM
- 2PM – 530PM

**Songs recorded (composer) (activities)**

- *Money (That's What I Want)* (Bradford and Gordy)
    - edit of takes 6 and 7
- *You Really Got A Hold On Me* (Robinson)
    - edit of takes 7, 10 and 11
- *Roll Over Beethoven* (Berry)
    - edit of takes 7 and 8
- *It Won't Be Long* (Lennon and McCartney)
    - edit of takes 17 and 21

**Songs mixed (version) (remix number and take)**

- *Devil In Her Heart* (mono)
    - remix (RM) 6 from take 6
- *Money (That's What I Want)* (mono)
    - remix (RM) 6/7 from edit of takes 6 and 7
- *You Really Got A Hold On Me* (mono)
    - remix (RM) 7/10/11 from edit of takes 7, 10 and 11
- *Please Mister Postman* (mono)
    - remix (RM) 9 from take 9
- *Till There Was You* (mono)
    - remix (RM) 8 from take 8
- *Roll Over Beethoven* (mono)
    - remix (RM) 7/8 from edit of takes 7 and 8
- *All My Loving* (mono)
    - *remix (RM) 14 from take 14*
- *It Won't Be Long* (mono)
    - remix (RM) 17/21 from edit of takes 17 and 21

**Studio Personnel**

- Producer: George Martin
- Balance engineer: Norman Smith
- Tape operator: Geoff Emerick

**Recording equipment**

*Recording console*

- REDD.51

*Primary tracking machine*

- TWIN-TRACK: 1/4" EMI BTR3

Mixdown machine

- MONO: 1/4" EMI BTR2

Outboard signal processors

- EMI RS114 Limiter
- EMI RS124 Altec Compressor
- EMI RS127 Presence Box
- EMI RS144 4-Way Mixer/Premix
- EMI RS92 Neumann Mic Equaliser

*Effects*

- Echo chamber (includes RS61 Low Level Amplifier with RS62 Power Supply and RS106A Echo Control Unit – Band Pass Filter)
- Tape echo/ repeat echo (STEED – send tape echo/echo delay

*Monitors*

Control room

- Altec 605A (Altec 612 Cabinet) with EMI RS141 Leak TL/25 Plus Amplifier

**Remixes**

Mono master remixes

- *Devil In Her Heart* (mono) (remix (RM) 6 from take 6)
- *Money (That's What I Want)* (mono) (remix (RM) 6/7 from edit of takes 6 and 7)
- *You Really Got A Hold On Me* (mono) (remix (RM) 7/10/11 from edit of takes 7, 10 and 11)
- *Please Mister Postman* (mono) (remix (RM) 9 from take 9)
- *Till There Was You* (mono) (remix (RM) 8 from take 8)
- *Roll Over Beethoven* (mono) remix (RM) 7/8 from edit of takes 7 and 8
- *All My Loving* (mono) (remix (RM) 14 from take 14)
- *It Won't Be Long* (mono) (remix (RM) 17/21 from edit of takes 17 and 21)

**Sources** - Lewisohn, Mark (1). p. 34. / Winn, John C. (3). p. 14

# September 11, 1963

**Time**
230PM – 1015PM

**Studio name and room**
EMI Recording Studios
Studio 2

- 230PM - 6PM
- 7PM – 1015PM

**Songs recorded (composer) (activities)**

- *I Wanna Be Your Man* (Lennon and McCartney)
    - take 1
- *Little Child* (Lennon and McCartney)
    - takes 1-2
- *All I've Got To Do* (Lennon and McCartney)
    - takes 1-14
    - superimposition take 15
- *Not A Second Time* (Lennon and McCartney)
    - takes 1-5
    - superimposition takes 6-9
- *Don't Bother Me* (Harrison)
    - takes 1-4
    - superimposition takes 5-7

**Studio Personnel**

- Producer: George Martin
- Balance engineer: Norman Smith
- Tape operator: Richard Langham

**Musicians (instruments played)**

- John Lennon (guitar, harmonica, percussion, vocals)

- Paul McCartney (bass, percussion, vocals)
- George Harrison (guitar, percussion, vocals)
- Ringo Starr (drums, percussion, vocals)

**Other musicians (instruments played)**

- George Martin (piano)

### Instruments

**Electric guitars**

*Lennon*

- 1958 Rickenbacker 325 Capri with Bigsby B5 vibrato (first model – repainted black)

*Harrison*

- 1962 Gretsch 6122 Chet Atkins Country Gentleman with Gretsch Bigsby B6G vibrato

**Acoustic guitars**

*Lennon/Harrison*

- 1962 Gibson J-160E

**Bass guitars**

*McCartney*

- 1961 Hofner 500/1

**Drums**

*Starr*

- 1963 Ludwig Oyster Black Pearl Downbeat (14" X 20" bass drum/ 8" X 12" rack tom/ 14" X 14" floor tom/ 14" X 5.5" Jazz Festival snare); Paiste, Zyn, Zildjian cymbals (20" ride/ 20" ride with 4-rivet "sizzle"/ 18" crash) Zildjian cymbals (14" model A hi-hats) (Ludwig Set 1)

**Percussion**

- Premier bongos
- Doumbek
- Wood Block
- Maracas
- Tambourine (Olympic or Ludwig)

**Pianos and keyboards**

- Steinway "Music Room" Model B Grand Piano (circa 1880s)

**Other**

- Hohner harmonica (Echo Vamper or Super Chromonica)

### Amplifiers

**Guitar**

*Lennon/Harrison*

- 1963 JMI Vox AC30/6 Twin Treble with "Top Boost" circuit, 30W with two 12" Vox Celestion Alnico Gray G12 T530 speakers

**Bass**

*McCartney*

- 1963 Vox AC30 head, 30W with Vox T60 speaker cabinet, with one 12", and one 15" Vox Celestion Alinco Blue speakers

## Recording equipment

*Recording console*

- REDD.37

*Primary tracking machine*

- TWIN-TRACK: 1/4" EMI BTR3

*Outboard signal processors*

- EMI RS114 Limiter
- EMI RS124 Altec Compressor
- EMI RS127 Presence Box
- EMI RS144 4-Way Mixer/Premix
- EMI RS92 Neumann Mic Equaliser

*Effects*

- Echo chamber (includes RS61 Low Level Amplifier with RS62 Power Supply and RS106A Echo Control Unit – Band Pass Filter)
- STEED (send tape echo/echo delay)

*Monitors*

Control room

- Altec 605A (Altec 612 Cabinet) with EMI RS141 Leak TL/25 Plus Amplifier

Studio

- RLS10 - "White Elephant"

*Microphones*

Vocals

- Neumann U48 or U47/48 (U47/8)

Electric guitar amplifiers

- Neumann U48, U47/48 (U47/8)
- Neumann KM54

Acoustic guitars

- Neumann U48 or U47/48 (U47/8)

Bass amplifier

- STC 4033-A

Drums

- Overhead - STC 4038
- Bass drum - STC 4033-A

Piano

- Neumann U48 or U47/48 (U47/8)

Other

- Neumann U48, U47/48 (U47/8)
- STC 4038

### Backing tracks

- *I Wanna Be Your Man* – backing track included Lennon on guitar; McCartney on bass; Harrison on guitar; Starr on drums and lead vocals
- *Little Child* – backing track included Lennon on guitar; McCartney on bass; Harrison on guitar; Starr on drums
- *All I've Got To Do* – backing track included Lennon on guitar and lead vocals; McCartney on bass and backing vocals; Harrison on guitar; Starr on drums
- *Not A Second Time* – backing track included Lennon on acoustic guitar; McCartney on bass; Harrison on acoustic guitar; Starr on drums
- *Don't Bother Me* – backing track of Harrison on guitar and lead vocals; Lennon on guitar; McCartney on bass; Starr on drums

### Superimpositions

- *All I've Got To Do* – superimpositions included McCartney and Harrison on backing vocals
- *Not A Second Time* – superimpositions included Lennon on double-tracked lead vocals and George Martin on piano
- *Don't Bother Me* – unknown superimpositions

### Notes

The work on *I Wanna Be Your Man, Little Child* and *Don't Bother Me* from this session was not used in any release versions of the songs.

**Sources -** Dowlding, William J. pp. 49, 50, 57. / Lewisohn, Mark (1). p. 35. / Ryan, Kevin and Brian Kehew. p. 359. / The Beatles. "*All I've Got To Do*". Rec.11 September 1963. The Beatles. FLAC audio file. / The Beatles. "*Little Child*". Rec.11 September 1963. The Beatles. FLAC audio file. / The Beatles. "*Not A Second Time*". Rec.11 September 1963. The Beatles. FLAC audio file. / Winn, John C. (3). pp. 15, 16.

## September 12, 1963

### Time

230PM - 1130PM

### Studio name and room

EMI Recording Studios
Studio 2

- 230PM – 630PM
- 7PM – 1130PM

### Songs recorded (composer) (activities)

- *A Message to Australia (spoken)*
    - takes 1-3
- *Open Message to Australia (spoken)*
    - take 1
- *Hold Me Tight (remake)* (Lennon and McCartney)
    - takes 20-24
    - superimposition takes 25-29
- *Don't Bother Me (remake)* (Harrison)
    - takes 10-13
    - superimposition takes 15-19
- *Little Child* (Lennon and McCartney)
    - takes 3-12
    - superimposition takes 13 - 15
    - edit piece takes 16-18
- *I Wanna Be Your Man* (Lennon and McCartney)
    - takes 2-7

**Songs mixed (version) (remix number and take)**

- *I Wanna Be Your Man* (mono)
    - remix (RM) 8-13 with simultaneous superimposition

**Studio Personnel**

- Producer: George Martin
- Balance engineer: Norman Smith
- Tape operator: Richard Langham

**Musicians (instruments played)**

- John Lennon (guitar, harmonica, tambourine, vocals)
- Paul McCartney (bass, claves, vocals)
- George Harrison (guitar, vocals)
- Ringo Starr (drums, bongo, vocals)

**Musicians (instruments played)**

- George Martin (organ)

**Instruments**

**Electric guitars**

*Lennon*

- 1958 Rickenbacker 325 Capri with Bigsby B5 vibrato (first model – repainted black)

*Harrison*

- 1962 Gretsch 6122 Chet Atkins Country Gentleman with Gretsch Bigsby B6G vibrato

**Bass guitars**

*McCartney*

- 1961 Hofner 500/1

**Drums**

*Starr*

- 1963 Ludwig Oyster Black Pearl Downbeat (14" X 20" bass drum/ 8" X 12" rack tom/ 14" X 14" floor tom/ 14" X 5.5" Jazz Festival snare); Paiste, Zyn, Zildjian cymbals (20" ride/ 20" ride with 4-rivet "sizzle"/ 18" crash) Zildjian cymbals (14" model A hi-hats) (Ludwig Set 1)

**Percussion**

- Arabian bongo
- Tambourine (Olympic or Ludwig)
- Woodblock

**Pianos and keyboards**

- Steinway "Music Room" Model B Grand Piano (circa 1880s)
- Hammond RT3 Organ (circa 1954-62)

**Other**

- Hohner harmonica (Echo Vamper or Super Chromonica)
- Hammond PR-40 tone cabinet

## Amplifiers

### Guitar

*Lennon/Harrison*

- 1963 JMI Vox AC30/6 Twin Treble with "Top Boost" circuit, 30W with two 12" Vox Celestion Alnico Gray G12 T530 speakers

### Bass

*McCartney*

- 1963 Vox AC30 head, 30W with Vox T60 speaker cabinet, with one 12", and one 15" Vox Celestion Alinco Blue speakers

## Recording equipment

*Recording console*

- REDD.37

*Primary tracking machine*

- TWIN-TRACK: 1/4" EMI BTR3

*Outboard signal processors*

- EMI RS114 Limiter
- EMI RS124 Altec Compressor
- EMI RS127 Presence Box
- EMI RS144 4-Way Mixer/Premix
- EMI RS92 Neumann Mic Equaliser

*Effects*

- Echo chamber (includes RS61 Low Level Amplifier with RS62 Power Supply and RS106A Echo Control Unit – Band Pass Filter)
- STEED (send tape echo/echo delay)

*Monitors*

Control room

- Altec 605A (Altec 612 Cabinet) with EMI RS141 Leak TL/25 Plus Amplifier

Studio

- RLS10 - "White Elephant"

*Microphones*

Vocals

- Neumann U48 or U47/48 (U47/8)

Electric guitar amplifiers

- Neumann U48, U47/48 (U47/8)
- Neumann KM54

Acoustic guitars

- Neumann U48 or U47/48 (U47/8)

Bass amplifier

- STC 4033-A

Drums

- Overhead - STC 4038
- Bass drum - STC 4033-A

Piano

- Neumann U48 or U47/48 (U47/8)

Other

- Neumann U48, U47/48 (U47/8)
- STC 4038

**Backing tracks**

- *Hold Me Tight* – backing track included McCartney on bass and lead vocals; Lennon on guitar and backing vocals; Harrison on guitar and backing vocals; Starr on drums
- *Don't Bother Me* – backing track included Lennon on guitar; McCartney on bass; Harrison on guitar and lead vocals; Starr on drums
- *Little Child* – backing track included Lennon on guitar; McCartney on bass; Harrison on guitar; Starr on drums
- *I Wanna Be Your Man* – backing track included Lennon on guitar and lead vocals; McCartney on bass and backing vocals; Harrison on guitar; Starr on drums and lead vocals

**Superimpositions**

- *Hold Me Tight* – superimpositions included McCartney on harmony lead vocals; Lennon and Harrison on backing vocals; handclaps
- *Don't Bother Me* – superimpositions included Harrison on double-tracked lead vocals; Lennon on tambourine; McCartney on wood block; Starr on doumbek
- *Little Child* – superimpositions included Lennon and McCartney on lead vocals; Lennon on harmonica; McCartney on piano
- *I Wanna Be Your Man* – superimposition included Martin on organ during remixing

**Edit pieces**

- *Little Child* – edit piece included Lennon on harmonica solo

**Notes**

*Hold Me Tight* and *Don't Bother Me* were recorded for a second time in this session. The original version of *Hold Me Tight* was recorded during the February 11th *Please Please Me* album session but that version went unreleased and no tape of the version exists.

**Sources -** Everett, Walter (1). p. 187. / Lewisohn, Mark (1). pp. 24, 36. / Ryan, Kevin and Brian Kehew. pp. 359, 360. / The Beatles. "*Don't Bother Me (take 10)*". Rec.12 September 1963. The Beatles. FLAC audio file. / The Beatles. "*Don't Bother Me (take 11)*". Rec.12 September 1963. The Beatles. FLAC audio file. / The Beatles. "*Don't Bother Me (take 12)*". Rec.12 September 1963. The Beatles. FLAC audio file. / The Beatles. "*Don't Bother Me (take 13)*". Rec.12 September 1963. The Beatles. FLAC audio file. / The Beatles. "*Don't Bother Me*". Rec.12 September 1963. The Beatles. FLAC audio file. / The Beatles. "*Hold Me Tight (rehearsal)*". Rec.12 September 1963. The Beatles. FLAC audio file. / The Beatles. "*Hold Me Tight (take 20)*". Rec.12 September 1963. The Beatles. FLAC audio file. / The Beatles. "*Hold Me Tight (take 21 called take 23)*". Rec.12 September 1963. The Beatles. FLAC audio file. / The Beatles. "*Hold Me Tight (take 22)*". Rec.12 September 1963. The Beatles. FLAC audio file. / The Beatles. "*Hold Me Tight (take 23)*". Rec.12 September 1963. The Beatles. FLAC audio file. / The Beatles. "*Hold Me Tight (take 24)*". Rec.12 September 1963. The Beatles. FLAC audio file. / The Beatles. "*Hold Me Tight (take 25)*". Rec.12 September 1963. The Beatles. FLAC audio file. / The Beatles. "*Hold Me Tight (take 26 and rehearsal)*". Rec.12 September 1963. The Beatles. FLAC audio file. / The Beatles. "*Hold Me Tight (take 27)*". Rec.12 September 1963. The Beatles.

FLAC audio file. / The Beatles. "*Hold Me Tight (take 28)*". Rec.12 September 1963. The Beatles. FLAC audio file. / The Beatles. "*Hold Me Tight (take 29)*". Rec.12 September 1963. The Beatles. FLAC audio file. / The Beatles. "*Hold Me Tight*". Rec.12 September 1963. The Beatles. FLAC audio file. / The Beatles. "*I Wanna Be Your Man*". Rec. 12, 30 September; 3, 23 October 1963. The Beatles. FLAC audio file. / The Beatles. "*Little Child*". Rec.12 September 1963. The Beatles. FLAC audio file. / Winn, John C. (3). pp. 16, 17.

# September 30, 1963

**Time**
10AM - 115PM

**Studio name and room**
EMI Recording Studios
Studio 2 (control room)

**Songs recorded (composer) (activities)**

- *Little Child* (Lennon and McCartney)
    - edit of takes 15 and 18
- *Hold Me Tight* (Lennon and McCartney)
    - edit of takes 26 and 29
- *Money (That's What I Want)* (mono)
    - remix (RM) 7 (versions 1-3) from the edit of takes 6 and 7 with simultaneous superimposition (see Notes)
- *I Wanna Be Your Man* (Lennon and McCartney)
    - superimposition takes 8-13 (see Songs mixed and Notes)

**Songs mixed (version) (remix number and take)**

- *All I've Got To Do* (mono)
    - remix (RM) 15 from take 15
- *Don't Bother Me* (mono)
    - remix (RM) 15 from take 15
- *Little Child* (mono)
    - unnumbered remix (RM) from edit of takes 15 and 18
- *I Wanna Be Your Man* (mono)
    - remix (RM) takes 8-13 from take 7 with simultaneous superimposition
- *Hold Me Tight* (mono)
    - remix (RM) 26 + (RM) 29 from edit of takes 26 and 29
- *Not A Second Time* (mono)
    - remix (RM) 9 from take 9
- *Money (That's What I Want)* (mono)
    - remix (RM) 7 (versions 1-3) from the edit of takes 6 and 7 with simultaneous superimposition (see Notes)

**Studio Personnel**

- Producer: George Martin
- Balance engineer: Norman Smith
- Tape operator: Geoff Emerick

**Other musicians (instruments played)**

- George Martin (piano, organ)

**Instruments**

**Pianos and keyboards**

- Steinway "Music Room" Model B Grand Piano (circa 1880s)
- Hammond RT3 Organ (circa 1954-62)

**Other**

- Hammond PR-40 tone cabinet

**Recording equipment**

*Recording console*

- REDD.37

*Primary tracking machine*

- TWIN-TRACK: 1/4" EMI BTR3

*Mixdown machine*

- MONO: 1/4" EMI BTR2

*Outboard signal processors*

- EMI RS114 Limiter
- EMI RS124 Altec Compressor
- EMI RS127 Presence Box
- EMI RS144 4-Way Mixer/Premix
- EMI RS92 Neumann Mic Equaliser

*Effects*

- Echo chamber (includes RS61 Low Level Amplifier with RS62 Power Supply and RS106A Echo Control Unit – Band Pass Filter)
- STEED (send tape echo/echo delay)

*Monitors*

Control room

- Altec 605A (Altec 612 Cabinet) with EMI RS141 Leak TL/25 Plus Amplifier

Studio

- RLS10 - "White Elephant"

Piano

- Neumann U48 or U47/48 (U47/8)

Other

- Neumann U48, U47/48 (U47/8)
- STC 4038

**Superimpositions**

- *Money (That's What I Want)* – superimposition included George Martin on piano (see Notes)
- *I Wanna Be Your Man* – superimposition included George Martin on organ (see Notes)

**Remixes**

Mono master remixes

- *All I've Got To Do* (mono) (remix (RM) 15 from take 15)
- *Don't Bother Me* (mono) (remix (RM) 15 from take 15)
- *Not A Second Time* (mono) (remix (RM) 9 from take 9)

**Notes**

George Martin's additional piano superimpositions on *Money (That's What I Want)* were done simultaneously with the mono remixes from the edit of takes 6 and 7. The previous remix of the same song completed on August 21st was considered superior and served as the master mono remix of the track.

Interestingly, the mono remixes of *I Wanna Be Your Man* with Martin's simultaneous superimposition of organ were numbered as takes 8-13, as opposed to RM 8-13. It was common during this period for the remix number (RM or RS number) to coincide with the take number from which it was derived. None of these remixes were released.

**Sources -** Everett, Walter (1). p. 188. / Lewisohn, Mark (1). p. 36. / Winn, John C. (3). p. 18.

# October 3, 1963

**Time**
7PM - 10PM

**Studio name and room**
EMI Recording Studios
Studio 2

**Songs recorded (composer) (activities)**

- *I Wanna Be Your Man* (Lennon and McCartney)
    - superimposition takes 14 and 15
- *Little Child* (Lennon and McCartney)
    - superimposition takes 19-21

**Studio Personnel**

- Producer: George Martin
- Balance engineer: Norman Smith
- Tape operator: Unknown

**Musicians (instruments played)**

- John Lennon (vocals)
- Paul McCartney (vocals)
- Ringo Starr (vocals, maracas)

**Other musicians (instruments played)**

- George Martin (organ)

**Instruments**

**Pianos and keyboards**

- Steinway "Music Room" Model B Grand Piano (circa 1880s)
- Hammond RT3 Organ (circa 1954-62)

**Percussion**

- Maracas

**Other**

- Hammond PR-40 tone cabinet

**Recording equipment**

*Recording console*

- REDD.37

*Primary tracking machine*

- TWIN TRACK: 1/4" EMI BTR3

*Outboard signal processors*

- EMI RS114 Limiter
- EMI RS124 Altec Compressor
- EMI RS127 Presence Box
- EMI RS144 4-Way Mixer/Premix
- EMI RS92 Neumann Mic Equaliser

*Effects*

- Echo chamber (includes RS61 Low Level Amplifier with RS62 Power Supply and RS106A Echo Control Unit – Band Pass Filter)
- STEED (send tape echo/echo delay)

*Monitors*

Control room

- Altec 605A (Altec 612 Cabinet) with EMI RS141 Leak TL/25 Plus Amplifier

Studio

- RLS10 - "White Elephant"

*Microphones*

Vocals

- Neumann U48 or U47/48 (U47/8)

Other

- Neumann U48, U47/48 (U47/8)
- STC 4038

**Superimpositions**

- *I Wanna Be Your Man* – superimposition included Starr on double-tracked lead vocals and maracas; Lennon and McCartney on backing vocals; Martin on organ
- *Little Child* – superimposition included Lennon on double-tracked lead vocals

**Sources -** Lewisohn, Mark (1). p. 36. / Winn, John C. (3). p. 18.

# October 17, 1963

**Time**
230PM – 10PM

**Studio name and room**
EMI Recording Studios
Studio 2

- 230PM - 530PM
- 530PM - 10PM

**Songs recorded (composer) (activities)**

- *The Beatles Christmas Record* (Various messages (speech))
    - unnumbered takes
- *You Really Got A Hold On Me* (Robinson)
    - take 12 (see Notes)
- *Another message* (speech)
- *I Want To Hold Your Hand* (Lennon and McCartney)
    - takes 1-17
    - superimposition to take 17
- *This Boy* (Lennon and McCartney)
    - takes 1-15
    - superimposition takes 16-17
    - edit of takes 15 and 17

**Studio Personnel**

- Producer: George Martin
- Balance engineer: Norman Smith
- Tape operator: Geoff Emerick

**Musicians (instruments played)**

- John Lennon (guitar, vocals)
- Paul McCartney (bass, vocals)
- George Harrison (guitar, vocals)
- Ringo Starr (drums)

## Instruments

### Electric guitars

*Lennon*

- 1958 Rickenbacker 325 Capri with Bigsby B5 vibrato (first model – repainted black)

*Harrison*

- 1962 Rickenbacker 425
- 1962 Gretsch 6122 Chet Atkins Country Gentleman with Gretsch Bigsby B6G vibrato

### Acoustic guitars

*Lennon/Harrison*

- 1962 Gibson J-160E

### Bass guitars

*McCartney*

- 1962-1963 Hofner 500/1

### Drums

*Starr*

- 1963 Ludwig Oyster Black Pearl Downbeat (14" X 20" bass drum/ 8" X 12" rack tom/ 14" X 14" floor tom/ 14" X 5.5" Jazz Festival snare); Paiste, Zyn, Zildjian cymbals (20" ride/ 20" ride with 4-rivet "sizzle"/ 18" crash) Zildjian cymbals (14" model A hi-hats) (Ludwig Set 1)

## Amplifiers

### Guitar

*Lennon/Harrison*

- 1963 JMI Vox AC30/6 Twin Treble with "Top Boost" circuit, 30W with two 12" Vox Celestion Alnico Gray G12 T530 speakers

### Bass

*McCartney*

- 1963 Vox AC30 head, 30W with Vox T60 speaker cabinet, with one 12", and one 15" Vox Celestion Alinco Blue speakers

## Recording equipment

*Recording console*

- REDD.37

Primary tracking machine

- TWIN-TRACK: 1/4" EMI BTR3
- FOUR-TRACK: 1" Telefunken M10

*Outboard signal processors*

- EMI RS114 Limiter
- EMI RS124 Altec Compressor
- EMI RS127 Presence Box
- EMI RS144 4-Way Mixer/Premix
- EMI RS92 Neumann Mic Equaliser

*Effects*

- Echo chamber (includes RS61 Low Level Amplifier with RS62 Power Supply and RS106A Echo Control Unit – Band Pass Filter)
- STEED (send tape echo/echo delay)

*Monitors*

Control room

- Altec 605A (Altec 612 Cabinet) with EMI RS141 Leak TL/25 Plus Amplifier

Studio

- RLS10 - "White Elephant"

*Microphones*

Vocals

- Neumann U48 or U47/48 (U47/8)

Electric guitar amplifiers

- Neumann U48, U47/48 (U47/8)
- Neumann KM54

Acoustic guitars

- Neumann U48 or U47/48 (U47/8)

Bass amplifier

- STC 4033-A

Drums

- Overhead - STC 4038
- Bass drum - STC 4033-A

Other

- Neumann U48, U47/48 (U47/8)
- STC 4038

**Backing Tracks**

- *I Want To Hold Your Hand* – backing track included Lennon on acoustic guitar and lead vocals; McCartney on bass and lead vocals; Harrison on guitar; Starr on drums
- *This Boy* – backing track included Lennon on acoustic guitar and lead vocals; McCartney on bass and lead vocals; Harrison on guitar and lead vocals; Starr on drums

**Superimpositions**

- *I Want To Hold Your Hand* – superimpositions included Harrison on guitar; Lennon and McCartney on backing vocals and handclaps
- *This Boy* – superimpositions included Lennon on double-tracked lead vocals; McCartney and Harrison on double-tracked backing vocals; Harrison on lead guitar

**Notes**

It is not known what work occurred on *You Really Got Hold On Me* during this session. Take 12 exists on a twin-track tape between recordings made for the annual Christmas fan club flexi-disc.

Everett notes Harrison superimposed a bass part on *I Want To Hold Your Hand* during this session. However, examination of both the

1963 and 1966 remixes do not reveal any additional bass performance. It is likely those such as Everett noting a bass part are actually referring to the baritone figure Harrison plays between stanzas of the verse (e.g., after the words, "...I think you'll understand.").

Emerick writes that the middle section of *This Boy* is actually an edit piece, and that initially Harrison performed a guitar solo during the middle eight of the song. Lewisohn also notes that the original tapes reveal a version of the song with a guitar solo in place. However, take 13 demonstrates the entire song in the same form as the final version (without an edit).

*This Boy* was edited during the session (an edit of takes 15 and 17), though the joining of two takes is not the same thing as the insertion of an edit piece. Edit pieces were typically parts of the song that needed improvement and were specifically noted by the engineers as such in their slating and documentation. It is entirely possible that one of the original takes, or takes 15 or 17 *did* contain a guitar solo that simply didn't make the cut.

With the recording of *I Want To Hold Your Hand*, The Beatles began using four-track primary tracking machines that would last until well into *The Beatles (The White Album)* and even for the initial work on the *Abbey Road* track, *Come Together*.

Two different four-tracks were present at EMI Recording Studios in 1963: the 1" Telefunken T9u and 1" Telefunken M10. According to an author interview with EMI engineer Richard Langham, the Telefunken T9u four-track was not used for primary tracking within the studio. It was instead used for remote sessions. A T9u installed within the studio was likely used for playback of these remote sessions. This unit was moved to Room 65 in mid-1965 where it remained until 1967, when replaced by a Studer J-37 four-track.

The Telefunken M10 was the machine that was used for recordings in the main three studios at EMI until the arrival of the Studer J-37 in 1965. The M10 and Studer J-37 shared duties in Studios 1 and 3 from mid-1965 until end of *Rubber Soul* sessions.

The M10 was replaced by the Studer J-37 for all studios post-*Rubber Soul*.

Assignments of primary tracking machines in this book reflect this timeline of application.

**Sources -** Emerick, Geoff. pp. 71-72, 75. / Everett, Walter (1). p. 198. / Lewisohn, Mark (1). p. 36. / Ryan, Kevin and Brian Kehew. pp. 220, 221. / The Beatles. "*I Want To Hold Your Hand (1966)*". Rec.17 October 1963. Mix. November 1963. The Beatles. FLAC audio file. / The Beatles. "*I Want To Hold Your Hand (RS1)*". Rec.17 October 1963. Mix. 21 October 1963. The Beatles. FLAC audio file. / The Beatles. "*I Want To Hold Your Hand (take 1)*". Rec.17 October 1963. The Beatles. FLAC audio file. / The Beatles. "*I Want To Hold Your Hand (take 2)*". Rec.17 October 1963. The Beatles. FLAC audio file. / The Beatles. "*I Want To Hold Your Hand (take 4)*". Rec.17 October 1963. The Beatles. FLAC audio file. / The Beatles. "*I Want To Hold Your Hand (take 9)*". Rec.17 October 1963. The Beatles. FLAC audio file. / The Beatles. "*I Want To Hold Your Hand (unknown take)*". Rec.17 October 1963. The Beatles. FLAC audio file. / The Beatles. "*I Want To Hold Your Hand*". Rec.17 October 1963. The Beatles. FLAC audio file. / The Beatles. "*This Boy (RS15)*". Rec.17 October 1963. The Beatles. FLAC audio file. /The Beatles. "*This Boy (take 2)*". Rec.17 October 1963. The Beatles. FLAC audio file. / The Beatles. "*This Boy (take 12)*". Rec.17 October 1963.

The Beatles. FLAC audio file. / The Beatles. "*This Boy (take 13)*". Rec.17 October 1963. The Beatles. FLAC audio file. / The Beatles. "*This Boy (take 15)*". Rec.17 October 1963. The Beatles. FLAC audio file. / The Beatles. "*This Boy (unknown take)*". Rec.17 October 1963. The Beatles. FLAC audio file. / Winn, John C. (3). pp. 19, 20.

# October 21, 1963

**Time**
10AM - 1PM

**Studio name and room**
EMI Recording Studios
Studio 1 (control room)

**Songs recorded (composer) (activities)**

- *This Boy* (Lennon and McCartney)
  - edit of remix mono (RM) 1 and 2

**Songs mixed (version) (remix number and take)**

- *I Want To Hold Your Hand* (mono)
  - remix (RM) 1 from take 17
- *This Boy* (mono)
  - remix (RM) 1 and 2 from edit of takes 15 and 17
- *I Want To Hold Your Hand* (stereo)
  - remix (RS) 17 from take 17
- *This Boy* (stereo)
  - remix (RS) 15 from edit of takes 15 and 17

**Studio Personnel**

- Producer: George Martin
- Balance engineer: Norman Smith
- Tape operator: Unknown

**Recording equipment**

*Recording console*

- REDD.37

*Primary tracking machine*

- FOUR-TRACK: 1" Telefunken M10

*Mixdown machine*

- MONO: 1/4" EMI BTR2
- STEREO: 1/4" EMI BTR3

*Outboard signal processors*

- EMI RS114 Limiter
- EMI RS124 Altec Compressor
- EMI RS127 Presence Box
- EMI RS144 4-Way Mixer/Premix
- EMI RS92 Neumann Mic Equaliser

*Effects*

- Echo chamber (includes RS61 Low Level Amplifier with RS62 Power Supply and RS106A Echo Control Unit – Band Pass Filter)
- STEED (send tape echo/echo delay)

*Monitors*

Control room

- Altec 605A (Altec 612 Cabinet) with EMI RS141 Leak TL/25 Plus Amplifier

**Remixes**

Mono master remixes

- *I Want To Hold Your Hand* (mono) (remix (RM) 1 from take 17)
- *This Boy* (mono) (remix (RM) from edit of RM1 and 2)

Stereo master remixes

- *I Want To Hold Your Hand* (stereo) (remix (RS) 17 from take 17)
- *This Boy* (stereo) (remix (RS) 15 from edit of takes 15 and 17)

**Sources**

- Lewisohn, Mark (1). p. 37. / Winn, John C. (3). p. 21.

# October 23, 1963

**Time**
10AM - 1PM

**Studio name and room**
EMI Recording Studios
Studio 2

**Songs recorded (composer) (activities)**

- *I Wanna Be Your Man* (Lennon and McCartney)
  - superimposition take 16

**Songs mixed (version) (remix number and take)**

- *I Wanna Be Your Man* (mono)
  - remix (RM) 16 from take 16
- *Little Child* (mono)
  - remix (RM) 21 from take 21
- *Hold Me Tight* (mono)
  - remix (RM) 26 from edit of takes 26 and 29

**Studio Personnel**

- Producer: George Martin
- Balance engineer: Norman Smith
- Tape operator: Unknown

**Musicians (instruments played)**

- Ringo Starr (percussion)

**Instruments**

**Percussion**

- Tambourine (Olympic or Ludwig)

**Recording equipment**

*Recording console*

- REDD.37

*Primary tracking machine*

- TWIN-TRACK: 1/4" EMI BTR3
- FOUR-TRACK: 1" Telefunken M10

*Mixdown machine*

- MONO: 1/4" EMI BTR2

*Outboard signal processors*

- EMI RS114 Limiter
- EMI RS124 Altec Compressor
- EMI RS127 Presence Box
- EMI RS144 4-Way Mixer/Premix
- EMI RS92 Neumann Mic Equaliser

*Effects*

- Echo chamber (includes RS61 Low Level Amplifier with RS62 Power Supply and RS106A Echo Control Unit – Band Pass Filter)
- STEED (send tape echo/echo delay)

*Monitors*

Control room

- Altec 605A (Altec 612 Cabinet) with EMI RS141 Leak TL/25 Plus Amplifier

Studio

- RLS10 - "White Elephant"

*Microphones*

Other

- Neumann U48 or U47/48 (U47/8)

**Superimpositions**

- *I Wanna Be Your Man* – superimposition included Starr on tambourine

**Mono master remixes**

- *I Wanna Be Your Man* (mono) remix (RM) 16 from take 16
- *Little Child* (mono) remix (RM) 21 from takes21
- *Hold Me Tight* (mono) remix (RM) 26 from edit of takes 26 and 29

**Sources -** Lewisohn, Mark (1). p. 37. / The Beatles. "*I Wanna Be Your Man*". Rec.11, 12, 30 September; 3, 23 October 1963. The Beatles. FLAC audio file. / Winn, John C. (3). p. 21.

# October 29, 1963

**Time**
10AM - 1PM

**Studio name and room**
EMI Recording Studios
Studio 3 (control room)

**Songs mixed (version) (remix number and take)**

- *It Won't Be Long* (stereo)
  - remix (RS) 17 from edit of takes 17 and 21
- *All I've Got To Do* (stereo)
  - remix (RS) 15 from take 15
- *All My Loving* (stereo)
  - remix (RS) 14 from take 14
- *Don't Bother Me* (stereo)
  - remix (RS) 15 from take 15
- *Little Child* (stereo)
  - remix (RS) 21 from take 21
- *Till There Was You* (stereo)
  - remix (RS) 8 from take 8
- *Please Mister Postman* (stereo)
  - remix (RS) 9 from take 9

- *Roll Over Beethoven* (stereo)
    - remix (RS) 7/8 from edit of takes 7 and 8
- *Hold Me Tight* (stereo)
    - remix (RS) 29 from edit of takes 26 and 29
- *You Really Got A Hold On Me* (stereo)
    - remix (RS) 7/10/11 from edit of takes 7, 10 and 11
- *I Wanna Be Your Man* (stereo)
    - remix (RS) 16 from take 16
- *Devil In Her Heart* (stereo)
    - remix (RS) 6 from take 6
- *Not A Second Time* (stereo)
    - remix (RS) 9 from take 9
- *Money (That's What I Want)* (stereo)
    - remix (RS) 7 from edit of takes 6 and 7

**Studio Personnel**

- Producer: George Martin
- Balance engineer: Norman Smith
- Tape operator(s): Geoff Emerick, B.T. (name unknown)

**Recording equipment**

*Recording console*

- REDD.51

*Primary tracking machine*

- TWIN-TRACK: 1/4" EMI BTR3
- FOUR-TRACK: 1" Telefunken M10

*Mixdown machine*

- STEREO: 1/4" EMI BTR3

*Outboard signal processors*

- EMI RS114 Limiter
- EMI RS124 Altec Compressor
- EMI RS127 Presence Box
- EMI RS144 4-Way Mixer/Premix
- EMI RS92 Neumann Mic Equaliser

*Effects*

- Echo chamber (includes RS61 Low Level Amplifier with RS62 Power Supply and RS106A Echo Control Unit – Band Pass Filter)
- STEED (send tape echo/echo delay)

*Monitors*

Control room

- Altec 605A (Altec 612 Cabinet) with EMI RS141 Leak TL/25 Plus Amplifier

**Remixes**

Stereo master remixes

- *It Won't Be Long* (stereo) (remix (RS) 17 from edit of takes 17 and 21)
- *All I've Got To Do* (stereo) (remix (RS) 15 from take 15)
- *All My Loving* (stereo) (remix (RS) 14 from take 14)
- *Don't Bother Me* (stereo) (remix (RS) 15 from take 15)
- *Little Child* (stereo) (remix (RS) 21 from take 21)
- *Till There Was You* (stereo) (remix (RS) 8 from take 8)
- *Please Mister Postman* (stereo) (remix (RS) 9 from take 9)

- *Roll Over Beethoven* (stereo) (remix (RS) 7/8 from edit of takes 7 and 8)
- *Hold Me Tight* (stereo) (remix (RS) 29 from edit of takes 26 and 29)
- *You Really Got A Hold On Me* (stereo) (remix (RS) 7/10/11 from edit of takes 7, 10 and 11)
- *I Wanna Be Your Man* (stereo) (remix (RS) 16 from take 16)
- *Devil In Her Heart* (stereo) (remix (RS) 6 from take 6)
- *Not A Second Time* (stereo) (remix (RS) 9 from take 9)

**Sources -** Lewisohn, Mark (1). p. 37. / Winn, John C. (3). p. 22.

# October 30, 1963

**Time**
230PM - 530PM

**Studio name and room**
EMI Recording Studios
Studio 3 (control room)

**Songs mixed (version) (remix number and take)**

- *Money (That's What I Want)* (stereo)
    - remix (RS) 7 from take 7

**Studio Personnel**

- Producer: George Martin
- Balance engineer: Norman Smith
- Tape operator: Anthony (Tony) Bridge

**Recording equipment**

*Recording console*

- REDD.51

*Primary tracking machine*

- TWIN-TRACK: 1/4" EMI BTR3

*Mixdown machine*

- STEREO: 1/4" EMI BTR3

*Outboard signal processors*

- EMI RS114 Limiter
- EMI RS127 Presence Box
- EMI RS144 4-Way Mixer/Premix EMI RS124 Altec Compressor
- EMI RS92 Neumann Mic Equaliser

*Effects*

- Echo chamber (includes RS61 Low Level Amplifier with RS62 Power Supply and RS106A Echo Control Unit – Band Pass Filter)
- STEED (send tape echo/echo delay)

*Monitors*

Control room

- Altec 605A (Altec 612 Cabinet) with EMI RS141 Leak TL/25 Plus Amplifier

## Remixes

Stereo master remixes

- *Money (That's What I Want)* (stereo) (remix (RS) 7 from take 7)

## Notes

The tape operator or second engineer role for this session has previously been credited by Lewisohn (and replicated extensively elsewhere) to an A.B. Lincoln. An author interview with engineer Richard Langham revealed that this credit was in error.

Lewisohn utilized EMI Recording Studios "Recording Sheets" which were used to track information about the sessions, including which engineers worked particular sessions, often expressed only by initials. This session credited an engineer with the initials "AB" (along with "NS", for Norman Smith).

According to Langham, "AB" actually refers to Anthony (Tony) Bridge, who is credited in this session and throughout this book wherever A.B. Lincoln was previously credited. An A.B. Lincoln did work for EMI Recording Studios; however, Langham recalls that he had left the studios prior to the time The Beatles started their tenure there.

**Sources -** Author interview. *Richard Langham*. Pelham, Ontario. 23 March 2013. / Lewisohn, Mark (1). p. 37. / Winn, John C. (3). p. 22.

# 1964 Recording Studios

## EMI Recording Studios

**Location**
London, England
3 Abbey Road
London NW8 9AY

**Studio name and room(s)**

EMI Recording Studios

- Studio 1
- Studio 2
- Studio 3

**Studio Personnel**

- Producer: George Martin
- Balance engineer: Norman Smith
- Tape operators: Richard Langham, Chris Neal, Geoff Emerick, Anthony (Tony) Bridge, Ken Scott, Ron Pender, Mike Stone

**Studio instrumentation**

*Percussion*

- Chocalho
- Claves
- ASBA congas
- Ludwig Clear Tone cowbell
- Ludwig Expando bongos
- Doumbek
- Ludwig Timpani
- Maracas
- Paiste cymbals
- Premier bongos
- Tambourine (Olympic or Ludwig)

*Pianos and keyboards*

- Steinway "Music Room" Model B Grand Piano (circa 1880s)
- 1905 Steinway Vertegrand (the "Mrs. Mills" upright piano) (#115519)
- Mannborg harmonium
- Challen Studio Piano (circa 1930s) (#861834 – Studio 2)
- Challen Studio Piano (circa 1930s) (Studio 3)
- Hammond RT3 Organ (circa 1954-1962)

*Other*

- Hammond PR-40 tone cabinet
- Leslie 122 speaker cabinet
- Leslie 147 speaker cabinet

**Recording equipment**

*Recording console*

- Studio 1 - REDD.37
- Studio 2 - REDD.51
- Studio 3 - REDD.51

*Primary tracking machine*

- FOUR-TRACK: 1" Telefunken T9u
- FOUR-TRACK: 1" Telefunken M10

*Mixdown machine*

- MONO: 1/4" EMI BTR2
- STEREO: 1/4" EMI BTR3
- MONO Tape Copying: ¼" Lyrec TR4

*Outboard signal processors*

- EMI RS106A Echo Control Unit – Band Pass Filter
- EMI RS114 Limiter
- EMI RS124 Altec Compressor
- EMI RS127 Presence Box
- EMI RS144 4-Way Mixer/Premix
- EMI RS158 Fairchild 666 Compressor
- EMI RS92 Neumann Mic Equaliser
- Fairchild 660 Limiter
- Plug-in EQ Boxes

*Effects*

- Echo chamber (includes RS61 Low Level Amplifier with RS62 Power Supply and RS106A Echo Control Unit – Band Pass Filter)
- Half-speed recording
- STEED (send tape echo/echo delay)

*Monitors*

Control room

- Altec 605A (Altec 612 Cabinet) with EMI RS141 Leak TL/25 Plus Amplifier

Studio

- RLS10 - "White Elephant"

*Microphones*

Vocals

- Neumann U48 or U47/48 (U47/8)

Electric guitar amplifiers

- Neumann U48, U47/48 (U47/8)
- Neumann KM54

Acoustic guitars

- Neumann U48 or U47/48 (U47/8)

Bass amplifier

- STC 4033-A (through June 1964)
- AKG D20 (after June 1964)

Drums

- Overhead - STC 4038
- Bass drum - STC 4033-A or AKG D20

- Overhead – AKG 19c
- Bass drum - AKG D20 (after June 1964)

Piano

- Neumann U48 or U47/48 (U47/8)

Other

- Neumann U48, U47/48 (U47/8)
- STC 4038

**Notes on studio equipment background, assignments, and applications**

In 1964, The Beatles' recordings for Parlophone at EMI Recording Studios were made on four-track Telefunken M10 primary tracking machines.

EMI Recording Studios' Record Engineering and Development Department (REDD) consoles were beautiful sounding, vacuum tube-based units. Technologically limited, they employed both fixed and variable-pan channels and limited desk inputs (10) and outputs (4) supplemented on the input side by EMI RS144 4-Way Mixer/Premix units. These consoles (in two iterations, the REDD.37 and REDD.51) served The Beatles for their entire career at EMI Recording Studios.

The EMI RS158 Fairchild 666 Compressor was available to engineers as of 1963. There is no direct evidence of their use on Beatles sessions during this period.

The EMI RS92 Neumann Mic Equaliser was used specifically with Neumann U47, U49 and U50 microphones to cut or boost certain frequencies. This capability was also found to be very useful by EMI engineers in relation to the studio's echo chambers and EMT plate reverbs. It is included in listings whenever those specific microphones are in use, as well as when echo chambers or the EMT reverbs are in use.

According to Ryan and Kehew, the EMI RS114 Limiter was not used in 1964 sessions after Fairchild 660 came into full use on *Beatles For Sale.*

Plug-in EQ Boxes were available to engineers at all EMI Recording Studios sessions, though specific boxes cannot be accurately assigned to any one session. Because of this, they are omitted from specific session listings.

The assignment of STEED (send tape echo/echo delay) occurs whenever an echo chamber is in use. According to Ryan and Kehew, the effect was commonly used to thicken the echo produced.

There were three echo chambers at EMI, two within the studios (Chamber 1, which was created for use with Studio 3, Chamber 2, which was used with Studio 2) and one chamber of the roof of the facility (Chamber 3, which was used with Studio 1). While designed with the needs of a certain studio in mind, any of the chambers could be used with any of the studios through the Siemens patch bay system. Therefore, echo chamber numbers are not specifically assigned to sessions in specific studios.

Echo chamber, tape echo/ repeat echo effects and half-speed recording effects continued to be employed on Beatles tracks during this period.

Norman Smith had previously recorded the echo chamber directly to tape when tracking, but as of 1964, he began to employ the effect at the remix stage instead, save for when multiple instruments were being recorded, as was the case with some backing tracks.

Vocals continued to be recorded using the Neumann U48 or U47/48 (U47/8) microphones.

In recording electric guitar amplifiers, Norman Smith-engineered sessions in 1964 utilized a combination of Neumann U48, U47/48 (U47/8) and Neumann KM54 microphones. As The Beatles had progressed to different amplifiers at this point, it was no longer as critical to differentiate microphones between the cabinets in order to achieve unique tones between the electric guitar performances.

The Neumann U48, U47/48 (U47/8) microphones' primary application in context of The Beatles' recordings were for vocals, acoustic guitars and amplifiers, though along with the STC 4038 they were also studio workhorses employed for everything from capturing orchestral parts to percussion and keyboard cabinets (like the Hammond PR-40 tone cabinet or Leslie speaker cabinets).

One change occurred in the middle of 1964 related to the mic'ing of Starr's Ludwig drum set. The STC 4038 used for overhead mic'ing was replaced by an AKG 19c, while the bass drum microphone, previously an STC 4033-A, was changed to a AKG D20 in September.

Among studio instrumentation that included numerous keyboards and percussion options, the Steinway "Music Room" Model B Grand Piano (one in both Studios 2 and 3) and Studio 2's Hammond RT3 Organ would play the largest roles in The Beatles' recording career, finding a place on virtually every album they recorded.

A complete list of all sources utilized for the identification and assignment of studio equipment is available in the Bibliography.

---

# Other studios

# EMI Pathe' Marconi Studios

**Location**
Paris, France
62 Rue De Sevres, Boulogne-sue-Seine
Paris 92

**Studio name and room**

EMI Pathe' Marconi Studios

**Studio Personnel**

- Producer: George Martin
- Balance engineer: Norman Smith
- Tape operator: Jacques Esmenjaud

**Recording equipment**

*Recording console*

- CLG Four Track

*Primary tracking machine*

- TWIN-TRACK: 1/4" EMI BTR3

- FOUR-TRACK: 1" Telefunken T9u or 1" Telefunken M10

*Mixdown machine*

- STEREO: 1" Telefunken T9u or 1" Telefunken M10

*Outboard signal processors*

- Custom-built processing equipment
- RS106A Echo Control Unit – Band Pass Filter
- EMI RS124 Altec Compressor
- EMI RS144 4-Way Mixer/Premix

*Effects*

- Unknown

*Monitors*

Control room

- Unknown

Studio

- Unknown

*Microphones*

Vocals

- Neumann U48 or U47/48 (U47/8)

Electric guitar amplifiers

- Neumann U47
- Neumann U48

Acoustic guitars

- Neumann U47
- Neumann U48

Bass amplifier

- Neumann U47
- Neumann U48

Drums

- Neumann U47
- Neumann U48

Other

- Neumann U47
- Neumann U48
- Neumann U67
- Neumann M49

**Notes on studio equipment background, assignments, and applications**

Only one session in January 1964 was recorded at EMI Pathe' Marconi Studios. The majority of the studio's technical details during this period are unknown.

# 1964

# Instruments and amplification

---

## Electric guitars

*Lennon*

- 1958 Rickenbacker 325 Capri with Bigsby B5 vibrato (first model – repainted black)
- 1964 Rickenbacker 325 Capri (second model – Black)
- 1964 Rickenbacker 1996

*Harrison*

- 1963 Gretsch PX6122 Chet Atkins Country Gentleman with Gretsch Bigsby B6G vibrato
- 1963 Gretsch 6119 Chet Atkins Tennessean with Gretsch Bigsby vibrato
- 1963 Rickenbacker 360-12 (12-string)

*McCartney*

- 1962 Epiphone ES-230TD, Casino with Selmer Bigsby B7 vibrato (strung left-handed)

## Acoustic guitars

*Lennon*

- 1964 Gibson J-160E
- 1964 Framus Hootenanny 5/024 (12-string)

*Harrison*

- 1962 Gibson J-160E
- Jose Ramirez Guitarra de Estudio (nylon string)
- Jose Ramirez A1 Segovia (nylon string)

*McCartney*

- 1964 Epiphone FT-79, Texan

## Bass guitars

*McCartney*

- 1962-1963 Hofner 500/1

## Drums

*Starr*

- 1963 Ludwig Oyster Black Pearl Downbeat (14" X 20" bass drum/ 8" X 12" rack tom/ 14" X 14" floor tom/ 14" X 5.5" Jazz Festival snare); Paiste, Zyn, Zildjian cymbals (20" ride/ 20" ride with 4-rivet "sizzle"/ 18" crash) Zildjian cymbals (14" model A hi-hats) (Ludwig Set 1) (through January 1964)
- 1964 Ludwig Oyster Black Pearl Downbeat (14" X 20" bass drum/ 8" X 12" rack tom/ 14" X 14" floor

tom/ 14" X 5.5" 1963 Jazz Festival snare); Paiste, Zyn, Zildjian cymbals (20" ride/ 20" ride with 4-rivet "sizzle"/ 18" crash) Zildjian cymbals (14" model A hi-hats) (Ludwig Set 2 – live performance set)

- 1964 Ludwig Oyster Black Pearl "Super Classic" (14" X 22" bass drum/ 9" X 13" rack tom/ 16" X 16" floor tom/ 1963 14" X 5.5" "Jazz Festival" snare); Paiste, Zyn, Zildjian cymbals (20" crash/ride; 20" Zyn 4-rivet "sizzle") Zildjian cymbals (18" crash/ride; 14" model A hi-hats) (Ludwig Set 3) (from June 1964)

**Pianos and keyboards**

- 1964 Hohner Pianet C

**Other**

- Hohner harmonica (Echo Vamper or Super Chromonica)

**Amplifiers**

**Guitar**

*Lennon/Harrison*

- 1963 JMI Vox AC30/6 Twin Treble with "Top Boost" circuit, 30W with two 12" Vox Celestion Alnico Gray G12 T530 speakers
- 1963 JMI Vox AC50 Small Box (Mk. I), 50W with Vox AC50 cabinet, with two 12" Vox Celestion Alnico Blue G12 T530 speakers and Goodmans Midax horn (through July 1964)
- 1964 JMI Vox AC100 Mk I, 100W with Vox AC100 cabinet, 4X12" Vox Celestion Alnico Silver T1088 speakers and 2X Goodmans Midax horns (after July 1964)

**Bass**

*McCartney*

- 1963 Vox AC100, 100W head with Vox AC100 custom cabinet, with two 15" Vox Celestion T1070 speakers

**Pianet**

- 1963 JMI Vox AC30/6 Twin Treble with "Top Boost" circuit, 30W with two 12" Vox Celestion Alnico Gray G12 T530 speakers

**Notes on instrument and amplification background, assignments and applications**

For electric guitars in 1964, Lennon played his 1958 Rickenbacker 325 guitar until February when it was replaced by a nearly identical 1964 Rickenbacker 325 Capri (Black).

Lennon's Gibson J-160E acoustic guitar was lost on November 25, 1963. Until its replacement in September of 1964, Lennon borrowed Harrison's 1962 J-160E for any recording sessions where he played acoustic guitar. He first used the 1964 Framus Hootenanny 5/024 acoustic 12-string on Beatles recordings in 1964.

For electric guitars in 1964, Harrison continued to play his 1963 Gretsch PX6122 Chet Atkins Country Gentleman with Gretsch Bigsby B6G vibrato and 1963 Gretsch 6119

Chet Atkins Tennessean with Gretsch Bigsby vibrato.

In February, he acquired a 1963 Rickenbacker 360-12 (12-string) electric guitar that became a key element in The Beatles' sound during this era.

For acoustic guitars, Harrison added two Jose Ramirez nylon string models; a Guitarra de Estudio and an A1 Segovia. The guitars were played by both Harrison and Lennon.

The Beatles were consistently obtaining updated gear, and Vox was especially eager to capitalize on their relationship with the band by providing the latest amplifiers. Updated guitar amplification comprised a 50-watt 1963 JMI Vox AC50 Small Box (Mk. I), with Vox AC50 cabinet (used through July) and a 100-watt 1964 JMI Vox AC100 Mk I, with Vox AC100 cabinet. The higher wattage amplifiers were not considered ideal by the audio engineers for recording purposes, and lower wattage rigs like the 30-watt 1963 JMI Vox AC30/6 Twin Treble with "Top Boost" introduced in 1963 continued to see use during the year. In addition to guitar amplification, the AC30/6 amplifier was used with the newly acquired 1964 Hohner Pianet C.

McCartney played his 1962-1963 Hofner 500/1 violin bass guitar during 1964.

McCartney brought both a new acoustic and electric guitar to his contributions in 1964. The acoustic guitar was a 1964 Epiphone FT-79, Texan. His new electric guitar was acquired at the end of the year; a 1962 Epiphone ES-230TD, Casino with Selmer Bigsby B7 vibrato (set up left-handed).

McCartney's bass amplifier was a 100-watt 1963 Vox AC100 with Vox AC100 custom cabinet. He had Vox modify the standard AC100 cabinet which originally contained four 12" speakers. In McCartney's customization, it was set up with two 15" Vox Celestion T1070 speakers.

Lennon and Harrison often (though not always) recorded their Gibson J-160E acoustic guitars through an amplifier during this period, though specifically for which performances is unknown. When an amplifier was utilized, an unamplified signal from the acoustic was blended with it. McCartney recalled, "They only used a tiny bit of electric, just for colour. If you turned it up too much you don't get any string noise, so the engineers and George Martin used to strike a balance between the colour of the electric thing and the natural acoustic." Whenever a Gibson J-160E acoustic guitar is assigned in this period, amplification is also assigned.

Starr had access to three Ludwig drum sets during 1964. At the beginning of the year, he continued to use his 1963 Ludwig Oyster Black Pearl Downbeat set (Ludwig Set 1); in February, this kit was supplemented with a 1964 model, virtually identical (Ludwig Set 2). Primarily used for concerts, the kit would appear on the post-career release, *The Beatles At The Hollywood Bowl* (1977). Then in June, he obtained yet another set: A 1964 Oyster Black

Pearl Super Classic set (Ludwig Set 3), this one with a larger bass drum; up to 22" from the 20" bass drum featured on Sets 1 and 2. Set 3 had one other modification identified by Starr's drum curator, Gary Astridge: he used 15" Zildigan model "A" hi-hats with the set at times, as opposed to the 14" version of the same cymbals. It is not known if the change was experimental or if it persisted, as Starr has previously noted he used the same 14" hi-hats for all his work with The Beatles. While this change should be taken into account, specific sessions where the 15" cymbals were used are unknown. For the purposes of this book, the 14" version is cited in association with Starr's work in the recording sessions.

The so-called Ludwig Set 3 remained his predominant set until 1969. At times, Starr would dampen his snare drum with a tea towel (this practise was initiated by Norman Smith in 1963 to thicken the sound of the snare and avoid the sharp sound of the drumstick hitting the rim, with the first photographic evidence of its application dating to September 1964).

Photographic evidence from August 11th, 1964 indicates Starr used a wood, 10" diameter Olympic model tambourine, though it's uncertain that this tambourine was the only one utilized in other 1964 sessions. The Beatles were also known to use Ludwig tambourines in the studio.

A 1964 Hohner Pianet C joined The Beatles' keyboard complement in 1964. This instrument was played by Lennon, McCartney, and Harrison during the year's work, and is evidence of the band branching out to discover new sounds even at this early date. The Pianet was a short scale (five-octave) electric piano played and recorded either through an amplifier or by direct injection.

A complete list of all sources utilized for the identification, specification and assignments of instruments and amplification is available in the Bibliography.

# Sessions

---

# 1964

## January 24, 1964

**Time**
10AM – 1045AM

**Studio name and room**
EMI Recording Studios
Studio 1 (control room)

**Songs recorded (composer) (activities)**

- *I Want To Hold Your Hand* (Lennon and McCartney)
    - tape copying of take 17

**Studio Personnel**

- Producer: N/A
- Balance engineer: Norman Smith
- Tape operator(s): Geoff Emerick, Anthony (Tony) Bridge

**Recording equipment**

*Recording console*

- REDD.37

*Primary tracking machine*

- FOUR-TRACK: 1" Telefunken M10

*Outboard signal processors*

- N/A

*Monitors*

Control room

- Altec 605A (Altec 612 Cabinet) with EMI RS141 Leak TL/25 Plus Amplifier

**Notes**
This tape copy of the backing track only (omitting vocals) was intended for use in France where arrangements had already been made to record German-language versions of both *I Want To Hold Your Hand* and *She Loves You.*

**Sources -** Lewisohn, Mark (1). p. 38.

# *A Hard Day's Night* sessions

## January 29, 1964

**Time**
10AM - 7PM

**Studio name and room**
EMI Pathe' Marconi Studios

**Songs recorded (composer) (activities)**

- *Komm, Gib Mir Deine Hand* (Lennon and McCartney with translation by Jean Nicolas and Heinz Hellmer)
    - takes 1-11
    - edit of takes 5 and 7
    - superimposition onto edit of takes 5 and 7
- *Sie Liebt Dich* (Lennon and McCartney with translation by Jean Nicolas and Lee Montogue)
    - takes 1-13
    - superimposition take 14
- *Can't Buy Me Love* (Lennon and McCartney)
    - takes 1-3

**Studio Personnel**

- Producer: George Martin
- Balance engineer: Norman Smith
- Tape operator: Jacques Esmenjaud

**Musicians (instruments played)**

- John Lennon (guitar, vocals)
- Paul McCartney (bass, vocals)
- George Harrison (guitar, vocals)
- Ringo Starr (drums)

**Instruments**

**Electric guitars**

*Lennon*

- 1958 Rickenbacker 325 Capri with Bigsby B5 vibrato (first model – Natural finish – repainted black)

*Harrison*

- 1963 Gretsch PX6122 Chet Atkins Country Gentleman with Gretsch Bigsby B6G vibrato
- 1963 Gretsch 6119 Chet Atkins Tennessean with Gretsch Bigsby vibrato

**Acoustic guitars**

*Lennon*

- 1962 Gibson J-160E

**Bass guitars**

*McCartney*

- 1962-1963 Hofner 500/1

**Drums**

*Starr*

- 1963 Ludwig Oyster Black Pearl (20" bass drum/ 12" rack tom/ 14" floor tom/ 14" snare); Zildjian cymbals (20" ride with 4-rivet "sizzle"/ 18" crash/ 14" model A hi-hats)

## Amplifiers

**Guitar**

*Lennon/Harrison*

- 1963 JMI Vox AC30/6 Twin Treble with "Top Boost" circuit, 30W with two 12" Vox Celestion Alnico Gray G12 T530 speakers
- 1963 JMI Vox AC50 Small Box (Mk. I), 50W with Vox AC50 cabinet, with two 12" Vox Celestion Alnico Blue G12 T530 speakers and Goodmans Midax horn

**Bass**

- 1963 Vox AC100, 100W head with Vox AC100 custom cabinet, with two 15" Vox Celestion T1070 speakers

## Recording equipment

*Recording console*

- CLG Four Track

*Primary tracking machine*

- TWIN-TRACK: 1/4" EMI BTR3
- FOUR-TRACK: 1" Telefunken T9u or 1" Telefunken M10

*Outboard signal processors*

- Custom-built processing equipment
- EMI RS124 Altec Compressor
- EMI RS144 4-Way Mixer/Premix

*Effects*

- Unknown

*Monitors*

Control room

- Unknown

Studio

- Unknown

*Microphones*

Vocals

- Neumann U48 or U47/48 (U47/8)

Electric guitar amplifiers

- Neumann U47
- Neumann U48

Acoustic guitars

- Neumann U47
- Neumann U48

Bass amplifier

- Neumann U47

- Neumann U48

Drums

- Neumann U47
- Neumann U48

Other

- Neumann U47
- Neumann U48
- Neumann U67
- Neumann M49

**Backing Tracks**

- *Sie Liebt Dich* – backing track included Lennon on guitar; McCartney on bass; Harrison on guitar; Starr on drums
- *Can't Buy Me Love* – backing track included Lennon on acoustic guitar and backing vocals; McCartney on bass and lead vocals; Harrison on guitar and backing vocals; Starr on drums

**Superimpositions**

- *Sie Liebt Dich* – superimposition of Lennon and McCartney on lead vocals; Harrison on backing vocals
- *Komm, Gib Mir Deine Hand* – superimposition of Lennon and McCartney on lead vocals; handclaps

**Notes**

There is little technical information available about the EMI Paris studios. What is known is noted above. Microphone selection is assumed to be standard to EMI Recording Studios.

The Beatles were on tour in Paris on this date and are assumed to be recording with their normally available equipment in this session.

*Komm, Gib Mir Deine Hand* was recorded to twin-track, with the original *I Want To Hold Your Hand* backing track occupying one track of the new tape and the new German-language vocals occupying the other.

As the original tapes for *She Loves You* had been destroyed, an entirely new recording of the German-language version was created from scratch.

Knublauch and Korinth note that while not documented, the two German-language versions of The Beatles' hits must have been mixed at some point during this session or at least prior to their German release on March 6th, 1964. The first record of them within the EMI tape logs dates to March 10th – four days after their public release.

Everett implies some distinct tonal differences between Harrison's 1963 Gretsch PX6122 Chet Atkins Country Gentleman and 1963 Gretsch 6119 Chet Atkins Tennessean that allow the listener to discern one available instrument over the other, though the precise tonal characteristics of amplified instruments are difficult to quantify based on subjective evidence, given the wide variation in tone settings on the guitars themselves, as well as those of the amplifiers.

In sessions through August 12th, 1964, Everett believed Harrison used the Country

Gentleman exclusively, though the Tennessean was available as of this session in Paris having been acquired around Christmas of 1963. Both guitars are considered to have been options for Harrison unless one or the other has been authoritatively identified as being used on a specific song.

**Sources -** Babiuk, Andy (1). pp. 108, 110. / Knublauch, Thorsten and Axel Korinth. pp. 322-325 / Lewisohn, Mark (1). p. 38. / Ryan, Kevin and Brian Kehew. p. 381. / The Beatles. "*Can't Buy Me Love (take 1)*". Rec.29 January 1964. The Beatles. FLAC audio file. / The Beatles. "*Can't Buy Me Love (take 2)*". Rec.29 January 1964. The Beatles. FLAC audio file. / The Beatles. "*Can't Buy Me Love (take 3)*". Rec.29 January 1964. The Beatles. FLAC audio file. / The Beatles. "*Can't Buy Me Love (take 4)*". Rec.29 January 1964. The Beatles. FLAC audio file. / The Beatles. "*Can't Buy Me Love*". Rec.29 January 1964. The Beatles. FLAC audio file. / The Beatles. "*Sie Liebt Dich*". Rec.29 January 1964. The Beatles. FLAC audio file. / Winn, John C. (3). pp. 24, 25.

# February 25, 1964

### Time

10AM – 530PM

### Studio name and room

EMI Recording Studios
Studio 2

- 10AM – 1PM
- 230PM – 530PM

### Songs recorded (composer) (activities)

- *You Can't Do That* (Lennon and McCartney)
  - takes 1-8
  - superimposition take 9
- *And I Love Her* (Lennon and McCartney)
  - takes 1 and 2
- *I Should Have Known Better* (Lennon and McCartney)
  - takes 1-3
- *Can't Buy Me Love* (Lennon and McCartney)
  - take 4

### Studio Personnel

- Producer: George Martin
- Balance engineer: Norman Smith
- Tape operator: Richard Langham

### Musicians (instruments played)

- John Lennon (guitar, harmonica, vocals)
- Paul McCartney (bass, cowbell, vocals)
- George Harrison (guitar, vocals)
- Ringo Starr (drums, bongos)

## Instruments

### Electric guitars

*Lennon*

- 1964 Rickenbacker 325 Capri (second model - Black)

*Harrison*

- 1963 Gretsch PX6122 Chet Atkins Country Gentleman with Gretsch Bigsby B6G vibrato
- 1963 Gretsch 6119 Chet Atkins Tennessean with Gretsch Bigsby vibrato
- 1963 Rickenbacker 360-12 (12-string)

### Acoustic guitars

*Lennon*

- 1962 Gibson J-160E

### Bass guitars

*McCartney*

- 1962-1963 Hofner 500/1

### Drums

*Starr*

- 1963 Ludwig Oyster Black Pearl Downbeat (14" X 20" bass drum/ 8" X 12" rack tom/ 14" X 14" floor tom/ 14" X 5.5" Jazz Festival snare); Paiste, Zyn, Zildjian cymbals (20" ride/ 20" ride with 4-rivet "sizzle"/ 18" crash) Zildjian cymbals (14" model A hi-hats) (Ludwig Set 1)

### Percussion

- Ludwig Expando bongos
- Ludwig Clear Tone cowbell

### Other

- Hohner harmonica (Echo Vamper or Super Chromonica)

## Amplifiers

### Guitar

*Lennon/Harrison*

- 1963 JMI Vox AC30/6 Twin Treble with "Top Boost" circuit, 30W with two 12" Vox Celestion Alnico Gray G12 T530 speakers
- 1963 JMI Vox AC50 Small Box (Mk. I), 50W with Vox AC50 cabinet, with two 12" Vox Celestion Alnico Blue G12 T530 speakers and Goodmans Midax horn

### Bass

*McCartney*

- 1963 Vox AC100, 100W head with Vox AC100 cabinet 2X15" Celestion T1070 speakers

### Recording equipment

*Recording console*

- REDD.51

*Primary tracking machine*

- FOUR-TRACK: 1" Telefunken M10

*Outboard signal processors*

- EMI RS114 Limiter
- EMI RS124 Altec Compressor
- EMI RS127 Presence Box
- EMI RS144 4-Way Mixer/Premix
- EMI RS92 Neumann Mic Equaliser

*Effects*

- Double tracking

*Monitors*

Control room

- Altec 605A (Altec 612 Cabinet) with EMI RS141 Leak TL/25 Plus Amplifier

Studio

- RLS10 - "White Elephant"

*Microphones*

Vocals

- Neumann U48 or U47/48 (U47/8)

Electric guitar amplifiers

- Neumann U48, U47/48 (U47/8)
- Neumann KM54

Acoustic guitars

- Neumann U48 or U47/48 (U47/8)

Bass amplifier

- STC 4033-A

Drums

- Overhead - STC 4038
- Bass drum - STC 4033-A

Other

- Neumann U48, U47/48 (U47/8)

### Backing tracks

- *You Can't Do That* – backing track included Lennon on guitar and lead vocals; McCartney on bass; Harrison on guitar; Starr on drums
- *And I Love Her* – backing track included Lennon on acoustic guitar; McCartney on bass and lead vocals; Harrison on 12-string electric guitar; Starr on drums
- *I Should Have Known Better* – backing track included Lennon on acoustic guitar, harmonica and lead vocals; McCartney on bass; Harrison on nylon string acoustic guitar; Starr on drums

### Superimpositions

- *Can't Buy Me Love* – superimpositions included McCartney on lead vocals; Harrison on guitar

- *You Can't Do That* – superimpositions included Lennon on double-tracked lead vocals; McCartney and Harrison on backing vocals; McCartney on cowbell; Starr on bongos

### Notes

Examination of audio from *Can't Buy Me Love* points to Harrison having double-tracked both the solo and the additional rhythm guitar parts he performed (the rhythm guitar can be heard in the right channel of the stereo remix during the introduction and choruses). The double-tracked rhythm guitar is played in octave modes, giving the impression of a 12-string guitar.

Lennon's 1962 Gibson J-160E was stolen in November 1963. For sessions after this date where he played an acoustic, he utilized Harrison's J-160E. Lennon replaced the guitar in September with a 1964 version of the same model.

Harrison noted in a 1987 interview with *Guitar Player* magazine that Lennon was the lead guitar player on *You Can't Do That.*

**Sources -** Babiuk, Andy (1). p. 102. / Dowlding, William J. p. 77. / Everett, Walter (1). pp. 223, 225. / Everett, Walter (2). p. 13. / Forte, Dan (1). / Lewisohn, Mark (1). pp. 38, 39. / Lewisohn, Mark (2). pp. 147, 148. / Miles, Barry. p. 162. / The Beatles. "*And I Love Her (take 2)*". Rec.25 February 1964. The Beatles. FLAC audio file. / The Beatles. "*You Can't Do That (take 6)*". Rec.25 February 1964. The Beatles. FLAC audio file. / The Beatles. *Anthology (Director's Cut)*. Dir. Bob Smeaton and Geoff Wonfor. Perf. The Beatles. Apple, 1996. DVD. / Winn, John C. (3). p. 25.

# February 26, 1964

### Time
10AM - 10PM

### Studio name and room
EMI Recording Studios

- Studio 2 (control room)
  - 10AM - 1PM)
- Studio 2
  - 230PM - 530PM
  - 7PM - 10PM

### Songs Recorded (composer) (activities)

- *I Should Have Known Better (remake)* (Lennon and McCartney)
  - takes 1-21
  - superimposition take 22
- *And I Love Her* (remake) (Lennon and McCartney)
  - takes 3-19
- *Can't Buy Me Love* (Lennon and McCartney)
  - edit of remix (RM) 1 and 2 from take 4
  - edit of remix 4 and 5 from take 4

### Songs mixed (version) (remix number and take)

- *You Can't Do That* (mono)
  - remix (RM) 1-3 from take 9
- *Can't Buy Me Love* (mono)
  - remix (RM) 1-5 from take 4

### Studio Personnel

- Producer: George Martin
- Balance engineer: Norman Smith

- Tape operator: Richard Langham

**Musicians (instruments played)**

- John Lennon (guitar, harmonica, vocals)
- Paul McCartney (bass, vocals)
- George Harrison (guitar)
- Ringo Starr (drums, claves, bongos)

## Instruments

**Electric guitars**

*Harrison*

- 1963 Rickenbacker 360-12 (12-string)

**Acoustic guitars**

*Lennon*

- 1962 Gibson J-160E

*Harrison*

- Jose Ramirez Guitarra de Estudio (nylon string)

Or

- Jose Ramirez A1 Segovia (nylon string)

**Bass guitars**

*McCartney*

- 1962-1963 Hofner 500/1

**Drums**

*Starr*

- 1963 Ludwig Oyster Black Pearl Downbeat (14" X 20" bass drum/ 8" X 12" rack tom/ 14" X 14" floor tom/ 14" X 5.5" Jazz Festival snare); Paiste, Zyn, Zildjian cymbals (20" ride/ 20" ride with 4-rivet "sizzle"/ 18" crash) Zildjian cymbals (14" model A hi-hats) (Ludwig Set 1)

**Percussion**

- Ludwig Expando bongos
- Claves

**Other**

- Hohner harmonica (Echo Vamper or Super Chromonica)

## Amplifiers

**Guitar**

*Lennon/Harrison*

- 1963 JMI Vox AC30/6 Twin Treble with "Top Boost" circuit, 30W with two 12" Vox Celestion Alnico Gray G12 T530 speakers
- 1963 JMI Vox AC50 Small Box (Mk. I), 50W with Vox AC50 cabinet, with two 12" Vox Celestion Alnico Blue G12 T530 speakers and Goodmans Midax horn

**Bass**

*McCartney*

- 1963 Vox AC100, 100W head with Vox AC100 custom cabinet, with two 15" Vox Celestion T1070 speakers

## Recording equipment

*Recording console*

- REDD.51

*Primary tracking machine*

- FOUR-TRACK: 1" Telefunken M10

Mixdown machine

- MONO: 1/4" EMI BTR2

Outboard signal processors

- EMI RS114 Limiter
- EMI RS124 Altec Compressor
- EMI RS127 Presence Box
- EMI RS144 4-Way Mixer/Premix
- EMI RS92 Neumann Mic Equaliser

*Effects*

- Echo chamber (includes RS61 Low Level Amplifier with RS62 Power Supply and RS106A Echo Control Unit – Band Pass Filter)
- STEED (send tape echo/echo delay)

*Monitors*

Control room

- Altec 605A (Altec 612 Cabinet) with EMI RS141 Leak TL/25 Plus Amplifier

Studio

- RLS10 - "White Elephant"

*Microphones*

Vocals

- Neumann U48 or U47/48 (U47/8)

Electric guitar amplifiers

- Neumann U48, U47/48 (U47/8)
- Neumann KM54

Acoustic guitars

- Neumann U48 or U47/48 (U47/8)

Bass amplifier

- STC 4033-A

Drums

- Overhead - STC 4038
- Bass drum - STC 4033-A

Other

- Neumann U48, U47/48 (U47/8)
- STC 4038

**Backing tracks**

- *I Should Have Known Better* – backing track included Lennon on acoustic guitar and lead vocals; McCartney on bass; Harrison on nylon string acoustic guitar; Starr on drums
- *And I Love Her* – backing track included Lennon on acoustic guitar; McCartney on bass and lead vocals; Harrison on nylon string acoustic guitar; Starr on drums; Starr on bongos and claves (from around take 8)

**Superimpositions**

- *I Should Have Known Better* – superimpositions included Lennon on double-tracked lead vocals and harmonica; Harrison on 12-string guitar

**Remixes**

Mono master remixes

- *Can't Buy Me Love* (mono) (remix (RM) 3 from take 4)
- *You Can't Do That* (mono) (remix (RM) 3 from take 9)

**Notes**

Winn noted tape box notation documents *Can't Buy Me Love* RM3 as the master remix for the UK and RM 4+5 for the US, though Lewisohn noted RM4 was used for both the US and UK. Both territories actually received RM3 as the mono master for the song. Lewisohn noted *I Should Have Known Better* commencing with take 4, while Barrett's logs indicate the song began with take 1.

**Sources -** Babiuk, Andy (1). p. 102. / Everett, Walter (1). pp. 225, 226. / Lewisohn, Mark (1). pp. 39, 40. / The Beatles. "*And I Love Her (take 11)*". Rec.26 February 1964. The Beatles. FLAC audio file. / The Beatles. "*I Should Have Known Better (take 11)*". Rec.26 February 1964. The Beatles. FLAC audio file. / The Beatles. "*I Should Have Known Better (takes 8-9)*". Rec.26 February 1964. The Beatles. FLAC audio file. / Winn, John C. (3). pp. 27, 28.

# February 27, 1964

**Time**
10AM - 530PM

**Studio name and room**
EMI Recording Studios
Studio 2

- 10AM – 1PM
- 230PM – 530PM

**Songs recorded (composer) (activities)**

- *And I Love Her* (second remake) (Lennon and McCartney)
    - take 20
    - superimposition take 21

- *Tell Me Why* (Lennon and McCartney)
    - takes 1-7
    - superimposition take 8
- *If I Fell* (Lennon and McCartney)
    - takes 1-14
    - superimposition take 15

**Studio Personnel**

- Producer: George Martin
- Balance engineer: Norman Smith
- Tape operator: Richard Langham

**Musicians (instruments played)**

- John Lennon (guitar, vocals)
- Paul McCartney (bass, vocals)
- George Harrison (guitar, claves, vocals)
- Ringo Starr (drums, bongos)

**Instruments**

**Electric guitars**

*Lennon*

- 1964 Rickenbacker 325 Capri (second model - Black)

*Harrison*

- 1963 Gretsch PX6122 Chet Atkins Country Gentleman with Gretsch Bigsby B6G vibrato
- 1963 Gretsch 6119 Chet Atkins Tennessean with Gretsch Bigsby vibrato
- 1963 Rickenbacker 360-12 (12-string)\

**Acoustic guitars**

*Lennon*

- 1962 Gibson J-160E

*Harrison*

- Jose Ramirez Guitarra de Estudio (nylon string)

Or

- Jose Ramirez A1 Segovia (nylon string)

**Bass guitars**

*McCartney*

- 1962-1963 Hofner 500/1

**Drums**

*Starr*

- 1963 Ludwig Oyster Black Pearl Downbeat (14" X 20" bass drum/ 8" X 12" rack tom/ 14" X 14" floor tom/ 14" X 5.5" Jazz Festival snare); Paiste, Zyn, Zildjian cymbals (20" ride/ 20" ride with 4-rivet "sizzle"/ 18" crash) Zildjian cymbals (14" model A hi-hats) (Ludwig Set 1)

**Percussion**

- Ludwig Expando bongos
- Claves

**Pianos and keyboards**

- Steinway "Music Room" Model B Grand Piano (circa 1880s)

## Amplifiers

### Guitar

*Lennon/Harrison*

- 1963 JMI Vox AC30/6 Twin Treble with "Top Boost" circuit, 30W with two 12" Vox Celestion Alnico Gray G12 T530 speakers
- 1963 JMI Vox AC50 Small Box (Mk. I), 50W with Vox AC50 cabinet, with two 12" Vox Celestion Alnico Blue G12 T530 speakers and Goodmans Midax horn

### Bass

*McCartney*

- 1963 Vox AC100, 100W head with Vox AC100 cabinet 2X15" Celestion T1070 speakers

## Recording equipment

*Recording console*

- REDD.51

*Primary tracking machine*

- FOUR-TRACK: 1" Telefunken M10

*Outboard signal processors*

- EMI RS114 Limiter
- EMI RS124 Altec Compressor
- EMI RS127 Presence Box
- EMI RS144 4-Way Mixer/Premix
- EMI RS92 Neumann Mic Equaliser

*Monitors*

Control room

- Altec 605A (Altec 612 Cabinet) with EMI RS141 Leak TL/25 Plus Amplifier

Studio

- RLS10 - "White Elephant"

*Microphones*

Vocals

- Neumann U48 or U47/48 (U47/8)

Electric guitar amplifiers

- Neumann U48, U47/48 (U47/8)
- Neumann KM54

Acoustic guitars

- Neumann U48 or U47/48 (U47/8)

Bass amplifier

- STC 4033-A

Drums

- Overhead - STC 4038
- Bass drum - STC 4033-A

Other

- Neumann U48, U47/48 (U47/8)
- STC 4038

**Backing tracks**

- *And I Love Her* – backing track included Lennon on acoustic guitar; McCartney on bass and lead vocals; Harrison on nylon acoustic guitar; Starr on bongos
- *Tell Me Why* – backing track included Lennon on acoustic guitar and lead vocals; McCartney on bass and backing vocals; Harrison on 12-string electric guitar and backing vocals; Starr on drums
- *If I Fell* – backing track included Lennon on acoustic guitar and lead vocals; McCartney on bass and lead vocals; Harrison on 12-string electric guitar; Starr on drums

**Superimpositions**

- *And I Love Her* – superimpositions included McCartney on double-tracked lead vocals; Starr on claves
- *Tell Me Why* – superimpositions included Lennon on double-tracked lead vocals; Unknown on piano (likely George Martin)
- *If I Fell* – superimpositions included Lennon and McCartney on double-tracked lead vocals; Harrison on 12-string electric guitar

**Sources** - Dowlding, William J. pp. 69, 71. / Everett, Walter (1). pp. 231, 233. / Lewisohn, Mark (1). p. 40. / The Beatles. "*And I Love Her*". Rec.27 February 1964. The Beatles. FLAC audio file. / The Beatles. "*If I Fell*". Rec.27 February 1964. The Beatles. FLAC audio file. / The Beatles. "*Tell Me Why (take 4)*". Rec.27 February 1964. The Beatles. FLAC audio file. / The Beatles. "*Tell Me Why*". Rec.27 February 1964. The Beatles. FLAC audio file. / Winn, John C. (3). pp. 28, 29.

# March 1, 1964

**Time**
10AM – 130PM

**Studio name and room**
EMI Recording Studios
Studio 2

**Songs recorded (composer) (activities)**

- *I'm Happy Just To Dance With You* (Lennon and McCartney)
    - takes 1-3
    - superimposition take 4
- *Long Tall Sally* (Blackwell, Johnson and Penniman)
    - take 1
- *I Call Your Name* (Lennon and McCartney)
    - takes 1-6
    - superimposition take 7
    - edit of takes 5 and 7

**Studio Personnel**

- Producer: George Martin
- Balance engineer: Norman Smith
- Tape operator: Richard Langham

**Musicians (instruments played)**

- John Lennon (guitar, vocals)
- Paul McCartney (bass, vocals)
- George Harrison (guitar, vocals)
- Ringo Starr (drums, cowbell)

**Other musicians (instruments played)**

- George Martin (piano)

## Instruments

### Electric guitars

*Lennon*

- 1964 Rickenbacker 325 Capri (second model - Black)

*Harrison*

- 1963 Gretsch PX6122 Chet Atkins Country Gentleman with Gretsch Bigsby B6G vibrato
- 1963 Gretsch 6119 Chet Atkins Tennessean with Gretsch Bigsby vibrato
- 1963 Rickenbacker 360-12 (12-string)

### Bass guitars

*McCartney*

- 1962-1963 Hofner 500/1

### Drums

*Starr*

- 1963 Ludwig Oyster Black Pearl Downbeat (14" X 20" bass drum/ 8" X 12" rack tom/ 14" X 14" floor tom/ 14" X 5.5" Jazz Festival snare); Paiste, Zyn, Zildjian cymbals (20" ride/ 20" ride with 4-rivet "sizzle"/ 18" crash) Zildjian cymbals (14" model A hi-hats) (Ludwig Set 1)

### Percussion

- Ludwig Clear Tone cowbell

### Pianos and keyboards

- Steinway "Music Room" Model B Grand Piano (circa 1880s)

## Amplifiers

### Guitar

*Lennon/Harrison*

- 1963 JMI Vox AC30/6 Twin Treble with "Top Boost" circuit, 30W with two 12" Vox Celestion Alnico Gray G12 T530 speakers
- 1963 JMI Vox AC50 Small Box (Mk. I), 50W with Vox AC50 cabinet, with two 12" Vox Celestion Alnico Blue G12 T530 speakers and Goodmans Midax horn

### Bass

*McCartney*

- 1963 Vox AC100, 100W head with Vox AC100 custom cabinet, with two 15" Vox Celestion T1070 speakers

## Recording equipment

*Recording console*

- REDD.51

*Primary tracking machine*

- FOUR-TRACK: 1" Telefunken M10

*Outboard signal processors*

- EMI RS114 Limiter

- EMI RS124 Altec Compressor
- EMI RS127 Presence Box
- EMI RS144 4-Way Mixer/Premix
- EMI RS92 Neumann Mic Equaliser

*Effects*

- Tape echo/ repeat echo

*Monitors*

Control room

- Altec 605A (Altec 612 Cabinet) with EMI RS141 Leak TL/25 Plus Amplifier

Studio

- RLS10 - "White Elephant"

*Microphones*

Vocals

- Neumann U48 or U47/48 (U47/8)

*Electric guitar amplifiers*

- Neumann U48, U47/48 (U47/8) or Neumann KM54

*Bass amplifier*

- STC 4033-A

*Drums*

- Overhead - STC 4038
- Bass drum - STC 4033-A

*Piano*

- Neumann U48 or U47/48 (U47/8)

Other

- Neumann U48, U47/48 (U47/8)
- STC 4038

**Backing tracks**

- *I'm Happy Just To Dance With You* – backing track included Lennon on guitar and backing vocals; McCartney on bass and backing vocals; Harrison on guitar and lead vocals; Starr on drums
- *Long Tall Sally* – backing track included Lennon on guitar; McCartney on bass and lead vocals; Harrison on guitar; Starr on drums; George Martin on piano
- *I Call Your Name* – backing track included Lennon on guitar and lead vocals; McCartney on bass; Harrison on 12-string electric guitar; Starr on drums

**Superimpositions**

- *I'm Happy Just To Dance With You* – superimpositions included Harrison on double-tracked lead vocals; Starr on tom-toms
- *I Call Your Name* – superimpositions included Lennon on double-tracked lead vocals; Starr on cowbell

**Sources -** Dowlding, William J. pp. 65, 70. / Everett, Walter (1). pp. 233, 234. / Lewisohn, Mark (1). p. 41. / The Beatles. "*I Call Your Name*". Rec.1 March 1964. The Beatles. FLAC audio file. / The Beatles. "*I'm Happy Just To Dance With You*". Rec.1 March 1964. The Beatles. FLAC audio file. / The Beatles. "*Long Tall Sally*". Rec.1

March 1964. The Beatles. FLAC audio file. / Winn, John C. (3). p. 29

# March 3, 1964

**Time**
10AM – 145PM

**Studio name and room**
EMI Recording Studios
Studio 1 (control room)

**Songs mixed (version) (remix number and take)**

- *I Should Have Known Better* (mono)
    - remix (RM) 1 from take 22
- *If I Fell* (mono)
    - remix (RM) 1 from take 15
- *Tell Me Why* (mono)
    - remix (RM) 1 from take 8
- *And I Love Her* (mono)
    - remix (RM) 1 from take 21
- *I'm Happy Just To Dance With You* (mono)
    - remix (RM) 1 from take 4
- *I Call Your Name* (mono)
    - remix (RM) 1 from edit of take 5 and 7

**Studio Personnel**

- Producer: George Martin
- Balance engineer: Norman Smith
- Tape operator: Anthony (Tony) Bridge

**Recording equipment**

*Recording console*

- REDD.37

*Primary tracking machine*

- FOUR-TRACK: 1" Telefunken M10

*Mixdown machine*

- MONO: 1/4" EMI BTR2

*Outboard signal processors*

- EMI RS114 Limiter
- EMI RS124 Altec Compressor
- EMI RS127 Presence Box
- EMI RS144 4-Way Mixer/Premix
- EMI RS92 Neumann Mic Equaliser

*Effects*

- Echo chamber (includes RS61 Low Level Amplifier with RS62 Power Supply and RS106A Echo Control Unit – Band Pass Filter)
- STEED (send tape echo/echo delay)

*Monitors*

Control room

- Altec 605A (Altec 612 Cabinet) with EMI RS141 Leak TL/25 Plus Amplifier

**Remixes**

Mono master remixes

- *I Should Have Known Better* (mono) (remix (RM) 1 from take 22)
- *If I Fell* (mono) (remix (RM) 1 from take 15)
- *Tell Me Why* (mono) (remix (RM) 1 from take 8)
- *And I Love Her* (mono) (remix (RM) 1 from take 21)
- *I'm Happy Just To Dance With You* (mono) (remix (RM) 1 from take 4)
- *I Call Your Name* (mono) (remix (RM) 1 from edit of take 5 and 7) (For US release)

**Sources -** Lewisohn, Mark (1). p. 41. / Winn, John C. (3). pp. 29, 30.

# March 4, 1964

**Time**
10AM - 11AM

**Studio name and room**
EMI Recording Studios
Studio 3 (control room)

**Songs mixed (version) (remix number and take)**

- *I Call Your Name* (Lennon and McCartney)
    - edit of remix (RM) 1 from edit of take 5 and 7

**Studio Personnel**

- Producer: George Martin
- Balance engineer: Unknown
- Tape operator(s): N/A

**Recording equipment**

*Recording console*

- Studio 3 - REDD.51

*Primary tracking machine*

- FOUR-TRACK: 1" Telefunken M10

*Mixdown machine*

- MONO: 1/4" EMI BTR2

*Outboard signal processors*

- EMI RS114 Limiter
- EMI RS124 Altec Compressor
- EMI RS127 Presence Box
- EMI RS144 4-Way Mixer/Premix
- EMI RS92 Neumann Mic Equaliser

*Monitors*

Control room

- Altec 605A (Altec 612 Cabinet) with EMI RS141 Leak TL/25 Plus Amplifier

**Notes**
From Barrett's notes ("Cut out from E51925-2T"), it is most likely that this session's work simply involved cutting the previous day's remix of *I Call Your Name* from its original reel

(numbered E51925-2T) and creating a new tape reel with the song as its only contents.

**Sources** - Lewisohn, Mark (1). p. 42. / Winn, John C. (3). p. 30.

# March 10, 1964

**Time**
10AM - 1PM

**Studio name and room**
EMI Recording Studios
Studio 2

**Songs recorded (composer) (activities)**

- *Can't Buy Me Love* (Lennon and McCartney)
    - superimposition onto take 4

**Songs mixed (version) (remix number and take)**

- *Can't Buy Me Love* (stereo)
    - remix (RS) 1 from take 4
- *Long Tall Sally* (stereo)
    - remix (RS) 1 from take 1
- *I Call Your Name* (stereo)
    - remix (RS) 1 from edit of takes 5 and 7
- *You Can't Do That* (stereo)
    - remix (RS) 1 from take 9
- *Long Tall Sally* (mono)
    - remix (RM) 1 from take 1
- *Komm, Gib Mir Deine Hand* (mono)
    - remix (RM) 1 from edit of takes 5 and 7
- *Sie Liebt Dich* (mono)
    - remix (RM) 1 from take 14

**Studio Personnel**

- Producer: George Martin
- Balance engineer: Norman Smith
- Tape operator: Geoff Emerick (see Notes)

**Other musicians (instruments played)**

- Norman Smith (drums)

**Instruments**

**Drums**

- Zildjian cymbals (14" model A hi-hats)

**Recording equipment**

*Recording console*

- REDD.51

*Primary tracking machine*

- FOUR-TRACK: 1" Telefunken M10

*Mixdown machine*

- MONO: 1/4" EMI BTR2
- STEREO: 1/4" EMI BTR3

*Outboard signal processors*

- EMI RS114 Limiter
- EMI RS124 Altec Compressor
- EMI RS127 Presence Box
- EMI RS144 4-Way Mixer/Premix
- EMI RS92 Neumann Mic Equaliser

*Effects*

- Echo chamber (includes RS61 Low Level Amplifier with RS62 Power Supply and RS106A Echo Control Unit – Band Pass Filter)
- STEED (send tape echo/echo delay)

*Microphones*

Drums

- Overhead - STC 4038

*Monitors*

Control room

- Altec 605A (Altec 612 Cabinet) with EMI RS141 Leak TL/25 Plus Amplifier

**Remixes**

Mono master remixes

- *Long Tall Sally* (mono) (remix (RM) 1 from take 1) (for US release)
- *Komm, Gib Mir Deine Hand* (mono) (remix (RM) 1 from edit of takes 5 and 7) (for German release) (see Notes)
- *Sie Liebt Dich* (mono) (remix (RM) 1 from take 14) (for German release) (see Notes)

Stereo master remixes

- *Can't Buy Me Love* (stereo) (remix (RS) 1 from take 4) (for UK release)
- *You Can't Do That* (stereo) (remix (RS) 1 from take 9) (for UK release)
- *Long Tall Sally* (stereo) (remix (RS) 1 from take 1) (for US release)
- *I Call Your Name* (stereo) (remix (RS) 1 from take 7) (for US release)

**Notes**

Knublauch and Korinth note that while not documented, the two German-language versions of The Beatles' hits must have been mixed either during the January 29th EMI session in Paris, or at least prior to their German release on March 6th, 1964, though the first record of them within the EMI tape logs dates to this March 10th session – four days after their public release. It is believed that the remixes simply entered the EMI system on this date.

Lewisohn noted that EMI documentation did not name the tape operator for this session. Emerick, however, recalled that this was the first session in which he sat behind the REDD console as balance engineer — if only for a short time. In his autobiography, he states that balance engineer Norman Smith noticed a technical issue with Starr's drum part for *Can't Buy Me Love* discovered during a remix session for the song (the issue being a loss in the high EQ that manifested itself with a dulling of the sound of the hi-hat on Starr's drum part).

While he does not mention the specific date for this session, he also states that Smith "...headed down into the studio to overdub a hastily set-up hi-hat onto a few bars of the song..." leaving Emerick at the controls for the superimposition.

Unlike the previous mono remix session for the song on February 26th (where Richard Langham, not Emerick, was the tape operator), no tracking activity was planned for this date. It is concluded that this is the date that Smith's contributions to the song were performed.

Audio examination demonstrates a slight difference in the drum work between the mono and stereo versions of the song. This also supports the conclusion that Smith's contributions occurred on this date. No mono remixing on the song occurred during this session.

The likelihood of Starr having contributed the hi-hat work on this day is low, considering the date and time of the session conflicts with the fact that The Beatles spent the day on location in Middlesex for the filming of scenes for their upcoming movie, *A Hard Day's Night.*

**Sources -** Emerick, Geoff. p. 81. / Knublauch, Thorsten and Axel Korinth. pp. 322-325 / Lewisohn, Mark (1). p. 42. / Lewisohn, Mark (2). p. 150. /The Beatles. *Can't Buy Me Love. A Hard Day's Night (mono).* George Martin, 1964. Vinyl, FLAC audio file. /The Beatles. *Can't Buy Me Love. A Hard Day's Night (stereo).* George Martin, 1964. Vinyl, FLAC audio file. /Winn, John C. (3). p. 31.

# March 12, 1964

**Time**
10AM - 12PM

**Studio name and room**
EMI Recording Studio
Studio 3 (control room)

**Songs mixed (version) (remix number and take)**

- *Komm, Gib Mir Deine Hand* (stereo)
  - remix (RS) 1 from edit of takes 5 and 7
- *Sie Liebt Dich* (stereo)
  - remix (RS) 1 from take 14

**Studio Personnel**

- Producer: George Martin
- Balance engineer: Norman Smith
- Tape operator: N/A

**Recording equipment**

*Recording console*

- REDD.51

*Primary tracking machine*

- FOUR-TRACK: 1" Telefunken M10

*Mixdown machine*

- STEREO: 1/4" EMI BTR3

*Outboard signal processors*

- EMI RS114 Limiter

- EMI RS124 Altec Compressor
- EMI RS127 Presence Box
- EMI RS144 4-Way Mixer/Premix
- EMI RS92 Neumann Mic Equaliser

*Effects*

- Echo chamber (includes RS61 Low Level Amplifier with RS62 Power Supply and RS106A Echo Control Unit – Band Pass Filter)
- STEED (send tape echo/echo delay)

*Monitors*

Control room

- Altec 605A (Altec 612 Cabinet) with EMI RS141 Leak TL/25 Plus Amplifier

**Sources -** Lewisohn, Mark (1). p. 42. / Winn, John C. (3). p. 32.

# April 16, 1964

**Time**
7PM - 10PM

**Studio name and room**
EMI Recording Studios
Studio 2

**Songs recorded (composer) (activities)**

- *A Hard Day's Night* (Lennon and McCartney)
  - takes 1-9
  - superimposition onto take 9

**Studio Personnel**

- Producer: George Martin
- Balance engineer: Norman Smith
- Tape operator: Geoff Emerick

**Musicians (instruments played)**

- John Lennon (guitar, vocals)
- Paul McCartney (bass, vocals)
- George Harrison (guitar)
- Ringo Starr (drums, woodblock)

**Other musicians (instruments played)**

- George Martin (piano)
- Norman Smith (bongos)

**Instruments**

**Electric guitars**

*Harrison*

- 1963 Gretsch PX6122 Chet Atkins Country Gentleman with Gretsch Bigsby B6G vibrato
- 1963 Gretsch 6119 Chet Atkins Tennessean with Gretsch Bigsby vibrato
- 1963 Rickenbacker 360-12 (12-string)

**Acoustic guitars**

*Lennon*

- 1962 Gibson J-160E

### Bass guitars

*McCartney*

- 1962-1963 Hofner 500/1

### Drums

*Starr*

- 1963 Ludwig Oyster Black Pearl Downbeat (14" X 20" bass drum/ 8" X 12" rack tom/ 14" X 14" floor tom/ 14" X 5.5" Jazz Festival snare); Paiste, Zyn, Zildjian cymbals (20" ride/ 20" ride with 4-rivet "sizzle"/ 18" crash) Zildjian cymbals (14" model A hi-hats) (Ludwig Set 1)

### Percussion

- Ludwig Expando bongos
- Ludwig Clear Tone cowbell

### Pianos and keyboards

- 1905 Steinway Vertegrand (the "Mrs. Mills" upright piano)

## Amplifiers

### Guitar

*Lennon/Harrison*

- 1963 JMI Vox AC30/6 Twin Treble with "Top Boost" circuit, 30W with two 12" Vox Celestion Alnico Gray G12 T530 speakers
- 1963 JMI Vox AC50 Small Box (Mk. I), 50W with Vox AC50 cabinet, with two 12" Vox Celestion Alnico Blue G12 T530 speakers and Goodmans Midax horn

### Bass

- 1963 Vox AC100, 100W head with Vox AC100 cabinet 2X15" Celestion T1070 speakers

## Recording equipment

*Recording console*

- REDD.51

*Primary tracking machine*

- FOUR-TRACK: 1" Telefunken M10

*Outboard signal processors*

- EMI RS114 Limiter
- EMI RS124 Altec Compressor
- EMI RS127 Presence Box
- EMI RS144 4-Way Mixer/Premix
- EMI RS92 Neumann Mic Equaliser

*Effects*

- Double-tracking
- Half-speed recording
- Echo chamber (includes RS61 Low Level Amplifier with RS62 Power Supply and RS106A Echo Control Unit – Band Pass Filter)
- STEED (send tape echo/echo delay)

*Monitors*

Control room

- Altec 605A (Altec 612 Cabinet) with EMI RS141 Leak TL/25 Plus Amplifier

Studio

- RLS10 - "White Elephant"

*Microphones*

Vocals

- Neumann U48 or U47/48 (U47/8)

Electric guitar amplifiers

- Neumann U48, U47/48 (U47/8)
- Neumann KM54

Acoustic guitars

- Neumann U48 or U47/48 (U47/8)

Bass amplifier

- STC 4033-A

Drums

- Overhead - STC 4038
- Bass drum - STC 4033-A

Piano

- Neumann U48 or U47/48 (U47/8)

Other

- Neumann U48, U47/48 (U47/8)
- STC 4038

**Backing tracks**

- *A Hard Day's Night* – backing track included Lennon on acoustic guitar and lead vocals; McCartney on bass and backing vocals; Harrison on 12-string electric guitar; Starr on drums

**Superimpositions**

- *A Hard Day's Night* – superimpositions included Lennon on double-tracked lead vocals; McCartney on double-tracked backing vocals; Norman Smith on bongos; Starr on cowbell; Lennon on acoustic guitar; Harrison on lead guitars; George Martin on piano

**Notes**

Take 9 of *A Hard Day's Night* included multiple superimpositions. At times, EMI engineers varied on their protocols regarding the numbering of takes and superimpositions. It was common during this period that superimpositions were numbered as additional takes. Clearly, as in this example, that wasn't always the case.

Audio examination indicates Harrison used the Rickenbacker 360-12 to record the rhythm track for *A Hard Day's Night*, but used one of his Gretsch guitars to play the solo. The 360-12 was used a final time to reinforce the final chord of the song.

Emerick noted that Martin played an "out-of-tune upright piano" for his part, doubling the solo of the song. The likely suspect was the 1905 Steinway Vertegrand piano, known for being intentionally left slightly out-of-tune (The so-called "Mrs. Mills" upright piano was named after an unlikely star, Parlophone recording artist Gladys Mills, who in her mid-40's made her mark as "Mrs. Mills" with piano sing-along versions of pop standards).

The solo for the song was recorded at half-speed.

**Sources -** Dowlding, William J. p. 68. / Emerick, Geoff. p. 84. / Everett, Walter (1). p. 236. / Lewisohn, Mark (1). p. 43. / Ryan, Kevin and Brian Kehew. pp. 380, 381. / The Beatles. "*A Hard Day's Night (take 1)*". Rec.16 April 1964. The Beatles. FLAC audio file. / The Beatles. "*A Hard Day's Night (take 2)*". Rec.16 April 1964. The Beatles. FLAC audio file. / The Beatles. "*A Hard Day's Night (take 3)*". Rec.16 April 1964. The Beatles. FLAC audio file. / The Beatles. "*A Hard Day's Night (take 4)*". Rec.16 April 1964. The Beatles. FLAC audio file. / The Beatles. "*A Hard Day's Night (take 5)*". Rec.16 April 1964. The Beatles. FLAC audio file. / The Beatles. "*A Hard Day's Night (take 6)*". Rec.16 April 1964. The Beatles. FLAC audio file. / The Beatles. "*A Hard Day's Night (take 7)*". Rec.16 April 1964. The Beatles. FLAC audio file. / The Beatles. "*A Hard Day's Night (take 8)*". Rec.16 April 1964. The Beatles. FLAC audio file. / The Beatles. "*A Hard Day's Night (take 9)*". Rec.16 April 1964. The Beatles. FLAC audio file. / The Beatles. "*A Hard Day's Night*". Rec.16 April 1964. The Beatles. FLAC audio file. / Winn, John C. (3). p. 32.

# April 20, 1964

**Time**
2PM – 315PM

**Studio name and room**
EMI Recording Studios
Studio 2 (control room)

**Songs mixed (version) (remix number and take)**

- *A Hard Day's Night* (mono)
  - remix (RM) 1 from take 9
- *A Hard Day's Night* (stereo)
  - remix (RS) 1 from take 9

**Studio Personnel**

- Producer: George Martin
- Balance engineer: Norman Smith
- Tape operator: Anthony (Tony) Bridge

**Recording equipment**

*Recording console*

- REDD.51

*Primary tracking machine*

- FOUR-TRACK: 1" Telefunken M10

*Mixdown machine*

- MONO: 1/4" EMI BTR2
- STEREO: 1/4" EMI BTR3

*Outboard signal processors*

- EMI RS114 Limiter
- EMI RS124 Altec Compressor
- EMI RS127 Presence Box
- EMI RS144 4-Way Mixer/Premix
- EMI RS92 Neumann Mic Equaliser

*Effects*

- Echo chamber (includes RS61 Low Level Amplifier with RS62 Power Supply and RS106A Echo Control Unit – Band Pass Filter)
- STEED (send tape echo/echo delay)

*Monitors*

Control room

- Altec 605A (Altec 612 Cabinet) with EMI RS141 Leak TL/25 Plus Amplifier

**Sources** - Lewisohn, Mark (1). p. 44. / Winn, John C. (3). p. 32.

# April 23, 1964

**Time**
430PM – 445PM

**Studio name and room**
EMI Recording Studios
Studio 2 (control room)

**Songs mixed (version) (remix number and take)**

- *A Hard Day's Night* (mono)
    - remix (RM) 10, from take 9

**Studio Personnel**

- Producer: George Martin
- Balance engineer: Norman Smith
- Tape operator: Unknown (see Notes)

**Recording equipment**

*Recording console*

- REDD.51

*Primary tracking machine*

- FOUR-TRACK: 1" Telefunken M10

*Mixdown machine*

- MONO: 1/4" EMI BTR2

*Outboard signal processors*

- EMI RS114 Limiter
- EMI RS124 Altec Compressor
- EMI RS127 Presence Box
- EMI RS144 4-Way Mixer/Premix

- EMI RS92 Neumann Mic Equaliser

*Effects*

- Echo chamber (includes RS61 Low Level Amplifier with RS62 Power Supply and RS106A Echo Control Unit – Band Pass Filter)
- STEED (send tape echo/echo delay)

*Monitors*

Control room

- Altec 605A (Altec 612 Cabinet) with EMI RS141 Leak TL/25 Plus Amplifier

### Remixes

Mono master remixes

- *A Hard Day's Night* (mono) (remix (RM) 10, from take 9)

### Notes

Lewisohn documents David Lloyd as the tape operator for this session. According to an author interview with Richard Langham, Lloyd had left EMI prior to the arrival of The Beatles.

**Sources -** Author interview. *Richard Langham*. London, UK. 15 August 2014. Via email. / Lewisohn, Mark (1). p. 44. / Winn, John C. (3). p. 33.

## May 22, 1964

### Time
10AM - 11AM

### Studio name and room
EMI Recording Studios
Studio 2

### Songs Recorded (composer) (activities)

- *You Can't Do That* (Lennon and McCartney)
  - superimposition take 10

### Studio Personnel

- Producer: George Martin
- Balance engineer: Norman Smith
- Tape operator: Anthony (Tony) Bridge, B.T. (identity unknown)

### Musicians (instruments played)

- George Martin (piano)

### Instruments

### Pianos and keyboards

- Steinway "Music Room" Model B Grand Piano (circa 1880s)

### Recording equipment

*Recording console*

- REDD.51

*Primary tracking machine*

- FOUR-TRACK: 1" Telefunken M10

*Outboard signal processors*

- EMI RS114 Limiter
- EMI RS124 Altec Compressor
- EMI RS127 Presence Box
- EMI RS144 4-Way Mixer/Premix
- EMI RS92 Neumann Mic Equaliser

*Monitors*

Control room

- Altec 605A (Altec 612 Cabinet) with EMI RS141 Leak TL/25 Plus Amplifier

Studio

- RLS10 - "White Elephant"

*Microphones*

Piano

- Neumann U48 or U47/48 (U47/8)

**Superimpositions**

- *You Can't Do That* – superimposition included George Martin on piano

**Notes**

Martin's piano work from this session went unused in released versions of *You Can't Do That.*

**Sources -** Lewisohn, Mark (1). p. 44. / Winn, John C. (3). p. 33.

# June 1, 1964

**Time**
230PM - 10PM

**Studio name and room**
EMI Recording Studios
Studio 2

- 230PM – 530PM
- 7PM – 10PM

**Songs Recorded (composer) (activities)**

- *Matchbox* (Perkins)
  - takes 1-4
  - superimposition take 5
- *I'll Cry Instead* (Lennon and McCartney)
  - "Section A" takes 1-5
  - edit of "Section A", take 6
  - "Section B" take 7
  - edit of "Section B", take 8
- *Slow Down* (Williams)
  - takes 1-3
  - superimposition takes 4, 5
- *I'll Be Back* (Lennon and McCartney)
  - takes 1-16
  - superimposition onto take 16

**Studio Personnel**

- Producer: George Martin
- Balance engineer: Norman Smith
- Tape operator: Ken Scott

**Musicians (instruments played)**

- John Lennon (guitar, vocals)
- Paul McCartney (bass, vocals)
- George Harrison (guitar, vocals)

- Ringo Starr (drums, tambourine, vocals)

### Other musicians (instruments played)

George Martin (piano)

## Instruments

### Electric guitars

*Lennon*

- 1964 Rickenbacker 325 Capri (second model - Black)

*Harrison*

- 1963 Gretsch PX6122 Chet Atkins Country Gentleman with Gretsch Bigsby B6G vibrato
- 1963 Gretsch 6119 Chet Atkins Tennessean with Gretsch Bigsby vibrato
- 1963 Rickenbacker 360-12 (12-string)

### Acoustic guitars

*Lennon*

- 1962 Gibson J-160E

*Harrison*

- Jose Ramirez Guitarra de Estudio (nylon string)

Or

- Jose Ramirez A1 Segovia (nylon string)

### Bass guitars

*McCartney*

- 1962-1963 Hofner 500/1

### Drums

*Starr*

- 1964 Ludwig Oyster Black Pearl "Super Classic" (14" X 22" bass drum/ 9" X 13" rack tom/ 16" X 16" floor tom/ 1963 14" X 5.5" "Jazz Festival" snare); Paiste, Zyn, Zildjian cymbals (20" crash/ride; 20" Zyn 4-rivet "sizzle") Zildjian cymbals (18" crash/ride; 14" model A hi-hats) (Ludwig Set 3)

### Percussion

- Tambourine (Olympic or Ludwig)

### Pianos and keyboards

- Steinway "Music Room" Model B Grand Piano (circa 1880s)

## Amplifiers

### Guitar

*Lennon/Harrison*

- 1963 JMI Vox AC30/6 Twin Treble with "Top Boost" circuit, 30W with two 12" Vox Celestion Alnico Gray G12 T530 speakers
- 1963 JMI Vox AC50 Small Box (Mk. I), 50W with Vox AC50 cabinet, with two 12" Vox Celestion Alnico Blue

G12 T530 speakers and Goodmans Midax horn

**Bass**

*McCartney*

- 1963 Vox AC100, 100W head with Vox AC100 custom cabinet, with two 15" Vox Celestion T1070 speakers

## Recording equipment

*Recording console*

- REDD.51

*Primary tracking machine*

- FOUR-TRACK: 1" Telefunken M10

*Outboard signal processors*

- EMI RS114 Limiter
- EMI RS124 Altec Compressor
- EMI RS127 Presence Box
- EMI RS144 4-Way Mixer/Premix
- EMI RS92 Neumann Mic Equaliser
- Fairchild 660 Limiter

*Effects*

- Double-tracking
- Echo chamber (includes RS61 Low Level Amplifier with RS62 Power Supply and RS106A Echo Control Unit – Band Pass Filter)
- STEED (send tape echo/echo delay)

*Monitors*

Control room

- Altec 605A (Altec 612 Cabinet) with EMI RS141 Leak TL/25 Plus Amplifier

Studio

- RLS10 - "White Elephant"

*Microphones*

Vocals

- Neumann U48 or U47/48 (U47/8)

Electric guitar amplifiers

- Neumann U48, U47/48 (U47/8)
- Neumann KM54

Acoustic guitars

- Neumann U48 or U47/48 (U47/8)

Bass amplifier

- AKG D20

Drums

- Overhead - STC 4038
- Bass drum - STC 4033-A

Piano

- Neumann U48, U47/48 (U47/8)

Other

- Neumann U48, U47/48 (U47/8)
- STC 4038

**Backing tracks**

- *Matchbox* – backing track included Starr on drums and lead vocals; Lennon on guitar; McCartney on bass; Harrison on guitar; George Martin on piano
- *I'll Cry Instead* – backing track included Lennon on acoustic guitar and lead vocals; McCartney on bass; Harrison on guitar; Starr on drums
- *Slow Down* – backing track included Lennon on guitar and lead vocals; McCartney on bass; Harrison on guitar; Starr on drums
- *I'll Be Back* – backing track included Lennon on acoustic guitar and lead vocals; McCartney on bass and backing vocals; Harrison on nylon string acoustic guitar; Starr on drums

**Superimpositions**

- *Matchbox* – superimpositions included on Starr on double-tracked lead vocals; Harrison on double-tracked guitar solo
- *I'll Cry Instead* – superimposition of Lennon on double-tracked lead vocals; Starr on tambourine
- *Slow Down* – superimposition included Lennon on double-tracked lead vocals
- *I'll Be Back* – superimpositions included Lennon and McCartney on double-tracked vocals; Harrison on nylon string acoustic guitar

**Notes**

Lewisohn does not note George Martin's contribution to *Matchbox*, though audio examination clearly points to his participation on the track.

Lewisohn also notes Starr's vocals being performed live, but audio examination demonstrates two distinct lead vocal tracks. It is assumed that while Starr performed the initial track live, it was later improved with superimposition onto take 5, and became the primary vocal in the remix.

It is not noted on which date superimpositions for *I'll Cry Instead* were created. Examination of the available audio indicates that the superimpositions were likely added independently to the A/B sectioning of the backing track. As no other sessions involving recording activity for the song were documented, these superimpositions are most likely to have occurred during this session.

Initial takes of *I'll Be Back* were not acoustic guitar-based, as was the finished track. While working out the arrangement and tempo of the tune, Lennon and Harrison both played electric guitars. Available audio evidence through take 3 reveals Lennon used his 1964 Rickenbacker 325 Capri, while Harrison played his 1963 Rickenbacker 360-12 12-string. It is not known at which point in the remaining takes the switch was made to acoustic guitars for the song.

Available as of late January 1964, the Fairchild 660 Limiter which would come to play a significant role in The Beatles' drum and vocal sounds may have been initially used on late *A Hard Day's Night* sessions according to Ryan and Kehew. A natural break in these sessions occurred between the recording of songs for the movie (finished April 16th) and recording of songs for the album B-side, which began with this day's session, nearly a month and a half later. For the purposes of this book the Fairchild 660 Limiter is assigned as part of the standard complement of outboard gear as of this date.

**Sources -** Dowlding, William J. p. 75. / Everett, Walter (1). p. 240-242. / Lewisohn, Mark (1). p. 44. / Ryan, Kevin and Brian Kehew. pp. 142, 381. / The Beatles. "*I'll Be Back (take 12)*". Rec.1 June 1964. The Beatles. FLAC audio file. / The Beatles. "*I'll Be Back (take 13)*". Rec.1 June 1964. The Beatles. FLAC audio file. / The Beatles. "*I'll Be Back (take 14)*". Rec.1 June 1964. The Beatles. FLAC audio file. / The Beatles. "*I'll Be Back (take 2)*". Rec.1 June 1964. The Beatles. FLAC audio file. / The Beatles. "*I'll Be Back (take 3)*". Rec.1 June 1964. The Beatles. FLAC audio file. / The Beatles. "*I'll Cry Instead*". Rec.1 June 1964. The Beatles. FLAC audio file. / The Beatles. "*Matchbox*". Rec.1 June 1964. The Beatles. FLAC audio file. / The Beatles. "*Slow Down*". Rec.1, 4 June 1964. The Beatles. FLAC audio file. / Winn, John C. (3). pp. 33, 34.

# June 2, 1964

**Time**
230PM - 10PM

**Studio name and room**
EMI Recording Studios
Studio 2

- 230PM – 530PM
- 7PM – 10PM

**Songs recorded (composer) (activities)**

- *Any Time At All* (Lennon and McCartney)
    - takes 1-7
    - superimposition takes 8-10
- *Things We Said Today* (Lennon and McCartney)
    - takes 1 and 2
- *When I Get Home* (Lennon and McCartney)
    - takes 1-10
    - superimposition take 11

**Studio Personnel**

- Producer: George Martin
- Balance engineer: Norman Smith
- Tape operator: Ken Scott

**Musicians (instruments played)**

- John Lennon (guitar, vocals)
- Paul McCartney (bass, cowbell, vocals)
- George Harrison (guitar, vocals)
- Ringo Starr (drums, tambourine)

## Instruments

### Electric guitars

*Lennon*

- 1964 Rickenbacker 325 Capri (second model - Black)

*Harrison*

- 1963 Gretsch PX6122 Chet Atkins Country Gentleman with Gretsch Bigsby B6G vibrato
- 1963 Gretsch 6119 Chet Atkins Tennessean with Gretsch Bigsby vibrato
- 1963 Rickenbacker 360-12 (12-string)

### Acoustic guitars

*Lennon/Harrison*

- 1962 Gibson J-160E

### Bass guitars

*McCartney*

- 1962-1963 Hofner 500/1

### Drums

*Starr*

- 1964 Ludwig Oyster Black Pearl "Super Classic" (14" X 22" bass drum/ 9" X 13" rack tom/ 16" X 16" floor tom/ 1963 14" X 5.5" "Jazz Festival" snare); Paiste, Zyn, Zildjian cymbals (20" crash/ride; 20" Zyn 4-rivet "sizzle") Zildjian cymbals (18" crash/ride; 14" model A hi-hats) (Ludwig Set 3)

### Percussion

- Tambourine (Olympic or Ludwig)
- Ludwig Clear Tone cowbell

## Amplifiers

### Guitar

*Lennon/Harrison*

- 1963 JMI Vox AC30/6 Twin Treble with "Top Boost" circuit, 30W with two 12" Vox Celestion Alnico Gray G12 T530 speakers
- 1963 JMI Vox AC50 Small Box (Mk. I), 50W with Vox AC50 cabinet, with two 12" Vox Celestion Alnico Blue G12 T530 speakers and Goodmans Midax horn

### Bass

*McCartney*

- 1963 Vox AC100, 100W head with Vox AC100 custom cabinet, with two 15" Vox Celestion T1070 speakers

## Recording equipment

*Recording console*

- REDD.51

*Primary tracking machine*

- FOUR-TRACK: 1" Telefunken M10

*Outboard signal processors*

- EMI RS114 Limiter
- EMI RS124 Altec Compressor
- EMI RS127 Presence Box
- EMI RS144 4-Way Mixer/Premix
- EMI RS92 Neumann Mic Equaliser
- Fairchild 660 Limiter

*Effects*

- Double-tracking
- Echo chamber (includes RS61 Low Level Amplifier with RS62 Power Supply and RS106A Echo Control Unit – Band Pass Filter)
- STEED (send tape echo/echo delay)

*Monitors*

Control room

- Altec 605A (Altec 612 Cabinet) with EMI RS141 Leak TL/25 Plus Amplifier

Studio

- RLS10 - "White Elephant"

*Microphones*

Vocals

- Neumann U48 or U47/48 (U47/8)

Electric guitar amplifiers

- Neumann U48, U47/48 (U47/8)
- Neumann KM54

Acoustic guitars

- Neumann U48 or U47/48 (U47/8)

Bass amplifier

- AKG D20

Drums

- Overhead - STC 4038
- Bass drum - STC 4033-A

Other

- Neumann U48, U47/48 (U47/8)
- STC 4038

**Backing tracks**

- *Any Time At All* – backing track included Lennon on acoustic guitar and lead vocals; McCartney on bass and backing vocals; Harrison on 12-string guitar; Starr on drums
- *Things We Said Today* – backing track included Lennon on acoustic guitar and backing vocals; McCartney on bass and lead vocals; Harrison on guitar; Starr on drums
- *When I Get Home* – backing track included Lennon on guitar and lead vocals; McCartney on bass and backing vocals; Harrison on guitar and backing vocals; Starr on drums

**Superimpositions**

- *Any Time At All* – superimpositions included Harrison on acoustic guitar; Starr on snare

- *When I Get Home* – superimpositions included Lennon on double-tracked lead vocals

**Sources -** Everett, Walter (1). pp. 246, 247. / Lewisohn, Mark (1). p. 44. / The Beatles. "*Any Time At All*". Rec.2 June 1964. The Beatles. FLAC audio file. / The Beatles. "*Things We Said Today*". Rec.2 June 1964. The Beatles. FLAC audio file. / The Beatles. "*When I Get Home*". Rec.2 June 1964. The Beatles. FLAC audio file. / Winn, John C. (3). p. 34, 35.

# June 3, 1964

**Time**
230PM - 10PM

**Studio name and room**
EMI Recording Studios
Studio 2

- 230PM – 530PM
- 7PM – 10PM

**Songs recorded (composer) (activities)**

- *You Know What To Do* (Harrison)
  - test take
  - demo take 1
- *You're My World* (Bindi, Paoli and Sigman)
  - unnumbered demo take
- *No Reply* (Lennon and McCartney)
  - unnumbered demo take
- *Any Time At All* (Lennon and McCartney)
  - superimposition onto take 10, called take 11
- *Things We Said Today* (Lennon and McCartney)
  - superimposition take 3

**Studio Personnel**

- Producer: George Martin
- Balance engineer: Norman Smith
- Tape operator: Ken Scott

**Musicians (instruments played)**

- John Lennon (guitar, piano, tambourine, vocals)
- Paul McCartney (bass, tambourine, vocals)
- George Harrison (guitar, tambourine, vocals)

**Instruments**

**Electric guitars**

*Lennon*

- 1964 Rickenbacker 325 Capri (second model - Black)

*Harrison*

- 1963 Gretsch PX6122 Chet Atkins Country Gentleman with Gretsch Bigsby B6G vibrato
- 1963 Gretsch 6119 Chet Atkins Tennessean with Gretsch Bigsby vibrato

**Bass guitars**

*McCartney*

- 1962-1963 Hofner 500/1

**Drums**

- 1964 Ludwig Oyster Black Pearl "Super Classic" (14" X 22" bass drum/ 9" X 13" rack tom/ 16" X 16" floor tom/ 1963 14" X 5.5" "Jazz Festival" snare); Paiste, Zyn, Zildjian cymbals (20" crash/ride; 20" Zyn 4-rivet "sizzle") Zildjian cymbals (18" crash/ride; 14" model A hi-hats) (Ludwig Set 3)

**Percussion**

- Tambourine (Olympic or Ludwig)

**Pianos and keyboards**

- Steinway "Music Room" Model B Grand Piano (circa 1880s)

## Amplifiers

**Guitar**

*Lennon/Harrison*

- 1963 JMI Vox AC30/6 Twin Treble with "Top Boost" circuit, 30W with two 12" Vox Celestion Alnico Gray G12 T530 speakers
- 1963 JMI Vox AC50 Small Box (Mk. I), 50W with Vox AC50 cabinet, with two 12" Vox Celestion Alnico Blue G12 T530 speakers and Goodmans Midax horn

**Bass**

*McCartney*

- 1963 Vox AC100, 100W head with Vox AC100 custom cabinet, with two 15" Vox Celestion T1070 speakers

## Recording equipment

*Recording console*

- REDD.51

*Primary tracking machine*

- FOUR-TRACK: 1" Telefunken M10

*Outboard signal processors*

- EMI RS114 Limiter
- EMI RS124 Altec Compressor
- EMI RS127 Presence Box
- EMI RS144 4-Way Mixer/Premix
- EMI RS92 Neumann Mic Equaliser
- Fairchild 660 Limiter

*Monitors*

Control room

- Altec 605A (Altec 612 Cabinet) with EMI RS141 Leak TL/25 Plus Amplifier

Studio

- RLS10 - "White Elephant"

*Microphones*

Vocals

- Neumann U48 or U47/48 (U47/8)

Electric guitar amplifiers

- Neumann U48, U47/48 (U47/8)
- Neumann KM54

Acoustic guitars

- Neumann U48 or U47/48 (U47/8)

Bass amplifier

- AKG D20

Drums

- Overhead - STC 4038
- Bass drum - STC 4033-A

Piano

- Neumann U48 or U47/48 (U47/8)

Other

- Neumann U48, U47/48 (U47/8)
- STC 4038

**Backing tracks**

- *You Know What To Do* – backing track included Harrison on guitar and guide vocal; Lennon on tambourine; McCartney on bass
- *You're My World* – unknown demo backing track included McCartney on vocal
- *No Reply* – backing track of Lennon on guitar and guide vocal; McCartney on bass and backing vocals; Unknown on drums

**Superimpositions**

- *Any Time At All* – superimpositions included Lennon on double-tracked lead vocals; McCartney on double-tracked backing vocals; Lennon on piano
- *Things We Said Today* – superimpositions included McCartney on double-tracked lead vocals; McCartney and Harrison on tambourines; Lennon on piano; Lennon on acoustic guitar

**Notes**

This session is not typically noted in the pantheon of EMI Recording Studios sessions for The Beatles. It started off as a rehearsal session for The Beatles with drummer Jimmy Nicol, who was to replace an ailing Ringo Starr at the last minute for live performances in Denmark, Holland, Hong Kong, Australia and New Zealand (June 3rd through 14th).

After working with Nicol for an hour, the remaining Beatles returned to demo two additional songs. *You Know What To Do* was a simple sketch of a new Harrison song, while *No Reply* would end up as an anchor tune for the next album, *Beatles For Sale*.

There is a great mystery and debate as to who the drummer is on the *No Reply* demo. Starr was in the hospital and Nicol was believed to be absent after the hour-long 3PM to 4PM rehearsal. The only unaccounted-for musician, Harrison had never been known to have drummed on any Beatles track until 1968, when he is believed to have been one of three drummers on *Back In The U.S.S.R.* Winn has speculated Harrison played bass on the tune, though to do so, he would have had to quickly figure out how to play McCartney's Hofner upside down.

While balance engineer Norman Smith was capable of playing drums, the demo contains his voice "slating" the track from the control room ("*No Reply*, take 1."). The most likely scenario is that Nicol wasn't absent at all and is in fact the drummer on the demo.

The only other song on this session was not so much a take as an artifact: McCartney busking 0:30 worth of Cilla Black's current hit, *You're My World.*

The latter half of the session was devoted to superimposition work on *Any Time At All* and *Things We Said Today.*

**Sources -** Everett, Walter (1). p. 248. / Lewisohn, Mark (2). pp. 160-164. / The Beatles. *No Reply (demo). Anthology.* George Martin, 1995. CD. / The Beatles. *You'll Know What To Do. Anthology.* George Martin, 1995. CD. / Winn, John C. (1). p. 186. / Winn, John C. (3). pp. 34, 35.

# June 4, 1964

**Time**
230PM - 7PM

**Studio name and room**
EMI Recording Studios
Studio 2

**Songs recorded (composer) (activities)**

- *I Call Your Name* (Lennon and McCartney)
    - edit of remix mono (RM) 1 and 2
- *Slow Down* (Lennon and McCartney)
    - superimposition onto take 5, called take 6
- *I'll Cry Instead*
    - edit of mono remix (RM) from takes 6 and 8

**Songs mixed (version) (remix number and take)**

- *Long Tall Sally* (mono)
    - remix (RM) 1 from take 1 (marked #2)
- *I Call Your Name* (mono)
    - remix (RM) 1 (#2) and 2 from takes 5 and 7
- *Matchbox* (mono)
    - remix (RM) 1 from take 5
- *Slow Down* (mono)
    - remix (RM) 1 from take 6
- *When I Get Home* (mono)
    - remix (RM) 1 from take 11
- *Any Time At All* (mono)
    - remix (RM) 1 from take 11
- *I'll Cry Instead* (Section A) (mono)
    - unnumbered remix (RM) from take 6

- *I'll Cry Instead* (Section B) (mono)
    - unnumbered remix (RM) from take 8
- *I'll Cry Instead* (mono)
    - remix (RM) 1 from edit of unnumbered remixes of Sections A and B

**Studio Personnel**

- Producer: George Martin
- Balance engineer: Norman Smith
- Tape operator: Richard Langham

**Other musicians (instruments played)**

- George Martin (piano)

**Instruments**

**Pianos and keyboards**

- Steinway "Music Room" Model B Grand Piano (circa 1880s)

**Recording equipment**

*Recording console*

- REDD.51

*Primary tracking machine*

- FOUR-TRACK: 1" Telefunken M10

*Mixdown machine*

- MONO: 1/4" EMI BTR2

*Outboard signal processors*

- EMI RS114 Limiter
- EMI RS124 Altec Compressor
- EMI RS127 Presence Box
- EMI RS144 4-Way Mixer/Premix
- EMI RS92 Neumann Mic Equaliser
- Fairchild 660 Limiter

*Effects*

- Echo chamber (includes RS61 Low Level Amplifier with RS62 Power Supply and RS106A Echo Control Unit – Band Pass Filter)
- STEED (send tape echo/echo delay)

*Monitors*

Control room

- Altec 605A (Altec 612 Cabinet) with EMI RS141 Leak TL/25 Plus Amplifier

Studio

- RLS10 - "White Elephant"

*Microphones*

Piano

- Neumann U48 or U47/48 (U47/8)

**Superimpositions**

- *Slow Down* – superimposition included George Martin on piano

**Remixes**

Mono master remixes

- *Long Tall Sally* (mono) (remix (RM) 1 from take 1 (marked #2))
- *I Call Your Name* (mono) (from edit of remix (RM) 1 (#2) and 2 from takes 5 and 7)
- *I'll Cry Instead* (mono) (remix (RM) 1 from edit of take 6 (Section A) and take 8 (Section B))
- *Matchbox* (mono) (remix (RM) 1 from take 5)
- *Slow Down* (mono) (remix (RM) 1 from take 6)

**Sources -** Lewisohn, Mark (1). p. 45. / Winn, John C. (3). pp. 34-36.

# June 9, 1964

**Time**
2PM – 545PM

**Studio name and room**
EMI Recording Studios
Studio 3 (control room)

**Songs recorded (composer) (activities)**

- *I Should Have Known Better* (Lennon and McCartney)
    - tape copying of RM1 from take 22
- *If I Fell* (Lennon and McCartney)
    - tape copying of remix mono (RM) 1 from take 15
- *Tell Me Why* (Lennon and McCartney)
    - tape copying of remix mono (RM) 1 from take 8
- *And I Love Her* (Lennon and McCartney)
    - tape copying of remix mono (RM) 1 from take 21
- *I'm Happy Just To Dance With You* (Lennon and McCartney)
    - tape copying of remix mono (RM) 1 from take 4
- *I'll Cry Instead* (Lennon and McCartney)
    - tape copying of remix (RM) 1 from edit of unnumbered remixes (RM) of Sections A and B
- *Can't Buy Me Love* (Lennon and McCartney)
    - tape copying of remix mono (RM) 3 from take 4
- *A Hard Day's Night* (Lennon and McCartney)
    - tape copying of remix mono (RM) 10 from take 9
    - edit of remix (RM) 10 from take 9

**Songs mixed (version) (remix number and take)**

- *Things We Said Today* (mono)
    - remix (RM) 1 from take 3

**Studio Personnel**

- Producer: George Martin
- Balance engineer: Norman Smith
- Tape operator: Ken Scott

**Recording equipment**

*Recording console*

- REDD.51

*Primary tracking machine*

- FOUR-TRACK: 1" Telefunken M10

*Mixdown machine*

- MONO: 1/4" EMI BTR2
- MONO Tape Copying: 1/4" Lyrec TR4

*Outboard signal processors*

- EMI RS114 Limiter
- EMI RS124 Altec Compressor
- EMI RS127 Presence Box
- EMI RS144 4-Way Mixer/Premix
- EMI RS92 Neumann Mic Equaliser
- Fairchild 660 Limiter

*Effects*

- Echo chamber (includes RS61 Low Level Amplifier with RS62 Power Supply and RS106A Echo Control Unit – Band Pass Filter)
- STEED (send tape echo/echo delay)

*Monitors*

Control room

- Altec 605A (Altec 612 Cabinet) with EMI RS141 Leak TL/25 Plus Amplifier

**Remixes**

Mono master remixes

- *Things We Said Today* (mono) (remix (RM) 1 from take 3)

**Notes**

This session involved tape copying of the current best versions of songs to be used by United Artists in the *A Hard Day's Night* film. The edit of the film's title song included an extra ending, which was intended for but never used by United Artists.

**Sources -** Lewisohn, Mark (1). p. 45. / Winn, John C. (3). pp. 36, 37

# June 10, 1964

**Time**
10AM – 11AM

**Studio name and room**
EMI Recording Studios
Studio 2 (control room)

**Songs mixed (version) (remix number and take)**

- *I'll Be Back* (mono)
  - remix (RM) 1 from take 16

**Studio Personnel**

- Producer: George Martin
- Balance engineer: Norman Smith
- Tape operator: Richard Langham

**Recording equipment**

*Recording console*

- REDD.51

*Primary tracking machine*

- FOUR-TRACK: 1" Telefunken M10

*Mixdown machine*

- MONO: 1/4" EMI BTR2

*Outboard signal processors*

- EMI RS114 Limiter
- EMI RS124 Altec Compressor
- EMI RS127 Presence Box
- EMI RS144 4-Way Mixer/Premix
- EMI RS92 Neumann Mic Equaliser
- Fairchild 660 Limiter

*Effects*

- Echo chamber (includes RS61 Low Level Amplifier with RS62 Power Supply and RS106A Echo Control Unit – Band Pass Filter)
- STEED (send tape echo/echo delay)

*Monitors*

Control room

- Altec 605A (Altec 612 Cabinet) with EMI RS141 Leak TL/25 Plus Amplifier

**Sources** - Lewisohn, Mark (1). p. 46.

# June 22, 1964

**Time**
10AM - 530PM

**Studio name and room**
EMI Recording Studios
Studio 1 (control room)

- 10AM – 1130AM
- 1130AM – 1PM
- 230PM – 530PM

**Songs recorded (composer) (activities)**

- *I Call Your Name* (stereo)
    - edit of remix (RS) 1 (#2) and RS3 from takes 5 and 7
- *I'll Cry Instead* (stereo)
    - edit of remix (RS) of Section A from take 6 and Section B from take 8

**Songs mixed (version) (remix number and take)**

- *Any Time At All* (mono)
    - remix (RM) 2 from take 11, for UK release
- *Any Time At All* (mono)
    - remix (RM) 3 from take 11, for US release
- *When I Get Home* (mono)
    - remix (RM) 2 from take 11, for UK release
- *When I Get Home* (mono)
    - remix (RM) 3 from take 11, for US release
- *I'll Be Back* (mono)
    - remix (RM) 2 from take 16, for UK release

- *I'll Be Back* (mono)
  - remix (RM) 3 from take 16, for US release
- *And I Love Her* (mono)
  - remix (RM) 2 from take 21
- *And I Love Her* (stereo)
  - remix (RS) 1 from take 21
- *When I Get Home* (stereo)
  - remix (RS) 1 from take 11
- *Any Time At All* (stereo)
  - remix (RS) 1 from take 11
- *I'll Be Back* (stereo)
  - remix (RS) 1 from take 16
- *If I Fell* (stereo)
  - remix (RS) 1 from take 15
- *A Hard Day's Night* (stereo)
  - remix (RS) 1 from take 9
- *I Should Have Known Better* (stereo)
  - remix (RS) 1 from take 22
- *I'm Happy Just To Dance With You* (stereo)
  - remix (RS) 1 from take 4
- *I Call Your Name* (stereo)
  - remix (RS) 1 (#2) and (RS) 3 from takes 5 and 7
- *Can't Buy Me Love* (stereo)
  - remix (RS) 1 from take 4
- *You Can't Do That* (stereo)
  - remix (RS) 1 from take 9
- *Tell Me Why* (stereo)
  - remix (RS) 1 from take 8
- *Things We Said Today* (stereo)
  - remix (RS) 1 from take 3
- *Matchbox* (stereo)
  - remix (RS) 1 from take 5
- *Slow Down* (stereo)
  - remix (RS) 1 from take 6
- *Long Tall Sally* (stereo)
  - remix (RS) 1 from take 1 (marked #2)
- *I'll Cry Instead* (stereo)
  - unnumbered remix (RS) of Section A from take 6
- *I'll Cry Instead* (stereo)
  - unnumbered remix (RS) of Section B from take 8

**Studio Personnel**

- Producer: George Martin
- Balance engineer: Norman Smith
- Tape operator: Geoff Emerick

**Recording equipment**

*Recording console*

- REDD.37

*Primary tracking machine*

- FOUR-TRACK: 1" Telefunken M10

*Mixdown machine*

- MONO: 1/4" EMI BTR2
- STEREO: 1/4" EMI BTR3

*Outboard signal processors*

- EMI RS114 Limiter
- EMI RS124 Altec Compressor
- EMI RS127 Presence Box
- EMI RS144 4-Way Mixer/Premix
- EMI RS92 Neumann Mic Equaliser
- Fairchild 660 Limiter

*Effects*

- Echo chamber (includes RS61 Low Level Amplifier with RS62 Power Supply and RS106A Echo Control Unit – Band Pass Filter)
- STEED (send tape echo/echo delay)

*Monitors*

Control room

- Altec 605A (Altec 612 Cabinet) with EMI RS141 Leak TL/25 Plus Amplifier

**Remixes**

Mono master remixes

- *Any Time At All* (mono) (remix (RM) 2 from take 11, for UK release)
- *Any Time At All* (mono) (remix (RM) 3 from take 11, for US release)
- *When I Get Home* (mono) (remix (RM) 2 from take 11, for UK release)
- *When I Get Home* (mono) (remix (RM) 3 from take 11, for US release)
- *I'll Be Back* (mono) (remix (RM) 2 from take 16, for UK release)
- *I'll Be Back* (mono) (remix (RM) 3 from take 16, for US release)
- *And I Love Her* (mono) (remix (RM) 2 from take 21)

Stereo master remixes

- *And I Love Her* (stereo) (remix (RS) 1 from take 21)
- *When I Get Home* (stereo) (remix (RS) 1 from take 11)
- *Any Time At All* (stereo) (remix (RS) 1 from take 11)
- *I'll Be Back* (stereo) (remix (RS) 1 from take 16)
- *If I Fell* (stereo) (remix (RS) 1 from take 15)
- *A Hard Day's Night* (stereo) (remix (RS) 1 from take 9)
- *I Should Have Known Better* (stereo) (remix (RS) 1 from take 22)
- *I'm Happy Just To Dance With You* (stereo) (remix (RS) 1 from take 4)
- *I Call Your Name* (stereo) (edit of remix (RS) 1 (#2) and (RS) 3 from takes 5 and 7
- *Tell Me Why* (stereo) (remix (RS) 1 from take 8)
- *Things We Said Today* (stereo) (remix (RS) 1 from take 3)
- *Matchbox* (stereo) (remix (RS) 1 from take 5)
- *Slow Down* (stereo) (remix (RS) 1 from take 6)
- *Long Tall Sally* (stereo) (unnumbered remix (RS) 1 (#2) from take 1)
- *I'll Cry Instead* (stereo) (unnumbered remix (RS) from edit of take 6 (Section A) and take 8 (Section B))

**Sources -** Lewisohn, Mark (1). p. 46. / Winn, John C. (3). pp. 37- 39.

# June 22, 1964

**Time**
545PM - 9PM

**Studio name and room**
EMI Recording Studios
Studio 2 (control room)

**Songs Recorded (composer) (activities)**

- *Slow Down* (Lennon and McCartney)
    - tape copying of remix (RM) 1 from take 6
- *Matchbox (Perkins)*
    - tape copying of remix (RM) 1 from take 5

- *Things We Said Today* (Lennon and McCartney)
    - tape copying of remix (RS) 1 from take 3

**Studio Personnel**

- Producer: George Martin
- Balance engineer: Norman Smith
- Tape operator: Geoff Emerick

**Recording equipment**

*Recording console*

- REDD.51

*Primary tracking machine*

- FOUR-TRACK: 1" Telefunken M10

*Mixdown machine*

- MONO: 1/4" EMI BTR2
- STEREO: 1/4" EMI BTR3
- MONO Tape Copying: 1/4" Lyrec TR4

*Monitors*

Control room

- Altec 605A (Altec 612 Cabinet) with EMI RS141 Leak TL/25 Plus Amplifier

**Sources -** Lewisohn, Mark (1). p. 46. / Winn, John C. (3). pp. 39.

# *Beatles For Sale* sessions

---

## August 11, 1964

**Time**
7PM - 11PM

**Studio name and room**
EMI Recording Studios
Studio 2

**Songs recorded (composer) (activities)**

- *Baby's In Black* (Lennon and McCartney)
    - takes 1-14
    - superimposition onto take 14
    - edit piece takes 1-13

**Studio Personnel**

- Producer: George Martin
- Balance engineer: Norman Smith
- Tape operator: Ron Pender

**Musicians (instruments played)**

- John Lennon (guitar, vocals)
- Paul McCartney (bass, vocals)
- George Harrison (guitar)
- Ringo Starr (drums, tambourine)

## Instruments

### Electric guitars

*Lennon*

- 1964 Rickenbacker 325 Capri (second model - Black)

*Harrison*

- 1963 Gretsch 6119 Chet Atkins Tennessean with Gretsch Bigsby vibrato

### Acoustic guitars

*Lennon*

- 1962 Gibson J-160E

### Bass guitars

*McCartney*

- 1962-1963 Hofner 500/1

### Drums

*Starr*

- 1964 Ludwig Oyster Black Pearl "Super Classic" (14" X 22" bass drum/ 9" X 13" rack tom/ 16" X 16" floor tom/ 1963 14" X 5.5" "Jazz Festival" snare); Paiste, Zyn, Zildjian cymbals (20" crash/ride; 20" Zyn 4-rivet "sizzle") Zildjian cymbals (18" crash/ride; 14" model A hi-hats) (Ludwig Set 3)

### Percussion

- Olympic tambourine

## Amplifiers

### Guitar

*Lennon/Harrison*

- 1963 JMI Vox AC30/6 Twin Treble with "Top Boost" circuit, 30W with two 12" Vox Celestion Alnico Gray G12 T530 speakers
- 1964 JMI Vox AC100 Mk I, 100W with Vox AC100 cabinet, 4X12" Vox Celestion Alnico Silver T1088 speakers and 2X Goodmans Midax horns

### Bass

*McCartney*

- 1963 Vox AC100, 100W head with Vox AC100 custom cabinet, with two 15" Vox Celestion T1070 speakers

## Recording equipment

*Recording console*

- REDD.51

*Primary tracking machine*

- FOUR-TRACK: 1" Telefunken M10

*Outboard signal processors*

- EMI RS114 Limiter
- EMI RS124 Altec Compressor

- EMI RS127 Presence Box
- EMI RS144 4-Way Mixer/Premix
- EMI RS92 Neumann Mic Equaliser
- Fairchild 660 Limiter

*Effects*

- Double-tracking

*Monitors*

Control room

- Altec 605A (Altec 612 Cabinet) with EMI RS141 Leak TL/25 Plus Amplifier

*Studio*

- RLS10 - "White Elephant"

*Microphones*

Vocals

- Neumann U48 or U47/48 (U47/8)

Electric guitar amplifiers

- Neumann U48, U47/48 (U47/8)
- Neumann KM54

Acoustic guitars

- Neumann U48 or U47/48 (U47/8)

Bass amplifier

- AKG D20

Drums

- Overhead – AKG 19c
- Bass drum - AKG D20

Other

- Neumann U48, U47/48 (U47/8)
- STC 4038

**Backing Tracks**

- *Baby's In Black* – backing track included Lennon on acoustic guitar and lead vocals; McCartney on bass and lead vocals; Harrison on guitar; Starr on drums

**Superimpositions**

- *Baby's In Black* – superimpositions included Lennon and McCartney on double-tracked lead vocals; Harrison on guitar; Starr on tambourine; Lennon on guitar

**Edit pieces**

- *Baby's In Black* – edit piece included Harrison on guitar for song's introduction

**Notes**

Harrison's guitar swells on *Baby's In Black* were accomplished by Lennon manually adjusting the volume pot of Harrison's guitar as he played.

The edit pieces created for the song's opening were not used in any release version.

**Sources** - Babiuk, Andy (1). p. 134. / Dean, Johnny. pp. 95, 97. / Everett, Walter (1). pp. 250, 254. / Lewisohn, Mark (1). p. 47. / Ryan, Kevin and Brian Kehew. p. 381. / The Beatles. "*Baby's In Black*". Rec.11 August1964. The Beatles. FLAC audio file. / Winn, John C. (3). p. 40.

# August 14, 1964

**Time**
7PM – 1115PM

**Studio name and room**
EMI Recording Studios
Studio 2

**Songs Recorded (composer) (activities)**

- *I'm A Loser* (Lennon and McCartney)
    - takes 1-8
    - superimposition onto take 8
- *Mr. Moonlight* (Johnson)
    - takes 1-4
- *Leave My Kitten Alone* (John, McDougal, Turner)
    - takes 1-5
    - superimposition onto take 5

**Songs mixed (version) (remix number and take)**

- *I'm A Loser* (mono)
    - remix (RM) 1, from take 8
- *Baby's In Black* (mono)
    - remix (RM) 1, from take 14

**Studio Personnel**

- Producer: George Martin
- Balance engineer: Norman Smith
- Tape operator: Ron Pender

**Musicians (instruments played)**

- John Lennon (guitar, vocals)
- Paul McCartney (bass, piano, vocals)
- George Harrison (guitar, vocals)
- Ringo Starr (drums, tambourine)

**Instruments**

**Electric guitars**

*Lennon*

- 1964 Rickenbacker 325 Capri (second model - Black)

*Harrison*

- 1963 Gretsch PX6122 Chet Atkins Country Gentleman with Gretsch Bigsby B6G vibrato
- 1963 Gretsch 6119 Chet Atkins Tennessean with Gretsch Bigsby vibrato

**Acoustic guitars**

*Lennon*

- 1964 Framus Hootenanny 5/024 (12-string)

**Bass guitars**

*McCartney*

- 1962-1963 Hofner 500/1

### Drums

*Starr*

- 1964 Ludwig Oyster Black Pearl "Super Classic" (14" X 22" bass drum/ 9" X 13" rack tom/ 16" X 16" floor tom/ 1963 14" X 5.5" "Jazz Festival" snare); Paiste, Zyn, Zildjian cymbals (20" crash/ride; 20" Zyn 4-rivet "sizzle") Zildjian cymbals (18" crash/ride; 14" model A hi-hats) (Ludwig Set 3)

### Percussion

- Tambourine (Olympic or Ludwig)

### Pianos and keyboards

- Steinway "Music Room" Model B Grand Piano (circa 1880s)

## Amplifiers

### Guitar

*Lennon/Harrison*

- 1963 JMI Vox AC30/6 Twin Treble with "Top Boost" circuit, 30W with two 12" Vox Celestion Alnico Gray G12 T530 speakers
- 1964 JMI Vox AC100 Mk I, 100W with Vox AC100 cabinet, 4X12" Vox Celestion Alnico Silver T1088 speakers and 2X Goodmans Midax horns

### Bass

- 1963 Vox AC100, 100W head with Vox AC100 custom cabinet, with two 15" Vox Celestion T1070 speakers

## Recording equipment

*Recording console*

- REDD.51

*Primary tracking machine*

- FOUR-TRACK: 1" Telefunken M10

*Mixdown machine*

- MONO: 1/4" EMI BTR2

*Outboard signal processors*

- EMI RS114 Limiter
- EMI RS124 Altec Compressor
- EMI RS127 Presence Box
- EMI RS144 4-Way Mixer/Premix
- EMI RS92 Neumann Mic Equaliser
- Fairchild 660 Limiter

*Effects*

- Double-tracking
- Echo chamber (includes RS61 Low Level Amplifier with RS62 Power Supply and RS106A Echo Control Unit – Band Pass Filter)
- STEED (send tape echo/echo delay)

*Monitors*

Control room

- Altec 605A (Altec 612 Cabinet) with EMI RS141 Leak TL/25 Plus Amplifier

Studio

- RLS10 - "White Elephant"

*Microphones*

Vocals

- Neumann U48 or U47/48 (U47/8)

Electric guitar amplifiers

- Neumann U48, U47/48 (U47/8)
- Neumann KM54

Acoustic guitars

- Neumann U48 or U47/48 (U47/8)

Bass amplifier

- AKG D20

Drums

- Overhead – AKG 19c
- Bass drum - AKG D20

Piano

- Neumann U47
- Neumann U48

Other

- Neumann U48 or U47/48 (U47/8)
- STC 4038

**Backing Tracks**

- *I'm A Loser* – backing track included Lennon on 12-string acoustic guitar, harmonica and lead vocals; McCartney on bass and backing vocals; Harrison on guitar; Starr on drums
- *Mr. Moonlight* – backing track included Lennon on guitar and lead vocals; McCartney on bass and backing vocals; Harrison on guitar; Starr on drums
- *Leave My Kitten Alone* – backing track included Lennon on guitar and lead vocals; McCartney on bass; Harrison on guitar; Starr on drums

**Superimpositions**

- *I'm A Loser* – superimpositions included Lennon and McCartney on double-tracked vocals; Harrison on guitar; Lennon on harmonica; Starr on tambourine
- *Leave My Kitten Alone* – superimpositions included Lennon on double-tracked lead vocals; Harrison on lead guitar; McCartney on piano; Starr on tambourine

**Notes**

The 12-string 1964 Framus Hootenanny 5/024 is not commonly thought to have become part of The Beatles' instrument complement until the *Help!* sessions in 1965. However, audio examination demonstrates Lennon playing a 12-string for this session on *I'm A Loser.*

A harmonica part is introduced on the same song during take 6, but for the final recording, the performance appears to be a superimposition, most likely performed in conjunction with the double-tracked vocals.

A 1987 article in *Guitar Player* magazine drawn from photographic evidence found in the monthly fan magazine, *Beatles Book*, reveals Harrison's 1963 Gretsch 6119 Chet Atkins Tennessean with Gretsch Bigsby vibrato was the guitar used on *I'm A Loser.*

Lennon's wonderful vocal introduction to *Mr. Moonlight* in take 4 would end up being edited into the remake of the song from October 18th.

**Sources -** Babiuk, Andy (1). p. 134. / Everett, Walter (1). pp. 250, 256, 257. / Lewisohn, Mark (1). p. 48. / Mytkowicz, Bob. / The Beatles. "*I'm A Loser (take 1) (Complete Control Room Monitor Mixes + Studio Sessions)*". Rec.14 August1964. The Beatles. FLAC audio file. / The Beatles. "*I'm A Loser (take 2) (Studio Sessions)*". Rec.14 August1964. The Beatles. FLAC audio file. / The Beatles. "*I'm A Loser (take 3) (Studio Sessions)*". Rec.14 August1964. The Beatles. FLAC audio file. / The Beatles. "*I'm A Loser (take 4) (Studio Sessions)*". Rec.14 August1964. The Beatles. FLAC audio file. / The Beatles. "*I'm A Loser (take 5) (Studio Sessions)*". Rec.14 August1964. The Beatles. FLAC audio file. / The Beatles. "*I'm A Loser (take 6) (Studio Sessions)*". Rec.14 August1964. The Beatles. FLAC audio file. / The Beatles. "*I'm A Loser (take 7) (Studio Sessions)*". Rec.14 August1964. The Beatles. FLAC audio file. / The Beatles. "*I'm A Loser (take 8) (Studio Sessions + Abbey Road Video Show)*". Rec.14 August1964. The Beatles. FLAC audio file. / The Beatles. "*I'm A Loser*". Rec.14 August1964. The Beatles. FLAC audio file. / The Beatles. "*Leave My Kitten Alone (take 4)*". Rec.14 August1964. The Beatles. FLAC audio file. / The Beatles. "*Leave My Kitten Alone (take 5)*". Rec.14 August1964. The Beatles. FLAC audio file. / The Beatles. "*Leave My Kitten Alone*". Rec.14 August1964. The Beatles. FLAC audio file. / The Beatles. "*Mr. Moonlight (take 1)*". *Anthology*. Perf. The Beatles. Apple, 1995. DVD. / The Beatles. "*Mr. Moonlight (take 2)*". *Anthology*. Perf. The Beatles. Apple, 1995. DVD. / The Beatles. "*Mr. Moonlight (take 4)*". Rec.14 August1964. The Beatles. FLAC audio file.

# August 23, 1964

**Time**
8PM - Unknown

**Location**
The Hollywood Bowl
2301 N Highland Ave, Los Angeles, CA, USA

**Songs recorded (composer) (activities)**

- *Twist And Shout* (Medley and Burns)
- *You Can't Do That* (Lennon and McCartney)
- *All My Loving* (Lennon and McCartney)
- *She Loves You* (Lennon and McCartney)
- *Things We Said Today* (Lennon and McCartney)
- *Roll Over Beethoven* (Berry)
- *Can't Buy Me Love* (Lennon and McCartney)
- *If I Fell* (Lennon and McCartney)
- *I Want To Hold Your Hand* (Lennon and McCartney)
- *Boys* (Dixon and Farrell)
- *A Hard Day's Night* (Lennon and McCartney)
- *Long Tall Sally* (Johnson, Penniman, Blackwell)

**Studio Personnel**

- Producer(s): Voyle Gilmore, George Martin
- Balance engineer: Hugh Davies
- Tape operator: Unknown

**Musicians (instruments played)**

- John Lennon (guitar, vocals)
- Paul McCartney (bass. vocals)
- George Harrison (guitar. vocals)
- Ringo Starr (drums, vocals)

## Instruments

**Electric guitars**

*Lennon*

- 1958 Rickenbacker 325 Capri (first model – Natural finish - repainted black)

*Harrison*

- 1963 Gretsch PX6122 Chet Atkins Country Gentleman with Gretsch Bigsby B6G vibrato
- 1963 Rickenbacker 360-12 (12-string)

**Bass guitars**

*McCartney*

- 1962-1963 Hofner 500/1

**Drums**

*Starr*

- 1964 Ludwig Oyster Black Pearl "Downbeat" (14" X 20" bass drum/ 8" X 12" rack tom/ 14" X 14" floor tom/ 1963 14" X 5.5" "Jazz Festival" snare); Paiste, Zyn, Zildjian cymbals (20" ride/ 20" ride with 4-rivet "sizzle"/ 18" crash) Zildjian cymbals (14" model A hi-hats) (Ludwig Set 2)

**Other**

- Hohner harmonica (Echo Vamper or Super Chromonica)

## Amplifiers

**Guitar**

*Lennon/Harrison*

- 1964 Vox AC100 Mk II, 100W with Vox AC100 cabinet, 4X12" Vox Alnico Celestion T530 speakers and 2X Goodmans Midax horns

**Bass**

McCartney

- 1963 Vox AC100, 100W head with Vox AC100 cabinet 2X15" Celestion T1070 speakers

## Recording equipment

*Recording console*

- Unknown

*Primary tracking machine*

- THREE-TRACK:1/2" Ampex 300

*Outboard signal processors*

- Unknown

*Effects*

- Unknown

*Monitors*

Control room

- Unknown

*Microphones*

Vocals

- Electro-Voice 666 or 667

Electric guitar amplifiers

- Electro-Voice 666 or 667

Bass amplifier

- Electro-Voice 666 or 667

Drums

- Electro-Voice 666 or 667 with Electro-Voice 668

**Notes**
The Ampex 300 is assigned as the primary tracking machine for this session based on the fact that these concerts are documented as being recorded on three-track, and that the Ampex 300 was the most common commercial three-track machine in use during this period.

Photographic evidence from the concert shows Electro-Voice 666 or 667 microphones were used for vocals and amplifiers as well as the kick drum. Ringo's overhead microphone also appears to be an Electro-Voice; this one a model 668.

**Sources -** Lewisohn, Mark (1). p. 48. / The Beatles. *Anthology (Director's Cut)*. Dir. Bob Smeaton and Geoff Wonfor. Perf. The Beatles. Apple, 1996. DVD.

# August 27, 1964

**Time**
Unknown

**Location**
1750 N Vine St., Los Angeles, CA, USA

**Studio name and room**
Capitol Records Studios

**Songs mixed (version) (remix number and take)**

- *Twist And Shout* (stereo)
- *You Can't Do That* (stereo)
- *All My Loving* (stereo)
- *She Loves You* (stereo)
- *Things We Said Today* (stereo)
- *Roll Over Beethoven* (stereo)
- *Can't Buy Me Love* (stereo)
- *If I Fell* (stereo)
- *I Want To Hold Your Hand* (stereo)
- *Boys* (stereo)
- *A Hard Day's Night* (stereo)
- *Long Tall Sally* (stereo)

**Studio Personnel**

- Producer: Voyle Gilmore
- Balance engineer: Hugh Davies

# September 29, 1964

### Time
230PM – 1045PM

### Studio name and room
EMI Recording Studios
Studio 2

- 230PM – 630PM
- 7PM – 1045PM

### Songs recorded (composer) (activities)

- *Every Little Thing* (Lennon and McCartney)
    - takes 1-4
- *I Don't Want To Spoil The Party* (Lennon and McCartney)
    - takes 1-9
    - superimposition onto take 9
- *What You're Doing* (Lennon and McCartney)
    - takes 1-7

### Studio Personnel

- Producer: George Martin
- Balance engineer: Norman Smith
- Tape operator(s): Ken Scott, Mike Stone

### Musicians (instruments played)

- John Lennon (guitar, vocals)
- Paul McCartney (bass, vocals)
- George Harrison (guitar, vocals)
- Ringo Starr (drums)

### Recording equipment

*Recording console*

- Unknown

*Primary tracking machine*

- THREE-TRACK:1/2" Ampex 300

*Mixdown machine*

- Unknown twin-track

*Outboard signal processors*

- Equalization, Limiting (unknown equipment makes or models)

*Effects*

- Reverb

*Monitors*

Control room

- Unknown

### Notes
The Ampex 300 is assigned as the primary tracking machine based on the fact that these concerts are documented as being recorded on three-track, and that the Ampex 300 was the most common commercial three-track machine in use during this period.

**Sources -** Lewisohn, Mark (1). p. 49. / The Beatles. *Anthology (Director's Cut)*. Dir. Bob Smeaton and Geoff Wonfor. Perf. The Beatles. Apple, 1996. DVD.

## Instruments

### Electric guitars

*Lennon*

- 1964 Rickenbacker 325-12 (12-string)

*Harrison*

- 1963 Gretsch PX6122 Chet Atkins Country Gentleman with Gretsch Bigsby B6G vibrato
- 1963 Gretsch 6119 Chet Atkins Tennessean with Gretsch Bigsby vibrato
- 1963 Rickenbacker 360-12 (12-string)

### Acoustic guitars

*Lennon*

- 1964 Gibson J-160E

### Bass guitars

*McCartney*

- 1962-1963 Hofner 500/1

### Drums

*Starr*

- 1964 Ludwig Oyster Black Pearl "Super Classic" (14" X 22" bass drum/ 9" X 13" rack tom/ 16" X 16" floor tom/ 1963 14" X 5.5" "Jazz Festival" snare); Paiste, Zyn, Zildjian cymbals (20" crash/ride; 20" Zyn 4-rivet "sizzle") Zildjian cymbals (18" crash/ride; 14" model A hi-hats) (Ludwig Set 3)

### Percussion

- Tambourine (Olympic or Ludwig)

## Amplifiers

### Guitar

*Lennon/Harrison*

- 1963 JMI Vox AC30/6 Twin Treble with "Top Boost" circuit, 30W with two 12" Vox Celestion Alnico Gray G12 T530 speakers
- 1964 JMI Vox AC100 Mk I, 100W with Vox AC100 cabinet, 4X12" Vox Celestion Alnico Silver T1088 speakers and 2X Goodmans Midax horns

### Bass

McCartney

- 1963 Vox AC100, 100W head with Vox AC100 custom cabinet, with two 15" Vox Celestion T1070 speakers

## Recording equipment

*Recording console*

- REDD.51

*Primary tracking machine*

- FOUR-TRACK: 1" Telefunken M10

*Outboard signal processors*

- EMI RS114 Limiter
- EMI RS124 Altec Compressor
- EMI RS127 Presence Box
- EMI RS144 4-Way Mixer/Premix
- EMI RS92 Neumann Mic Equaliser
- Fairchild 660 Limiter

*Monitors*

Control room

- Altec 605A (Altec 612 Cabinet) with EMI RS141 Leak TL/25 Plus Amplifier

Studio

- RLS10 - "White Elephant"

*Microphones*

Vocals

- Neumann U48 or U47/48 (U47/8)

Electric guitar amplifiers

- Neumann U48, U47/48 (U47/8)
- Neumann KM54

Acoustic guitars

- Neumann U48 or U47/48 (U47/8)

Bass amplifier

- AKG D20

Drums

- Overhead – AKG 19c
- Bass drum - AKG D20

Other

- Neumann U48, U47/48 (U47/8)
- STC 4038

**Backing Tracks**

- *Every Little Thing* – backing track included Lennon on acoustic guitar and lead vocals; McCartney on bass and backing vocal; Harrison on 12-string guitar; Starr on drums
- *I Don't Want To Spoil The Party* – backing track included Lennon on acoustic guitar and lead vocals; McCartney on bass and backing vocals; Harrison on guitar; Starr on drums
- *What You're Doing* – backing track included Lennon on 12-string guitar; McCartney on bass; Harrison on 12-string guitar; Starr on drums

**Superimpositions**

- *I Don't Want To Spoil The Party* – superimpositions included Lennon, McCartney, and Harrison on backing vocals; Starr on tambourine

**Notes**

Takes of *What You're Doing* recorded during this session and on the following day mark the only appearance of Lennon's 1964 Rickenbacker 325-12 (12-string) electric guitar on a Beatles session.

The song was remade in its entirety on October 26th, when Lennon exchanged the Rickenbacker for his Gibson J-160E acoustic guitar.

A 1987 article in *Guitar Player* magazine drawn from photographic evidence found in the monthly fan magazine, *Beatles Book*, indicates Harrison played his 1963 Gretsch PX6122 Chet Atkins Country Gentleman with Gretsch Bigsby B6G vibrato on *I Don't Want To Spoil The Party*.

**Sources -** Everett, Walter (1). pp. 258, 260. / Lewisohn, Mark (1). p. 49. / Lewisohn, Mark (2). p. 172. / Mytkowicz, Bob. / The Beatles. "*Every Little Thing*". Rec.29, 30 September 1964. The Beatles. FLAC audio file. / The Beatles. "*I Don't Want To Spoil The Party*". Rec.29 September 1964. The Beatles. FLAC audio file. / The Beatles. "*What You're Doing (take 11)*". Rec.29 September 1964. The Beatles. FLAC audio file. / The Beatles. "*What You're Doing (take 5)*". Rec.29 September 1964. The Beatles. FLAC audio file. / Winn, John C. (3). p. 42.

# September 30, 1964

**Time**
230PM – 1030PM

**Studio name and room**
EMI Recording Studios
Studio 2

- 230PM – 530PM
- 630PM – 1030PM

**Songs recorded (composer) (activities)**

- *Every Little Thing (remake)* (Lennon and McCartney)
    - takes 5-9
    - superimposition onto take 9
- *What You're Doing* (Lennon and McCartney)
    - takes 8-11
- *No Reply* (Lennon and McCartney)
    - takes 1-8
    - superimposition onto take 8

**Studio Personnel**

- Producer: George Martin
- Balance engineer: Norman Smith
- Tape operator(s): Ken Scott, Mike Stone

**Musicians (instruments played)**

- John Lennon (guitar, vocals)
- Paul McCartney (bass, vocals)
- George Harrison (guitar, vocals)
- Ringo Starr (drums, percussion)

**Other musicians (instruments played)**

- George Martin (piano)

## Instruments

### Electric guitars

*Lennon*

- 1963 Rickenbacker 360-12 (12-string)

*Harrison*

- 1963 Gretsch PX6122 Chet Atkins Country Gentleman with Gretsch Bigsby B6G vibrato
- 1963 Gretsch 6119 Chet Atkins Tennessean with Gretsch Bigsby vibrato
- 1963 Rickenbacker 360-12 (12-string)

### Acoustic guitars

*Lennon*

- 1964 Gibson J-160E

*Harrison*

- 1962 Gibson J-160E

### Bass guitars

*McCartney*

- 1962-1963 Hofner 500/1

### Drums

*Starr*

- 1964 Ludwig Oyster Black Pearl "Super Classic" (14" X 22" bass drum/ 9" X 13" rack tom/ 16" X 16" floor tom/ 1963 14" X 5.5" "Jazz Festival" snare); Paiste, Zyn, Zildjian cymbals (20" crash/ride; 20" Zyn 4-rivet "sizzle") Zildjian cymbals (18" crash/ride; 14" model A hi-hats) (Ludwig Set 3)

### Percussion

- Ludwig Timpani

### Pianos and keyboards

- Steinway "Music Room" Model B Grand Piano (circa 1880s)

## Amplifiers

### Guitar

*Lennon/Harrison*

- 1964 JMI Vox AC100 Mk I, 100W with Vox AC100 cabinet, 4X12" Vox Celestion Alnico Silver T1088 speakers and 2X Goodmans Midax horns

### Bass

*McCartney*

- 1963 Vox AC100, 100W head with Vox AC100 custom cabinet, with two 15" Vox Celestion T1070 speakers

## Recording equipment

*Recording console*

- REDD.51

*Primary tracking machine*

- FOUR-TRACK: 1" Telefunken M10

*Outboard signal processors*

- EMI RS114 Limiter
- EMI RS124 Altec Compressor
- EMI RS127 Presence Box
- EMI RS144 4-Way Mixer/Premix
- EMI RS92 Neumann Mic Equaliser
- Fairchild 660 Limiter

*Effects*

- Double tracking

*Monitors*

Control room

- Altec 605A (Altec 612 Cabinet) with EMI RS141 Leak TL/25 Plus Amplifier

Studio

- RLS10 - "White Elephant"

*Microphones*

Vocals

- Neumann U48 or U47/48 (U47/8)

Electric guitar amplifiers

- Neumann U48, U47/48 (U47/8)

Acoustic guitars

- Neumann U48 or U47/48 (U47/8)

Bass amplifier

- AKG D20

Drums

- Overhead – AKG 19c
- Bass drum - AKG D20

Piano

- Neumann U48 or U47/48 (U47/8)

Other

- Neumann U48, U47/48 (U47/8)
- STC 4038

**Backing Tracks**

- *Every Little Thing* – backing track included Lennon on 12-string guitar and lead vocals; McCartney on bass and backing vocal; Harrison on acoustic guitar; Starr on drums
- *What You're Doing* – backing track included Lennon on 12-string guitar and lead vocals; McCartney on bass and lead vocals; Harrison on 12-string guitar; Starr on drums
- *No Reply* – backing track included Lennon on acoustic guitar and lead vocals; McCartney on bass and backing vocals; Harrison on acoustic guitar; Starr on drums

**Superimpositions**

- *Every Little Thing* – superimpositions included Lennon or Harrison on 12-string guitar; Starr on timpani; George Martin on piano

- *No Reply* – superimpositions included Lennon on double-tracked lead vocals; McCartney on double-tracked backing vocals; handclaps; Starr on drum overdub (bass drum and crash only); George Martin on piano

**Notes**

Takes of *What You're Doing* from this session and those from the previous day mark the only recorded appearance of Lennon's 1964 Rickenbacker 325-12 (12-string) guitar.

The song was remade in its entirety on October 26th, when Lennon exchanged the Rickenbacker for his Gibson J-160E acoustic guitar.

Early takes of *No Reply* feature George Martin on piano and McCartney duplicating Lennon's lead vocal line for the verses of the song.

For the final track, Martin's piano contribution is scaled back and superimposed, while Lennon doubles his own lead vocal for the verses.

**Sources** - Everett, Walter (1). pp. 258, 260, 261. / Lewisohn, Mark (1). p. 49. / Ryan, Kevin and Brian Kehew. p. 380. / The Beatles. "*Every Little Thing*". Rec.29, 30 September 1964. The Beatles. FLAC audio file. / *The Beatles. "No Reply (take 1)".* Anthology. Perf. The Beatles. Apple, 1995. DVD. / The Beatles. "*No Reply (take 2)". Anthology*. George Martin, 1995. CD. / The Beatles. "*No Reply*". Rec.30 September 1964. The Beatles. FLAC audio file. / The Beatles. "*What You're Doing". Beatles For Sale.* George Martin. 1964. Vinyl, FLAC audio file. / Winn, John C. (3). p. 43.

# October 6, 1964

**Time**
3PM - 10PM

**Studio name and room**
EMI Recording Studios
Studio 2

- 3PM – 645PM
- 7PM – 10PM

**Songs recorded (composer) (activities)**

- *Eight Days A Week* (Lennon and McCartney)
    - takes 1-13
    - superimposition onto take 13

**Studio Personnel**

- Producer: George Martin
- Balance engineer: Norman Smith
- Tape operator(s): Ken Scott, Mike Stone

**Musicians (instruments played)**

- John Lennon (guitar, vocals)
- Paul McCartney (bass, vocals)
- George Harrison (guitar, vocals)
- Ringo Starr (drums)

**Instruments**

**Electric guitars**

*Harrison*

- 1963 Gretsch PX6122 Chet Atkins Country Gentleman with Gretsch Bigsby B6G vibrato

- 1963 Gretsch 6119 Chet Atkins Tennessean with Gretsch Bigsby vibrato
- 1963 Rickenbacker 360-12 (12-string)

### Acoustic guitars

*Lennon*

- 1964 Gibson J-160E

*Harrison*

- 1962 Gibson J-160E

### Bass guitars

*McCartney*

- 1962-1963 Hofner 500/1

### Drums

*Starr*

- 1964 Ludwig Oyster Black Pearl "Super Classic" (14" X 22" bass drum/ 9" X 13" rack tom/ 16" X 16" floor tom/ 1963 14" X 5.5" "Jazz Festival" snare); Paiste, Zyn, Zildjian cymbals (20" crash/ride; 20" Zyn 4-rivet "sizzle") Zildjian cymbals (18" crash/ride; 14" model A hi-hats) (Ludwig Set 3)

## Amplifiers

### Guitar

*Lennon/Harrison*

- 1963 JMI Vox AC30/6 Twin Treble with "Top Boost" circuit, 30W with two 12" Vox Celestion Alnico Gray G12 T530 speakers
- 1964 JMI Vox AC100 Mk I, 100W with Vox AC100 cabinet, 4X12" Vox Celestion Alnico Silver T1088 speakers and 2X Goodmans Midax horns

### Bass

*McCartney*

- 1963 Vox AC100, 100W head with Vox AC100 custom cabinet, with two 15" Vox Celestion T1070 speakers

## Recording equipment

*Recording console*

- REDD.51

*Primary tracking machine*

- FOUR-TRACK: 1" Telefunken M10

*Outboard signal processors*

- EMI RS114 Limiter
- EMI RS124 Altec Compressor
- EMI RS127 Presence Box
- EMI RS144 4-Way Mixer/Premix
- EMI RS92 Neumann Mic Equaliser
- Fairchild 660 Limiter

*Effects*

- Echo chamber (includes RS61 Low Level Amplifier with RS62 Power Supply and RS106A Echo Control Unit – Band Pass Filter)
- STEED (send tape echo/echo delay)

*Monitors*

Control room

- Altec 605A (Altec 612 Cabinet) with EMI RS141 Leak TL/25 Plus Amplifier

Studio

- RLS10 - "White Elephant"

*Microphones*

Vocals

- Neumann U48 or U47/48 (U47/8)

Electric guitar amplifiers

- Neumann U48, U47/48 (U47/8)
- Neumann KM54

Acoustic guitars

- Neumann U48 or U47/48 (U47/8)

Bass amplifier

- AKG D20

Drums

- Overhead – AKG 19c
- Bass drum - AKG D20

Other

- Neumann U48 or U47/48 (U47/8)

**Backing tracks**

- *Eight Days A Week* – backing track included Lennon on acoustic guitar and lead vocals; McCartney on bass and lead vocals; Harrison on guitar; Starr on drums

**Superimpositions**

- *Eight Days A Week* – superimpositions included Harrison on guitar; Lennon on double-tracked lead vocals; McCartney on backing vocals; group handclaps

**Sources** -Dowlding, William J. p. 88. / Everett, Walter (1). p. 261. / Lewisohn, Mark (1). p. 49. / The Beatles. "*Eight Days A Week* ". Rec.6 October 1964. The Beatles. FLAC audio file. / The Beatles. "*Eight Days A Week (take 2)". Anthology*. George Martin, 1995. CD. / The Beatles. "*Eight Days A Week (take 4)". Anthology*. George Martin, 1995. CD. / The Beatles. "*Eight Days A Week (take 5)". Anthology*. George Martin, 1995. CD. / Winn, John C. (3). p. 43.

# October 8, 1964

**Time**
230PM - 6PM

**Studio name and room**
EMI Recording Studios
Studio 2

### Songs recorded (composer) (activities)

- *She's A Woman* (Lenner and McCartney)
    - takes 1-7
    - superimposition onto take 6

### Studio Personnel

- Producer: George Martin
- Balance engineer: Norman Smith
- Tape operator(s): Ken Scott, Mike Stone

### Musicians (instruments played)

- John Lennon (guitar)
- Paul McCartney (bass, piano, vocals)
- George Harrison (guitar)
- Ringo Starr (drums, chocalho)

### Instruments

### Electric guitars

*Lennon*

- 1964 Rickenbacker 325 Capri (second model - Black)

*Harrison*

- 1963 Gretsch PX6122 Chet Atkins Country Gentleman with Gretsch Bigsby B6G vibrato
- 1963 Gretsch 6119 Chet Atkins Tennessean with Gretsch Bigsby vibrato

### Bass guitars

*McCartney*

- 1962-1963 Hofner 500/1

### Drums

*Starr*

- 1964 Ludwig Oyster Black Pearl "Super Classic" (14" X 22" bass drum/ 9" X 13" rack tom/ 16" X 16" floor tom/ 1963 14" X 5.5" "Jazz Festival" snare); Paiste, Zyn, Zildjian cymbals (20" crash/ride; 20" Zyn 4-rivet "sizzle") Zildjian cymbals (18" crash/ride; 14" model A hi-hats) (Ludwig Set 3)

### Percussion

- Chocalho

### Pianos and keyboards

- Steinway "Music Room" Model B Grand Piano (circa 1880s)

## Amplifiers

### Guitar

*Lennon/Harrison*

- 1963 JMI Vox AC30/6 Twin Treble with "Top Boost" circuit, 30W with two 12" Vox Celestion Alnico Gray G12 T530 speakers
- 1964 JMI Vox AC100 Mk I, 100W with Vox AC100 cabinet, 4X12" Vox Celestion Alnico Silver T1088 speakers and 2X Goodmans Midax horns

### Bass

*McCartney*

- 1963 Vox AC100, 100W head with Vox AC100 custom cabinet, with two 15" Vox Celestion T1070 speakers

## Recording equipment

*Recording console*

- REDD.51

*Primary tracking machine*

- FOUR-TRACK: 1" Telefunken M10

*Outboard signal processors*

- EMI RS114 Limiter
- EMI RS124 Altec Compressor
- EMI RS127 Presence Box
- EMI RS144 4-Way Mixer/Premix
- EMI RS92 Neumann Mic Equaliser
- Fairchild 660 Limiter

*Effects*

- Double-tracking

*Monitors*

Control room

- Altec 605A (Altec 612 Cabinet) with EMI RS141 Leak TL/25 Plus Amplifier

Studio

- RLS10 - "White Elephant"

*Microphones*

Vocals

- Neumann U48 or U47/48 (U47/8)

Electric guitar amplifiers

- Neumann U48, U47/48 (U47/8) or Neumann KM54

Acoustic guitars

- Neumann U48 or U47/48 (U47/8)

Bass amplifier

- AKG D20

Drums

- Overhead – AKG 19c
- Bass drum - AKG D20

Piano

- Neumann U48 or U47/48 (U47/8)

Other

- Neumann U48, U47/48 (U47/8)

### Backing tracks

- *She's A Woman* – backing track included Lennon on guitar; McCartney on bass and lead vocals; Starr on drums

### Superimpositions

- *She's A Woman* – superimpositions included McCartney on double-tracked vocals; McCartney on piano; Harrison on double-tracked guitar solo; Starr on chocalho

**Sources -** Everett, Walter (1). p. 266. / Lewisohn, Mark (1). p. 49. / Ryan, Kevin and Brian Kehew. p. 381. / The Beatles. "*She's A Woman (take 1)*". Rec.8 October 1964. The Beatles. FLAC audio file. / The Beatles. "*She's A Woman (take 2)*". Rec.8 October 1964. The Beatles. FLAC audio file. / The Beatles. "*She's A Woman (take 3)*". Rec.8 October 1964. The Beatles. FLAC audio file. / The Beatles. "*She's A Woman (take 4)*". Rec.8 October 1964. The Beatles. FLAC audio file. / The Beatles. "*She's A Woman (take 5, called take 7)*". Rec.8 October 1964. The Beatles. FLAC audio file. / The Beatles. "*She's A Woman (take 6) (EP Collection + Anthology (Audifon)*". Rec.8 October 1964. The Beatles. FLAC audio file. / The Beatles. "*She's A Woman*". Rec.8 October 1964. The Beatles. FLAC audio file. / Winn, John C. (3). p. 44.

# October 12, 1964

### Time
10AM - 3PM

### Studio name and room
EMI Recording Studios
Studio 2 (control room)

- 10AM – 1030AM
- 230PM – 3PM

### Songs mixed (version) (remix number and take)

- *She's A Woman* (mono)
    - remix (RM) 1 from take 6
- *She's A Woman* (stereo)
    - remix (RS) 1 from take 6
- *Eight Days A Week* (mono)
    - remix (RM) 1 from take 13

### Studio Personnel

- Producer: George Martin
- Balance engineer: Norman Smith
- Tape operator: Ken Scott

### Recording equipment

*Recording console*

- REDD.51

*Primary tracking machine*

- FOUR-TRACK: 1" Telefunken M10

*Mixdown machine*

- MONO: 1/4" EMI BTR2

- STEREO: 1/4" EMI BTR3

*Outboard signal processors*

- EMI RS114 Limiter
- EMI RS124 Altec Compressor
- EMI RS127 Presence Box
- EMI RS144 4-Way Mixer/Premix
- EMI RS92 Neumann Mic Equaliser
- Fairchild 660 Limiter

*Effects*

- Echo chamber (includes RS61 Low Level Amplifier with RS62 Power Supply and RS106A Echo Control Unit – Band Pass Filter)
- STEED (send tape echo/echo delay)

*Monitors*

Control room

- Altec 605A (Altec 612 Cabinet) with EMI RS141 Leak TL/25 Plus Amplifier

**Remixes**

Mono master remixes

- *She's A Woman* (mono) (remix (RM) 1 from take 6)

Stereo master remixes

- *She's A Woman* (stereo) (remix (RS) 1 from take 6)

**Sources** - Lewisohn, Mark (1). p. 50. / Winn, John C. (3). p. 44.

# October 16, 1964

**Time**
230PM - 530PM

**Studio name and room**
Studio 1 (control room)

**Songs mixed (version) (remix number and take)**

- *No Reply* (mono)
    - remix (RM) 1 and 2 from take 8

**Studio Personnel**

- Producer: George Martin
- Balance engineer: Norman Smith
- Tape operator: Anthony (Tony) Bridge

**Recording equipment**

*Recording console*

- REDD.37

*Primary tracking machine*

- FOUR-TRACK: 1" Telefunken M10

*Mixdown machine*

- MONO: 1/4" EMI BTR2

*Outboard signal processors*

- EMI RS114 Limiter
- EMI RS124 Altec Compressor
- EMI RS127 Presence Box

- EMI RS144 4-Way Mixer/Premix
- EMI RS92 Neumann Mic Equaliser
- Fairchild 660 Limiter

*Effects*

- Echo chamber (includes RS61 Low Level Amplifier with RS62 Power Supply and RS106A Echo Control Unit – Band Pass Filter)
- STEED (send tape echo/echo delay)

*Monitors*

Control room

- Altec 605A (Altec 612 Cabinet) with EMI RS141 Leak TL/25 Plus Amplifier

**Remixes**

Mono master remixes

- *No Reply* (mono) (remix (RM) 2 from take 8)

**Sources -** Lewisohn, Mark (1) p. 50.

# October 18, 1964

**Time**
230PM – 1130PM

**Studio name and room**
EMI Recording Studio
Studio 2

**Songs recorded (composer) (activitics)**

- *Eight Days A Week* (Lennon and McCartney)
    - edit piece takes 14-15
- *Kansas City/Hey-Hey-Hey-Hey!* (Lieber and Stoller/ Penniman)
    - takes 1 and 2
    - superimposition onto takes 1 and 2
- *Mr. Moonlight (remake)* (Johnson)
    - takes 5-8
    - superimposition onto take 8

- *I Feel Fine* (Lennon and McCartney)
    - takes 1-9
    - superimposition onto take 9
- *I'll Follow The Sun* (Lennon and McCartney)
    - takes 1-8
    - superimposition onto take 8
- *Everybody's Trying To Be My Baby* (Perkins)
    - take 1
    - superimposition onto take 1
- *Rock And Roll Music* (Berry)
    - take 1
- *Words Of Love* (Holly)
    - takes 1-3
    - superimposition onto take 3

**Studio Personnel**

- Producer: George Martin
- Balance engineer: Norman Smith
- Tape operator: Geoff Emerick

**Musicians (instruments played)**

- John Lennon (guitar, percussion, vocals)
- Paul McCartney (bass, organ, guitar, vocals)
- George Harrison (guitar, percussion, vocals)
- Ringo Starr (drums, tambourine, percussion)

**Other musicians (instruments played)**

- George Martin (piano)

**Instruments**

**Electric guitars**

*Lennon*

- 1964 Rickenbacker 325 Capri (second model - Black)

*Harrison*

- 1963 Gretsch PX6122 Chet Atkins Country Gentleman with Gretsch Bigsby B6G vibrato
- 1963 Gretsch 6119 Chet Atkins Tennessean with Gretsch Bigsby vibrato
- 1963 Rickenbacker 360-12 (12-string)

**Acoustic guitars**

*Lennon*

- 1964 Gibson J-160E

*Harrison*

- 1962 Gibson J-160E

**Bass guitars**

*McCartney*

- 1962-1963 Hofner 500/1

**Drums**

*Starr*

- 1964 Ludwig Oyster Black Pearl "Super Classic" (14" X 22" bass drum/ 9" X 13" rack tom/ 16" X 16" floor tom/ 1963 14" X 5.5" "Jazz Festival" snare); Paiste, Zyn, Zildjian cymbals (20" crash/ride; 20" Zyn 4-rivet "sizzle") Zildjian cymbals (18" crash/ride; 14" model A hi-hats) (Ludwig Set 3)

**Percussion**

- Tambourine (Olympic or Ludwig)
- Wood Block
- African Drum
- Suitcase
- Premier bongos
- ASBA congas
- Hand-drumming

**Pianos and keyboards**

- Steinway "Music Room" Model B Grand Piano (circa 1880s)
- Hammond RT3 Organ (circa 1954-1962)

**Other**

- Hammond PR-40 tone cabinet

**Amplifiers**

**Guitar**

*Lennon/Harrison*

- 1963 JMI Vox AC30/6 Twin Treble with "Top Boost" circuit, 30W with two 12" Vox Celestion Alnico Gray G12 T530 speakers
- 1964 JMI Vox AC100 Mk I, 100W with Vox AC100 cabinet, 4X12" Vox Celestion Alnico Silver T1088 speakers and 2X Goodmans Midax horns

**Bass**

- 1963 Vox AC100, 100W head with Vox AC100 custom cabinet, with two 15" Vox Celestion T1070 speakers

**Recording equipment**

*Recording console*

- REDD.51

*Primary tracking machine*

- FOUR-TRACK: 1" Telefunken M10

*Mixdown machine*

- MONO: 1/4" EMI BTR2
- STEREO: 1/4" EMI BTR3

*Outboard signal processors*

- EMI RS114 Limiter
- EMI RS124 Altec Compressor
- EMI RS127 Presence Box
- EMI RS144 4-Way Mixer/Premix
- EMI RS92 Neumann Mic Equaliser
- Fairchild 660 Limiter

*Effects*

- Double-tracking
- Tape echo/ repeat echo

*Monitors*

Control room

- Altec 605A (Altec 612 Cabinet) with EMI RS141 Leak TL/25 Plus Amplifier

Studio

- RLS10 - "White Elephant"

*Microphones*

Vocals

- Neumann U48 or U47/48 (U47/8)

Electric guitar amplifiers

- Neumann U48, U47/48 (U47/8)
- Neumann KM54

Acoustic guitars

- Neumann U48 or U47/48 (U47/8)

Bass amplifier

- AKG D20

Drums

- Overhead – AKG 19c
- Bass drum - AKG D20

Piano

- Neumann U48 or U47/48 (U47/8)

Other

- Neumann U48, U47/48 (U47/8)
- STC 4038

**Backing tracks**

- *Mr. Moonlight* – backing track included Lennon on guitar and lead vocals; McCartney on bass and backing vocals; Harrison on guitar; Starr on congas
- *Kansas City/Hey-Hey-Hey-Hey!* – backing track included Lennon on guitar; McCartney on bass and lead vocals; Harrison on guitar; Starr on drums
- *I Feel Fine* – backing track included Lennon on acoustic guitar; McCartney on bass; Harrison on guitar; Starr on drums
- *I'll Follow The Sun* – backing track included McCartney on bass and lead vocals; Lennon on acoustic guitar and backing vocals; Harrison on guitar; Starr on percussion (hand-drumming)
- *Everybody's Trying To Be My Baby* – backing track included Lennon on acoustic guitar; McCartney on bass; Harrison on guitar and lead vocals; Starr on drums
- *Rock And Roll Music* – backing track included Lennon on guitar and lead vocals; McCartney on bass; Harrison on acoustic guitar; Starr on drums; Martin on piano
- *Words Of Love* – backing track included Lennon on guitar; McCartney on bass; Harrison on guitar; Starr on drums

**Superimpositions**

- *Mr. Moonlight* – superimpositions included Lennon on double-tracked lead vocals; McCartney on double-tracked backing vocals; McCartney on organ; Harrison on African drum
- *Kansas City/Hey-Hey-Hey-Hey!* – superimpositions included Lennon, McCartney, and Harrison on backing vocals and handclaps; George Martin on piano
- *I Feel Fine* – superimposition included Lennon on double-tracked lead vocals; Lennon, McCartney, and Harrison on backing vocals; Harrison on guitar
- *I'll Follow The Sun* – superimpositions included Harrison on guitar
- *Everybody's Trying To Be My Baby* – superimpositions included Harrison on double-tracked lead vocals; Starr on tambourine
- *Words Of Love* – superimposition included Harrison on lead guitar; Lennon, McCartney, and Harrison on double-tracked vocals and handclaps

**Edit pieces**

- *Eight Days A Week* – edit pieces included Harrison on 12-string guitar and Starr on drums for song introduction and ending. Only the ending edit piece was used.

**Notes**

The feedback guitar note that begins *I Feel Fine* was played by Lennon with his 1964 Gibson J-160E played through one of the Vox amplifiers. Lennon recalled in an interview, "That's me completely. Including the electric guitar lick and the record with the first feedback anywhere."

Emerick recalls that Lennon, McCartney, and Harrison sang the lead vocals for *Words of Love* together on the same microphone. The guitar solo on the song was double-tracked.

A 1987 article in *Guitar Player* magazine drawn from photographic evidence found in the monthly fan magazine, *Beatles Book*, indicates Harrison's 1963 Gretsch 6119 Chet Atkins Tennessean with Gretsch Bigsby vibrato was the guitar used on *Words Of Love.*

The repeat echo applied to Harrison's vocals on *Everybody's Trying To Be My Baby* and Lennon's vocals on *Rock And Roll Music* were recorded directly to the track.

**Sources -** Dowlding, William J. p. 86, 91. / Emerick, Geoff. pp. 93, 95-96, 97. / Everett, Walter (1). pp. 250, 257, 265, 268. / Everett, Walter (2). p. 13. / Lewisohn, Mark (1). p. 50. / Miles, Barry and Pearce Marchbank. p. 80. / Mytkowicz, Bob. / Ryan, Kevin and Brian Kehew. p. 381. / The Beatles. "*Everybody's Trying To Be My Baby*". Rec.18 October 1964. The Beatles. FLAC audio file. / The Beatles. "*I Feel Fine (take 1) (Studio Sessions)*". Rec.18 October 1964. The Beatles. FLAC audio file. / The Beatles. "*I Feel Fine (take 2) (Studio Sessions)*". Rec.18 October 1964. The Beatles. FLAC audio file. / The Beatles. "*I Feel Fine (take 3) (Studio Sessions)*". Rec.18 October 1964. The Beatles. FLAC audio file. / The Beatles. "*I Feel Fine (take 4) (Studio Sessions)*". Rec.18 October 1964. The Beatles. FLAC audio file. / The Beatles. "*I Feel Fine (take 5) (Studio Sessions)*". Rec.18 October 1964. The Beatles. FLAC audio file. / The Beatles. "*I Feel Fine (take 6) (Studio Sessions)*". Rec.18 October 1964. The Beatles. FLAC audio file. The Beatles. "*I Feel Fine (take 7) (Studio Sessions)*". Rec.18 October 1964. The Beatles. FLAC audio file. The Beatles. "*I Feel Fine (take 8) (Sgt. Pepper: A History Of The Beatle Years)*". Rec.18 October 1964. The Beatles. FLAC audio file. / The Beatles. "*I Feel Fine (take 9) (Studio Sessions)*". Rec.18 October 1964. The Beatles. FLAC audio file. / The Beatles. "*I Feel Fine*". Rec.18 October 1964. The Beatles. FLAC audio file. / The Beatles. "*I'll Follow The Sun*". *Beatles For Sale.* Rec.18 October 1964. The Beatles. FLAC audio file. / The Beatles. *"Kansas City/Hey-Hey-Hey-Hey! (take 2)". Anthology.* George Martin, 1995. CD. / The Beatles. "*Kansas City/Hey-Hey-Hey-Hey!*". Rec.18 October 1964. The Beatles. FLAC audio file. / The Beatles. "*Mr. Moonlight*". Rec.18 October 1964. The Beatles. FLAC audio file. / The Beatles. "*Rock And Roll Music*". *Beatles For Sale.* Rec.18 October 1964. The Beatles. FLAC audio file. / The Beatles. "*Words Of Love*". *Beatles For Sale.* Rec.18 October 1964. The Beatles. FLAC audio file. / Winn, John C. (3). pp. 43, 45, 46.

# October 21, 1964

**Time**

230PM – 545PM

**Studio name and room**

EMI Recording Studios
Room 65

**Songs mixed (version) (remix number and take)**

- *I'll Follow The Sun* (mono)
    - remix (RM) 1 from take 8

- *I Feel Fine* (mono)
    - remix (RM) 1-4 from take 9
- *She's A Woman* (mono)
    - remix (RM) 2 from take 6
- *Everybody's Trying To Be My Baby* (mono)
    - remix (RM) 1 from take 1

**Studio Personnel**

- Producer: George Martin
- Balance engineer: Norman Smith
- Tape operator: Ron Pender

**Recording equipment**

*Recording console*

- REDD.51

*Primary tracking machine*

- FOUR-TRACK: 1" Telefunken M10

*Mixdown machine*

- MONO: 1/4" EMI BTR2
- STEREO: 1/4" EMI BTR3

*Outboard signal processors*

- EMI RS124 Altec Compressor
- EMI RS127 Presence Box
- EMI RS144 4-Way Mixer/Premix
- EMI RS92 Neumann Mic Equaliser
- Fairchild 660 Limiter

*Effects*

- Echo chamber (includes RS61 Low Level Amplifier with RS62 Power Supply and RS106A Echo Control Unit – Band Pass Filter)
- STEED (send tape echo/echo delay)

*Monitors*

Control room

- Altec 605A (Altec 612 Cabinet) with EMI RS141 Leak TL/25 Plus Amplifier

**Remixes**

Mono master remixes

- *I'll Follow The Sun* (mono) (remix (RM) 1 from take 8)
- *I Feel Fine* (mono) (remix (RM) 3 from take 9)
- *I Feel Fine* (mono) (remix (RM) 4 from take 9) (for US Release)
- *She's A Woman* (mono) (remix (RM) 2 from take 6) (for US Release)
- *Everybody's Trying To Be My Baby* (mono) (remix (RM) 1 from take 1)

**Sources -** Lewisohn, Mark (1) p. 51. / Winn, John C. (3). p. 44.

# October 22, 1964

**Time**
11AM - 12PM

**Studio name and room**
EMI Recording Studios
Studio 1 (control room)

**Songs mixed (version) (remix number and take)**

- *I Feel Fine* (mono)
    - remix (RM) 5 from take 9

**Studio Personnel**

- Producer: George Martin
- Balance engineer: Norman Smith
- Tape operator: Ron Pender

**Recording equipment**

*Recording console*

- REDD.37

*Primary tracking machine*

- FOUR-TRACK: 1" Telefunken M10

*Mixdown machine*

- MONO: 1/4" EMI BTR2

*Outboard signal processors*

- EMI RS124 Altec Compressor
- EMI RS127 Presence Box
- EMI RS144 4-Way Mixer/Premix
- EMI RS92 Neumann Mic Equaliser
- Fairchild 660 Limiter

*Effects*

- Echo chamber (includes RS61 Low Level Amplifier with RS62 Power Supply and RS106A Echo Control Unit – Band Pass Filter)
- STEED (send tape echo/echo delay)

*Monitors*

Control room

- Altec 605A (Altec 612 Cabinet) with EMI RS141 Leak TL/25 Plus Amplifier

**Sources -** Lewisohn, Mark (1). p. 51.

# October 26, 1964

**Time**
10AM - 10PM

**Studio name and room**
EMI Recording Studios

- Studio 2 (control room)
    - 10AM – 1245PM
    - 1245PM-105PM
- Studio 2
    - 430PM – 630PM
    - 730PM – 10PM

**Songs recorded (composer) (activities)**

- *Honey Don't* (Perkins)
    - takes 1-5

- *What You're Doing* (remake) (Lennon and McCartney)
    - takes 13-19
    - superimposition onto take 19
- *Another Beatles Christmas Record* (Lennon, McCartney, Harrison, Star)
    - "Christmas Message" takes 1-5
    - edit of takes 1 through 5
    - "Speech" takes 1 and 2
    - "Marching"

**Songs mixed (version) (remix number and take)**

- *I Don't Want To Spoil The Party* (mono)
    - remix (RM) 1 from take 9
- *Rock And Roll Music* (mono)
    - remix (RM) 1 from take 1
- *Words Of Love* (mono)
    - remix (RM) 1 from take 3
- *Baby's In Black* (mono)
    - remix (RM) 2 from take 14
- *I'm A Loser* (mono)
    - remix (RM) 2 from take 8
- *Kansas City/Hey-Hey-Hey-Hey!* (mono)
    - remix (RM) 1 from take 1
- *Kansas City/Hey-Hey-Hey-Hey!* (stereo)
    - remix (RS) 1 from take 1

**Studio Personnel**

- Producer: George Martin
- Balance engineer: Norman Smith
- Tape operator(s): Tony Clark, Anthony (Tony) Bridge

**Musicians (instruments played)**

- John Lennon (guitar, piano, vocals)
- Paul McCartney (bass, vocals)
- George Harrison (guitar, vocals)
- Ringo Starr (drums, vocals)

**Instruments**

**Electric guitars**

*Harrison*

- 1963 Gretsch PX6122 Chet Atkins Country Gentleman with Gretsch Bigsby B6G vibrato
- 1963 Gretsch 6119 Chet Atkins Tennessean with Gretsch Bigsby vibrato
- 1963 Rickenbacker 360-12 (12-string)

**Acoustic guitars**

*Lennon*

- 1964 Gibson J-160E
- 1964 Framus Hootenanny 5/024 (12-string)

**Bass guitars**

*McCartney*

- 1962-1963 Hofner 500/1

**Drums**

*Starr*

- 1964 Ludwig Oyster Black Pearl "Super Classic" (14" X 22" bass drum/ 9" X 13" rack tom/ 16" X 16" floor tom/ 1963 14" X 5.5" "Jazz Festival" snare); Paiste, Zyn, Zildjian cymbals (20" crash/ride; 20" Zyn 4-rivet "sizzle") Zildjian cymbals (18" crash/ride; 14" model A hi-hats) (Ludwig Set 3)

### Pianos and keyboards

- Steinway "Music Room" Model B Grand Piano (circa 1880s)

## Amplifiers

### Guitar

*Lennon/Harrison*

- 1963 JMI Vox AC30/6 Twin Treble with "Top Boost" circuit, 30W with two 12" Vox Celestion Alnico Gray G12 T530 speakers
- 1964 JMI Vox AC100 Mk I, 100W with Vox AC100 cabinet, 4X12" Vox Celestion Alnico Silver T1088 speakers and 2X Goodmans Midax horns

### Bass

*McCartney*

- 1963 Vox AC100, 100W head with Vox AC100 custom cabinet, with two 15" Vox Celestion T1070 speakers

## Recording equipment

*Recording console*

- REDD.51

*Primary tracking machine*

- FOUR-TRACK: 1" Telefunken M10
- MONO: 1/4" EMI BTR2

*Mixdown machine*

- MONO: 1/4" EMI BTR2
- STEREO: 1/4" EMI BTR3

*Outboard signal processors*

- EMI RS114 Limiter
- EMI RS127 Presence Box
- EMI RS144 4-Way Mixer/Premix EMI RS124 Altec Compressor
- EMI RS92 Neumann Mic Equaliser
- Fairchild 660 Limiter

*Effects*

- Echo chamber (includes RS61 Low Level Amplifier with RS62 Power Supply and RS106A Echo Control Unit – Band Pass Filter)
- STEED (send tape echo/echo delay)

*Monitors*

Control room

- Altec 605A (Altec 612 Cabinet) with EMI RS141 Leak TL/25 Plus Amplifier

Studio

- RLS10 - "White Elephant"

*Microphones*

Vocals

- Neumann U48 or U47/48 (U47/8)

Electric guitar amplifiers

- Neumann U48, U47/48 (U47/8)
- Neumann KM54

Acoustic guitars

- Neumann U48 or U47/48 (U47/8)

Bass amplifier

- AKG D20

Drums

- Overhead – AKG 19c
- Bass drum - AKG D20

**Backing tracks**

- *Honey Don't* – backing track included Starr on drums and lead vocals; Lennon on 12-string acoustic guitar; Harrison on guitar; McCartney on bass
- *What You're Doing* – backing track included Lennon on acoustic guitar and backing vocals; McCartney on bass and lead vocals; Harrison on 12-string guitar and backing vocals; Starr on drums

**Superimpositions**

- *Honey Don't* – superimpositions included Starr on tambourine
- *What You're Doing* – superimpositions included McCartney on double-tracked lead vocals; Lennon on piano; Harrison on guitar

**Remixes**

Mono master remixes

- *I Don't Want To Spoil The Party* (mono) (remix (RM) 1 from take 9)
- *Rock And Roll Music* (mono) (remix (RM) 1 from take 1)
- *Words Of Love* (mono) (remix (RM) 1 from take 3)
- *Baby's In Black* (mono) (remix (RM) 2 from take 14)
- *I'm A Loser* (mono) (remix (RM) 2 from take 8)
- *Kansas City/Hey-Hey-Hey-Hey!* (mono) (remix (RM) 1 from take 1)

Stereo master remixes

- *Kansas City/Hey-Hey-Hey-Hey!* (stereo) (remix (RS) 1 from take 1)

**Notes**

While George Martin often provided the piano parts on The Beatles' songs from this period (and Everett makes a detailed case for his work on this session), subjective review of the audio evidence points to Lennon being the piano player on *What You're Doing.* The part reveals none of the virtuosity typically evident in Martin's playing, but does demonstrate the sort of simple, staccato attack that Lennon used on later tracks like *I'm Down.*

This is one of the first instances when The Beatles sat in on a remixing session. From this session on, band members were in attendance for the creation of the majority of the mono remixes of their songs.

Up until the late 1960s, stereo remixes were still somewhat of a novelty in the UK, and The Beatles rarely attended remix-only sessions related to them. A very marginal amount of time was spent on the stereo remixes of a particular track in comparison to the work performed on the mono remixes.

A 1987 article in *Guitar Player* magazine drawn from photographic evidence found in the monthly fan magazine, *Beatles Book*, indicates Harrison's 1963 Gretsch 6119 Chet Atkins Tennessean with Gretsch Bigsby vibrato was the guitar used on *Honey Don't*.

**Sources -** Lewisohn, Mark (1). p. 51. / Mytkowicz, Bob. / The Beatles. "*Honey Don't*". Rec.26 October 1964. The Beatles. FLAC audio file. / The Beatles. "*What You're Doing*". Rec.26 October 1964. The Beatles. FLAC audio file. / Winn, John C. (3). pp. 46-48.

# October 27, 1964

**Time**
10AM - 1PM

**Studio name and room**
EMI Recording Studios
Studio 2 (control room)

- 10AM – 1230PM
- 1230PM – 1PM

**Songs recorded (composer) (activities)**

- *Mr. Moonlight* (Johnson)
  - edit of remix mono (RM) 1 and 2
- *Eight Days A Week* (Lennon and McCartney)
  - edit of remix mono (RM) 2 and 3
  - edit of remix stereo (RS) 1 and 2

**Songs mixed (version) (remix number and take)**

- *What You're Doing* (mono)
  - remix (RM) 1 from take 19
- *Mr. Moonlight* (mono)
  - remix (RM) 1 and 2 from takes 4 and 8
- *Honey Don't* (mono)
  - remix (RM) 1 from take 5
- *Every Little Thing* (mono)
  - remix (RM) 1 from take 9
- *Eight Days A Week* (mono)
  - remix (RM) 2 and 3 from takes 13 and 15
- *Eight Days A Week* (stereo)
  - remix (RS) 1 and 2 from takes 13 and 15
- *Every Little Thing* (stereo)
  - remix (RS) 1 from take 9
- *Honey Don't* (stereo)
  - remix (RS) 1 from take 5
- *What You're Doing* (stereo)
  - remix (RS) 1 from take 19

**Studio Personnel**

- Producer: George Martin
- Balance engineer: Norman Smith
- Tape operator: Ken Scott

**Recording equipment**

*Recording console*

- REDD.51

*Primary tracking machine*

- FOUR-TRACK: 1" Telefunken M10

*Mixdown machine*

- MONO: 1/4" EMI BTR2
- STEREO: 1/4" EMI BTR3

*Outboard signal processors*

- EMI RS124 Altec Compressor
- EMI RS127 Presence Box
- EMI RS144 4-Way Mixer/Premix
- EMI RS92 Neumann Mic Equaliser
- Fairchild 660 Limiter

*Effects*

- Echo chamber (includes RS61 Low Level Amplifier with RS62 Power Supply and RS106A Echo Control Unit – Band Pass Filter)
- STEED (send tape echo/echo delay)

*Monitors*

Control room

- Altec 605A (Altec 612 Cabinet) with EMI RS141 Leak TL/25 Plus Amplifier

**Remixes**

Mono master remixes

- *What You're Doing* (mono) (remix (RM) 1 from take 19)
- *Mr. Moonlight* (mono) (edit of remix (RM) 1 and 2 from takes 4 and 8)
- *Honey Don't* (mono) (remix (RM) 1 from take 5)
- *Every Little Thing* (mono) (remix (RM) 1 from take 9)
- *Eight Days A Week* (mono) (edit of remix (RM) 2 and 3 from takes 13 and 15)

Stereo master remixes

- *Eight Days A Week* (stereo) (edit of remix (RS) 1 and 2 from takes 13 and 15)
- *Every Little Thing* (stereo) (remix (RS) 1 from take 9)
- *Honey Don't* (stereo) (remix (RS) 1 from take 5)
- *What You're Doing* (stereo) (remix (RS) 1 from take 19)

**Sources -** Lewisohn, Mark (1). p. 52. / Winn, John C. (3). pp. 46, 49.

# November 4, 1964

**Time**
10AM - 1PM

**Studio name and room**
EMI Recording Studios
Studio 2 (control room)

**Songs recorded (composer) (activities)**

- *Mr. Moonlight* (Johnson)
    - edit of remix stereo (RS) 1 and 2

**Songs mixed (version) (remix number and take)**

- *I'll Follow The Sun* (stereo)
    - remix (RS) 1 from take 8
- *Everybody's Trying To Be My Baby* (stereo)
    - remix (RS) 1 from take 1
- *Rock And Roll Music* (stereo)
    - remix (RS) 1 from take 1
- *Words Of Love* (stereo)
    - remix (RS) 1 from take 3
- *Mr. Moonlight* (stereo)
    - remix (RS) 1 and 2 from takes 4 and 8
- *I Don't Want To Spoil The Party* (stereo)
    - remix (RS) 1 from take 9
- *I'm A Loser* (stereo)
    - remix (RS) 1 from take 8
- *Baby's In Black* (stereo)
    - remix (RS) 1 from take 14
- *No Reply* (stereo)
    - remix (RS) 1 from take 8
- *I Feel Fine* (stereo)
    - remix (RS) 1 from take 9

**Studio Personnel**

- Producer: George Martin
- Balance engineer: Norman Smith
- Tape operator: Mike Stone

**Recording equipment**

*Recording console*

- REDD.51

*Primary tracking machine*

- FOUR-TRACK: 1" Telefunken M10

*Mixdown machine*

- MONO: 1/4" EMI BTR2
- STEREO: 1/4" EMI BTR3

*Outboard signal processors*

- EMI RS124 Altec Compressor
- EMI RS127 Presence Box
- EMI RS144 4-Way Mixer/Premix
- EMI RS92 Neumann Mic Equaliser
- Fairchild 660 Limiter

*Effects*

- Echo chamber (includes RS61 Low Level Amplifier with RS62 Power Supply and RS106A Echo Control Unit – Band Pass Filter)
- STEED (send tape echo/echo delay)

*Monitors*

Control room

- Altec 605A (Altec 612 Cabinet) with EMI RS141 Leak TL/25 Plus Amplifier

**Remixes**

Stereo master remixes

- *I'll Follow The Sun* (stereo) (remix (RS) 1 from take 8)
- *Everybody's Trying To Be My Baby* (stereo) (remix (RS) 1 from take 1)
- *Rock And Roll Music* (stereo) (remix (RS) 1 from take 1)
- *Words Of Love* (stereo) (remix (RS) 1 from take 3)

- *Mr. Moonlight* (stereo) (remix (RS) 1 and 2 from takes 4 and 8)
- *I Don't Want To Spoil The Party* (stereo) (remix (RS) 1 from take 9)
- *I'm A Loser* (stereo) (remix (RS) 1 from take 8)
- *Baby's In Black* (stereo) (remix (RS) 1 from take 14)
- *No Reply* (stereo) (remix (RS) 1 from take 8)
- *I Feel Fine* (stereo) (remix (RS) 1 from take 9)

**Sources -** Lewisohn, Mark (1). p. 52. / Winn, John C. (3). pp. 47, 49.

# Other sessions 1966

---

## November 7, 1966

**Time**
230PM - 530PM

**Studio name and room**

EMI Recording Studios
Studio 1 (control room)

**Songs mixed (version) (remix number and take)**

- *I Want To Hold Your Hand* (stereo)
  - remix (RS) 1 from take 17

**Studio Personnel**

- Producer: George Martin
- Balance engineer: Geoff Emerick
- Tape operator: Mike Stone

**Recording equipment**

*Recording console*

- REDD.37

*Primary tracking machine*

- FOUR-TRACK: 1" Studer J-37

*Mixdown machine*

- STEREO: 1/4" EMI BTR3

*Outboard signal processors*

- EMI RS124 Altec Compressor
- EMI RS127 Presence Box
- EMI RS56 Universal Tone Control (Curve Bender)
- EMI RS92 Neumann Mic Equaliser
- Fairchild 660 Limiter

*Effects*

- Echo chamber (includes RS61 Low Level Amplifier with RS62 Power Supply and RS106A Echo Control Unit – Band Pass Filter)
- STEED (send tape echo/echo delay)

*Monitors*

Control room

- Altec 605A (Altec 612 Cabinet) with EMI RS141 Leak TL/25 Plus Amplifier

**Remixes**

Stereo master remixes

- *I Want To Hold Your Hand* (stereo) (remix (RS) 1 from take 17)

**Sources -** Lewisohn, Mark (1). p. 86. / Winn, John C. (3). p. 89.

# November 8, 1966

**Time**
4PM - 530PM

**Studio name and room**
EMI Recording Studios
Room 53

**Songs mixed (version) (remix number and take)**

- *She Loves You* (stereo)
    - remix (RS) 1 and 2 from mono single master tape

**Studio Personnel**

- Producer: N/A
- Balance engineer: Geoff Emerick
- Tape operator(s): N/A

**Recording equipment**

*Recording console*

- RS147

*Primary tracking machine*

- FOUR-TRACK: 1" Telefunken M10

*Mixdown machine*

- MONO: 1/4" EMI BTR2

*Outboard signal processors*

- EMI RS124 Altec Compressor
- EMI RS127 Presence Box
- EMI RS56 Universal Tone Control (Curve Bender)
- EMI RS92 Neumann Mic Equaliser
- Fairchild 660 Limiter

*Monitors*

Control room

- RS143 (Dr. Dutton Loudspeaker)

**Remixes**

Stereo master remixes

- *She Loves You* (stereo) (remix (RS) 1 from mono single master tape)

**Sources -** Lewisohn, Mark (1). p. 86.

# November 10, 1966

**Time**
200PM - 430PM

**Studio name and room**
EMI Recording Studios
Room 65

**Songs recorded (composer) (activities)**

- *This Boy* (Lennon and McCartney)
    - edit of remix stereo (RS) 1 and 2

**Songs mixed (version) (remix number and take)**

- *This Boy* (stereo)
    - remix (RS) 1 and 2 from takes 15 and 17
- *Day Tripper* (stereo)
    - remix (RS) 2 from take 3
- *We Can Work It Out* (stereo)
    - remix (RS) 2 from take 2

**Studio Personnel**

- Producer: N/A
- Balance engineer: Peter Bown
- Tape operator: Graham Kirkby

**Recording equipment**

*Recording console*

- REDD.37

*Primary tracking machine*

- FOUR-TRACK: 1" Studer J-37

*Mixdown machine*

- STEREO: 1/4" EMI BTR3

*Outboard signal processors*

- EMI RS124 Altec Compressor
- EMI RS127 Presence Box
- EMI RS158 Fairchild 666 Compressor
- EMI RS56 Universal Tone Control (Curve Bender)
- EMI RS92 Neumann Mic Equaliser
- Fairchild 660 Limiter

*Effects*

- Echo chamber (includes RS61 Low Level Amplifier with RS62 Power Supply and RS106A Echo Control Unit – Band Pass Filter)
- STEED (send tape echo/echo delay)

*Monitors*

Control room

- Altec 605A (Altec 612 Cabinet) with EMI RS141 Leak TL/25 Plus Amplifier

**Remixes**

Stereo master remixes

- *Day Tripper* (stereo) (remix (RS) 2 from take 3)
- *We Can Work It Out* (stereo) (remix (RS) 2 from take 2)

**Sources -** Lewisohn, Mark (1). p. 86. / Winn, John C. (3). p. 90.

# Appendix 3 – Mono and Stereo Master Remixes (for UK release)

**(In order of completion)**

## Mono remixes

**"Please Please Me" era**

- *How Do You Do It* — unnumbered remix from take 2), created on 9/4/1962; unreleased
- *P.S. I Love You* — unnumbered remix from take 10, created on 9/11/1962; released on *Love Me Do* b/w *P.S. I Love You* (Single), *Please Please Me* (LP) and *All My Loving* (EP)
- *Love Me Do* (remake) — unnumbered remix from take 18, created on 9/11/1962; released on *Love Me Do* b/w *P.S. I Love You* (Single) and *The Beatles Hits* (EP)
- *Please Please Me* — unnumbered remix from unknown take; created on 11/30/1962; released on *Please Please Me* b/w *Ask Me Why* (Single), *Please Please Me* (LP) and *The Beatles Hits* (EP)
- *Ask Me Why* — unnumbered remix from take 6); created on 11/30/1962; released on *Please Please Me* b/w *Ask Me Why* (Single) and *All My Loving* (EP)
- *Ask Me Why* — unnumbered remix from take 6; created on 2/25/1963; released on *Please Please Me* (LP)
- *Anna (Go To Him)* — unnumbered remix from take 3; created on 2/25/1963; released on *Please Please Me* (LP) and *The Beatles (No. 1)* (EP)
- *Boys* — unnumbered remix from take 1; created on 2/25/1963; released on *Please Please Me* (LP)
- *Chains* — unnumbered remix from take 1; created on 2/25/1963; released on *Please Please Me* (LP) and *The Beatles (No. 1)* (EP)
- *Misery* — unnumbered remix from take 16; created on 2/25/1963; released on *Please Please Me* (LP) and *The Beatles (No. 1)* (EP)
- *Do You Want To Know A Secret* — unnumbered remix from take 8; created on 2/25/1963; released on *Please Please Me* (LP) and *Twist And Shout* (EP)
- *There's A Place* — unnumbered remix from take 13; created on 2/25/1963; released on *Please Please Me* (LP) and *Twist And Shout* (EP)
- *I Saw Her Standing There* — unnumbered remix from edit of takes 9 and 12; created on 2/25/1963; released on *Please Please Me* (LP) and *The Beatles (No. 1)* (EP)
- *Twist And Shout* — unnumbered remix from take 1; created on 2/25/1963; released on *Please Please Me* (LP) and *Twist And Shout* (EP)
- *A Taste Of Honey* — unnumbered remix from take 7; created on 2/25/1963; released on *Please Please Me* (LP) and *Twist And Shout* (EP)

- *Baby It's You* — unnumbered remix from take 5; created on 2/25/1963; released on *Please Please Me* (LP)
- *Thank You Girl* — unnumbered remix from edit of takes 6, 13, 17, 20, 21, and 23; created on 3/13/1963; released on *From Me To You* b/w *Thank You Girl* (Single) and *The Beatles Hits* (EP)
- *From Me To You* — unnumbered remix from edit of takes 12, 8, 9, and 10, with take 8; created on 3/14/1963; released on *From Me To You* b/w *Thank You Girl* (Single), *The Beatles Hits* (EP), and *A Collection Of Beatles Oldies* (LP)

### "With The Beatles" era

- *She Loves You* — unnumbered remix from edit of unknown take numbers; created on 7/4/1963; released on *She Loves You* b/w *I'll Get You* (Single), *The Beatles Million Sellers* (EP), *A Collection Of Beatles Oldies* (LP)
- *I'll Get You* — unnumbered remix from unknown take number; created on 7/4/1963; released on *She Loves You* b/w *I'll Get You* (Single)
- *Devil In Her Heart* — RM 6 from take 6; created on 8/21/1963; released on *With The Beatles* (LP)
- *Money (That's What I Want)* — RM 6/7 from edit of takes 6 and 7; created on 8/21/1963; released on *With The Beatles* (LP) and *All My Loving* (EP)
- *You Really Got A Hold On Me* — RM 7/10/11 from edit of takes 7, 10 and 11; created on 8/21/1963; released on *With The Beatles* (LP)
- *Please Mister Postman* — RM 9 from take 9; created on 8/21/1963; released on *With The Beatles* (LP)
- *Till There Was You* — RM 8 from take 8; created on 8/21/1963; released on *With The Beatles* (LP)
- *Roll Over Beethoven* — RM 7/8 from edit of takes 7 and 8; created on 8/21/1963; released on *With The Beatles* (LP)
- *All My Loving* — RM 14 from take 14; created on 8/21/1963; released on *With The Beatles* (LP) and *All My Loving* (EP)
- *It Won't Be Long* — RM 17/21 from edit of takes 17 and 21; created on 8/21/1963; released on *With The Beatles* (LP)
- *I Wanna Be Your Man* — RM 16 from take 16; created on 10/23/1963; released on *With The Beatles* (LP)
- *Little Child* — RM 21 from take 21; created on 10/23/1963; released on *With The Beatles* (LP)
- *Hold Me Tight* — RM 26 from take 26; created on 10/23/1963; released on *With The Beatles* (LP)
- *All I've Got To Do* — RM 15 from take 15; created on 9/30/1963; released on *With The Beatles* (LP) and *All My Loving* (EP)
- *Don't Bother Me* — RM 15 from take 15; created on 9/30/1963; released on *With The Beatles* (LP)
- *Not A Second Time* —RM 9 from take 9; created on 9/30/1963; released on *With The Beatles* (LP)

- *I Want To Hold Your Hand* — RM 1 from take 17; created on 10/21/1963; released on *I Want To Hold Your Hand* b/w *This Boy* (Single), *The Beatles Million Sellers* (EP) and *A Collection Of Beatles Oldies* (LP)
- *This Boy* — unnumbered remix from edit of RM1 and 2 from edit of takes 15 and 17; created on 10/21/1963; released on *I Want To Hold Your Hand* b/w *This Boy* (Single)

## "A Hard Day's Night" era

- *Can't Buy Me Love* — RM 3 from take 4; created on 2/26/1964; released on *Can't Buy Me Love* b/w *You Can't Do That* (Single), *The Beatles Million Sellers* (EP) and *A Collection Of Beatles Oldies* (LP)
- *You Can't Do That* — RM 3 from take 9; created on 2/26/1964; released on *Can't Buy Me Love* b/w *You Can't Do That* (Single) and *A Hard Day's Night* (LP)
- *I Should Have Known Better* — RM 1 from take 22; created on 3/3/1964; released on *A Hard Day's Night* (LP) and *A Hard Day's Night (extracts from the film)* (EP)
- *If I Fell* — RM 1 from take 15; created on 3/3/1964; released on *A Hard Day's Night* (LP) and *A Hard Day's Night (extracts from the film)* (EP)
- *Tell Me Why* — RM 1 from take 8; created on 3/3/1964; released on *A Hard Day's Night* (LP) and *A Hard Day's Night (extracts from the film)* (EP)
- *And I Love Her* — RM 1 from take 21; created on 6/22/1964; released on *A Hard Day's Night* (LP) and *A Hard Day's Night (extracts from the film)* (EP)
- *I'm Happy Just To Dance With You* — RM 1 from take 4; created on 3/3/1964; released on *A Hard Day's Night* (LP)
- *Komm, Gib Mir Deine Hand* — RM 1 from edit of takes 5 and 7; created on unknown date between 1/29 and 3/6/1964; For German release
- *Sie Liebt Dich* — RM 1 from take 14; created on unknown date between 1/29 and 3/6/1964; For German release
- *A Hard Day's Night* — RM 10, from take 9; created on 4/23/1964; released on *A Hard Day's Night* b/w *Things We Said Today* (Single), *A Hard Day's Night* (LP) and *A Collection Of Beatles Oldies* (LP)
- *Long Tall Sally* — RM 1 from take 1 (marked #2); created on 6/4/1964; released on *Long Tall Sally* (EP)
- *I Call Your Name* — RM 1 (#2) and 2 from takes 5 and 7; created on 6/4/1964; released on *Long Tall Sally* (EP)
- *I'll Cry Instead* — RM 1 from edit of take 6 (Section A) and take 8 (Section B); created on 6/4/1964; released on *A Hard Day's Night* (LP) and *A Hard Day's Night (extracts from the album)* (EP)
- *Matchbox* — RM 1 from take 5; created on 6/4/1964; released on *Long Tall Sally* (EP)
- *Slow Down* — RM 1 from take 6; created on 6/4/1964; released on *Long Tall Sally* (EP)
- *Things We Said Today* — RM 1 from take 3; created on 6/9/1964; released on *A Hard Day's Night* b/w *Things We Said Today* (Single), *A Hard Day's Night* (LP) and *A Hard Day's Night (extracts from the album)* (EP)

- *Any Time At All* — RM 2 from take 11; created on 6/22/1964; released on *A Hard Day's Night* (LP) and *A Hard Day's Night (extracts from the album)* (EP)
- *When I Get Home* — RM 2 from take 11; created on 6/22/1964; released on *A Hard Day's Night* (LP) and *A Hard Day's Night (extracts from the album)* (EP)
- *I'll Be Back* — RM 2 from take 16; created on 6/22/1964; released on *A Hard Day's Night* (LP)
- *And I Love Her* — RM 2 from take 21; created on 6/22/1964; released on *A Hard Day's Night* (LP)

### "Beatles For Sale" era

- *She's A Woman* — RM 1 from take 6; created on 10/12/1964; released on *I Feel Fine* b/w *She's A Woman* (Single)
- *No Reply* — RM 2 from take 8; created on 10/16/1964; released on *Beatles For Sale* (LP) and *Beatles For Sale* (EP)
- *I'll Follow The Sun* — RM 1 from take 8; created on 10/21/1964; released on *Beatles For Sale* (LP) and *Beatles For Sale No. 2* (EP)
- *I Feel Fine* — RM 3 from take 9); created on 10/21/1964; released on *I Feel Fine* b/w *She's A Woman* (Single), *The Beatles Million Sellers* (EP) and *A Collection Of Beatles Oldies* (LP)
- *Everybody's Trying To Be My Baby* — RM 1 from take 1; created on 10/21/1964; released on *Beatles For Sale* (LP)
- *I Don't Want To Spoil The Party* — RM 1 from take 9; created on 10/26/1964; released on *Beatles For Sale* (LP) and *Beatles For Sale No. 2* (EP)
- *Rock And Roll Music* — RM 1 from take 1; created on 10/26/1964; released on *Beatles For Sale* (LP) and *Beatles For Sale* (EP)
- *Words Of Love* — RM 1 from take 3; created on 10/26/1964; released on *Beatles For Sale* (LP) and *Beatles For Sale No. 2* (EP)
- *Baby's In Black* — RM 2 from take 14; created on 10/26/1964; released on *Beatles For Sale* (LP) and *Beatles For Sale No. 2* (EP)
- *I'm A Loser* — RM 2 from take 8; created on 10/26/1964; released on *Beatles For Sale* (LP) and *Beatles For Sale* (EP)
- *Kansas City/Hey-Hey-Hey-Hey!* — RM 1 from take 1; created on 10/26/1964; released on *Beatles For Sale* (LP)
- *What You're Doing* — RM 1 from take 19; created on 10/27/1964; released on *Beatles For Sale* (LP)
- *Mr. Moonlight* — RM 1 and 2 from takes 4 and 8; created on 10/27/1964; released on *Beatles For Sale* (LP)
- *Honey Don't* — RM 1 from take 5; created on 10/27/1964; released on *Beatles For Sale* (LP)
- *Every Little Thing* — RM 1 from take 9; created on 10/27/1964; released on *Beatles For Sale* (LP)
- *Eight Days A Week* — edit of RM 2 and 3 from takes 13 and 15; created on 10/27/1964; released on *Beatles For Sale* (LP) and *Beatles For Sale* (EP)

- *Ticket To Ride* — RM 1 from take 2; created on 2/18/1965; released on *"Ticket To Ride" b/w "Yes It Is"* (Single), *Help!* (LP) and *A Collection Of Beatles Oldies* (LP)

# Stereo remixes

### "Please Please Me" era

- *Anna (Go To Him)* — unnumbered remix from take 3; created on 2/25/1963; released on *Please Please Me* (LP)
- *Boys* — unnumbered remix from take 1; created on 2/25/1963; released on *Please Please Me* (LP)
- *Chains* — unnumbered remix from take 1; created on 2/25/1963; released on *Please Please Me* (LP)
- *Misery* — unnumbered remix RS from take 16; created on 2/25/1963; released on *Please Please Me* (LP)
- *Baby It's You* — unnumbered remix from take 5; created on 2/25/1963; released on *Please Please Me* (LP)
- *Do You Want To Know A Secret* — unnumbered remix from take 8; created on 2/25/1963; released on *Please Please Me* (LP)
- *There's A Place* — unnumbered remix from take 13; created on 2/25/1963; released on *Please Please Me* (LP)
- *I Saw Her Standing There* — unnumbered remix from edit of takes 9 and 12; created on 2/25/1963; released on *Please Please Me* (LP)
- *Twist And Shout* — unnumbered remix from take 1; created on 2/25/1963; released on *Please Please Me* (LP)
- *A Taste Of Honey* — unnumbered remix from take 7; created on 2/25/1963; released on *Please Please Me* (LP)
- *Ask Me Why* — unnumbered remix from take 6; created on 2/25/1963; released on *Please Please Me* (LP)
- *Please Please Me* — unnumbered remix from edit of takes 16, 17, 18; created on 2/25/1963; released on *Please Please Me* (LP)
- *Love Me Do* — unnumbered remix from 09/11/1962 session; created on 2/25/1963; released on *Please Please Me* (LP)
- *P.S. I Love You* — unnumbered remix from 09/11/1962 session; created on 2/25/1963; released on *Please Please Me* (LP)

### "With The Beatles" era

- *Thank You Girl* — unnumbered remix from edit of takes 6, 13, 17, 20, 21, and 23; created on 3/13/1963; unreleased

- *From Me To You* — unnumbered remix from edit of takes 12, 8, 9, and 10; created on 3/14/1963; released on *A Collection Of Beatles Oldies* (LP)
- *I Want To Hold Your Hand* — RS 17 from take 17; created on 10/21/1963; released on *A Collection Of Beatles Oldies* (LP)
- *This Boy* — RS 15 from edit of takes 15 and 17; created on 10/21/1963; unreleased
- *It Won't Be Long* — RS 17 from edit of takes 17 and 21; created on 10/29/1963; released on *With The Beatles* (LP)
- *All I've Got To Do* — RS 15 from take 15; created on 10/29/1963; released on *With The Beatles* (LP)
- *All My Loving* — RS 14 from take 14; created on 10/29/1963; released on *With The Beatles* (LP)
- *Don't Bother Me* — RS 15 from take 15; created on 10/29/1963; released on *With The Beatles* (LP)
- *Little Child* — RS 21 from take 21); created on 10/29/1963; released on *With The Beatles* (LP)
- *Till There Was You* — RS 8 from take 8; created on 10/29/1963; released on *With The Beatles* (LP)
- *Please Mister Postman* — RS 9 from take 9; created on 10/29/1963; released on *With The Beatles* (LP)
- *Roll Over Beethoven* — RS 7/8 from edit of takes 7 and 8; created on 10/29/1963; released on *With The Beatles* (LP)
- *Hold Me Tight* — RS 29 from edit of take 29; created on 10/29/1963; released on *With The Beatles* (LP)
- *You Really Got A Hold On Me* — RS 7/10/11 from edit of takes 7, 10 and 11; created on 10/29/1963; released on *With The Beatles* (LP)
- *I Wanna Be Your Man* — RS 16 from take 16; created on 10/29/1963; released on *With The Beatles* (LP)
- *Devil In Her Heart* — RS 6 from take 6; created on 10/29/1963; released on *With The Beatles* (LP)
- *Not A Second Time* — RS 9 from take 9; created on 10/29/1963; released on *With The Beatles* (LP)
- *Money* (That's What I Want) — RS 7 from edit of takes 7; created on 10/30/1963; released on *With The Beatles* (LP)

### "A Hard Day's Night" era

- *Komm, Gib Mir Deine Hand* — RM 1 from edit of takes 5 and 7; created on unknown date between 1/29 and 3/12/1964; unreleased
- *Sie Liebt Dich* — RM 1 from take 14; created on unknown date between 1/29 and 3/12/1964; unreleased
- *Can't Buy Me Love* — RS 1 from take 4; created on 3/10/1964; released on *A Hard Day's Night* (LP) and *A Collection Of Beatles Oldies* (LP)
- *You Can't Do That* — RS 1 from take 9; created on 3/10/1964; released on *A Hard Day's Night* (LP)

- *And I Love Her* — RS 1 from take 21; created on 6/22/1964; released on *A Hard Day's Night* (LP)
- *When I Get Home* — RS 1 from take 11; created on 6/22/1964; released on *A Hard Day's Night* (LP)
- *Any Time At All* — RS 1 from take 11; created on 6/22/1964; released on *A Hard Day's Night* (LP)
- *I'll Be Back* — RS 1 from take 16; created on 6/22/1964; released on *A Hard Day's Night* (LP)
- *If I Fell* — RS 1 from take 15; created on 6/22/1964; released on *A Hard Day's Night* (LP)
- *A Hard Day's Night* — RS 1 from take 9; created on 6/22/1964; released on *A Hard Day's Night* (LP) and *A Collection Of Beatles Oldies* (LP)
- *I Should Have Known Better* — RS 1 from take 22; created on 6/22/1964; released on *A Hard Day's Night* (LP)
- *I'm Happy Just To Dance With You* — RS 1 from take 4); created on 6/22/1964; released on *A Hard Day's Night* (LP)
- I *Call Your Name* — edit of RS 1 (#2) and RS3 from takes 5 and 7; created on 6/22/1964; unreleased
- *Tell Me Why* — RS 1 from take 8); created on 6/22/1964; released on *A Hard Day's Night* (LP)
- *Things We Said Today* — RS 1 from take 3; created on 6/22/1964; released on *A Hard Day's Night* (LP)
- *Matchbox* — RS 1 from take 5; created on 6/22/1964; unreleased
- *Slow Down* — RS 1 from take 6; created on 6/22/1964; unreleased
- *Long Tall Sally* — RS 1 (#2) from take 1); created on 6/22/1964; unreleased
- *I'll Cry Instead* — unnumbered remix (RS) from edit of take 6 (Section A) and take 8 (Section B); created on 6/22/1964; released on *A Hard Day's Night* (LP)

### "Beatles For Sale" era

- *She's A Woman* — RS 1 from take 6; created on 10/12/1964; unreleased
- *Kansas City/Hey-Hey-Hey-Hey!* — RS 1 from take 1; created on 10/26/1964; released on *Beatles For Sale* (LP)
- *Eight Days A Week* — edit of RS 1 and 2 from takes 13 and 15; created on 10/27/1964; released on *Beatles For Sale* (LP)
- *Every Little Thing* — RS 1 from take 9); created on 10/27/1964; released on *Beatles For Sale* (LP)
- *Honey Don't* — RS 1 from take 5; created on 10/27/1964; released on *Beatles For Sale* (LP)
- *What You're Doing* — RS 1 from take 19; created on 10/27/1964; released on *Beatles For Sale* (LP)
- *I'll Follow The Sun* — RS 1 from take 8; created on 11/4/1964; released on *Beatles For Sale* (LP)
- *Everybody's Trying To Be My Baby* — RS 1 from take 1; created on 11/4/1964; released on *Beatles For Sale* (LP)

- *Rock And Roll Music* — RS 1 from take 1; created on 11/4/1964; released on *Beatles For Sale* (LP)
- *Words Of Love* — RS 1 from take 3; created on 11/4/1964; released on *Beatles For Sale* (LP)
- *Mr. Moonlight* — edit of RS 1 and 2 from takes 4 and 8; created on 11/4/1964; released on *Beatles For Sale* (LP)
- *I Don't Want To Spoil The Party* — RS 1 from take 9; created on 11/4/1964; released on *Beatles For Sale* (LP)
- *I'm A Loser* — RS 1 from take 8; created on 11/4/1964; released on *Beatles For Sale* (LP)
- *Baby's In Black* — RS 1 from take 14; created on 11/4/1964; released on *Beatles For Sale* (LP)
- *No Reply* — RS 1 from take 8; created on 11/4/1964; released on *Beatles For Sale* (LP)

# Appendix 4 – Electric guitars

| Electric Guitars | Used from date | Used to date | Main player | In service |
|---|---|---|---|---|
| 1958 Rickenbacker 325 Capri with Bigsby B5 vibrato (first model – natural finish – repainted black) Note: Kaufmann vibrato used between August 1960 and August 1961 | 15 October 1960 | 12 February 1964 | Lennon | 1961-1964 |
| 1957 Gretsch G6128 Duo Jet with Gretsch Bigsby B3 vibrato | 1 July 1961 | - | Harrison | 1961-1964 |
| 1958/1959 Resonet Futurama | 20 November 1959 | - | Harrison | 1961 |
| 1962 Gretsch 6122 Chet Atkins Country Gentleman with Gretsch Bigsby B6G vibrato | 23 June 1963 | 31 October 1963 | Harrison | 1961-1963 |
| 1962 Rickenbacker 425 | 17 September 1963 | - | Lennon/ Harrison | 1961-1964 |
| 1963 Gretsch PX6122 Chet Atkins Country Gentleman with Gretsch Bigsby B6G vibrato | 1 November 1963 | 14 February 1965 | Harrison | 1961-1965 |
| 1963 Gretsch 6119 Chet Atkins Tennessean with Gretsch Bigsby vibrato | 23 December 1963 | 1 March 1965 | Harrison | 1964-1965 |
| 1963 Rickenbacker 360-12 (12-string) | 7 February 1964 | 14 February 1965 | Harrison | 1964-1965 |
| 1964 Rickenbacker 1996 | 7 February 1964 | - | Lennon | 1964 |
| 1964 Rickenbacker 325 Capri (second model - black) | 13 February 1964 | - | Lennon | 1964-1965 |

| Electric Guitars | Used from date | Used to date | Main player | In service |
|---|---|---|---|---|
| 1962 Epiphone ES-230TD, Casino with Selmer Bigsby B7 vibrato (strung left-handed) | 15 December 1964 | - | McCartney | 1964-1969 |

# Appendix 5 – Acoustic guitars

| Acoustic Guitars | Used from date | Used to date | Main player | In service |
|---|---|---|---|---|
| 1962 Gibson J-160E | 4 September 1962 | 1 December 1963 | Lennon | 1961-1963 |
| 1962 Gibson J-160E | 4 September 1962 | 24 July 1968 | Harrison | 1961-1968 |
| Jose Ramirez Guitarra de Estudio (nylon string) | 26 February 1964 | 31 December 1967 | Harrison | 1964-1966 |
| Jose Ramirez A1 Segovia (nylon string) | 26 February 1964 | 31 December 1967 | Harrison | 1964-1967 |
| 1964 Gibson J-160E | 1 September 1964 | 30 July 1969 | Lennon | 1964-1969 |
| 1964 Epiphone FT-79, Texan | 15 December 1964 | 1 November 1967 | McCartney | 1964- 1968 |
| 1964 Framus Hootenanny 5/024 (12-string) | 14 August 1964 | 26 July 1969 | Lennon/ Harrison | 1964-1969 |

# Appendix 6 – Bass guitars

| Bass Guitars | Used from date | Used to date | Main player | In service |
|---|---|---|---|---|
| 1961 Hofner 500/1 | 1 April 1961 | 4 October 1963 | McCartney | 1961-1963, 1968-1969 |
| 1962-1963 Hofner 500/1 | 4 October 1963 | - | McCartney | 1964-1969 |

# Appendix 7 – Drums

| Drums | Used from date | Used to date | Main player | In service |
|---|---|---|---|---|
| 1960 Premier 58 Mahogany Duroplastic (14" X 20" bass drum/ 8" X 12" rack tom/ 16" floor tom/ 14"X4" "Royal Ace" snare); Ajax, Paiste Stambul or Kurts cymbals (20" ride/ 18" crash/ 14" hi-hats) | 1 July 1957 | 1 June 1963 | Starr | 1961-1963 |
| 1960 Premier 54 Marine Pearl (14" X 22" bass drum/ 8" X 12" rack tom/ 16" X 16" floor tom/ 14" X 5.5" "Super Ace" snare) Zyn cymbals (16" crash / 18" custom "sizzle" ride), Zildjian cymbals (18" crash/ 14" hi-hats) | 1 September 1960 | 6 June 1962 | Best | 1961-1963 |

| Drums | Used from date | Used to date | Main player | In service |
|---|---|---|---|---|
| 1963 Ludwig Oyster Black Pearl Downbeat (14" X 20" bass drum/ 8" X 12" rack tom/ 14" X 14" floor tom/ 14" X 5.5" Jazz Festival snare); Paiste, Zyn, Zildjian cymbals (20" ride/ 20" ride with 4-rivet "sizzle"/ 18" crash) Zildjian cymbals (14" model A hi-hats) (Ludwig Set 1) | 7 January 1963 | 31 January 1964 | Starr | 1961-1964 |
| 1956 Ludwig Black Diamond Pearl Buddy Rich Super Classic (14" X 22" bass drum/ 9" X 13" rack tom/ 16" X 16" floor tom/ 14" X 5.5" snare); Unknown cymbals (20" ride/ 18" crash/ 14" hi-hats) | 11 September 1962 | 11 September 1962 | White | 1962 |
| 1964 Ludwig Oyster Black Pearl "Downbeat" (14" X 20" bass drum/ 8" X 12" rack tom/ 14" X 14" floor tom/ 1963 14" X 5.5" "Jazz Festival" snare); Paiste, Zyn, Zildjian cymbals (20" ride/ 20" ride with 4-rivet "sizzle"/ 18" crash) Zildjian cymbals (14" model A hi-hats) (Ludwig Set 2 – live performance set) | 1 February 1964 | 1 June 1964 | Starr | 1964 |
| 1964 Ludwig Oyster Black Pearl "Super Classic" (14" X 22" bass drum/ 9" X 13" rack tom/ 16" X 16" floor tom/ 1963 14" X 5.5" "Jazz Festival" snare); Paiste, Zyn, Zildjian cymbals (20" crash/ride; 20" Zyn 4-rivet "sizzle") Zildjian cymbals (18" crash/ride; 14" model A hi-hats) (Ludwig Set 3) | 2 June 1964 | 1 January 1969 | Starr | 1964- 1968 |

# Appendix 8 – Percussion

| Percussion | Main player | In service |
|---|---|---|
| Tambourine (Olympic or Ludwig) | Starr | 1961-1969 |
| Premier bongos | Starr | 1961-1965, 1967-1969 |
| Maracas | Starr | 1961-1970 |
| Ludwig timpani | Starr | 1961-1964, 1967-1968 |
| Doumbek | Starr | 1961-1964 |
| Ludwig Expando bongos | Starr | 1964 |
| Cowbell | Starr | 1964-1967 |

# Appendix 9 – Pianos and keyboards

| Pianos and Keyboards | Used from date | Used to date | In service | In Studios |
|---|---|---|---|---|
| Celeste (Schiedmayer (unknown year) or Mustel (1953)) | 20 February 1963 | - | 1961-1963, 1967-1969 | 1,2,3 |
| Steinway "Music Room" Model B Grand Piano (circa 1880s) | 20 February 1963 | 8 December 1969 | 1961-1969 | 2,3 |
| Hammond RT3 Organ (circa 1954-62) | 30 September 1963 | 21 April 1969 | 1961-1969 | 2 |
| 1964 Hohner Pianet C | 18 October 1964 | 8 August 1968 | 1964-1966, 1968-1969 | 1,2,3 |

| Pianos and Keyboards | Used from date | Used to date | In service | In Studios |
|---|---|---|---|---|
| 1905 Steinway Vertegrand (the "Mrs. Mills" upright piano) | 19 February 1965 | 9 July 1969 | 1961-1969 | 2,3 |
| Mannborg harmonium | 20 October 1965 | 16 July 1969 | 1964-1966, 1968-1969 | 1,2,3 |

# Appendix 10 – Other instruments

| Other Instruments | Main player | In service |
|---|---|---|
| Hammond PR-40 tone cabinet | - | 1961-1965, 1967-1968 |
| Hohner harmonica (Echo Vamper or Super Chromonica) | Lennon | 1961-1965 |
| Leslie 122 speaker cabinet | - | 1964, 1966-1969 |
| Leslie 147 speaker cabinet | - | 1964-1965, 1969 |

# Appendix 11 – Guitar amplifiers

| Guitar Amplifiers | Used from date | Used to date | Main player | In service |
|---|---|---|---|---|
| 1960 Fender Narrow Panel Deluxe (Tweed) 15W with one 12" Jensen P12R or Jensen P12Q speaker (pre-EMI Studios) | 15 October 1960 | 27 July 1962 | Lennon | 1961-1963 |
| 1960 Gibson GA-40T (Tweed), 16W with one 12" Jensen P12Q speaker (pre-EMI Studios) | 1 April 1961 | 27 July 1962 | Harrison | 1961-1963 |
| 1962 JMI Vox AC30/6 Twin (original fawn colour) with "Top Boost" circuit, 30W with two 12" Vox Celestion Alinco Blue G12 T530 speakers | 27 July 1962 | 3 March 1963 | Lennon/ Harrison | 1961-1963 |
| 1962 JMI Vox AC30/6 Twin (re-covered black) with "Top Boost" circuit, 30W with two 12" Vox Celestion Alinco Blue G12 T530 speakers | 4 March 1963 | 13 July 1963 | Lennon/ Harrison | 1961-1963 |
| 1963 JMI Vox AC30/6 Twin Treble with "Top Boost" circuit, 30W with two 12" Vox Celestion Alnico Gray G12 T530 speakers | 8 July 1963 | 3 December 1965 (with Vox organ until 5 April 1966) | Lennon/ Harrison | 1961-1965 |
| 1963 JMI Vox AC50 Small Box (Mk. I), 50W with Vox AC50 cabinet, with two 12" Vox Celestion Alnico Blue G12 T530 speakers and Goodmans Midax horn | 24 December 1963 | 31 July 1964 | Lennon/ Harrison | 1964 |

| Guitar Amplifiers | Used from date | Used to date | Main player | In service |
|---|---|---|---|---|
| 1964 JMI Vox AC100 Mk I, 100W with Vox AC100 cabinet, with four 12" Vox Celestion Alnico Silver T1088 speakers and 2X Goodmans Midax horns | 9 August 1964 | 1 October 1965 | Lennon/ Harrison | 1964-1965 |

# Appendix 12 – Bass amplifiers

| Bass Amplifiers | Used from date | Used to date | Main player | In service |
|---|---|---|---|---|
| 1960 Selmer Truvoice Stadium, 15W head with one 10" speaker | 1 April 1961 | 2 April 1961 | McCartney | 1961-1963 |
| 1960 Selmer Truvoice Stadium, 15W head with 1961 Barber "Coffin" cabinet, with one 15" speaker | 1 October 1961 | 2 October 1961 | McCartney | 1961-1963 |
| Leak Point One preamplifier and Leak TL-12 Plus amplifier with Tannoy Dual Concentric 15" speaker and cabinet | 6 June 1962 | 7 June 1962 | McCartney | 1961-1963 |
| Quad II/22 (circa 1959-61), 15W (modified to 40W with Quad model 22 preamplifier) head with 1961 Barber "Coffin" cabinet, with one 15" speaker (first EMI Studios sessions) | 27 July 1962 | 28 July 1962 | McCartney | 1961-1963 |
| 1963 Vox T60 head, 60W with Vox T60 speaker cabinet, with one 12", and one 15" Vox Celestion Alinco Blue speakers | 1April 1963 | 2 April 1963 | McCartney | 11961-1963 |

| Bass Amplifiers | Used from date | Used to date | Main player | In service |
|---|---|---|---|---|
| 1963 Vox AC30 head, 30W with Vox T60 speaker cabinet, with one 12", and one 15" Vox Celestion Alinco Blue speakers | 8 July 1963 | 9 July 1963 | McCartney | 1961-1963 |
| 1963 Vox AC100, 100W head with Vox AC100 custom cabinet, with two 15" Vox Celestion T1070 speakers | 24 December 1963 | 30 August 1965 | McCartney | 1964-1965 |

# Appendix 13 – EMI Studios outboard equipment usage

| Outboard Equipment | Used from date | Used to date | In service |
|---|---|---|---|
| EMI RS114 Limiter | 6 June 1962 | 1 June1964 | 1961-1970 |
| EMI RS124 Altec Compressor | 6 June 1962 | - | 1961-1970 |
| EMI RS127 Presence Box | 6 June 1962 | - | 1961-1970 |
| EMI RS144 4-Way Mixer/Premix | 6 June 1962 | - | 1961-1970 |
| EMI RS92 Neumann Mic Equaliser | 6 June 1962 | - | 1961-1970 |
| Plug-in EQ Boxes | 6 June 1962 | - | 1961-1970 |
| EMI RS158 Fairchild 666 Compressor | 1 January 1963 | 1 March 1967 | 1963-1967 |
| Fairchild 660 Limiter | 24 January 1964 | | 1964-1970 |

# Appendix 14 – EMI Studios microphones and usage

| Microphones | Application in Beatles sessions | In service |
|---|---|---|
| Neumann U47 | Used for vocals, acoustic guitars, grand pianos, percussion, guitar amplifiers, speaker cabinets, and orchestral sections. | 1961-1970 |
| Neumann U48 | Used for vocals, acoustic guitars, grand pianos, percussion, guitar amplifiers, speaker cabinets, and orchestral sections. | 1961-1970 |
| Neumann U47/48 (U47/8) | Used for vocals, acoustic guitars, grand pianos, percussion, guitar amplifiers, speaker cabinets, and orchestral sections. Initially, U47s had cardioid and omni patterns. These were modified in 1963 to cardioid and figure-8 patterns, thus accounting for the U47/U48 and U47/8 designations | 1961-1970 |
| Neumann KM54 | Used for guitar and bass amplifiers, acoustic guitars, vocals | 1961-1964, 1967-1968 |
| STC 4033-A | Used for bass drum, bass amplifiers | 1961-1964 |
| AKG D20 | Used for bass drum, bass amplifiers | 1963-1969 |
| STC 4038 | Used for drum overhead, bass amplifiers, speaker cabinets, brass sections, guitar amplifiers, and some vocals | 1961-1964, 1967, 1969 |

| Microphones | Application in Beatles sessions | In service |
| --- | --- | --- |
| AKG 19c | Used for drum overhead, floor tom drum, rack tom drum, pianos, percussion, orchestral sections, and vocals | 1964-1970 |

# Appendix 15 – Explanation of technical equipment

**Compressor** – A device that allows recording engineers to control the dynamic range of an audio signal. By "compressing" the range between the quietest and loudest sounds (typically boosting the quiet sounds and attenuating the loudest sounds), the engineer can refine or enhance the sounds either when recording or remixing a song. EMI Recording Studios used a number of compressors during The Beatles' tenure, including the EMI RS124 Altec Compressor, EMI RS158 Fairchild 666 Compressor, and EMI RS168 Prototype Zener Diode Compressor/Limiter.

**DIT Box (Direct Injection Transformer)** – A device that allows an instrument to be connected directly to the recording console, bypassing the requirement for either speakers to amplify the sound or microphones to capture them.

**Echo chambers** – at EMI there were three rooms containing reflective surfaces where an audio speaker and microphone was set up. The audio signal requiring echo was sent to the speaker, where it reflected through the room. This reflection, and the delay created between the time the original signal enters the room and its reflection is heard by the microphone, creates an echo. This result was routed back to the recording console where it was added to the original signal at the discretion of the session's producer.

**Equaliser** – A device that allows recording engineers to adjust a range of audio frequencies, either through reducing or boosting the target frequencies. Referred to by the shorthand EQ, equalisation works to add definition and clarity to an audio source by reducing problematic frequencies and reinforcing pleasing frequencies. EMI Recording Studios utilized EQ features built in to their REDD and TG boards, external EQ units like the EMI RS92 Neumann Mic Equaliser, EMI RS127 Presence Box, Plug-in EQ Boxes and the EMI RS56 Universal Tone Control (Curve Bender).

**Limiter** - A device that allows recording engineers to control the maximum or peak volume level of a signal, essentially capping the volume at a predetermined point. A form of compression, limiting utilizes very high ratios of compression to insure peak signal levels remain contained. The engineer can refine or enhance sounds either when recording or remixing a song through "limiting". EMI Recording Studios used a number of limiters during The Beatles' tenure, including the EMI RS114 Limiter, Fairchild 660 Limiter, and EMI RS168 Prototype Zener Diode Compressor/Limiter.

**Mixer/Premixer** – A supplementary audio input device that extended the number of inputs available to a recording console. The EMI RS144 4-Way Mixer/Premix was able to handle four additional channels of audio, summed to a single channel at output. Thus, the engineer "premixed" the signals before being sent to the console.

**Mixdown machine** – The tape recording device used to capture the result of a remix. EMI Recording Studios utilized both monaural (BTR2) and stereo (BTR3) machines.

**Monitors** – Speakers or headphone speakers that allow the performer, engineer and producer to listen to the work occurring in the studio.

**Outboard signal processors** – A term used for studio equipment that is external to the recording console. Outboard signal processors are used to enhance or modify the audio signal. An example of this would be a compressor, which affects the audio signal by narrowing its dynamic range, reducing the difference between the loudest and quietest aspects of the audio signal. Compressors, limiters and equalizers were the primary pieces of outboard gear utilized during The Beatles' sessions at EMI Recording Studios.

**Presence box** – A specialized equalization (EQ) unit used by EMI Recording Studios to boost or cut frequencies occurring in the treble range. This ability to refine the high-frequency signals recorded or remixed allowed engineers to add definition to the sounds they were working with.

**Primary tracking machine** – The audio tape recording device used to capture an original performance. EMI Recording Studios utilized monaural, twin-track, twin-track stereo, four-track and eight-track machines during the period in which The Beatles worked there. The number of "tracks" a machine has reflects the total number of sound outputs that can be sent to remix. However, any one track can hold any number of sound *inputs* (e.g., an entire orchestra can be captured on a single track).

**Recording console** – A central piece of studio equipment that is used to control and manipulate the audio inputs and outputs of a studio, including but not limited to microphones, direct inputs, outboard effects and processors. The sum of this manipulation is routed from the console to the studio's tape machines either for tracking, superimposition or remixing.

# Glossary

**Backing track** – The base performance of a song. In early Beatles sessions, a backing track might include both instruments and vocals, though later in their career it would primarily be comprised of a handful of instruments that would give the song its structure and tempo.

**Banding** – The assembly of recorded material into a particular running order prior to disc cutting for an album or EP release.

**Double-tracking** – The process of recording a duplicate performance of an existing performance. The Beatles commonly double-tracked vocals and guitar parts. As two live performances are never identical, double-tracking creates a natural phasing in the resulting audio that adds a pleasing thickening to an audio signal.

**Effects** – Any enhancement to an audio signal that utilizes a specific additional process or external equipment outside compression, equalization or limiting (though these tools could be employed in the creation of effects). Examples of effects used for The Beatles' recordings during the eras covered in this book include echo chambers, tape echo, tape delay, and half-speed recording.

**Half-speed recording** – The process of recording a performance to a primary tracking machine running at half its normal speed. When played back at normal speed, the recorded part would be transposed in both pitch and speed. The Beatles utilized this effect when a performance was either too challenging to be executed at regular speed (i.e., the guitar solo for *A Hard Day's Night*).

**Mock stereo remix** – A final remix created by duplicating a mono audio track on a secondary track and then using audio equalization to create different tonal qualities between the two tracks while maintaining the integrity of the original track's sound.

**Remixing** – The balancing, equalization, compression/limiting, final effects processing and reduction of multiple sound sources to their final form for release. The Beatles' release remixes were created for monaural (or "mono" single channel/signal path) or stereophonic (or "stereo" dual channel/signal path) release. In EMI Recording Studios parlance, these were referred to as "remix mono" (or RM) and "remix stereo" (or RS).

**Tape echo/ repeat echo, Tape delay –** An effect where an input signal is routed to a tape machine other than the primary tracking machine during the recording or remixing process. The signal is recorded onto the second machine and after a short delay as the tape passes its playback head, the signal from the playback head is returned to the recording console and combined with the original signal prior to being routed to either the primary tracking machine, or mixdown machine. A single, fixed delay was referred to as "tape echo." With the addition of a feedback loop from the playback to the record head on the secondary machine (an EMI BTR2) and signal level control, the echo could be made to regenerate to the point of feedback (as demonstrated by the backing vocals for *Paperback Writer*); this was referred to as "repeat echo." Variations in the duration of time between the original signal echo beyond these two effects based on variations of the tape speed on the secondary machine were referred to as "tape delay" effects. A short delay created a "slapback" or "slap" echo.

**STEED (send tape echo/echo delay)** – An EMI Recording Studios exclusive effect where an audio signal destined for the echo chamber was first delayed by being routed to a BTR2 tape machine. The "repeat" was created by the originally delayed signal being returned to the BTR2 – over and over again if desired. The interval of delay could be adjusted in duration and proximity to the original signal depending on the desired result by manipulation of the tape speed from the BTR2. STEED was also used to "thicken" the reverb sound of the chambers in general and the effect was almost always in use whenever an echo chamber was.

**Superimposition** – The addition of a recorded performance to a previously recorded performance ("overdub" in contemporary terminology). Superimpositions are used to build a complete arrangement for a song from a backing track when all parts are not able to be recorded simultaneously. The Beatles commonly superimposed vocals, percussion, keyboards, solos and orchestrations on their songs.

**Tracking** – The process of recording audio.

# Bibliography

**1961 - 1963**

Sessions and studios


- Forte, Dan (1). "The Jungle Music and Posh Skiffle of George Harrison." *Guitar Player (#11)* Nov. 1987. Print.
- Gottfridsson, Hans Olof (1997). *The Beatles from Cavern to Star-Club: The Illustrated Chronicle, Discography and Price Guide 1957-62*. Print.
- Inglis, Ian (2012). *The Beatles in Hamburg*. London: Reaktion. Print.
- Lewisohn, Mark (1) (1988). *The Beatles Recording Sessions*. New York: Harmony Books. Print.
- Lewisohn, Mark (2) (1992). *The Complete Beatles Chronicle*. Chicago: Chicago Review Press. Print.
- Lewisohn, Mark (3) (2013). *The Beatles: All These Years Volume 1; Tune In*. New York: Crown Archetype. Print.
- MacDonald, Ian (2005). *Revolution in the Head: The Beatles' Records and the Sixties* (Second Revised ed.). London: Pimlico (Rand). Print.
- Martin, George and Jeremy Hornsby (1979). *All You Need Is Ears*. New York: St. Martin's. Print.
- Massey, Howard (2015). *The Great British Recording Studios*. Milwaukee: Hal Leonard books. Print.
- Norman, Philip (1981). *Shout!: The Beatles in Their Generation*. New York: Simon & Schuster, Print.
- Ryan, Kevin and Brian Kehew (2008) *Recording The Beatles*. Kansas City: Curvebender Publishing. Print.
- Winn, John C. (1) (2008). *Way Beyond Compare. The Beatles' Recorded Legacy*. New York: Three Rivers. Print.
- Winn, John C. (3) (2005). *Lifting Latches. The Beatles' Recorded Legacy*. Sharon, VT: Multiplus. Print.


Instrumentation


- "62_hofner." *62_hofner*. The Beatles Gear. http://www.thebeatlesgear.com/. 21 Aug. 2016.
- "Alnico. *Celestion Blue*." Celestion. http://celestion.com. 27 Mar. 2014.
- "Andy White's Beatles Drum Set." *Not So Modern Drummer*. https://www.notsomoderndrummer.com/. 15 Sept. 2015.
- "Beatles Book Photo Library." *Beatles Book Photo Library*. www.beatlesbookphotolibrary.com. 25 June 2014.
- "Gibson.Com: 1959 ES-175." *Gibson.com: Gibson Custom 1959 ES-175*. http://gibson.com. 17 Oct. 2014.

- "Harmonica." *Hohner*. http://www.playhohner.com. 01 Apr. 2014.
- "Vintage Snare Drums Online Ludwig Drum Sets - Vintage Ludwig Drum Sets - Vintage Ludwig Drums - Ludwig Drum Company." *Vintage Drum Guide*. www.vintagedrumguide.com/. 05 Oct. 2016.
- Astridge, Gary. "Ringo's Beatle Kits." *Ringosbeatlekits*. http://www.ringosbeatlekits.com. 3 Apr. 2013.
- Babiuk, Andy (1) (2001). *Beatles Gear*. Backbeat Books. Print.
- Babiuk, Andy (2) (2015). *Beatles Gear: All the Fab Four's Instruments from Stage to Studio--the Ultimate Edition*. Backbeat Books. Print.
- Dowlding, William J (1989). *Beatlesongs*. New York, NY: Simon & Schuster. Print.
- Everett, Walter (1) (2001). *The Beatles As Musicians - The Quarrymen Through Rubber Soul*. New York, NY. Oxford University Press. Print.
- Forte, Dan (2). "George's Guitar Gallery." *Guitar Player (#11)* Nov. 1987: Print.
- Hahlbeck, Gary. "The VOX Showroom - JMI Vox 1960 AC-30/6 - Fawn Vinyl." *The VOX Showroom - JMI Vox 1960 AC-30/6* - Fawn Vinyl. http://www.voxshowroom.com. 04 Apr. 2014.
- Hahlbeck, Gary. "The VOX Showroom - JMI Vox T60 Bass Amplifier." *The VOX Showroom - JMI Vox T60 Bass Amplifier*. http://www.voxshowroom.com. 08 Apr. 2014.
- Hahlbeck, Gary. "The VOX Showroom - The AC-30/6 Twin W/brown Fret Cloth." *The VOX Showroom - The AC-30/6 Twin W/brown Fret Cloth*. http://www.voxshowroom.com. 04 Apr. 2014.
- Hahlbeck, Gary. "The VOX Showroom - Vox AC-50 Mk I Two Input Amplifier Head - 1964." *The VOX Showroom - Vox AC-50 Mk I Two Input Amplifier Head - 1964*. http://www.voxshowroom.com. 04 Apr. 2014.
- Hahlbeck, Gary. "The VOX Showroom - www.voxshowroom.com." *The VOX Showroom - www.voxshowroom.com*. http://www.voxshowroom.com. 5 May. 2012.
- Hunter, David. "Classic Amps: The 1950s Gibson GA-40 Les Paul amplifier." *Classic Amps: The 1950s Gibson GA-40 Les Paul amplifier*. http://gibson.com. 2009. 27 Mar. 2014.
- Ludwig Drums. *Ludwig Drums 1963 Brochure*. Chicago: Ludwig Drums, 1963. Print.
- Miles, Barry (1997). *Paul McCartney: Many Years from Now*. New York: H. Holt. Print.
- Missin, Pat. "What Harmonica Did John Lennon Use to Play the Intro to "Love Me Do" and Other Songs by The Beatles?" *What Harmonica Did John Lennon Use to Play the Intro to "Love Me Do" and Other Songs by The Beatles?* http://www.patmissin.com/ffaq/q29.html. 20 Feb. 2011.
- Mytkowicz, Bob. "Fab Gear! The Guitars of The Beatles." *Guitar Player (#11)* Nov. 1987. Print.
- Premier. *Premier Drums 1960 Brochure*. London: Premier, 1960. Print.
- "THE FUTURAMA GUITAR STORY." *Futurama Electric Guitars*. www.vintagehofner.co.uk/hofnerfs/futurama/fut.html. 3 January 2019. Web.
- Vail, Mark (2002). *The Hammond Organ: Beauty in the B*. Backbeat Books. Print.
- Ware, Mark. "Fender Narrow Panel Tweed Deluxe | Ampwares." *Fender Narrow Panel Tweed Deluxe | Ampwares*. http://ampwares.com. 20 Mar. 2014.

Other

- The Beatles. *Anthology*. Dir. Bob Smeaton and Geoff Wonfor. Perf. The Beatles. Apple, 2003. DVD.

**1964**

Sessions and studios

- "Capitol Records Studios Circa 1960." *Preservation Sound.* www.preservationsound.com/. 11 Feb. 2013.
- Dean, Johnny (2005). *The Best of the Beatles Book*. London: Beat Publications. Print.
- Forte, Dan (1). "The Jungle Music and Posh Skiffle of George Harrison." *Guitar Player (#11)* Nov. 1987. Print.
- Knublauch, Thorsten and Axel Korinth (2008). *Komm, Gib Mir Deine Hand - Die Beatles in Deutschland 1960-1970*. Norderstedt: on Demand, 2008. Print.
- Lewisohn, Mark (1) (1988). *The Beatles Recording Sessions*. New York: Harmony Books. Print.
- Lewisohn, Mark (2) (1992). *The Complete Beatles Chronicle*. Chicago: Chicago Review Press. Print.
- MacDonald, Ian (2005). *Revolution in the Head: The Beatles' Records and the Sixties* (Second Revised ed.). London: Pimlico (Rand). Print.
- Martin, George and Jeremy Hornsby (1979). *All You Need Is Ears*. New York: St. Martin's. Print.
- Massey, Howard (2015). *The Great British Recording Studios*. Milwaukee: Hal Leonard Books. Print.
- Ryan, Kevin and Brian Kehew (2008) *Recording The Beatles*. Kansas City: Curvebender Publishing. Print.
- Scott, Ken (2012). *Abbey Road to Ziggy Stardust: Off-the-record with The Beatles, Bowie, Elton, and so much more*. Alfred Music Publishing Co., Inc. Print.
- Winn, John C (1) (2008). *Way Beyond Compare. The Beatles' Recorded Legacy*. New York: Three Rivers. Print.
- Winn, John C. (3) (2005). *Lifting Latches. The Beatles' Recorded Legacy*. Sharon, VT: Multiplus. Print.

Instrumentation

- "62_hofner." *62_hofner*. The Beatles Gear. http://www.thebeatlesgear.com/. 21 Aug. 2016.
- "Beatles Book Photo Library." *Beatles Book Photo Library*. www.beatlesbookphotolibrary.com. 25 June 2014.
- "Celestion Silver Alnicos - T1088." *Celestion Silver Alnicos - T1088*. http://www.voxac100.org. 03 Apr. 2014.
- "Harmonica." *Hohner*. http://www.playhohner.com/instruments/harmonica/. 01 Apr. 2014.

- "Rare Beatles Vox Guitar Sells for $408,000." *Guitar World*. http://www.guitarworld.com. 20 May 2013.
- "Vintage Snare Drums Online Ludwig Drum Sets - Vintage Ludwig Drum Sets - Vintage Ludwig Drums - Ludwig Drum Company." *Vintage Drum Guide*. https://www.ludwig-drums.com. 05 Oct. 2016.
- "VOX Legends » The Beatles and VOX." *VOX*. http://www.voxamps.com. 08 Apr. 2014.
- Astridge, Gary. "Ringo's Beatle Kits." *Ringosbeatlekits*. http://www.ringosbeatlekits.com. Web. 3 Apr. 2013.
- Babiuk, Andy (1) (2001). *Beatles Gear*. Backbeat Books. Print.
- Babiuk, Andy (2) (2015). *Beatles Gear: All the Fab Four's Instruments from Stage to Studio--the Ultimate Edition*. Backbeat Books. Print.
- Dowlding, William J. (1989). *Beatlesongs*. New York, NY: Simon & Schuster. Print.
- Electro-Voice. *Indestructible?* N.p.: Electro-Voice, 1965. Print.
- Everett, Walter (1) (2001). *The Beatles As Musicians - The Quarrymen Through Rubber Soul*. New York, NY. Oxford University Press. Print.
- Forte, Dan (2). "George's Guitar Gallery." *Guitar Player (#11)* Nov. 1987. Print.
- Hahlbeck, Gary. "The VOX Showroom - The AC-100 MkI." *The VOX Showroom - The AC-100 MkI*. http://www.voxshowroom.com. 04 Apr. 2014.
- Hahlbeck, Gary. "The VOX Showroom - The AC-30/6 Twin W/brown Fret Cloth." *The VOX Showroom - The AC-30/6 Twin W/brown Fret Cloth*. http://www.voxshowroom.com. 04 Apr. 2014
- Hahlbeck, Gary. "The VOX Showroom - Vox AC-50 Mk I Two Input Amplifier Head - 1964." *The VOX Showroom - Vox AC-50 Mk I Two Input Amplifier Head - 1964*. http://www.voxshowroom.com. 04 Apr. 2014.
- Hahlbeck, Gary. "The VOX Showroom - www.voxshowroom.com." *The VOX Showroom - www.voxshowroom.com*. http://www.voxshowroom.com. 05 May. 2012.
- Miles, Barry (1997). *Paul McCartney: Many Years from Now*. New York: H. Holt. Print.
- Miles, Barry and Pearce Marchbank (1978). *Beatles in Their Own Words*. New York: Delilah/Putnam. Print
- Mytkowicz, Bob. "Fab Gear! The Guitars of The Beatles." *Guitar Player (#11)* Nov. 1987. Print.
- Peleolazar, Brendan. *ASBADRUMS.COM*. http://asbadrums.com. 09 Jan. 2015.
- Vail, Mark (2002). *The Hammond Organ: Beauty in the B*. Backbeat Books. Print.

Other

- The Beatles. *Anthology*. Dir. Bob Smeaton and Geoff Wonfor. Perf. The Beatles. Apple, 2003. DVD.

**Author interviews**

- Ken Scott – March, September, October, December 2014, January 2015 and February 2016. Via email.

- Richard Langham – January, February, March, April, December 2013. Via email. March 23, 2013, Pelham, Ontario. January, February, July, August 2014. Via email.
- Gary Astridge – September 2018. Via email.
- Ben Rowling – October 2020. Via email.

## Discography


- "OneMojoFilter.com."*OneMojoFilter.com*. http:// OneMojoFilter.com. Web. Feb.-Mar. 2013.
- "The Beatles Record Collection." *The Beatles Record Collection*. http://yokono.co.uk. Web. 4 Apr. 2015.
- @beatlesbible. "Beatles Discography: United Kingdom." *The Beatles Bible*. https://www.beatlesbible.com/. Web. 14 Mar. 2015.
- Calkin, Graham. "The Beatles Complete U.K. Discography." *The Beatles Complete U.K. Discography*. http://www.jpgr.co.uk. 27 Web. Oct. 2012.
- "The Beatles Club - My Bonnie." Digital image. *The Beatles Club*. http://the-beatles.club/wp-content/uploads/1964/04/the-beatles-germany-single-polydor-nh-24-673-the-first-commercial-pressing-of-a-beatles-record-tony-sheridan-the-beat-brothers.jpg. Web. 31 May 2017.
- "Please Please Me album – original label.." Digital image. *Beatle Net*. http://www.beatle.net/wp-content/uploads/UK0139.jpg. Web. 31 May 2017.


## Photographic reference


- "Beatle Photo Blog."*Beatle Photo Blog*. http://beatlephotoblog.com. Web. 8 Sept. 2016.
- "TheBeatleSource - The Savage Young Beatles."*TheBeatleSource - The Savage Young Beatles*. http://www.beatlesource.com. Web. 17 Feb. 2012.
- @beatlesbible. "Beatles Photo Gallery." *The Beatles Bible* https://www.beatlesbible.com. Web. 14 Mar. 2015.


## Miscellaneous Audio


- "The Beatles Interviews Database." *Beatles Ultimate Experience*. http://www.beatlesinterviews.org. Web. 9 Oct. 2012.
- Phillips, Dave. "DAVE PHILLIPS' Podcast." *PodOmatic*. https://www.podomatic.com. Web. 27 Aug. 2011.

# Index

# ABOUT THE AUTHOR

Jerry Hammack is a Canadian-American musician, producer, recording engineer and author living in Toronto, Ontario, Canada.

**Other Books by Jerry Hammack**

The Beatles Recording Reference Manual — Volume 2 — Help! through Revolver (1965-1966)

The Beatles Recording Reference Manual — Volume 3 — Sgt. Pepper's Lonely Hearts Club Band through Magical Mystery Tour (late 1966-1967)

The Beatles Recording Reference Manual — Volume 4 — The Beatles through Yellow Submarine (1968- early 1969)

The Beatles Recording Reference Manual — Volume 5 — Let It Be through Abbey Road (1969-1970)

Made in the USA
Middletown, DE
24 May 2021

40316796R00239